MONETARY INTEGRATION IN WESTERN EUROPE:
EMU, EMS AND BEYOND

Butterworths European Studies is a series of monographs providing authoritative treatments of major issues in modern European political economy.

General Editor

François Duchêne — Director, Sussex European Research Centre, University of Sussex, England

Consultant Editors

David Allen — Department of European Studies, University of Loughborough, England

Hedley Bull — Montague Burton Professor of International Relations, University of Oxford, England

Wolfgang Hager — Visiting Professor, European University Institute, Florence, Italy

Stanley Hoffmann — Professor of Government and Director, Centre for European Studies, Harvard University, USA

Roger Morgan — Head of European Centre for Political Studies, Policy Studies Institute, London, England

Donald Puchala — Professor of Government and Director, Institute on Western Europe, Columbia University, USA

Susan Strange — Professor of International Relations, London School of Economics, England

William Wallace — Director of Studies, Royal Institute of International Affairs, London, England

Hans Maull — Journalist, Bavarian Radio, Munich. Formely European Secretary, Trilateral Commission, Paris

Already Published

Europe and World Energy by Hanns Maull

Forthcoming Titles

European Political Co-operation
European Environmental Policy: East and West
The Defence of Western Europe
The Mediterranean Basin: A Study in Political Economy
The Making of the European Monetary System
The EEC and the Developing Countries
Pay Inequalities in the European Community

Monetary Integration in Western Europe:
EMU, EMS and Beyond

D. C. Kruse

Assistant Treasurer
International Department
Bankers Trust Company
New York

Butterworths

LONDON   BOSTON
Durban   Sydney   Toronto   Wellington

United Kingdom	Butterworth & Co (Publishers) Ltd
London	88 Kingsway, WC2B 6AB
Australia	Butterworths Pty Ltd
Sydney	586 Pacific Highway, Chatswood, NSW 2067
	Also at Melbourne, Brisbane, Adelaide and Perth
Canada	Butterworth & Co (Canada) Ltd
Toronto	2265 Midland Avenue, Scarborough, Ontario, M1P 4S1
New Zealand	Butterworths of New Zealand Ltd
Wellington	T & W Young Building, 77–85 Customhouse Quay, 1, CPO Box 472
South Africa	Butterworth & Co (South Africa) (Pty) Ltd
Durban	152–154 Gale Street
USA	Butterworth (Publishers) Inc
Boston	10 Tower Office Park, Woburn, Massachusetts 01801

All rights reserved. No part of this publication may be reproduced or transmitted in any form or by any means, including photocopying and recording, without the written permission of the copyright holder, application for which should be addressed to the Publishers. Such written permission must also be obtained before any part of this publication is stored in a retrieval system of any nature.

This book is sold subject to the Standard Conditions of Sale of Net Books and may not be re-sold in the UK below the net price given by the Publishers in their current price list.

First published 1980

© Butterworth & Co (Publishers) Ltd 1980

ISBN 0 408 10666 2

British Library Cataloguing in Publication Data

Kruse, D C
  Monetary integration in Western Europe. –
  (Butterworths European studies)
  1. Monetary unions   2. Monetary policy –
  European Economic Community countries
  I. Title
  332.4'556'094   HG3894   80-40980

ISBN 0-408-10666-2

Typeset by Butterworths Litho Preparation Department
Printed in USA

TO My Father

Acknowledgements

In preparing this book I have received assistance from individuals and institutions too numerous to permit personal acknowledgement here. To them I wish to express my deep gratitude for providing information, responding to my questions, sharing their thoughts and insights, and suggesting improvements and refinements to my work. Without their interest, encouragement, and understanding this book would never have been written.

To the Marshall Aid Commemoration Commission I would like to extend a very special word of appreciation for giving me the opportunity to pursue my postgraduate studies at the University of Sussex. In this stimulating environment I was able to indulge my interest in European monetary affairs and produce the dissertation out of which this book has grown. Desmond Cohen and Roy Price were unfailing sources of guidance and advice, and the ideas presented here have been greatly enriched by their incisive comments and suggestions.

An internship in the cabinet of Wilhelm Haferkamp at the Commission of the European Communities afforded me an invaluable opportunity to observe the workings of the Community institutions firsthand and to gather information about the EMU Project under ideal circumstances. Dr Franz Froschmaier and Dr Manfred Wegner helped refine my understanding of the dynamics of the Community system and contributed a penetrating analysis of the political realities in the area of economic and monetary unification. I am especially indebted to my fellow interns in the cabinet for providing a congenial atmosphere in which to exchange ideas as well as channelling much useful material in my direction.

Tim Howe ably assisted me in shortening and revising the text, and Debbie Cooper and Marianne Farrell did yeoman service in producing the final manuscript under severe time pressure. François Duchêne has infused this work with his extensive knowledge of the European Community and his keen insights into international relations.

Note on the Text

Throughout this book data are expressed in the currency in which they were originally compiled; except for some balance of payments figures expressed in dollars or European units of account, this is generally the currency of the country to which they pertain. Besides avoiding the problems in deciding which exchange rate to use, especially in a period when rates varied quite significantly with time, this approach has the advantage of presenting information in terms of the same unit in which data about other dimensions of the economy are expressed: the significance of a given inflow of foreign funds is clearest when seen in the context of the country's total money supply or overall payments position. To facilitate comparisons among countries as well as to provide an indication of how exchange rates moved over the period 1968–79, the table in the Appendix gives the official parities or, where appropriate, the average exchange rate, among European currencies, the dollar, and the European unit of account.

Expressing data in national currencies also serves a a useful reminder that the information presented in this book generally comes from national sources and hence incorporates the statistical idiosyncrasies of each country. As the way in which the same term is defined may vary between countries, the broadly defined money supply, M_2, for example, being regarded in Germany as encompassing notes and coins in circulation, demand deposits, and term accounts with original maturities of up to four years, while in France it includes all term accounts and savings accounts at banking institutions as well, it is clear that figures from different countries are not, strictly speaking, comparable. Fortunately, the discrepancies introduced by such definitional differences are relatively small and generally do not significantly affect the inferences that can be made.

In any event, a strong case can be made on several grounds for using national data. First, for many types of statistics, figures published by national authorities are the only ones available. Second, they measure the variables of significance in a given country. In other words, the variations in national definitions reflect differences in the structure of individual economies that cause the set of elements that should be included to obtain, for example, a meaningful measure of the money supply to change from country to country. Third, it is these national statistics that are considered by national authorities in assessing the performance of their economy and in deciding on the policies they will follow. For a book that is first and foremost concerned with policy-making by national authorities, it is clear that presenting the data compiled by the countries concerned, and expressed in terms of their currencies, is the only tenable course of action.

Contents

1 Introduction — 1

2 The motivation for EMU: European integration — 13

3 The motivations for EMU: national interest — 31

4 The birth of the EMU project — 54

5 Exchange rate concertation: first faltering steps — 81

6 Exchange rate concertation: the snake in the tunnel — 111

7 Exchange rate concertation: the snake — 135

8 Completion of the Common Market interregional transfers and economic policy co-ordination — 174

9 Conclusion — 200

10 European and monetary union in the aftermath of the oil crisis — 221

Index — 267

CHAPTER ONE
Introduction

My annals have it so:
A thing my mother saw,
Nigh eighty years ago
With happiness and awe.

Sight never to forget:
Solemn against the sky
In stately silhouette
Ten emus walking by.

One after one they went
In line and without haste:
On their unknown intent,
Ten emus grandly paced.

She, used to hedged-in fields
Watched them go filing past
Into the great Bush Wilds
Silent and vast[1].

It is an ironic quirk of fate that economic and monetary union, the goal that gave rise to the present 'European Monetary System', should have as its acronym 'EMU', for the Australian bird of that name bears an uncanny resemblance to the project on which the European Community embarked at the end of the 1960s. Like the emu, economic and monetary union has impressive dimensions, in terms not only of the size of the undertaking but also of the magnitude of the achievement its attainment would represent, an accomplishment which would have extensive ramifications on the economic, political and social systems of the member states. Perhaps as a result of their proportions, the most prominent characteristic of both the emu and EMU is their inability to get off the ground. And both are clearly endangered species.

The comparison between the two emus is more than just whimsical, for it does provide valuable insights into the efforts to achieve economic and monetary union in the Community. With the lucidity and succinctness peculiar to poetry, these four stanzas contain a trenchant analysis of the EMU project and the reasons for its failure. The 1969 Hague Summit, which formally set EMU as a goal for the Community as well as opening the door for the admission of new members, has had a lasting influence on the Community: the decisions made there determined the course of European integration for years to come. Moreover, the poem highlights the most significant attribute of the commitment to work towards economic and monetary union made by the heads of state. 'In stately silhouette, ten emus walking by . . . on their unknown intent,' encapsulates the fundamental cause of the failure of this endeavour: each national government as well as the Commission has its own conception of EMU, reflecting its individual interests. They could agree on a general goal described in decidely vague terms, but when the time came for specific actions, the member states were unable to overcome their differences. The result was the abandonment of the EMU Project. Yet the Community did not entirely abandon its goal of economic and monetary union and did not revert back to being nine more or less autonomous and 'hedged-in' economies. Instead, it resolved to continue moving forward on this vast undertaking and five years later embarked on a new initiative, the 'European Monetary System'.

Perhaps the most important achievement of the efforts to work towards EMU has been that it has conferred on the member states a much fuller understanding of what economic and monetary union really means in the context of the European Community. At the very outset is should be made clear that neither EMU nor its offshoot EMS bears any relation to the European Monetary Agreement, which replaced the European Payments Union on the restoration of convertibility in January 1959. 'EMU', economic and monetary union, is a term referring specifically to the goal that the European Community set for itself at the Hague Summit and more precisely to the particular set of initiatives on which it embarked, known as the EMU project. No mention of EMU is therefore to be found in economic theory. 'Economic union' however is defined in general terms: 'an agreement between two or more nations involving the pursuance of common economic policies in such matters as customs duties, fiscal and monetary regulations, internal taxation, and related subjects'[2]. The conditions for a monetary union, as defined by Allen are

> 'a single currency, or if there are several currencies, these currencies must be fully convertible, one into the other, at immutably fixed exchange rates, creating effectively a single currency [plus] an arrangement whereby monetary policy for the union, including control of high-powered money and regulations affecting the commercial banks' ability to create money, is determined at the union level, leaving no national autonomy in monetary policy . . . [and] a single external exchange-rate policy'[3].

The latter conditions, however, can be deduced from the first criterion.

Making use of the traditional distinction between the flows of goods and services, of the factors of production, and of the means of payment, economic union thus encompasses all three areas in which economies can interact, while monetary union takes in only one factor of production, namely capital, and the means of payment.

From these definitions it is obvious that monetary union is subsumed under economic union. The question therefore arises why the word 'monetary' was ever included in 'economic and monetary union'. In part, this terminology reflects a misconception which has developed as a result of the fact that central banks are generally regarded as controlling *monetary* policy and governments as conducting *economic* policy. The formulation 'economic *and* monetary union' is, however, primarily a result of the particular circumstances surrounding this endeavour. The Council resolution of 22 March 1971 set the final goal in EMU as creating a Community that

(1) constitue une zone à l'interieur de laquelle les personnes, les biens, les services, et les capitaux circulent librement et sans distortion de concurrence, sans pour autant engendrer des déséquilibres structurels et régionaux et dans les conditions propres à permettre aux agents économiques de développer leur activité à l'échelle communautaire;

(2) forme un ensemble monétaire individualisé au sein du système international, caracterisé par la convertibilité totale et irréversible des monnaies, l'élimination des marges de fluctuation des cours de change, la fixation irrévocable des rapports de parité, conditions indispensables à la création d'une monnaie unique, et comportant une organisation communautaire des banques centrales;

(3) détienne dans le domaine économique et monétaire les compétences et responsabilités permettant à ses institutions d'assurer la gestion de l'union. A cette fin, les décisions de politique économique requises sont prises au niveau communautaire et les pouvoirs nécessaires sont attribués aux institutions de la Communauté[4].

In other words, economic and monetary union was defined as the free and unrestricted movement of goods, services, and the factors of production; the existence of a common currency area; and that degree of common economic policy-making requisite to the smooth functioning of the union. However, the Treaty of Rome, which laid the basis for the creation of the EEC in 1958, already provided specifically for

(1) l'élimination, entre les Etats membres, des droits de douane et des restrictions quantatives à l'entrée et à la sortie des marchandises, ainsi que de toutes autres mesures d'effet équivalent,

(2) l'établissement d'un tarif douanier commun et d'une politique commerciale commune envers les Etats tiers,
(3) l'abolition entre les Etats membres, des obstacles à la libre circulation des personnes, des services, et des capitaux[5].

Consequently the establishment of a *monetary* union and the co-ordination of *economic* policies were the two substantive elements in this endeavour, and were reflected as such in the expression 'economic *and* monetary union'.

The definition embodied in the Council resolution of 22 March 1971 provides a good foundation on which to base a more detailed description of the meaning of EMU in the Community, but it is vague, especially on institutional issues, reflecting the divergence of views among the member states. For instance, it lays down that the Community is to possess the 'compétences et responsabilités permettant à ses institutions d'assurer la gestion de l'union'[6], but does not specify which economic policies are to be made by, or what powers are to be transferred to, the Community. It is, however, possible to deduce the nature of the relationships among the member states that was envisaged in EMU by examining the environment in which economic and monetary union is to be achieved, specifically by referring to the Treaty of Rome and the Community system it established. For this purpose it will be useful to consider in turn the economic relations among the member states in terms of the flow of goods and services, factors of production and payments.

The meaning of economic and monetary union in the European Community is clear as far as the interchange of goods and services is concerned. There is to be free trade. Specifically, all national barriers to the movement of goods and services in response to market forces, such as tariffs, quantitative restrictions, import deposits, taxes or subsidies that affect trade, export credit schemes and discriminatory government procurement policies, are to be eliminated. This is to take place in the context of a Community that will not only have formed a customs union but also will have taken the necessary steps to prevent national policies from distorting the goods and service markets, as envisaged in the Treaty of Rome[7]. To this end, the member states had in 1969 already begun to harmonize their systems of indirect taxation, to adopt common health and safety standards, to furnish foreign aid spendable in any Community country and to institute a common policy on monopolies and competition, as well as the more visible actions of eliminating internal tariffs, introducing a common external tariff and establishing a common agricultural policy.

Similarly, in terms of the factors of production, EMU means not only the removal of the barriers to factor mobility but also the co-ordination of national policies to ensure that resources are allocated to their employment of greatest efficiency. As the Treaty of Rome and subsequent declarations have made clear, the Community is to be a common market within which workers can seek employment, professional qualifications are recognized, investments can be freely made, and companies can establish branches without regard to national boundaries[8]. To prevent inter-country policy differences from distorting factor markets, national governments are to take steps such as harmonizing the systems of direct taxation and abrogating discriminatory regulations governing access to capital markets[9]. In addition, the Community is to promote actively factor mobility – both sectorally and geographically – through its social, regional and agricultural programmes, with special emphasis on retraining workers and providing aid to ease the inevitable adjustments through a system of financial assistance at the Community level, i.e. inter-national transfers.

The relationship among the member states in terms of payments that is to characterize economic and monetary union cannot be delineated with such precision or certainty because here the Community is moving onto new ground, where the Treaty of Rome and past interpretations offer little guidance. It is, however, possible to deduce from the Council resolution of 22 March 1971 the elements that are implicit in EMU. According to the Council's definition, EMU means fixed and immutable exchange rates and unrestricted convertibility among the currencies of the member states. This is the minimum condition for a monetary union, but there are strong practical arguments for a Community currency, as only this would underline the irreversibility of the venture. Whether there is one currency or many, EMU implies a common external monetary policy: there can be only one set of exchange rates with third countries, and realistically there can be only one system of exchange controls. Were the member states to impose varying forms of exchange control, only the most liberal would be operative because all transactions would be channelled through this currency. The actual pooling of foreign reserves is not strictly implicit in this system. But because it is a *sine qua non* of EMU that the maintenance of the established parities be above suspicion, it is clear that if these assets are not held in common, there must be some mechanism to ensure that they are available to the countries needing them[10].

Similarly, EMU implies a common Community monetary policy. Given the high degree of international capital mobility, there could essentially be only one set of interest rates in the Community under conditions of unrestricted convertibility of currencies. Consequently, while the national central banks might remain and perhaps even retain a limited amount of autonomy, as in the case of the individual Federal Reserve Banks in the United States, their powers would be severely circumscribed, particularly their ability to finance government deficits by 'printing money'. The broad lines of monetary policy would be laid down at the Community level, and this would entail the transfer of control over monetary policy to supranational institutions[11].

Furthermore, economic and monetary union would mean the co-ordination of policy in the field of economic affairs as a whole. The Community is already committed to doing so, as the member states have recognized that their high level of economic interdependence greatly limits the ability of any individual national government to control domestic conditions effectively*. Moreover, in an economic and monetary union, national governments would not have available to them instruments such as exchange rate modifications, payments controls, alterations in interest rates, tariffs and import deposits that can be used to influence directly the flow of goods, services and the factors of production. In order to maintain economic conditions that would foster confidence in the parity system and in interconvertibility, it would therefore be essential that the demand management policies of the members be co-ordinated. In practice, individual governments might retain considerable freedom of action, because they could determine the particular mix of fiscal, wage–price and other macroeconomic policies appropriate in a particular situation. Nevertheless, economic and monetary union would imply a significant loss of power, for the imperative of laying down the broad lines of economic policy at the Community level would mean that they could no longer exercise final control over economic affairs.

Finally, economic and monetary union in the European Community implies the existence of a system of interregional transfers to palliate the adjustments necessitated by the fixation of exchange rates and to compensate those regions adversely affected by the creation of a common currency area. Such a mechanism would redistribute the gains from increased efficiency so that each region on balance profited from economic unification. Even though it is more an expression of the political reality that each member state must gain from its participation than an indication of the existence of a single Community welfare function, this careful balancing of benefits is an important element of the Community system. It is reflected in the budgetary arrangements under which the countries with the strongest economies, assumed to be the major beneficiaries of integration, are expected to finance a disproportionately large share of the Community's spending, which is directed preferentially towards their less prosperous partners. It is even more apparent in the creation of a European Investment Bank to channel funds to areas lagging behind in economic development.

The set of characteristics described above is clearly the minimum

---

* In an economic and monetary union, the economies of the member states would be even more closely integrated than they are at present. As the marginal propensity to import would be relatively high – especially for the small, open economies such as Belgium where the average propensity to import is already around 50% – each government would be faced with a situation where the income effects of a change in, for example, taxation would be quite small, while the effect on the balance of payments could be very considerable. Conversely, domestic conditions would be greatly influenced by policy decisions made in other Community countries[12].

consistent with the concept of economic and monetary union in the Community. Other elements could be added to produce a more expansive definition of EMU, but these would go beyond that which is implicit in the Council resolution of 22 March 1971, and more importantly would obscure the four essential elements of EMU*. Moreover, because the countries of the European Community clearly place a premium on the retention of national sovereignty, or at least its trappings, it would be inappropriate to define EMU to include a greater transfer of authority than in fact appears necessary for it to be viable. More importantly, in analysing an endeavour that, after all, failed, there are distinct conceptual advantages in defining the objective in the most minimal terms, because this focuses attention on the inability to achieve the critical elements. Consequently we will define economic and monetary union as the free and unrestricted movement of goods and services, together with the harmonization of government policies to prevent market distortions; the free and unrestricted movement of the factors of production and the co-ordination of national policies to ensure that the allocation of resources is based on the highest marginal productivity; and immutably fixed exchange rates and unlimited convertibility, together with a common monetary policy, the common determination of the broad lines of economic policy and a system of interregional transfers.

Reformulating this definition to correspond to the categories generally used, economic and monetary union in the context of the European Community means

(1) the establishment of a common market along the lines envisaged by the Treaty of Rome, characterized in particular by the free and unrestricted movement of goods, services, and the factors of production, and the pursuit of economic policies compatible with the efficient operation of market forces;†
(2) the creation of a monetary union, characterized in particular by the irrevocable fixation of parities and unrestricted convertibility;
(3) the institution of common economic policy-making, characterized in particular by the transfer of authority over monetary policy and the general orientation of economic policy to Community institutions;

---

* Many authorities include the existence of a Community budget large in size relative to individual national budgets and financed directly from taxation in the set of characteristics of EMU. While it seems probable that such arrangements would be present in an economic and monetary union in the Community, they are not implicit in the concept of EMU. A large Community budget would offer certain advantages, such as providing a union-wide automatic stabilization mechanism through progressive taxation and transfer payments and maximizing the benefits of concerted monetary and fiscal action. Perhaps more important politically, it would allow interregional transfers to be made without visible budget entries. Nevertheless, a successful and lasting EMU could be achieved without budgetary centralization[13].

† It is assumed throughout this chapter that social costs and values have been integrated into the market mechanism so that the unrestricted operation of market forces acts to optimize social welfare.

(4) the introduction of a system of interregional transfers, characterized in particular by the richer areas providing financial assistance to the less prosperous regions to ease the process of the transition to an economic union.

These characteristics define precisely and concisely the objectives of the Community's first set of efforts to work towards economic and monetary union, the EMU Project launched in the aftermath of the Hague Summit. In contrast, the objectives of the European Monetary System, which replaced the defunct EMU Project in 1979 as the focus of the Community's endeavours in this area, cannot be ennumerated in such specific terms. The ultimate goal of the Community, and hence of the EMS, remains the establishment of an economic and monetary union. But whereas the EMU Project aimed at *achieving EMU*, EMS has the much less ambitious intent of *fostering progress towards EMU*, primarily by promoting greater stability in intra-Community exchange rates and concomitantly stimulating greater co-ordination of national economic policies. Precisely because EMS is to bring about an evolution in the economic interrelationships among the member states which will give rise to new and as yet undetermined forms of interaction, and because the initiatives that develop in response to particular circumstances will reflect the opportunities and realities of future situations, the specific steps to be taken and the precise objectives cannot be set down in advance.

As with EMU, one can achieve a fuller understanding of EMS, in terms both of its present constitution and its future development, by examining the circumstances in which it was conceived and the environment in which it is to function. This is the purpose of this book. It is, however, appropriate to anticipate some of the conclusions that will be reached and to suggest the main elements of the EMS system so that they can serve as a framework for the material presented in the following chapters. The European Monetary System essentially incorporates and carries on the efforts in the exchange rate field generally known as the snake. It fosters and promotes

(1) greater exchange rate stability within the Community by (a) setting fixed but changeable parities for the currencies of the member states, (b) limiting their day-to-day fluctuations to ±2¼% through the multilateral intervention arrangements, and (c) providing mutual financial assistance through the European Monetary Co-operation Fund;
(2) the pooling of national reserves in the European Monetary Co-operation Fund and ultimately the European Monetary Fund;
(3) the use of the European Unit of Account both for intra-Community settlements and as a possible alternative to the U.S. dollar as a reserve asset; and

(4) a greater exchange of information and a more intense co-ordination of economic policies as a result of the obligations in the exchange rate field, specifically through the indicator of divergence, which signals the need for a given country to take action to reduce the pressure on its currency.

As is indeed evident from its name, the European Monetary System focuses primarily on one of the three ways in which economies are traditionally viewed as interacting, but it clearly encompasses much more. Consequently, it is only appropriate that in a book dealing with EMS the broad spectrum of subjects falling under the heading of economic and monetary integration in the Community be considered. From the definition of economic and monetary union given before, it is clear that four principal topics will be covered. The efforts to create a monetary union and to institute common economic policy-making will be the focus of attention with the establishment of a common market and the introduction of a system of interregional transfers being considered as they relate to EMU. Unfortunately in the real world it is not feasible to distinguish between steps that bring economic relationships among a group of countries closer to these four charateristics *with the definite intent to work towards EMU*, which is properly the process of economic and monetary unification, and those advances along the same path directed towards other ends, which are really part of the broader phenomenon of economic integration. Because the heads of state of the European Community formally committed themselves to the creation of an economic and monetary union, the only feasible approach is to regard all progress towards establishing a monetary union, a common set of economic policies, a common market, and a system of interregional transfers, however motivated, as constituting economic and monetary unification. Consequently, EMU does not raise new topics, for these four elements fall within the purview of what is generally regarded as economic policy. Rather, EMU provides a new perspective; it places existing issues in a new context. In the last analysis, the subject of this book is the making of economic policy in the European Community.

This has two important consequences. First, because the economic policies pursued by any government form an interrelated and interdependent set, it will not be possible to consider only those developments and actions that are directly related to EMU. Decisions in one area affect the course of events in others and cannot be dissociated from them. Second, while EMU may furnish an interesting framework in which to study economic policy-making, it is probably not an important factor influencing the actual making of decisions. Although national governments may be sincerely committed to economic and monetary union, it is a long-run rather than immediate objective. Because economic policy in the member states is made almost exclusively on the basis of short-term considerations for the obvious reason that the political system creates a time-frame of at most five years, it is clear that a goal such as EMU carries little weight. Even were EMU to offer substantial long-term benefits for all the member states, it would be politically unrealistic to expect steps in this direction unless the balance of costs and benefits were favourable in the short term. The implication is that advances in concerting exchange rates, co-ordinating economic policies, forming a common market and instituting a system of interregional transfers, if they actually occur, will come by virtue of their own merits. In other words, progress in economic and monetary unification depends on the short-term benefits it is seen to offer, and this is a function of its compatibility with national economic policies. Consequently, in focusing on the four specific aspects of EMU, we will concentrate on the economic strategy of individual member states, i.e. the overall approach selected by the government in its conduct of economic affairs.

This text falls into three basic sections. Chapters 2–4 examine the origins and nature of the attempt to create an economic and monetary union in the European Community. In this formative period, efforts in this direction proceed essentially apart from the actual conduct of economic policy. However, the experience of the recent past and current policies unite with political considerations concerning European integration to foster the birth of the EMU Project. Chapters 2 and 3 study the motivations for this endeavour. Chapter 4 analyses the process by which the vague commitment made by the heads of state at the Hague was transformed into a set of specific initiatives and examines the Community's strategy for achieving EMU, which reflected but failed to reconcile the fundamental differences between national policy goals and hence national positions on the critical issues raised by economic and monetary unification.

Chapters 5–8 examine the effect of the EMU Project on the conduct of economic affairs, focusing on the relationships among the member states in the four areas relevant to economic and monetary unification. As the progress made on each of these fronts is analysed in turn, it becomes clear that the fate of the EMU Project will be determined by the economic strategy adopted by each national government and that its success will depend in the last analysis on the nine countries pursuing policies that allow their relationships to evolve in the direction of economic union.

Chapters 9 and 10 explore the reasons for the failure of the EMU Project and assesses the prospects for future advances in this area. In Chapter 9 some general conclusions about the process of economic and monetary integration in the Community are made and the forces acting for and against EMU are examined. Based on this analysis, the actions that can most productively be taken are suggested and compared with the steps the Community countries are likely to take. Finally the developments that have occurred since the demise of the EMU Project are discussed and their culmination in the inauguration of the European Monetary System described in Chapter 10. It concludes with an assessment of the significance of EMS and its implications for the future economic relationships among the member states.

Throughout the book, the focus of attention is clearly on the governments of the six, later the nine, member states. This only reflects the reality that power in the Community is concentrated primarily at the national level. It is also a fact of life that France and Germany, together with Britain after its accession in 1973, were the dominant countries in the Community and hence that any steps towards eonomic and monetary union had to receive their endorsement. For this reason, the economic policies of the British, French and German governments are analysed in particular detail. If at times it seems that more emphasis is being placed on developments in Britain, France or Germany than at the overall Community level, it is because the course of economic and monetary unification was determined in London, Paris and Bonn, not Brussels. Economic integration is in the last analysis a product of actions at the national level.

Paradoxically, the phenomenon of European integration can best be studied by examining developments at the national level, for it is the decisions of national governments and the parameters of the system in which these are made that determine the political and economic relationships among countries. Consequently, a book such as this, which is essentially a study of national economic policy-making, can at the same time illuminate the process of international economic integration and more generally of European integration. EMU is a subject that merits study in and of itself; for this reason, as well as for conceptual clarity and unity, the points that are made and the conclusions that are drawn will refer primarily to economic and monetary unification. Nevertheless, as economic and monetary unification is but one aspect of the integration process, it is clear that the ideas advanced here are equally applicable to the more general phenomenon, as will be evident from the striking similarity between situations in the EMU field and in other areas of Community activity. The connections between this specific endeavour and the larger process of European integration will be considered later, but it is important to stress at the outset that the material presented can be studied at several levels. The analysis of the attempt to create an economic and monetary union in the context of the European Community is in a very real sense as much a study of European integration as it is of national economic policy.

1 Mary Elizabeth Fullerton, 'Emus'. In Douglas Stewart (compiler) *Poetry in Australia*, University of California Press, Berkeley and Los Angeles, 1965, Volume 1, p.193
2 Harold S. Sloan and Arnold J. Zurcher, *Dictionary of Economics*, p.146
3 Polly Reynolds Allen, *Organization and Administration of a Monetary Union*, Princeton Studies in International Finance, No. 38, 1976
4 *Journal officiel des Communautés européennes* (hereafter cited as *Journal officiel*) C28, 27 March 1971, p.2

5 *Traité instituant la Communauté économique européene* (hereafter cited as *EEC Treaty*). In *Traités instituant les Communautés européenes*, 1973, Art. 3, p.179
6 *Journal officiel*, C28, 27 March 1971, p.2
7 *EEC Treaty*, Pt. Two, Titles I and II, and Part Three, Titles I and II, pp.190–218, 241–268
8 *EEC Treaty* (Part Two, Title Three), pp.219–234
9 *EEC Treaty* (Part Three, Titles I, III, and IV), pp.241–256, 269–280
10 Allen, *Organization and Administration of a Monetary Union*, pp.14–18
11 *Report to the Council and the Commission on the realization by stages of Economic and Monetary Union in the community* (hereafter cited as *Werner Report*). In Bulletin (of the European Communities) supplement, November 1970, p.13
12 This argument is made with particular force and clarity in the *Commission Memorandum to the Council on the Co-ordination of Economic Policies and Monetary Co-operation within the Community*. In *Bulletin* (of the European Communities), Supplement, March 1969, p.5
13 The case for budgetary centralization is made in Douglas Dosser, 'The Community Budget and the Member States' Budgets'. In *Study Group I*, Pt. Two, C. A contrary view is expressed in the *Werner Report*, pp.10–13

CHAPTER TWO

The Motivations for EMU: European Integration

Plans to create an economic and monetary union among the countries of the European Community formally originated at the summit meeting of its heads of state in the Hague on 1 and 2 December 1969, but they had their roots in developments over the past decade. In Chapter 2 we examine one of the forces militating for EMU, the process of European integration, and try to demonstrate how, in the particular conditions of the late 1960s, the efforts towards this integration came to be identified with economic and monetary union. In Chapter 3 the other principal force acting to promote economic and monetary integration, that of national interest, is considered, and the way in which the different national aims of the six independent countries came to coincide with EMU in the period leading up to the Hague Summit.

The Treaty of Rome

In examining the relation between economic and monetary unification and European integration, the obvious point of departure is the Treaty of Rome. Unfortunately, neither economic nor monetary union is explicitly mentioned in the Treaty, and the provisions referring to their constituent elements may at first seem contradictory. Although the establishment of a true 'common market' logically implies the introduction of a common currency or its equivalent, the Treaty of Rome does not commit the signatory governments to the maintenance of fixed and unchangeable parities. Article 107 does specify that 'each Member State [shall] treat its policy with regard to rates of exchange as a matter of common concern'[1], but it also allows for parity changes if needed 'to ensure the equilibrium of its overall balance of payments and to maintain confidence in its currency, while taking care to ensure a high level of employment and a stable level of prices'[2]. Because these are the usual reasons for alterations in the exchange rate and because the management of economic affairs remains by implication the preserve of national authorities[3], it is clear that nothing in the Treaty of Rome can be construed as imposing constraints on the member states' exchange rate policies or indicating that such limitations are requisite to the creation of a common market.

Nevertheless the Treaty of Rome does provide specifically for the introduction of most of the other elements necessary for a monetary union. Convertibility between EEC currencies is not to be restricted for the purposes of 'any payments connected with the movement of goods, services, or capital, and any transfers of capital or earnings to the extent that the movement of goods, services, capital, and persons between Member States has been liberalized pursuant to this Treaty'[4]; and exchange controls may not be applied to current transactions except 'where a sudden crisis in the balance of payments occurs'[5] and where assistance from the Community is either insufficient or not immediately available. Furthermore, 'to the extent necessary to ensure the proper functioning of the common market . . . all restrictions on the movement of capital belonging to persons resident in member states and any discrimination based on the nationality or on the place of residence of the parties or on the place where such capital is invested' are to be abolished[6]. At the same time, the member states are to work towards 'the progressive co-ordination of [their] exchange policies in respect of the movement of capital between these States and third countries'[7].

As to policy co-ordination, the Treaty of Rome sets as one of its objectives 'the application of procedures by which the economic policies of Member States can be co-ordinated and disequilibria in their balance of payments remedied'[8], and expressly states that the 'Member States shall . . . co-ordinate their respective economic policies to the extent necessary to attain the objectives of this Treaty'[9]. Further, the Treaty provides for the creation of a Monetary Committee 'to keep under review the monetary and financial situation of the Member States and of the Community and the general payments system of the Member States . . . in order to promote co-ordination of the policies of Member States in the monetary field to the full extent needed for the functioning of the common market'[10]. Additionally the member states are to 'regard their conjunctural policies as a matter of common concern'[11]. In the case of a member state experiencing payments difficulties, the Treaty foresees 'mutual assistance' by means of the Community adopting 'a concerted approach to or within any other international organization to which Member States may have recourse' in requesting aid and 'the granting of limited credits by other Member States, subject to their agreement'[12].

Thus, while the Treaty of Rome does not commit its signatories to monetary union in practice or indeed in principle, the effect of its provisions is nevertheless to create a system in which all the elements of monetary union are present, with the notable exception of fixed and immutable exchange rates. That the Treaty should go so far in this direction reflects the recognition that unrestricted convertibility and economic policy co-ordination are essential to the free movement of goods, services and the factors of production. Fixed and unchangeable exchange rates are no less important, as trade would be impeded by the uncertainty about import costs and export earnings inherent in a situation where alterations in exchange rates are possible. Although this risk can generally be covered through the use of the forward exchange markets, the costs incurred, which may amount to as much as 10 per cent of the total value of the transaction, represent a surcharge on international trade acting to distort the flow of goods and services. Indeed, even with fixed and immutable exchange rates, the difficulties in pricing in foreign currencies, the transaction costs of changing money from one currency to another and the working balances immobilized in different currencies would still represent barriers to free trade within the Community unless there were a common currency.

In spite of this the Treaty of Rome carefully avoids commitments to creating a monetary union. That an issue of such obvious importance to the successful operation of the Common Market should have been omitted reflects the political realities of 1956 and 1957. At that time it was clear that European countries would not accept any provision limiting their autonomy in determining exchange rates. That the French government was not prepared to enter into the customs union without special safeguards to protect its domestic producers provides a revealing insight into official attitudes at this juncture[13]. But while government sensibilities restricted the measures that could be embodied in the Treaty, its drafters were confident that when, in the future, progress in establishing the common market had reached the point where the need for fixed and immutable exchange rates had become evident, the member states would be prepared to move in this direction. The result was a text which allows for far more ambitious progress in economic integration than that for which it actually provides.

In this, the Treaty of Rome reflects the neo-functionalist strategy out of which it itself developed. After the failure of efforts to proceed directly towards a politically united Europe by means of the Council of Europe and the European Defence Community, the European integration movement changed its strategy and tried to work indirectly towards its final goal through economic integration. The ultimate object of the Treaty – implicit throughout but never actually expressed – was the creation of a united Europe. In this strategy the growing economic links among the member states envisaged in the Treaty of Rome were expected to foster closer political ties and culminate in the creation of a single political, economic and social unit.

This approach permeates the Treaty of Rome, where the system actually set up, characterized by a customs union, a common agricultural policy and a certain amount of co-operation in other areas, is only a pale shadow of the system specifically envisaged. This system is seen to encompass the free movement of the factors of production, a common transport policy, an EEC competition policy, the harmonization of tax and legal systems to the extent they influenced commercial activity, a European social policy and – through the European Atomic Energy Community – a common energy policy. Political considerations limited the targets that could be set explicitly in the

Treaty, but the EEC was still seen as developing from a common market into a full economic union: this was perceived as the logical, and indeed the virtually inevitable, extension of the process which would begin with the construction of the customs union.

The preamble makes it clear that there were two key motives in proceeding towards EMU, one economic and the other political. The economic case was based on the same logic as that for establishing the Common Market: economic integration was regarded as desirable because it was thought that a more efficient utilization of resources would occur as factors of production were allocated to the use in which they earned the highest return once market forces were freed from artificial constraints. The establishment of a common market was a first step in this direction; economic union would be the culmination. It should be emphasized that this increase in welfare refers only to the total *market* value of production and only to the area as a *whole*. Where social values diverge appreciably from market values, as for instance in the case of a premium on environmental quality or a desire for regional balance, economic integration will not necessarily lead to an actual gain in welfare. Even were the creation of an economic union to increase the welfare of the group as a whole, there is no guarantee that this would benefit every member state. Countries adversely affected could, of course, be compensated so that the total gain was more equally distributed, but this policy presupposes the existence of a transfer mechanism.

On political grounds, the argument for intensifying the economic integration of the member states was that by strengthening the links among national economies it would foster a sense of community and stimulate greater interaction and co-operation among national governments. In this neo-functionalist strategy, economic integration was seen not only as an end in itself, with significant benefits, but also as a means of proceeding towards the greater goal of a united Europe. It is for these reasons that the goal of creating an economic union among the signatories is such an important, if unstated, element in the Treaty of Rome.

Monetary integration before the Barre Report

While the goal of creating an economic and monetary union was implicit in the Treaty of Rome, it was certainly not one of its most immediate objects. Economic and monetary affairs were consequently not viewed as an area for Community activity during the transition period of 12 years, when efforts were focused on establishing the customs union and the Common Agricultural Policy. Developments during the EEC's first decade reflected this attitude. A Monetary Committee was established on 18 March 1958 in accordance with the Treaty's provisions. A short-term economic policy committee was created on 9 March 1960 to monitor the demand management policies of the six member states, which were having growing effects on the economic conditions within the other States as the share of intra-Community trade in GNP increased steadily[14]. Otherwise, economic and monetary affairs were generally neglected.

As early as 1962, however, the need for progress in monetary integration in order to complement and buttress the nascent customs union was explicitly recognized in the Commission's Action Programme for the Second Stage. This document argued along two lines. First, it asserted that the 'coordination des politiques nationales, qui, à la limite, tend à leur unification', envisaged in the Treaty of Rome, 'serait incomplète et risquerait par conséquent d'être inefficace, si une action comparable n'était pas menée quant aux politiques monétaires'[15]; it then outlined the general problems that would arise from the pursuit of divergent monetary policies in a common market. Second, the Action Programme emphasized that the absence of progress in monetary unification could jeopardize the accomplishments of the first four years and particularly 'la cohésion du Marché commun, car celle-ci ne pourrait marquer d'être affectée profondément par des troubles monétaires sérieux'[16]. While the customs union and the CAP had so far not been endangered, parity changes could have a devastating effect on the Community:

'Toute modification [de parité] importante provoquerait, dans les échanges entre des pays que ne protégera plus aucune barrière douanière des bouleversements si profonds, et entraînerait en raison du prix d'intervention commautaire garanti pour les céréales et pour d'autres produits agricoles de base, des changements si soudains dans les prix des produits agricoles – et par conséquent dans les revenus des agriculteurs – que le Marché commun lui–meme pourrait être mis en cause.'[17]

The Commission therefore concluded that since 'le traité a prévu une politique commerciale commune, mais pas de politique monétaire commune, c'est là évidemment une lacune qu'il faut essayer de combler'[18].

In an excellent example of the neo-functionalist mechanism in operation, the Commission submitted proposals on 24 June 1963 to fill this gap. Although it argued that the growing links 'entre les politiques monétaires nationales d'une part et le processus d'intégration d'autre part, impose aux pays intéressés de coopérer toujours plus étroitement en matière de politique monétaire', the Commission did not suggest the creation of a monetary union or question that for the present national authorities should make 'les décisions qu'ils jugeront les meilleures dans l'intérêt national'[19]. Rather it limited its recommendations to the minimum necessary to achieve the targets set in the Action Programme, proposing the establishment of institutions that would promote the requisite co-ordination of national policies in four area crucial to the Common Market – domestic monetary policy, international monetary policy, exchange rate policy and budgetary policy. The Council of Ministers considered these proposals at its meeting of 8 May 1964 and agreed to enact their main provisions. With this, the Community made its first major sally into the field of monetary integration.

In agreeing to the expansion of Community activity into monetary affairs, the Council significantly altered the Commission's proposals in all but one of the fields, and the resulting initiatives were therefore considerably less ambitious. The formation of a committee composed of the five central bank governors to facilitate the interchange of information and the co-ordination of credit and exchange policies was approved virtually as submitted[20]. The Monetary Committee was mandated to hold consultations on the major issues in international monetary affairs, particularly the reform of the system and the provision of assistance to countries in balance of payments difficulties, but the member states were not obliged to adopt a common position or, in emergencies, even to hold discussions at all[21]. This reluctance of the national governments to commit themselves to working together extended to budgetary policy as well. A committee on budgetary policy was to be established, but it was to report to the Council and to the Commission, instead of working directly with national officials actually involved in preparing budgets – as originally intended – and consequently it would directly influence policy formulation very little[22]. The member states accepted that 'les modifications éventuelles de parité peuvent avoir des conséquences sur la réalisation et le fonctionnement du Marché commun', and undertook to hold consultations 'préalablement à toute modification de la parité de change de la monnaie d'un ou de plusieurs États membres'[23]. However, a vague formula was substituted for the specific procedures suggested by the Commission, and while the Commission was to be involved in the consultation process, the formal commitment took the form, significantly, of an intergovernmental declaration, not a Council decision. While the member governments might recognize the need for exchange rate co-ordination, if not fixity, they still subscribed to the Treaty of Rome's view that exchange rate policy was properly in the domain of the national authorities, not the Community.

Besides these measures contained in the Action Programme, the only other progress in economic and monetary unification during the first 10 years of the Community's existence was the creation of the Medium-Term Economic Policy Committee on 15 April 1964[24]. This body was meant to promote co-ordination of medium-term policies, specifically by preparing a five-year plan for the Community as a whole that incorporated a common set of goals and targets. Yet as with monetary and budgetary policy, the Council decision provided for consultation rather than co-ordination. Information was to be exchanged and problems discussed, but there was no commitment to achieving a Community policy. As this catalogue of meager actions indicates, progress in monetary integration during the Community's first decade was desultory, essentially limited to implementing the provisions of the Treaty of Rome.

Although it was acknowledged in theory that the imperatives of European integration required advances in monetary integration, this failed to be translated into practice because of the particular conditions in Europe between 1958 and 1968. During this period special circumstances rendered the neo-functionalist mechanism inoperative. The case for economic and monetary unification rested primarily on the need for fixed and immutable parities and unrestricted convertibility. Except for the revaluations of the guilder and the mark in 1961, however, exchange rates among its five currencies had remained fixed and exchange controls had generally been relaxed. Under these circumstances

> 'the considerable progress made in the establishment of a customs union and in the field of agriculture engendered the feeling that monetary manipulations have become unlikely, if not impossible. The fixing of common agricultural prices, their expression in forms of a unit of account, reinforced this feeling so much more that economic and monetary relationships within the Community were harmonious between 1960 and 1967, at least in appearance. A climate of false security was created and this explains that insufficient attention was given to the co-ordination of economic policies and to monetary solidarity in the Community.'[25]

In such a situation it was difficult to argue convincingly that monetary unification was needed, as even the Commission had to admit. That fixed exchange rates would persist indefinitely and capital restrictions disappear without specific efforts could be disputed, but national governments were disinclined to take steps towards monetary union until the necessity had been demonstrated.

Two other circumstances also inhibited progress in monetary integration during the Community's first 10 years. First, the Community institutions were so busy implementing the specific provisions of the Treaty of Rome that they could not have considered proposals for action in the field of monetary affairs before 1963. Quite simply, the establishment of a customs union and the introduction of the Common Agricultural Policy took precedence over other endeavours and demanded the virtually exclusive attention of the Commission and the Council. Even had the limited decision-making capacity of the system not been a constraint, the Commission would probably have been reluctant to embark on an initiative in economic and monetary affairs until these other enterprises were completed because of the political climate and the potential consequences of a failure at this stage. Second, by the time efforts in the monetary field could realistically have been contemplated, the crisis of June 1965 had brought activity to a standstill. In a situation where the very existence of the Community hung in the balance, it was understandable that the thoughts of monetary integration were temporarily forgotten.

These obstacles gradually disappeared in the late 1960s. The Community survived the crisis, although the role of the Commission was circumscribed and the principle of unanimity in the Council tacitly accepted. With its existence no longer in question, the Community could turn its attention to establishing the single economic unit envisaged in the Treaty of Rome. The customs union and the Common Agricultural Policy had already been achieved, so the decision-making organs were free to concentrate on other projects. Indeed these very accomplishments militated for progress in monetary unification since the absence of exchange rate fixity constituted a potential danger to the customs union and the CAP. Perhaps the critical change at the end of the 1960s, however, was that fixed exchange rates could no longer be taken for granted. Events in the second half of the decade had shattered the confident assumptions of previous years and emphasized the importance of monetary unification in a common market.

The devaluation of the pound in November 1967 ended a period of almost seven years during which there had been no changes in the parities of the major world currencies. The significance of sterling's devaluation extended far beyond its immediate effect on international trade and finance, considerable as that may have been, for it heralded the breakdown of the postwar international monetary system. The heart of the reserve currency system set up at Bretton Woods in 1944 was the free interconvertibility of gold and U.S. dollars. With the passage of time, this relation had come under increasing strain as the dollar came to be widely regarded as overvalued. Partly because of the deterioration in the American current balance, exacerbated by the burden of the Vietnam conflict, the United States's gold reserves had dwindled over the years, casting doubt on the American ability to maintain convertibility at the official rate of $ 35 per ounce of fine gold.

The United States, working through the Gold Pool, was in fact able to satisfy the demand for gold, even after the devaluation of the pound has shifted the focus of the speculative attack onto the dollar, but as the gold reserve in Fort Knox continued to decline, the American government began to press for a loosening of the bond between gold and the dollar. Such proposals understandably caused alarm both within the United States and abroad, for they were regarded (correctly) as an assault on the foundations of the Bretton Woods system. It was against this backdrop that the Commission launched its first major initiative in the field of monetary affairs since the adoption of the proposals in the Action Programme almost four years before.

In February 1968 the Commission submitted a memorandum to the finance ministers of the Six analysing the events of previous months and their implications for the Community. The still vivid memory of the circumstances under which the British Government had had to devalue the pound prompted the Commission to suggest 'the setting up, as part of the Community, of mutual assistance machinery under Articles 108 and 109 of the Treaty'[26]. Pointing out that the effects of sterling's devaluation on trade patterns were already causing concern to the member states and asserting that the consequences of a parity change in a Community currency could only be greater as half of the Six's 'foreign' trade was intra-Community the Commission argued that exchange rates had to be regarded as a matter of common interest and 'the possibility of Member States undertaking to make no change in their currency parities, except by common accord' seriously considered[27]. The Commission was therefore concerned by suggestions (emanating from the IMF among others) for introducing a larger element of flexibility into the system, especially in terms of the potential danger to the Common Market and particularly the Common Agricultural Policy. In an effort to forestall a move in this direction, it recommended that the member states study 'the adoption of identical ranges of fluctuations in respect of non-member countries, not only to facilitate commercial and financial relations within the Community, but also to make possible a common position for the Member States should non-member countries adopt floating exchange rates'[28].

In addition to these proposals intended to safeguard the common market, the Commission's memorandum also contained two suggestions for improving the functioning of present arrangements. The first recommendation, called for the study of 'the definition of a European unit of account which would be used in all fields of Community action requiring a common denominator'; at the time the Community was employing a different unit of account for virtually each of its activities, a nightmarish situation[29]. The second, proposing 'the elimination, for the currencies of the Member States, of day-to-day fluctuations around the parities', was designed to eliminate difficulties that had developed in the operation of the Common Agricultural Policy*[30].

---

* Even without parity changes, movements of exchange rates within the bands on either side of the par value complicate the operation of the Community intervention system, under which national governments, acting on behalf of the Community, enter the markets to prevent prices of certain commodities falling below a commonly agreed level. Although these intervention prices are officially expressed in units of account, they are converted into national currencies at the official rate of exchange for practical purposes; in other words, the intervention level in each country is fixed in terms of its currency. As long as actual exchange rates coincide with the official parities, the prices at all intervention centres will be equal, but in practice exchange rates fluctuate around parity – and under the European Monetary Agreement these movements could give rise to divergences of as much as 1½% between intervention levels in different countries. Centres in 'strong' currency countries would attract large flows of foreign produce, engendering considerable storage and accounting problems, as well as wasting resources on transportation[31].

The Commission's memorandum was forgotten in the rush of events in spring and summer 1968, and not examined by the Council until September, when it was referred to the Monetary Committee and the Committee of Central Bank Governors for further consideration. By then, however, it had been overtaken by events. At the international level, the introduction of the two-tier gold market in March had brought a temporary solution to the problem of the dollar's convertibility, postponed the collapse of the Bretton Woods system and momentarily diverted attention from the American payments dilemma. At the European level, the May crisis in France had radically transformed the economic situation in the Community and confronted the Six with new and pressing challenges. Stating that it 'would be failing in its duty if it did not inform the Council of its concern and submit its opinions on problems facing the Community'[32], the Commission presented a second memorandum on 5 December 1968. In this memorandum the specific policies it considered necessary to respond to the developments of past months were outlined. This later report contained few new ideas, and indeed the suggestions for introducing a single unit of account and eliminating fluctuations had vanished, to reappear at a later date. Its proposals for co-ordinating economic policies, especially exchange rate and conjunctural, i.e. short-term counter-cyclical, policies and instituting a system of mutual financial assistance were now focused instead on those aspects of monetary integration relevant to the contemporary situation and how these could be of benefit to the member states.

The Barre Report

In the course of examining the Commission's memorandum of 5 December at its meeting seven days later, the Council 'recognized the need for fuller alignment of economic policies in the Community and for an examination of the scope for intensifying monetary co-operation'[33]. It was to these two issues that the Commission addressed itself in a third memorandum, dated 12 February 1969, 'on the Co-ordination of Economic Policies and Monetary Co-operation within the Community'. Better known as the Barre Report, this was the Community's first attempt to formulate a systematic, coherent approach to monetary integration. While the proposals contained in the Barre Report constituted a first step beyond the common market, it must be stressed that they were advanced in response to developments during the previous year and the problems thus created for the Community. They may have had the effect of starting the Six on the road to an economic and monetary union, but this was not their intent. EMU, after all, had not been proposed, much less accepted, as a goal for the member states. Consequently, while representing a milestone in the Community's development, the Barre Report cannot be regarded as the Commission's earliest set of proposals for economic and monetary unification. The Barre Report is concerned not with future goals but with past acccomplishments; it is not a call for further integration in order to create an economic union, but rather the last of the Commission reports urging monetary co-operation in order to safeguard the precious achievements of the previous decade, the customs union and the CAP.

The Barre Report argued that progress in two areas, co-ordinating economic policies and instituting a system of mutual financial assistance, was essential. It asserted that because of the high level of economic interdependence among the member states, decisions about exchange rates, demand levels and credit conditions in one country had a significant effect on conditions throughout the Community. Hence it was imperative that economic policies be co-ordinated: if the Six pursued conflicting policies, not only could a chaotic situation arise in which no country attained its goals, but there was also the danger that governments, in a futile attempt to reach their national targets, might resort to actions threatening the existence of the customs union.

'Therefore the Community cannot stop at the point which it has reached. Either, under the pressure of diverging forces which are already apparent, it will – paradoxically – allow its unity to slacken at the very time when the tariff union has been achieved after much effort . . . or by achieving sufficient alignment of the national economic policies within the existing institutions, the Community will consolidate and develop the result obtained so far to the benefit of all the member countries.'[34]

That national short-term economic policies in a common market would have to be compatible had of course been recognized in the Treaty of Rome, and the Monetary, Budgetary, Short- and Medium-term Policy and Central Bank Governors Committees had been established in an effort to promote co-operation among the appropriate national authorities. Regular discussions and exchanges of information were taking place within this institutional framework. However, these consultations invariably occurred after decisions had been made, so they could hardly be regarded as fostering any real co-ordination. The Barre Report proposed to vitalize these procedures by requiring that

des consultations préalables [hitherto necessary only in the case of exchange rate modifications] ont lieu au sujet des décisions ou mesures importants d'un Etat membre en matière de politique économique courante qui ont une incidence notable sur son équilibre interne et externe et/ou sur les économies des autres Etats membres'[35].

The Barre Report further argued that co-ordination of short-term economic policies would be incomplete unless it were complemented by similar action in the field of medium-term policy. This did not mean 'adopting identical policies in every member country, but ensuring that the policies are sufficiently mutually consistent when studied at the level of the Community'[36]. As in the case of short-term policies, the Community had already set up committees to foster the co-ordination of medium-term policies, but once again the consultations occurred after the crucial decisions had been made at the national level. The first medium-term plan approved by the Council on 11 April 1967 had been a useful exercise in examining the problems facing the Community as a whole, and in pointing out the major options available to member states, but it had little influence on the policies actually pursued. In fact it contained no quantitative targets[37]. The Barre Report recommended that this process be made an effective mechanism for bringing about co-ordination, in particular by formulating quantitative medium-term objectives based on the needs of the Community as a unit and not on an amalgamation of national aims. In addition, the Commission called upon the Council to review in autumn 1969 the member states' performance in growth, price stability and the balance of payments as well as the likely shape of future developments and to consider taking appropriate action if needed.

The second major area in which the Barre Report advanced proposals was mutual financial assistance. As the Commission argued,

> 'Even if the co-ordination proposed in this memorandum worked effectively, it would not preclude unforeseen accidents. No Community Member State is immune to such occurrences, which could quickly jeopardize its external financial position. In such circumstances, there is a serious risk for the Community that the State affected will resort to unilateral safeguard measures.'[38]

To preclude such a threat to the customs union, the Commission proposed a system of mutual assistance, under which any member state experiencing a drain on its reserves could borrow funds from its partners. Although aid of this kind was already available through the IMF and various bilateral swap agreements, the Commission maintained that the creation of an EEC mechanism was desirable because this would affirm the Community's identity: it was, after all, appropriate that a member state in payments difficulty should turn first to its partners. Moreover, a Community assistance system could be used to reinforce the procedures for co-ordinating economic policies by making aid contingent on general conformance with Community targets. The Commission conceded that a Community system would not be able to provide assistance on the same scale as the existing international arrangements, which it would in any case complement and not replace. But at the same time it asserted that this did not mean a European mechanism was superfluous, because it was intended more to forestall crises than to resolve them. Because payments difficulties could be either chronic or acute, the Barre Report suggested that aid be provided in two forms. Conditional medium-term financial assistance would be available to countries with fundamental structural problems, while short-term monetary support would be furnished unconditionally to member states experiencing a balance of payments crisis.

The Barre Report thus contained two interrelated sets of proposals for economic policy co-ordination and mutual financial assistance. Each of its recommendations responded to a particular need that had become apparent in the previous year. Yet, together they constituted a coherent whole, complementing and reinforcing each other. In other words, the Barre Report combined a practical response to the Community's immediate needs with a reasoned analysis of the progress in monetary integration requisite to the successful functioning of the customs union and the Common Agricultural Policy.

The proposals contained in the Barre Report were nevertheless considered separately by the Council. Only the recommendation for increased co-ordination of short and medium-term economic policies elicited general agreement, and even so the measures approved on 17 July 1969 were much less ambitious than the Commission had suggested. Henceforth, there were to be consultations among the Six *before* a member state took any action in the field of short-term policy affecting its external or internal balance, resulting in an appreciable divergence from the Community's medium-term aims, or having a substantial influence on the economies of the other five countries. However, the final decision still rested with the national authorities, who were under no obligation to take account of the discussions, or even to hold them were the need for action regarded as too pressing[39].

Yet while actual progress in monetary integration might be slight, that there could be any advance at all reflected the changes in the internal situation in the Community that had occurred during its first 10 years. The 1965–66 crisis had been resolved; the customs union and the Common Agricultural Policy were in place; and, perhaps most important, the devaluation of sterling, the crisis in the international monetary system, the splitting of the gold market and the developments in France had shattered the confident assumptions that exchange rate alterations were a thing of the past. The member states now recognized that a certain amount of progress in monetary integration was indispensable to safeguard the accomplishments of the Community's first decade and that this could be achieved only by specific initiatives to this end.

EMU as the instrument for further integration

A second motivation for proceeding towards EMU emerged as the 1960s drew to a close. Over the previous 10 years, the creation of a customs union and the establishment of the Common Agricultural Policy had been the means for bringing about the integration of the member states. By the end of 1968 both of these projects were essentially completed, and the Community needed a new endeavour that would serve as the instrument for further integration. For this role economic and monetary unification was both an obvious and an attractive candidate.

Economic and monetary unification was an atractive instrument for bringing about the further integration of the member states because of two perceptions, one of the economic consequences and the other of the political implications of EMU. These assessments will be presented and – since certain aspects are at the least open to dispute – examined in turn. In economic terms, economic and monetary unification was regarded as an excellent way of promoting European integration because it was seen as increasing the aggregate welfare of the member states. The logic was the same as in the Treaty of Rome: the elimination of national barriers to the free movement of goods, services and the factors of production would lead to a more efficient allocation of resources and thereby to greater output. Specifically, the establishment of a monetary union was perceived as fostering a more rational programme*, intensifying competition and enhancing specialization by removing marketing uncetainties due to possible exchange rate movements, and increasing price stability by reducing fluctuations, which with the ratchet effect exerted upward pressure on the price level[40, 41].
price level[40, 41].

Whether the removal of barriers to free trade and unrestricted factor movements would in fact result in a more efficient utilization of resources is at the very least open to question; the ethnic, linguistic and social obstacles to factor movements, over which national authorities have little influence, could prevent resource allocation being determined solely by marginal productivity. It seems, therefore, even more dubious that EMU would lead to an increase in aggregate welfare. As Grubel states,

---

* The ruling out of changes in exchange rates was seen as promoting a more efficient pattern of investment since it would be possible to determine with greater certainty the uses of capital that would provide the highest return. It is certainly true that the problems resulting from potential variations in exchange rates in comparing alternative investment are very real. Virtually all multinational companies have experienced difficulties in calculating the profitability of individual units, let alone evaluating competing investment projects, even with the use of sophisticated analytical techniques supplemented by extensive recourse to computers. Under such circumstances, it is almost inevitable that production and investment decisions will not lead to the optimal utilization of resources. Yet one can argue that in a monetary union inappropriate exchange rates could result in the free movement of factors misallocating resources and reducing the Community's welfare. Whether the establishment of a monetary union will increase welfare depends therefore on the degree to which exchange rates accurately reflect relative values of currencies; its proponents generally argue that its advantages would outweigh the costs of potential misallocations, but they have assumed that the movement of factors would resolve imbalances – and at the lowest cost.

'Empirically it appears that the constraint on the use of monetary and fiscal policy in pursuit of optimum trade-offs and full employment [in a monetary union] is conceived by countries as implying a heavy welfare loss.

Even countries willing to form a common market, such as the nations of western Europe, have resisted any agreements which force them to peg permanently and irrevocably the relative values of their currencies.'[42]

And even were EMU to lead to gains in aggregate welfare, it would be politically impossible to establish a redistribution mechanism such that all nine member states would gain economically. In sum, the view that EMU would benefit 'everyone', no matter how strongly held by governments, must be treated with great skepticism.

Besides the welfare gains it was supposed to bring, economic and monetary unification was perceived as offering the Community an opportunity to acquire greater popular appeal. Too often the Community and the integration process were criticized for having little direct effect on the ordinary citizen. The irrevocable fixation of exchange rates, perhaps even the introduction of a common currency, would be of direct and tangible benefit not just to those engaged in international trade and finance but also to the growing masses spending their vacations in other member states. Moreover, a common currency would be a highly visible symbol of the Community's identity. Just as important, the efforts to overcome structural problems and reduce regional differences would give the Community a more human face. 'Die EG–Sozialpolitik hat sich in der Vergangenheit zu einseitig an ökonomischen Kriterien wie "Vermeidung von Wettbewerbsverzerrungen" oder "Abbau von Mobilitatshemmnissen" orientiert.' With economic and monetary unification, the Community could embark on more ambitious programmes to improve the quality of life for its residents, a possibility that had 'Hoffnungen auf eine vermehrte Einbeziehung gesellschaftlicher Kategorien in das Zielbündel der WWU geweckt'[43].

Significant as the economic motivations for economic and monetary unification may have been, these were overshadowed by political considerations. After all, the ultimate goal of European integration was the creation of a politically united Europe. Indeed, in terms of the neo-functionalist strategy, economic unification was not an end in itself, but a means to this political end. Economic unification was seen as desirable to the extent that it promoted co-operation among national governments, forged links among economies and concomitantly among peoples, and generally contributed to the integration of Europe, *independent* of any economic benefits that might accrue to the Community in the process.

From this neo-functionalist perspective, economic and monetary unification was a most attractive instrument for fostering the further integration of the member states because it entailed increasing co-ordination of economic policies, culminating in central control of monetary and certain aspects of budgetary policy. In the initial stages, policy-making at the Community level might take the form of representatives of national governments operating in a confederal framework and arriving at decisions on the basis of unanimous agreement, but eventually the need for quick and decisive responses in critical situations could be expected to erode gradually the ability of an individual member state to block Community action. Were unanimity no longer necessary in practice, the Community would have progressed to a federal system. Ultimately, EMU required that there be only one decision-making body, not six or nine, and this implied the existence of Community institutions endowed with real powers. Such a transfer of authority from the nation state to the Community would represent a major step towards political union, especially as the policy areas involved, such as the level of prices and the rate of unemployment, were of great political importance.

The institutional implications of this transfer of authority were potentially even more significant than the transfer itself in terms of political integration, for accompanying these changes in the locus of power would be pressures for more democratic control over the institutions responsible for making Community economic policy. These might be satisfied in any number of ways, of which directly electing and increasing the powers of the European Parliament is merely the most obvious. Whatever the method chosen, however, the effect would be to transform and strengthen substantially the Community institutions[44].

It should be pointed out that the relation between economic and political integration was perceived as dynamic, not static: the political motivation for proceeding towards EMU was not that the forging of an economic and monetary union would entail the formation of a political union but that advances towards EMU were regarded as contributing in symbolic, decision-making and institutional terms to progress towards political integration. This distinction may at first seem pedantic, but it is important, for too often it has been asserted that economic and monetary union was a Trojan horse for 'springing' political union on the member states[45].

Although it may contain certain elements of truth, the assertion that economic and monetary union was seen as a means of working by stealth towards political union in an environment that precluded any initiatives in direct advancement of this aim is simply preposterous. It is an incredible notion that by getting the member states to agree to complex, technical proposals, such as reducing the size of the margins within which Community currencies fluctuated against each other, they could be manoeuvred into committing themselves to a series of steps leading inexorably to political union. It is extremely improbable that national authorities would not perceive the consequences implicit in technical proposals, and it is really a feat of imagination to see the nation states of the 1960s and 1970s being forced to cede powers to Community institutions against their will because of Council resolutions or even because of decisions in the Court of Justice. Moreover, such a strategy would be fraught with risk, for should the member states repeal or merely flout their previous decisions, which would have been the likely outcome, this would have had disastrous consequences for European integration, and for the EEC in particular.

Economic and monetary unification was motivated by the belief that it could be a means of furthering political integration, not that it would result in political union. There was no suggestion of any rigid link between progress in these two endeavours, depending as they did on different factors. It follows as a corrollary therefore that political union was seen as being achieved only as a result of a conscious and explicit decision on the part of the member states. This same view that progress in European integration would have to be founded on the support of the Community countries permeates the Treaty of Rome. The Treaty reflected the neo-functionalist approach, recognizing that each advance would have to have the endorsement of every member state. This perception – central to the integrationist logic – is both an admission of weakness and an affirmation of strength. To attempt to coerce national governments would have been lunacy given the political realities, but to do so was regarded as unnecessary because the benefits of European integration would cause the member states to work together in their own national interests. To build a united Europe on the basis of consensus would be a long, difficult and frustrating task, but the Treaty of Rome is imbued with the conviction that there is no other way and the confidence that the logic of integration would ultimately prevail.

As the Community entered its second decade, then, the logic of European integration had resulted in two motivations for economic and monetary unification. The Barre Report was the most important expression of the first, the perception that monetary integration was necessary to protect what had already been acheved in both economic and political terms. The second reason, that monetary integration was crucial to further advances in European integration, was manifest as the Community neared the end of the transition period and began to examine the balance-sheet of its first decade and to chart its course for the next 10 years. Thus, as the Hague Summit approached, considerations of European integration militated strongly for initiatives in the field of economic and monetary affairs, for economic and monetary integration had come to be recognized as an essential part of the efforts to create a truly united Europe.

1. *Traité instituant la Communauté économique européene* [hereafter cited as *EEC Treaty*]. In *Traités instituant les Communautés européennes*, 1973, Art. 107, Para. 1, p.261
2. *EEC Treaty*, Art. 104, pp.259–260
3. *EEC Treaty*, Art. 145, pp.293–294
4. *EEC Treaty*, Art. 106, Para. 1, p.260
5. *EEC Treaty*, Art. 109, Para. 1, p.263
6. *EEC Treaty*, Art. 67, Para. 1, p.231
7. *EEC Treaty*, Art. 70, Para. 1, p.232
8. *EEC Treaty*, Art. 3[g], p.180
9. *EEC Treaty*, Art. 6, Para. 1, p.181
10. *EEC Treaty*, Art. 105, Para. 2, p.260
11. *EEC Treaty*, Art. 103, Para. 1, p.259
12. *EEC Treaty*, Art. 108, Para. 2a and b, pp.262–263
13. Herbert G. Grubel, 'The Theory of Optimum Currency Areas'. *Canadian Journal of Economics*, III, 1970, pp.318–324
14. *Journal officiel des Communautés européennes* [hereafter cited as *Journal officiel*], 17, 6 October 1958, p.390
15. EEC Commission, *Mémorandum sur le Programme d'Action de la Communauté pendant la deuxième étape*, 1962, p.63
16. *Mémorandum sur la Programme d'Action de la Communauté pendant la deuxième étape*, p.64
17. *Mémorandum sur la Programme d'Action de la Communauté pendant la deuxième étape*, p.63
18. *Mémorandum sur le Programme d'Action de la Communauté pendant la deuxième étape*, p.64
19. 'Communication de la Commission au Conseil transmise le 24 Juin 1963 – Coopération Monétaire et Financière au Sein de la CEE'. Quoted in Louis Cartou, *La Politique Monétaire de la CEE*, Armand Colin, Paris, 1970, p.43
20. *Journal officiel*, 77, 21 May 1964, p.1206
21. *Journal officiel*, 77, 21 May 1964, p.1207
22. *Journal officiel*, 77, 21 May 1964, p.1205
23. *Journal officiel*, 77, 21 May 1964, p.1226
24. *Journal officiel*, 64, 22 April 1964, p.1031
25. 'Exposé de M. Barre au Parlement européen sur la situation économique de la Communauté au début de 1970', Strasbourg, 9 February 1970. Quoted in Bela Balassa, 'Monetary Integration in the European Common Market'. In Alexander Swoboda (ed.), *Europe and the Evolution of the International Monetary System*, Institut Universitaire de Hautes Etudes Internationales, Geneva, 1973, p.96
26. Commission Memorandum to the Council on the Co-ordination of Economic Policies and Monetary Cooperation within the Community [12 February 1969] [hereafter cited as the *Barre Report*]. In *Bulletin*, supplement, (March 1969) p.4
27. *Barre Report*, p.3
28. *Barre Report*, p.3
29. *Barre Report*, p.4
30. *Barre Report*, p.3
31. Leonhard Gleske, Währungspolitik und Agrarmarkt in der Europäischen Wirtschaftsgemeinschaft', *Europe-Archiv*, XXV, (1970) pp.15–23
32. *Barre Report*, p.4
33. *Barre Report*, p.3
34. *Barre Report*, p.6
35. Communautés européennes, Comité monétaire, *Onzième Rapport d'Activité*, 1968/1969, p.14, and *Barre Report*, pp.10–11
36. *Barre Report*, p.7
37. *Journal officiel*, 79, 25 April 1967, pp.1513–1567 ('Programme de Politique Economique à Moyen Terme')
38. *Barre Report*, p.7
39. *Journal officiel*, XII:L183, 25 July 1969, p.41
40. Grubel, 'The Theory of Optimum Currency Areas', pp.319–322
41. Tibor Scitovsky, *Economic Theory and Western European Integration*, Allen and Unwin, London, 1958, p.110–135
42. Herbert C. Grubel, 'The Theory of Optimal Regional Association'. In H. G. Johnson and Alexander K. Swoboda (eds.), *The Economics of Common Currencies*, Allen and Unwin, London, 1973, p.110
43. Bildungswerk Europäische Politik, *Gutachten zur Übergangsphase der Wirtschafts- und Währungsunion*, Bildungswerk Europäische Politik, Bonn, 1973, p.2, and European Communities, Commission, *European Economic Integration and Monetary Unification*, European Communities, Brussels, 1973, p.7
44. R. Broad and R. J. Jarrett, *Community Europe Today*, Oswald Wolff, London, 1972, pp.241–242
45. Pierre Werner, 'De l'Union économique et monétaire à l'Union politique', *Europe Documents*, No. 656, 1 March 1972

CHAPTER THREE

The Motivations for EMU: National Interest

At the same time that progress towards economic and monetary union was coming to be regarded as vital to the process of European integration, the Community countries were coming to see in economic and monetary unification a means of promoting their individual national interests. Unlike the symbiotic relationship existing between economic integration and European unification, however, there was no reason *a priori* why the forging of a single economic unit should necessarily be perceived as being in a given country's best interests. That at the end of the 1960s national governments viewed progress toward EMU as advantageous and desirable reflected the view that, in this particular set of circumstances, it could further the achievement of national aims. This assessment was based on a practical evaluation of the benefits that could be obtained from specific elements of EMU; significantly it did not reflect an attraction to economic and monetary union as a conceptual whole. Since objectives varied from country to country, certain elements of EMU appealed more in one situation than in another and the final calculation of benefit was therefore different in each case. Ironically, this meant that governments could support EMU for diametrically opposed reasons. In this chapter various characteristics of EMU are examined in turn and the ways in which they became identified with the diverse national interests of the member states on the eve of the Hague Summit are explored.

Attractions of fixed exchange rates

The most salient feature of economic and monetary union is the existence of immutably fixed exchange rates among the currencies of the member states. As was mentioned in Chapter 2, fixed and unchanging exchange rates within the Community had almost come to be taken for granted for most of the 1960s. Towards the end of that decade, however, this situation changed as the parities of first the pound in 1967 and then the franc and the mark in 1969 were adjusted. In these altered circumstances, economic and monetary unification attracted interest as a means of eliminating exchange rate movements. That European governments should have wished to endow exchange rates with both a permanent and a fixed character may at first appear implausible. This would have deprived them of an important instrument for operating, through relative prices, on the balance of payments and consequently forced adjustments to be made through other, more domestically objectionable measures[1]. Certainly at this time the Six were opposed to floating exchange rates, both in theory and in practice. True, that in response to market forces Germany did allow the value of the mark to fluctuate between 30 September and 10 November 1969, but this action was taken as a last resort under exceptional circumstances: over DM 6000 million had entered Germany from abroad in the month of September, DM 1000 million on 24 September alone[2]. In any case, it was purely temporary. Yet the rejection of floating did not necessarily imply the endorsement of permanently fixed parities: the system envisaged in the IMF Articles of Agreement, to which all the member states subscribed, was one of fixed but adjustable parities.

In practice, however, the Bretton Woods system had been characterized by fixed and relatively immobile exchange rates. Although the authors' original intent might have been that adjustments should take place as necessary, the experience of the 20 years that followed was of few, but rather substantial, alterations for the simple reason that governments viewed parity changes as political liabilities. Electorates invariably considered any adjustment, upwards or downwards, as an indication of the failure of the government's economic policies, regardless of whether exchange rate stability was a conceptually valid criterion for evaluating the conduct of economic affairs. It is in this context that the attraction of EMU is to be seen. The governments of the member states were obviously not about to commit themselves to a system of fixed and unchangeable parities, for there were clearly circumstances where revaluation or devaluation, whatever its disadvantages, was the least politically costly course. The interest of national governments in EMU was based rather on the attractiveness of a system in which parity changes would literally be a thing of the past.

The corollary of this governmental aversion to parity changes was that they were delayed until unavoidable in the hope that they might not, after all, be necessary. Such exchange rate adjustments as there were in the 1950s and 1960s tended therefore to occur well after the need for them had become apparent, frequently under the pressure of a speculative attack, and to be of relatively large magnitude. The devaluation of the franc in August 1969 and the revaluation of the mark two months later displayed all of these characteristics. An examination of these episodes not only provides valuable insights into the reasons for which governments perceived parity changes as political liabilities but also reveals the means by which the authorities sought to avoid them.

Although it is extremely difficult to identify the factors 'responsible' for a parity change, it is generally accepted that divergences from world price trends were at the root of the 1969 French and German exchange rate modifications. In both cases these deviations from international performance were evident by mid 1968. In France the Accords of Grenelle in the aftermath of the May 1968 crisis had resulted in wage increases averaging 4½–5%, with effect from 1 June, and a further 2½–3%, with effect from 1 October. This rise in labour costs was soon reflected in the price index, whose monthly rate of increase almost tripled – from 0.3 to 0.8% – between August and October 1968[3]. In part as a consequence of this upsurge, the GDP deflator averaged 4.5% in France as against 2.86% for the OECD countries taken as a whole during the period 1958–70[4]. In Germany, on the other hand, prices rose 5% less than the average increase for all OECD countries over the period 1965–68[5].

The first signs of trouble on the balance of payments began appearing in early 1968. The French current account, which recorded a surplus of almost FFr 600 million in the first quarter, moved sharply into the red, registering a deficit of FFr 1200 million in the second quarter and over FFr 3000 million in both the third and the fourth[6]. In Germany, the current account surplus declined until fourth quarter 1968, but the persistent surplus of more than DM 1500 million marks per quarter during a period of high domestic demand was causing growing concern to the authorities, especially as the economy approached the limits of its productive capacity[7]. Fully one year before the exchange rates were modified, then, the need for such an adjustment had become discernible. Indeed, as early as 1967 the Wissenschaftliche Beirat beim Bundeswirtschaftsministerium had warned that as a continued divergence in the German price performance from world trends would create inflationary tensions and embarrassing payments surpluses, a revaluation should be considered and the requisite contingency plans prepared[8].

Despite the indications of fundamental disequilibrium in their balance of payments, the two Governments strongly rejected the contention that parity changes were necessary, arguing that the phenomena cited above were only temporary. The French government maintained that the higher labour costs would be offset to a great extent by increased productivity as economic activity grew, and that the current account results for the second and third quarters were at least in part the product of the May upheaval and hence could be expected to improve, especially if the official price projections were correct[9]. The German authorities, for their part, asserted that the disappearance of the current account surplus could be expected to lag several months behind the upsurge in aggregate domestic demand and pointed out that the official reserve balance was much less favourable than the current account[10].

By the end of 1968, however, these arguments were no longer so convincing. French prices were rising quickly, soaring 2½% between November and December, despite contractual agreements between most major industries and the Government limiting the rate of price increases, and despite government subsidies to industry of FFr 3000–4000 million through the abolition of payroll tax (worth 3½–4% on the wage bill) and VAT rebates on the value of stocks held on 1 January 1968. Moreover, the current account deficit widened to over FFr 3000 million in the fourth quarter[11]. Germany, in contrast, experienced a rise of only 2% in retail prices in the year to October 1968, and registered a record current account surplus of over DM 4500 million in the fourth quarter, even though evidence of conditions of excess demand was accumulating[12]. Some of the 21% increase in the value of exports during this quarter was a result of speculative purchases, especially after the introduction of the export tax, which allowed for the exemption of goods shipped before 23 December pursuant to prior contracts; most of the increase, however, would appear to have been due to the price competitiveness of German products[13].

Although the authorities might continue to maintain that the existing parities were still appropriate, the exchange markets were more impressed by the economic indicators. As early as February 1968, DM 2200 million flowed into Germany from abroad, but this seems to have been caused by mistrust of the dollar rather than speculation on the mark. In any event, the short-term capital account recorded a deficit of well over DM 1000 million for the first quarter as a whole, and the Bundesbank was confident that any foreign funds remaining would leave rapidly once the international monetary problems had been resolved[14]. Precisely the opposite occurred, however. The short-term capital account moved strongly into surplus from the spring on, and the German authorities were able to prevent a corresponding increase in official reserves only by keeping interest rates at very low levels to encourage the re-exportation of capital by banks and other financial institutions[15]. France was confronted with the opposite problem, as over $1500 million was estimated to have left France via the capital account during the May crisis[16]. The French government responded by imposing exchange controls on 31 May, prohibiting the acquisition of assets abroad, in the form of bank accounts, securities or property, without the prior authorization of the Banque de France[17], and this, together with the resolution of the national crisis, stemmed the decline in the country's reserved. Yet confidence in the existing exchange rates was far from restored, as the French authorities discovered when they were compelled to allow the day-to-day interest rate to rise from 6 to 8% to contain the outflow that followed the removal of exchange controls on 5 September.

As the fourth quarter progressed, the signs of the need for parity adjustments became more and more conclusive, and the first major wave of speculation occurred in November 1968. The slow exodus of capital from France, amounting to some FFr 3000 million for September and October, rapidly gathered momentum, and even though the Banque de France attempted to stop the haemorrhaging by raising the discount rate 1% on 12 November and adding 1% to the reserve requirement on sight deposits three days later, removing some FFr 2200 million in liquidity in all, the drain on the reserves assumed alarming proportions, leaving the French government little alternative but to close the exchange markets on 20 November[18]. The German authorities followed suit the next day, after they too had found monetary action powerless to halt the capital flows which had brought DM 9400 million into the Federal Republic during November[19]. The following weekend, 23–24 November, the finance ministers of Britain, France and Germany, the countries principally involved in the crisis, assembled in Bonn in an attempt to resolve the situation.

Despite the mass of evidence, in terms of divergent price trends, growing payments imbalances and, most recently, speculative pressure indicating that the existing exchange rates were inappropriate, the French and German governments resolutely refused to consider modifying their parities at the Bonn Conference. In part, this reflected a determination not to 'reward' the speculators, but the critical factor was the implacable opposition of both Governments on political grounds. General de Gaulle rejected devaluation out of hand. Aside from the damage such a course of action would have done to France's prestige abroad, it would have had considerable political costs at home because the Government had publicly committed itself to maintaining the parity of the franc. Devaluation would have been tantamount to an admission that the Government's economic strategy had failed[20]. Moreover, it would have had an inflationary effect on prices not without its political dangers in the post-May atmosphere. The Kiesinger government was likewise unalterably opposed to a revaluation of the mark, for it had associated itself too strongly with the position that the mark was not undervalued. In addition, appreciation of the mark had several specific political disadvantages. For example, because of the way the Common Agricultural Policy operated, it would reduce farmers' income[21].

That political considerations effectively precluded a parity change did not, however, obviate the need to restore the French and German balances of payments to equilibrium. It merely meant that other methods would have to be used to bring about the necessary adjustment. Thus, the French government moved to restrain price increases by eliminating the payroll tax and to reduce domestic demand – regarded as excessive in the fourth quarter – by increasing taxes by FFr 2600 million, cutting FFr 2500 million from government spending and limiting bank lending on 31 December to 104% and on 31 January 1969 to 101% of its level on 30 September 1968. In addition, exchange controls were reintroduced in a much more stringent form. Not only were capital exports prohibited without prior authorization from the Banque de France, but imports could not be paid for until received, forward purchases of foreign currencies required special approval and the proceeds of sales abroad had to be converted into francs within a fixed period of time[22]. The German authorities, for their part, manipulated indirect taxation, granting a 4% rebate on imports and levying a 4% surcharge on all exports except agricultural products covered by the CAP, as of 20 November. This 4% *de facto* revaluation of the commercial mark was complemented by the introduction of a reserve requirement of 100% on the increase in non-residents' bank deposits above the level of 15 November 1968[23].

The measures taken in both countries were successful in their immediate object of restoring confidence in the existing exchange rates. The exchanges re-opened in calm conditions on 25 November, and within two weeks DM 3300 million had flowed out of Germany. Yet by spring 1969, indications were growing that these expedients had not corrected the fundamental imbalance in the French and German payments positions. The French trade deficit grew from FFr 1628 million in the fourth quarter 1968 to FFr 2188 million in the first quarter 1969 and then skyrocketed to FFr 3722 million in the second quarter. This was in response to an upsurge in domestic demand in the last quarter 1968 and again in the second quarter 1969 which outstripped even the rapid increases in production and gave prices a further upwards push[24]. The implications of these developments were not lost on the exchange markets: despite the rigorous exchange controls, the terms of payment turned sharply against France by an estimated $800 million in the year ending 30 June 1969[25]. Once again, mistrust of the franc was setting in.

This time, however, the French government was in no position to ignore the growing weight of evidence that the franc was overvalued. Official reserves, which had totalled FFr 34 000 million at the start of 1968, had declined to FFr 13 000 million by November 1968, and had fallen still further to only FFr 10 000 million by the middle of 1969 – in part because of General de Gaulle's resignation on 28 April[26]. Yet the President's departure from office cut two ways. On the one hand, the trauma of the elections caused an exodus of capital which exacerbated the country's payments position; on the other, the installation of a new government afforded an opportunity for a change in economic strategy. The incoming administration, not under the same commitments as its predecessor, would be able to consider various approaches to the country's problems with a greater degree of detachment. In particular, the Pompidou government would not feel that its prestige depended on maintaining the parity of the franc, and it attached much less importance to the effects of a devaluation on France's standing abroad than had the General. With the body of evidence clearly indicating that the franc was overvalued and that the only way to 'restaurer les équilibres sans avoir à recourir à une politique de déflation génératrice de stagnation et de chômage' was to devalue the currency[27], the question confronting the government was not whether the franc should be devalued but when and by how much. Quite simply, the choice was between carrying out a controlled devaluation under conditions selected by the authorities or waiting until a crisis forced it on them. And this decision had to be made soon, for devaluation could not be put off much longer. The German elections scheduled for September set a rigid time limit, for if the necessary adjustment had not been carried out by then, there was the virtual certainty of speculative capital flows which would create a crisis situation. On 10 August 1969, the franc was devalued by 11.1%.

The devaluation was accompanied by a series of measures to help strengthen the balance of payments. Prices were frozen from 8 August until 15 September; an additional FFr 1200 million in public investment was transferred to the cyclical fund; government hiring was suspended; the base for the calculation of corporation tax was increased from 80 to 90% of profits; accelerated depreciation was no longer allowed for tax purposes; the investment incentives introduced in the aftermath of the May crisis were to end in March instead of December 1970; a minimum down payment of 50% was required for hire purchase; and a bonus of 1½% was to be paid on the amount by which savings deposits for the period 1 September 1969 – 31 May 1970 on average exceeded the level between January and August 1969[28].

The combination of the devaluation and these measures resulted in a rapid and marked improvement in the balance of payments. The deficit on the goods and services account fell from over FFr 3500 million in the second quarter to less than FFr 500 million in the third and moved into surplus by more than FFr 1000 million in the fourth. Although part of this turnround was a result of the stronger competitive position of French products in world markets, it primarily reflected a large change in the terms of payment as confidence in the franc was restored. The recovery of the current account, which moved into surplus in the first quarter of 1970, together with high interest rates, led to a growth in official reserves of some FFr 850 million in the last quarter of 1969 and almost FFr 3000 million in each of the first two quarters of 1970[29]. If any doubt remained, the prompt and satisfying effects of the devaluation confirmed that this was indeed the medicine that the French economy needed.

The Kiesinger government displayed the same unyielding opposition to a parity change as General de Gaulle, with the significant difference that it was in a much better position to maintain this stance because it did not face the prospect of its reserves being depleted. Thus, while it might concede that the 'temporary' border tax measures were not about to be rescinded, it could afford to ignore the facts that between 1962 and the end of 1969, prices in the Federal Republic rose 7½% less than they did in Germany's overseas markets and that the trade surplus which had shrunk to DM 2770 million in the first quarter of 1969, as a result of the November measures, increased to record levels of almost DM 4000 million in each of the two following quarters[30, 31]. The exchange markets were, however, more impressed by objective indicators. A growing undercurrent of mistrust in the mark's parity developed, surfacing during the financial upheaval following General de Gaulle's resignation at the end of April 1969. In the following two weeks DM 16 700 million in foreign funds entered the Federal Republic. Unmoved, the German government on 9 May reaffirmed its determination to maintain the existing parity and easily compelled the market to accept its decision. Yet almost half of the foreign capital which had flowed into the country was not repatriated, a clear indication that confidence had not been restored[32].

If the widespread expectation of a revaluation and the concomitant inflow of funds posed no threat to the authorities in terms of reserves, it did seriously impair their ability to manage the economy, because any attempt to restrain demand, by either fiscal or monetary means, was likely to produce an inlow of funds from abroad and an expansion of domestic liquidity. As the signs of overheating multiplied in the summer and fall of 1969, the Federal cabinet became divided over the issue of altering the exchange rate. Although the Government did not waver in its rejection of a revaluation, the revelation of this controversy, together with the prospect of the 28 September elections producing a new government not committed to maintaining the parity triggered a wave of speculation in early September[33]. By 24 September DM 6000 million had flowed into Germany, of which more than DM 2000 million was concentrated in the final three days. The authorities responded by closing the foreign exchange markets on 25 and 26 September. When the markets re-opened on 29 September, the speculative inflow continued unabated, with the Bundesbank having to absorb over DM 1000 million in foreign currencies before the exchanges were closed for a second time[34]. Unencumbered by previous statements that the mark was not overvalued, the Social-Democratic government that had replaced the Grand Coalition decided to float the mark with effect from 30 September and subsequently fixed the parity at $ 1 = DM 3.66. The new rate, considerably higher than the floating rate, was justified on the grounds that the border taxes were being repealed and hence that the new exchange rate would have to allow for the differences between German and international prices that had arisen over the past eight years[35].

As in France, the parity changes resulted in a rapid run-down of speculative positions. Between 1 October and 20 November, some DM 11 000 million in foreign capital was repatriated. As a result, the dangerously high level of liquidity started to decline, and with the ebbing of speculative pressure, the authorities were able, for the first time in 18 months, to pursue the contractionary policies needed to restrain domestic demand[36]. The success of the revaluation and the skilful manner in which it was carried out not only paid economic dividends; it also enhanced the prestige of the new government and particularly that of the Finance and Economics Minister, Karl Schiller. As in France, what was amazing was not that the remedy was so successful, but that its application was so long postponed. The evidence that the franc was overvalued and the mark was undervalued had become conclusive by the end of 1968[37]. Yet the exchange rate adjustments were only completed in October 1969. For almost a year, the two governments had used a whole series of expedients to try to avoid or at least delay taking this decisive step. only after both had been replaced and even then only under circumstances which left them no realistic alternative were the parity changes finally carried out.

In both cases, the reason for this resolute opposition to exchange rate adjustments was clear: whatever the net economic benefits, revaluation or devaluation was perceived as entailing large political costs. The French and German governments had staked their prestige on maintaining the existing exchange rates and were well aware that they could not adopt a course of devaluation or revaluation with impunity; they would be admitting that they had been wrong. Moreover, as the maintenance of the parity was an important object as well as a key element in their economic policies, they would effectively be conceding that they had failed in their management of the economy. Quite simply, the French government could not have devalued the franc without tacitly acknowledging that its post-1968 economic strategy had not worked. Yet even had the ministers not taken such a strong stand against an alteration of the exchange rate and even had the preservation of the parity not been such a central issue in economic policy, there were important reasons for not resorting to this particular medicine.

Although a modification of the exchange rate might be in a country's best economic interests, it nevertheless entailed very real economic costs – for the entire economy and for particular sectors – that could translate into political liabilities. The adjustment costs of shifting resources from one employment into another could be considerable, in terms of lost production as well as the more personal costs of unemployment, retraining and perhaps relocation[38]. The long-term advantages might well outweigh these immediate welfare losses, but governments in general have a short time horizon, extending only to the next general election. Moreover, the gains and losses would not necessarily be equally distributed throughout the economy. The export sector, for instance, would be especially hard hit by a revaluation, a consideration not politically insignificant in Germany with its relatively high percentage of employment in export-oriented industries. Of course, costs and benefits could, in theory, be redistributed so that the net welfare change was shared equally. However, aside from the practical problems of designing and introducing such a mechanism, it is a political reality that those who lost from this transfer would be unfavourably disposed towards the Government, even if on balance they would be better off than had the adjustment not been made.

Large as the direct political and economic costs of parity changes might be, the accompanying measures to restore payments equilibrium could be even greater liabilities, for parity changes were invariably coupled with moves to modify the level and composition of demand, an area of high political sensitivity. Revaluation or devaluation might reduce the adjustments in demand needed to achieve external balance, but this did not make those that were still required any more palatable. The August 1969 devaluation of the franc was carried out precisely because it was a means of avoiding the massive reduction of demand, resulting in *stagnation et chômage*, which would have otherwise been required to correct the imbalance in the French payments position[39]. Yet a reduction in domestic absorption was still indispensable. To ensure that the resources required to strengthen the balance of payments were made available so that the Government's target of equilibrium on the trade account by mid 1970 would be met, domestic demand could not rise by more than about 3% in real terms in 1970[40]. Because it was clear that even with the marked increase in savings, demand would not stay within these limits, the government was faced with the necessity of increasing taxes and/or cutting expenditure. Although the post-devaluation budget measures aimed at maintaining a high level of aggregate demand and reduced disposable income by far less than would have been required without the devaluation, they did cut sharply into the net income of households from the fourth quarter onwards[41]. The Government knew it would be held accountable for this. Likewise, the measures taken in late 1969 to restrain domestic demand in Germany were a liability to the Government. The need to stop the accelerating cycle of wage and price increases was recognized – indeed the revaluation was praised for allowing the authorities to take action to restrain inflationary pressures – but the steps taken to reduce demand were severely criticized as pushing the economy towards recession[42].

Thus, for both the French and German governments, parity changes and the accompanying measures entailed substantial political costs, even though they were in the country's best long-term economic interests. It is therefore hardly surprising that governments generally saw exchange rate adjustments as a last resort. That parity changes should be such a liability to any but perhaps a newly-elected government might appear unjustified – much as blaming the doctor for the unpleasantness of the medicine – but the incontrovertible fact remains that most governments wished to avoid exchange rate modifications. European governments were therefore attracted to EMU as a means of consigning this unpopular policy instrument to the scrapheap of history. Moreover, in 1969 the maintenance of fixed and immutable exchange rates did not appear so unrealistic. There was a high degree of confidence that the new European parities would prove durable and that the series of payments crises dating from 1967 had now come to an end. After all, the new exchange rates for the franc and the mark had been accepted by the market as definitive, and the French and German payments imbalances were rapidly on the way to being resolved. Thus, the proposals for EMU came onto the stage of European affairs at a very opportune moment, as the governments were both interested in eliminating exchange rate movements – or more accurately proscribing them – and convinced that this was feasible.

Advantages of a Community mutual financial support system

At the same time that EMU interested national governments as a means of doing away with parity changes, it also attracted attention as a way of introducing a system of mutual financial assisance. Only through a network of credit arrangements with other countries could central banks hope to defend parities in the face of capital movements greatly exceeding their reserves. Governments had long recognized the benefits of helping each other in international monetary affairs, a recognition reflected in the establishment of such institutions as the IMF. Both the scope and the degree of existing co-operation were, however, far from ideal. In order to prevent a temporary outflow of funds in excess of a country's reserves compelling it, even though its payments position was fundamentally sound, to change its parity or to adopt policies in neither its own nor the world's interest, central banks would lend funds to each other during payments crises. Indeed there was a tacit agreement among the industrialized countries that no government would, because of a lack of reserves, be forced into altering its exchange rate against its will[43]. Yet despite attempts in such bodies as the OECD, there was no real co-ordination of national monetary policies to prevent disruptive interest-induced flows of funds, and the provision of assistance was contingent on the approval of the authorities concerned. By the end of the 1960s, when massive international capital movements had become a fact of life, it was clear that a much broader and deeper co-operation was needed[44, 45].

The exchange crises of 1967–69 revealed both the value and the limitations of the existing forms of co-operation. In terms of aid provided, the results were impressive: Germany alone provided Britain with bilateral and multilateral assistance totalling over DM 2000 million in 1967, as well as making a DM 1600 million line of credit available in 1968. In addition, the Bundesbank placed DM 4500 million at the disposal of the French authorities in 1968[46]. All told over $ 3000 million in international support was made available to France, of which more than half was actually used[47]. Yet perhaps a more important indication of the worth of the international assistance system was that it enabled the French to defend the parity of the franc throughout 1968 and to devalue it in 1969 *'hors de toute pression extérieure immédiate'*[48].

If the mutual assistance system had functioned well, its shortcomings had also become obvious. The provision of funds was not automatic, and delays at critical moments could result from the need to arrange lines of credit or activate the machinery for multilateral assistance. More important, even though aid might invariably be forthcoming, that there was no guarantee that it would be furnished could act to depress further confidence in the currency under pressure. As an attempt to remedy these failings in the system, a mechanism for recycling reserves within the Group of Ten was informally proposed on 10 February 1969. These arrangements eliminated practically all of the causes of delay, but they stopped short of actually guaranteeing assistance[49]. Although this omission would not in practice have made any real difference in the provision of aid, certain countries regarded a formal commitment as important for reasons of market psychology, and for them economic and monetary union exerted an attraction because it entailed automatic mutual assistance.

EMU had a further appeal in this connection in that it was seen as a means of introducing a system of mutual assistance that would not only provide automatic support but also challenge American dominance in monetary affairs. At first, it may be difficult to understand how excluding the United States, which provided the largest share of assistance during payments crises, could be regarded as desirable, because this would seem to weaken the mechanism. Yet it was precisely the pre-eminence of the United States in international monetary affairs and the role of the dollar as the primary intervention currency which made the creation of a new Community monetary assistance mechanism so attractive to certain member states. It was seen as a way of asserting European independence from the United States[50]. Moreover, it would do so without penalizing the Six because the new arrangements would complement, not replace, the old. In other words, it was an opportunity for certain countries, especially France, to make political capital at very low real cost. Interest in the mutual assistance aspect of EMU however was primarily due to the fact that it responded to the need to expand and strengthen the mutual assistance system; the challenge to American dominance was an incidental bonus.

Opportunity to challenge American dominance

Yet the perception that EMU could be a means towards ending the American hegemony in international monetary affairs was a significant factor militating in favour of EMU on both political and economic grounds. The French in particular disliked the privileged position the Bretton Woods arrangements conferred on the dollar and argued that the United States was exploiting this situation to acquire real assets abroad in exchange for non-convertible dollars[51, 52]. The formation of an economic and monetary union would at the minimum allow the member states to hold their reserves in assets other than dollars, while the introduction of a common European currency would not only strengthen the Community's identity, in particular in relation to the United States, but also challenge the supremacy of the dollar as the international intervention and reserve currency[53]. Realistically, it was doubtful whether the Community countries could overcome the American dominance in international monetary affairs. However, by acting in concert they could at least have a greater effect on the international forces that affected them and thereby significantly reduce American influence on European economic affairs.

The idea of the Community acting as a unit in international economic affairs had a particular appeal in the political climate on the eve of the Hague Summit, as recent events had demonstrated that the Member States had interests which were distinct from, and sometimes in conflict with, those of the United States. For instance, on the question of issuing SDRs, which the American government strongly supported, the German government voted affirmatively but was concerned lest the introduction of these new reserve assets should increase the – in German eyes – excessively high level of international liquidity and thereby further reduce the pressure on countries in payments deficit to take corrective action[54]. The French authorities had even greater reservations about the new 'international currency', which, in their view, 'ne saurait apporter à lui seul, une solution satisfaisante aux problèmes de l'équilibre des règlements internationaux, puisqu'il ne fait que compléter la gamme des palliatifs imaginés pour atténuer les difficultés les plus pressantes'[55]. Such variations in official attitudes towards SDRs notwithstanding, the Belgian, Dutch, French, German, and, indeed, the Italian positions all displayed a staunch desire to strengthen discipline in the international monetary system, especially by reinforcing the obligation of convertibility into gold. On this point they came into conflict with the American authorities.

The fundamental disagreement over the role of gold reflected differences far deeper than conflicting views on the way in which the international monetary system should function: the demands for convertibility into gold were unmistakably directed towards the dollar and were a transparent attempt to force the United States to change its domestic economic policies by requiring that it restore its balance of payments to equilibrium[56, 57].

The basic problem, in the European view, was the policy of 'benign neglect': American economic policies were set on the basis of domestic considerations, without regard to their repercussions at the international level. This had led to demand outstripping supply in the United States since the middle of the 1960s with two consequences of particular concern to its major trading partners, Europe and Japan: there had been a gradual deterioration in the balance of payments and a steady rise in prices. These developments had transmitted inflationary impulses abroad, on both the demand and cost sides. And while it would be an exaggeration to claim that the United States had 'exported' inflation to western Europe, the American appetite for imports had been an important contributing factor[58]. Moreover, for certain countries it was adding insult to injury that one of the major reasons for the excessive demand and the payments deficit of the United States should be the American intervention in Vietnam, which they opposed on political grounds, but were in some sense being forced to finance through the acquisition of large amounts of dollars. The European governments recognized that they could exert little direct influence on the demand management policies pursued in Washington and still less on the conduct of the Vietnam War. They hoped, however, that by putting pressure on the United States to reduce its payments deficit, they could moderate the expansionary pressures on their economies and perhaps even diminish American activity in Indochina. Hence their interest in convertibility as a means of limiting the United States's ability to run a balance of payments deficit and their attraction to EMU, since if they were to have a decisive influence on the United States, it was indispensable that they act as a unit.

Advantages of co-ordinating economic policies

So far the issues considered have been international in character, involving relations between two or more countries. In these instances there were tangible benefits from co-operation and discernible common Community interests which acted to bring the member states together. As we now turn to issues internal to the member states, and specifically to that set of motivations for EMU that arose from its offering a way to exert an influence on the domestic economic policies of other governments the commonality of interest disappears and the differences among the member states emerge more sharply.

The co-ordination of domestic economic policies was an element which increasingly attracted national governments to EMU at the end of the 1960s. It was not, of course, the prospect of a common set of economic policies which motivated them. A Community short-term economic policy, such as a uniform monetary policy, was totally unrealistic and unacceptable given the dissimilar conditions and different objectives of the individual economies[59]. It was, indeed, precisely the divergence between the interests of the Six which gave common policy-making its fascination, for it was perceived as a means of exerting an influence on other countries' policies so as to make them conform more closely to one's own interests. As recent events had demonstrated, the high degree of economic interdependence among the Six meant that national governments could effectively control domestic conditions only if they could influence policy decisions made beyond their borders.

As the most open of the Community economies, with approximately half of its GNP being exported, Belgium–Luxembourg was very conscious of its dependence on decisions made abroad, especially those of its partners in the Community, who together absorbed about two-thirds of its exports[60]. A contraction of demand in these countries had an immediate and appreciable impact on the level of economic activity in Belgium, where the fall in demand in France and Germany in 1966–67 resulted in the nation's worst postwar recession up to that time, as well as a substantial balance of payments deficit. Moreover, the authorities in Brussels were limited in their ability to offset impulses from abroad: efforts to stimulate the economy proved ineffective because much of the effect was dissipated abroad. In any event, because of their effect on the balance of payments, they had to be largely delayed until after reflationary action had been taken in other Community countries; the subsequent recovery was more a result of the resurgence of demand in the United States, Britain and Germany than of any Belgian initiatives[61]. Under these circumstances it is hardly surprising that the Belgian government would grasp at an opportunity to influence the short-term economic policies of its bigger partners.

Although the French economy was much less vulnerable to developments abroad and the authorities better able to control the level of domestic economic activity because exports constituted less than 15% of GNP, the French government was also interested in influencing the conjunctural policies of the other Community countries, especially Germany, which alone absorbed almost 20% of French exports. The rapid decline in sales to the Federal Republic beginning in May 1966, as a consequence of the recession in Germany, was a major cause of the slowdown on the other side of the Rhine, just as the recovery in Germany was an important factor in the subsequent upswing in French production starting towards the end of 1967[62]. Yet the significance of exports to the French economy went far beyond their immediate effect on the level of economic activity, for they were vital as a source of foreign exchange, the lack of which had plagued the French economy for decades and imposed a large constraint on the actions of successive governments[63, 64]. Although the 1969 parity changes, by creating the prospect of a strong balance of payments position, temporarily reduced interest in influencing the economic policies of other member states, the French government continued to be attracted by this aspect of EMU. At the same time, however, it recognized the potential threat this posed to its freedom of action in economic affairs and strongly opposed the idea of formulating conjunctural policies at the Community level[65].

If the Belgian and French governments were interested in EMU as a means of influencing the demand policies pursued in Germany, conjunctural policy co-ordination held no less attraction for the authorities in Bonn for two main reasons. First, ever since the hyperinflation episode of the interwar period, price stability had been one of the principal aims of economic policy[66]. Attainment of this goal was, however, jeopardized by the poor performance of Germany's trading partners in this respect, for under a system of fixed exchange rates any country whose price level rose less rapidly than the international average would be subjected to inflationary pressures from abroad in the form of an insatiable demand for its products. The upward pressure on prices could, of course, be temporarily resisted by contracting domestic demand and sterilizing the monetary inflows, but 'in Kleinen

Ländern früher, in grösseren Ländern später wird die Restriktionspolitik schliesslich doch zum Scheitern verurteilt sein'[67]. Events in 1968 and 1969 fully confirmed the Wissenschaftliche Beirat's assertion that without international co-ordination of demand and price policies the only way to check the spread of inflation was through parity changes. The German experience in the late 1960s suggested, however, that even exchange rate adjustments could not completely insulate a country from more rapid price increases abroad: although German exports did become more expensive abroad in the aftermath of the revaluation, there was at best only a slight pause in the rise of the price of imports in the Federal Republic[68].

Second, the opportunity to exercise control over the conjunctural policies of the other member states attracted the German government not only because it was seen to be a prerequisite for achieving price stability at home but also because it was regarded as necessary to safeguard the customs union of which Germany was a major beneficiary. As the events of 1968 had shown, divergent price trends constituted a potential threat to the free movement of goods throughout the Community. Countries with inflation rates chronically higher than those of their neighbours were likely to experience a deterioration of their trade balance and if this led to what the authorities regarded as a severe drain on the reserves, it was by no means inconceivable that tariffs, quantitative controls, import deposits, or a multitude of other restrictions on imports might be imposed. France had, after all, resorted to import controls in the aftermath of the May 1968 crisis and so, for that matter, had the United Kingdom. True, the French restrictions had been lifted by August 1969, but this did not lessen the German concern that unless the differences between the rates of inflation in the member states were reduced, similar action might be taken again – and with a less pleasant conclusion.

The recognition that the high degree of economic interdependence prevented individual governments acting independently from effectively controlling domestic economic conditions militated in favour of EMU not only by making national governments keen to influence the policies of other member states but also by reducing opposition to the notion of a common monetary policy. European governments had in the past been hostile to such an idea, because they regarded the monetary variables (such as interest rates and money supply) as having too direct an influence on the nation's economic well-being to permit the conduct of monetary affairs to be transferred to the Community, especially because economic conditions and hence the appropriate monetary policies varied significantly among the six countries. The emergence of large-scale international capital movements in the course of the 1960s, as the growth of the Eurodollar market together with the increased international mobility of funds acted to integrate national capital markets, however, created a situation in which the ability of national governments to pursue an independent course in monetary affairs was impaired. Quite simply, credit conditions were being determined more and more by forces beyond the control of national authorities, and this increased the incentive for the member states to work together at the same time that it lessened the objections to limiting an already restricted national autonomy[70, 71].

The constraints that international capital movements imposed on the control of domestic monetary conditions were perhaps most strikingly illustrated by the experience of Germany in the 12 months before the October 1969 revaluation of the mark. As output began to strain against the limits of the country's productive capacity and inflationary pressures started to appear in the last quarter of 1968, the Bundesbank came to regard the level of domestic liquidity as excessive. It recognized, however, that any attempt to tighten the money supply would merely result in large inflows of interest-sensitive capital and, through its effect on domestic price and demand conditions, strengthen expectations of a revaluation, thereby stimulating further inflows. Under such conditions, 'keine inländische Anstrengung zur Restriktion . . . anhaltenden Erfolg haben konnte, es sei denn, die Freizügigkeit und Integration des internationalen Waren – und Kapitalverkehrs wäre eingeschränkt worden'[72]. The danger of provoking capital inflows limited the scope for initiatives in fiscal policy as well, because any reduction in aggregate demand, could be expected not only to slow the rate of price increases but also to increase the current account surplus. Thus, the vulnerability of the external flank effectively hamstrung both monetary and fiscal policy. Moreover, recognition of the dilemma facing the authorities itself became an important factor stimulating expectations of a revaluation. Recognizing the futility of trying to moderate domestic demand, the authorities resolved instead to reduce the balance of payments surpluses by discouraging capital inflows and promoting long-term capital exports. Interest rates were consequently allowed to fluctuate in response to market conditions at levels sometimes near zero and generally below comparable Eurodollar rates adjusted for the mark's exchange rate premium. Such a policy of accommodation ran counter, of course, to the needs of the domestic situation, but the Bundesbank had little real alternative[73, 74].

Although the problems faced by the French authorities in the year prior to the August 1969 devaluation of the franc were generally opposite to those in Germany, here too monetary conditions were strongly influenced by forces emanating from outside the country. In order to prevent an outflow of funds that the reserves could not sustain, the Banque de France had to keep interest rates closely aligned to trends in the Eurodollar market, allowing day-to-day rates to rise from 4 to 9% between January 1968 and August 1969[75]. Yet the scope for pursuing an independent monetary policy was greater than in Germany because exchange control and structural factors acted to insulate French monetary conditions from external influences. Consequently, money market rates, while influenced by Eurocurrency levels, could diverge by 2–3%[76]. Moreover, because the major source of re-financing for banks at this time was the discount market, the Banque de

France was able to fix the cost of credit to some extent independently of rates on the money market and also to make funds available at reduced rates for special purposes, such as export finance, commercial credit, and housing[77, 78]. The compartmentalized nature of the French financial system clearly facilitated the authorities' task in maintaining conditions of monetary ease to aid the recovery from the May 1968 crisis while guarding against the outflow of capital. Nevertheless, there was a limit to the 'autonomy' enjoyed by the Banque de France, for external constraints, albeit not inconsistent with domestic needs, forced a steady rise in the discount rate from 3½ to 6% during 1968[79].

international environment, to establish credit conditions appropriate to the domestic situation, but here too the authorities were unable to conduct a truly independent monetary policy. The upward trend in world interest rates during most of 1968 and 1969 was broadly compatible with the contractionary stance assumed by the Banque Nationale de Belgique in response to the rise in prices and salaries that started in second half 1968. Nevertheless, despite a system of exchange controls, the danger of international capital flows did restrict the room for official manoeuvre[80]. As early as December 1968, the discount rate had to be raised ¾% to stem a disturbing capital outflow, and increases totalling a further 3% were necessary by September 1969, in addition to ceilings on bank lending. Even so, it remained profitable to re-lend funds abroad. The authorities tried to reduce the haemorrhaging of reserves by limiting the banks' foreign positions and their recourse to the discount facility, but the continuing outflow finally forced the tightening of credit conditions the Banque Nationale had hoped to avoid[81].

In these three countries, then, the experiences of 1968 and 1969 had demonstrated that the international mobility of capital placed limits on the monetary conditions that could be maintained in any country: any policy that caused interest rates to diverge substantially from international, and specifically Eurodollar, rates would in the absence of offsetting exchange rate expectations result in an equilibrating flow of funds. This did not mean that there could be only one Community-wide set of interest rates. International capital mobility was by no means perfect, and because of factors such as poor information and exchange risks, appreciable differentials could exist without giving rise to capital movements. But the room for variation was not infinite. Sooner or later, the equilibrating mechanism would come into action, even in the face of attempts to isolate national capital markets by administrative action, for money, like water, always finds its own level. Stringent exchange controls did not prevent an outflow of over FFr 3500 million from France in the aftermath of General de Gaulle's resignation[82]. The 100% reserve requirement the Bundesbank placed on the growth of non-resident bank accounts did reduce the inflows to banks, but only because capital flowed in by other routes, such as the purchase of German securities: banks, which had channelled two-thirds of the inflow in autumn 1968, received just one-quarter of the influx in spring 1969[83]. And the Belgian authorities could have told their German counterparts that any attempt to block these new routes would have been equally inefficacious, for even with an elaborate two-tiered exchange system, Belgium had seen its reserves decline by almost BFr 10 000 million during the first nine months of 1969, even though the customs statistics showed a deficit of less than BFr 3000 million[84]. The lesson was clear. Direct controls might be an obstacle to international capital movements, but they were certainly not an effective barrier behind which national governments could recover their ability to pursue an independent line in monetary policy.

Indeed on the evidence of 1968 and 1969 the ability of national authorities to control monetary conditions within their their boundaries was, if anything, decreasing. International capital movements had greatly increased in size during this period, so that whereas some DM 9500 million was estimated to have entered Germany during the November 1968 crisis, the comparable figure was almost DM 17 000 million in the spring and a further DM 10 000 million in the fall of 1969[85]. The obvious implication was that a country allowing a substantial covered interest differential to emerge could expect short-term capital movements on a scale which could not only place great pressure on the exchange rate but also bring about a change in domestic monetary conditions. The forces would, of course, be greatest in small, financially 'open' countries, but by the end of the 1960s all the members of the European Community had come to recognize that such external constraints prevented them from pursuing a truly independent course in monetary policy.

This realization may have lessened their opposition to a common monetary policy, as they saw the 'loss' of sovereignty in its proper perspective, and increased their interest in co-operation in economic affairs in order to further their own aims. It had not, however, led the member states to favour a common Community monetary policy. The reason was quite simple: even if it were not so objectionable as it once had been, a common monetary policy still held no attraction for the member states. The experience of 1968 and 1969 had not demonstrated that a single Community set of interest rates or a uniform rate of growth in the money supply would have brought political or economic benefits; on the contrary, events had made it clear that it would have entailed substantial costs. External constraints might have produced a certain similarity of policy in the member states and the realities of the situation might have encouraged the Six to act as a unit at the international level, but the desire of national governments to move in divergent directions had been too obvious and the differences in their goals too marked to suggest a common monetary policy would have been anything less than disastrous.

In other words, a central element of EMU was regarded not only as undesirable but also unattainable. At a more fundamental level, the differences between the member states in terms both of their objectives and of their circumstances that are evident in this chapter raise serious doubts about the prospects for economic and monetary union. That France should have a particularly high, and Germany an especially low rate of price increases, that external forces should impose a tighter constraint on German interest rates than French, or that France and Italy should be more attracted by a system of short-term mutual assistance are all manifestations of the divergences in national interests among the Community countries. That such basic differences should exist among the member states clearly did not augur well for the success of EMU.

The reaction of the member states to the idea of interregional transfers hardly painted a more encouraging picture. Understandably, each country's position reflected whether it expected to contribute or receive funds. In the case of most member states there was little doubt, and Belgium, Germany, Italy, Luxembourg and the Netherlands behaved predictably. The French stance, however, merits greater consideration, for France, whose future role as a net donor or beneficiary was most open to question, displayed the greatest interest in such a mechanism. It was, of course, natural that France, with its above-average rate of inflation should have been a strong proponent of a system designed to mitigate balance of payments difficulties within the Community. The experience of 1968–69, when the French government had been forced to abandon its programme of growth, modernization and full employment because of pressure on the franc was too recent a memory. Although the authorities in Paris were confident that the actions taken to rationalize productive structures and improve the functioning of the economy would restrain the upward movement in prices and that the 12½% devaluation of August 1969 – far greater than the 6–8% needed to compensate for the differences between France's price performance and that of her trading partners – would keep the balance of payments in surplus, they were still strongly attracted by a system to reduce regional imbalances within the Community[86]. Both France and the Community as a whole were seen as benefiting from such a mechanism. An interregional transfer system would obviously operate to France's advantage if she were a net recipient; even if she were not, it would indirectly serve French interests, for France was unlikely to be a major contributor and would therefore gain on balance from avoiding payments crises, trade restrictions or deflationary measures that might endanger French export sales, growth and healthy demand conditions at home. The Community would benefit from a higher aggregate level of employment, the avoidance of trade restrictions and, most important in French eyes, the modernization of its economic structures. With perhaps more than a touch of self-interest, the French authorities asserted that curbing demand in regions of high inflation was a *pis-aller*, arguing that in placing external balance ahead of economic growth, modernization as well as growth was being sacrificed, because the level of investment required to transform productive structures would be forthcoming only in conditions of high and sustained demand. And without modernizing the means of production, the French authorities argued, there was no way to achieve a lasting reduction in inflationary propensities[87, 88, 89]. It was an intriguing theory, but in the final analysis, national interest determined the French position, as indeed those of all the member states.

Once again it was clear that the appeal of EMU to the member states lay in its ability to act as a means of furthering national interests. It was precisely this belief that economic and monetary unification might serve as the vehicle for the attainment of specific national goals which aroused the interest of the European countries. The events of 1968 and 1969 had transformed the outlook of the national governments. Attitudes revealed to be unrealistic or outmoded had been abandoned and in their place new aims substituted. This redefinition of national interest in each of the member states was the key to the favourable responses to the idea of EMU, for these new targets happened to coincide with specific elements of economic and monetary unification. The aspects of EMU that appealed to individual member states differed from one to another reflecting the divergences in national objectives. That there was no interest in common policies except as a means of obtaining control over the policies and actions of the other Community countries was itself eloquent testimony to the insurmountable differences between conditions and goals in the six economies. Yet far from casting doubt on the future of economic and monetary unification, these very differences militated in its favour, for integration was seen as a force to be used to dominate, not unite. In other words, the process of constructing an economic and monetary union was seen as a way of achieving avowedly national aims, and dissimilar, indeed conflicting, as these might be, the member states were united in their interest in this new project. From these disparate motivations emerged on the eve of the Hague Summit a political climate favourable to the proposals for the construction of an economic and monetary union within the European Community.

1 Fred Hirsch, 'The political economics of European monetary integration', *The World Today*, **XXVIII**, 10 October 1972, pp. 424–433
2 *Monatsberichte der Deutschen Bundesbank* (hereafter cited as *Monatsberichte*), October 1969, pp. 5–6
3 'Le rapport économique et financier (du Projet de Loi de Finances pour 1969) (hereafter cited as 'Le rapport économique et financier') in Ministère de l'Economie et des Finances (France), *Statistiques et Etudes Financières*, **XX**, November 1968, pp. 1170–1175
4 OECD, *Economic Surveys, France*, 7–12 (1971)
5 *Geschäftsbericht der Deutschen Bundesbank für das Jahr* (hereafter cited as *Geschäftsbericht*), p. 19
6 France, Ministère de l'Economie et des Finances, *Notes Bleues* (Supplement), *Statistiques et Etudes Financières*, **54**, February 1970 p. 1
7 *Geschäftsbericht*, 1968, pp. 10–18

8 *Jahreswirtschaftsbericht 1968 der Bundesregierung* (hereafter cited as *Jahreswirtschaftsbericht*) p.28
9 'Le rapport économique et financier', *Statistiques et Etudes Financières*, **XX**, 1969, pp. 1192–1199, 1226–1233
10 *Monatsberichte*, August 1968, p.1
11 OECD, *Economic Surveys, France*, 1968, pp.23–30
12 *Monatsberichte*, October 1968, pp.3–6
13 *Monatsberichte*, February 1969, pp.5–9, 35–42
14 *Monatsberichte*, May 1968, pp.39–50
15 *Monatsberichte*, August 1968, pp.41–52
16 'Le rapport économique et financier', *Statistiqués et Etudes Financières*, **XXI**, 1969, pp.1170–1175
17 OECD, *Economic Surveys, France*, 1968, pp.28–31
18 OECD, *Economic Surveys, France*, 1968, pp.28–31
19 *Monatsberichte*, November–December 1968, pp.3–4
20 'Le rapport économique et financier', *Statistiqués et Etudes Financières*, **XXI**,1969, pp.1165–1167, 1192–1199
21 Leonhard Gleske, 'Währungspolitik und Agrarmarkt in der Europäischen Wirtschaftsgemeinschaft', *Europe–Archiv*, **XXV**, 1970, pp.22–23
22 'Währungspolitik und Agrarmarkt in der Europäischen Wirtschaftsgemeinschaft', pp.22–23
23 *Monatsberichte*, November–December 1968, pp.3–4
24 'Le rapport économique et financier', *Statistiqués et Etudes Financières*, **XXII**, 1970, pp.5–12
25 Banque de France, *Compte rendu*, 1969, (Exercice 1969) [hereafter cited as *Compte rendu*] pp.8–12, 43–46
26 *Compte rendu*, 1968, pp.25–26
27 'Le rapport économique et financier', *Statistiqués et Etudes Financières*, **XXII**, 1970, p.12
28 *Le Rapport Annuel du Conseil National du Crédit* (France) [hereafter cited as CNC] 1969, pp.17–21
29 *Compte rendu*, 1969, pp.8–12
30 *Geschäftsbericht*, 1969, p.17
31 *Monatsberichte*, December 1971, p.68*
32 *Monatsberichte*, June 1969, pp.5–8
33 See, for instance, *Geschäftsbericht*, 1969, Pt. I, and OECD, *Economic Surveys, Germany*, 1969, pp.24–27
34 *Monatsberichte*, October 1969, pp.5–7
35 *Geschäftsbericht*, 1969, pp.16–19
36 *Monatsberichte*, November 1969, pp.5–8
37 Germany, Sachverständigenrat zur Begutachtung der gesamtwirtschaftlichen Entwicklung, 'Binnenwirtschaftliche Stabilität und aussenwirtschaftliches Gleichgewicht', (Sondergutachten vom 30. Juni 1969), in *Im Sog des Booms*, 109–118 (Jahresgutachten 1969/1970)Germany, Council of Experts, 'Domestic Stability and External Balance', Special Report dated 30 June 1969 in *Im Sog des Booms* (Annual Report 1969/70)
38 On the costs of factor movements, see J. E. Meade, *Trade and Welfare*, Oxford University Press, London (1955), Chap. XXII
39 'Le rapport économique et financier', *Statiqués et Etudes Financières*, **XXII**, 1970, p.12
40 'Le rapport économique et financier, *Statiqués et Etudes Financières*, **XXII**, 1970, pp.31–35
41 OECD, *Economic Surveys, France*, 1969, pp.18–23
42 *Geschäftsbericht*, 1969, pp.24–26
43 Fred Hirsch, *Money International*, Penguin Books, Harmondsworth, 1969, Chap. 12
44 *Report to the Council and the Commission on the realisation by stages of Economic and Monetary Union in the Community* [Werner Report], in *Bulletin* (of the European Communities), supplement, November 1970, p.8
45 *Commission Memorandum to the Council on the Co-ordination of Economic Policies and Monetary Co-operation Within the Community* [Barre Report], 12 February 1969, pp.6–9
46 *Jahreswirtschaftsbericht*, 1969, p.26
47 *Compte rendu*, 1969, pp.12–14 and *Geschäftsbericht*, 1968, pp.40–44
48 *Compte rendu*, 1969, p.6
49 *Geschäftsbericht*, 1968, pp.35–36
50 Bela Balassa, 'Monetary Integration in the European Common Market'. In Alexander K. Swoboda (ed.), *Europe and the Evolution of the International Monetary System*, Institut Universitaire de Hautes Etudés Internationalés, 1973, p.95
51 Guy Berger, Le Conflit entre l'Europe et les États-Unis', *Revue Francaise de Science Politique*, **XXII**(2), April 1972, pp.348–358
52 Hirsch, *Money International*, pp.499–503
53 T. Peeters, 'The Europa Scheme' and Robert A. Mundell, 'Why Europe?'. In European Communities' Commission, *European Economic Integration and Monetary Unification*, 1973, Appendices

54 *Geschäftsbericht*, 1969, pp. 40–42
55 *Compte rendu*, 1969, p. 18
56 Berger, 'Le Conflit entre l'Europe et les États-Unis', pp. 348–358
57 Edward L. Morse, 'La Politique Américaine de Manipulation de la Crise', *Revue Francaise de Science Politique*, **XXII**(2), April 1972, pp. 359–381
58 Susan Strange, 'The Dollar Crisis 1971', *International Affairs*, **XLVIII**(2), April 1972, pp. 191–200
59 Bela Balassa and Stephen Resnick, *Monetary Integration and the Consistency of Policy Objectives in the European Common Market*, Department of Political Economy of the Johns Hopkins University Working Paper in Economics #7, esp. pp. 14–18
60 Belgium, Ministère des Affaires Economiques, *l'Economie belge en 1968*, p. 337
61 Banque Nationale de Belgique, *Annual Report 1968*, pp. 30–32
62 'Le rapport économique et financier', Statistiques et Etudes Financières, **XIX**, November 1967, pp. 1446–1451
63 Commissariat Général du Plan d'Equipement et de la Productivité, Ve-Plan, Rapport Général de la Commission de l'Economie Générale et du Financement, pp. 82–116
64 Commissariat Général du Plan d'Equipement et de la Productivité, VIe-Plan de Developpement Economique et Social, 1971–75, pp. 9–30
65 'Le rapport économique et financier', *Statiqués et Etudes Financières*, **XXII**, 1970, pp. 13–14
66 Albert, 'La désunion monétaire européenne', *Revue francaise de Science Politique*, **XXII**, (2), April 1972, pp. 385–387
67 *Jahreswirtschaftsbericht*, 1968, p. 27
68 *Geschäftsbericht*, 1969, p. 22
69 European Communities Commission, *European Economic Integration and Monetary Unification*, 1973, pp. 4–18
70 The issue of economic interdependence is explored in detail in Richard N. Cooper, *The Economics of Interdependence*, 1968
71 The subject of a European capital market is thoroughly examined in European Economic Community, *The Development of a European Capital Market*, 1967, (Segré Report)
72 EEC, *The Development of a European Capital Market*, p. 13
73 EEC, *The Development of a European Capital Market*, pp. 1–15
74 *Geschäftsbericht*, 1968, pp. 50–57
75 *CNC*, 1968, pp. 32–37
76 *CNC*, 1969, pp. 25–31
77 European Communities, Monetary Committee, *La politique monétaire*, 1972, pp. 162–169
78 *Compte rendu*, 1969, pp. 28–32, 54–59
79 *CNC*, 1968, pp. 24–27
80 Banque Nationale de Belgique, *Annual Report 1968*, pp. 11–21
81 Banque Nationale de Belgique, *Annual Report 1969*, pp. 7–13
82 *CNC*, 1969, p. 26
83 *Monatsberichte*, June 1969, p. 5
84 Banque Nationale de Belgique, *Annual Report 1969*, pp. 72–73
85 *Monatsberichte*, November–December 1968, p. 3; September, 1969, pp. 33–41; November 1969, pp. 31–35
86 Conversation with Professor Jacques Delors, 9 March 1976
87 Commissariat Général du Plan d'Equipement et de la Productivité, VIe Plan de Développement Economique et Social, 1971–1975, esp. pp. 9–19
88 OECD, *Economic surveys, France*, 1970, pp. 48–55
89 OECD, *Economic Surveys, France*, 1971, pp. 5–25

CHAPTER FOUR
The Birth of the EMU Project

Chapters 2 and 3 have examined the motives behind the attempt to create an economic and monetary union among the countries of the European Community and have shown how the forces of European integration and of national interest came to militate strongly in favour of this as the 1960s came to a close. Against this background we will now trace the development of the EMU Project, from its conception at the Hague Summit of December 1969, through its gestation in the Werner Committee to its birth on 22 March 1971. Chapter 4 will focus on the efforts to prepare a plan for the economic and monetary unification of the Community and will concentrate on analysing the process by which the different and frequently conflicting positions of the six national governments were moulded into a consensus on the nature of the final goal and on the first steps that the member states should take towards this objective.

The Hague Summit

The Hague Summit of 1 and 2 December 1969 marks a major turning point in the life of the European Community. The transition period had ended in July 1968, and with the customs union and the Common Agricultural Policy established, the projects specifically laid down in the Treaty of Rome had been completed. Further progress in European integration would consequently have to come from initiatives in new fields and directions. The Hague Summit was thus an occasion for the Six 'to draw up a balance sheet of the work that had been achieved, to manifest their determination to carry it on, and to lay down broad guidelines for the future'[1].

In charting the course for the next decade, the heads of state envisaged the Community developing along two lines. First, it would be enlarged: the Hague Summit paved the way for the admission of new members, approving 'the opening of negotiations between the Community on the one hand and applicant States on the other hand'[2]. Second, it would become more integrated: the links among the member states were to be intensified by the extension of the Community system into new areas. This mixture of 'expansion et approfondissement' reflected the essential compromise achieved at the Hague. The objections to the entry of other European states, principally Great Britain, had been lifted, but only on the condition that the present level of integration be deepened so that enlargement would not lead to stagnation or even regression to a free trade area. The heads of state were therefore faced with the task of specifying the ways in which the ties between the Community countries would be strengthened and particularly of selecting the major initiatives that were to be taken in the Community's second decade[3].

It is against this background that the heads of state 'reaffirmed their wish to carry on more rapidly with the further development necessary to reinforce the Community and its development into an economic union'[4]. That the decision to set EMU as a goal was made as part of a larger commitment to progressing towards a more united Europe has two crucial implications. First, the EMU Project was launched primarily for reasons of European integration. The considerations of national interest discussed in Chapter 3 were vitally important because it was essential that EMU be perceived to benefit each individual country. Nevertheless the driving force for the EMU Project was the set of motivations described in Chapter 2. That the summit set EMU as one of the Community's principal goals was primarily because this endeavour was seen as promoting the economic and political integration of the member states.

This is of capital significance because there is a critical assumption in this logic that is so obvious it is generally ignored: it was simply assumed that the creation of a united Europe was desirable and hence that any step in this direction was advantageous. In other words, it was taken on faith that the creation of an economic and monetary union was in the best interests of the member states, that the free and unconstrained operation of market forces throughout the Community would result in overall welfare gains, that the Six or even the Ten constituted an optimal currency area, and so on. Yet there was no evidence that this was in fact the case. On the contrary, it was clear at the time that there were strong grounds for suspecting that EMU would entail a diminution in Community welfare, at least in the short run. This was because whatever benefits certain of its aspects might offer, some of its key elements, such as a common monetary policy, conflicted with the interests of the Community countries. The heads of state, however, regarded economic integration as desirable by definition and consequently did not consider these thorny issues. That the EMU Project was conceived without reference to the realities of the situation in which it was launched was to have profound implications for its future.

The second implication of EMU being conceived as part of a larger effort to intensify the integration of the member states is that the commitment to economic and monetary union was very diffuse. This is in some sense a corollary of the first, for the fact that economic and monetary union was simply assumed to be in the interests of the Community suggests that there was little scrutiny of EMU's specific attributes. The heads of state set broad goals and mapped out in general terms the areas into which the Community should extend its activities, but they left the formulation of specific plans to the Council of Ministers. In view of the wide range of subjects to be considered, this was the only feasible approach, for to have considered details at the summit might well have hampered agreement. Yet while vagueness promoted consensus, it also introduced a considerable amount of uncertainty as to what had actually been agreed. Each state had its own, different, definition of economic and monetary union. The practical significance of the summit accord and the progress in European integration in which it was likely to result was therefore exceedingly difficult to assess.

The real significance of the Hague Summit, however, is that it marks the start of the EMU Project. The commitment in principle to the economic and monetary unification of the member states is the foundation for Community activity in this field and forms the basis for the efforts of the following four years. That it might rest on unchallenged assumptions and vague agreements open to conflicting interpretations does not affect the essential fact that, for the first time, at the Hague Summit the heads of state of the Community countries manifested the political will to proceed towards the creation of an economic monetary union.

While the Hague Summit marked the beginning of the EMU Project, the Community had nevertheless made several earlier forays into the field of economic and monetary affairs[5]. The course of economic and monetary integration in the Community cannot therefore be traced by concentrating exclusively on the EMU Project, i.e. the set of initiatives arising as a direct consequence of the Hague Summit, for this would ignore other important developments in this field. While advances made in the context of formally distinct projects or by different organizational units might technically be occurring in isolation, they exerted a strong influence on each other and in practical terms formed part of a single, interdependent set of efforts. Any attempt to present a picture of this multi-dimensional pattern of events is bound to be complicated and at times confusing, but it is indispensable to see developments in their larger context and to understand the links among various elements of the same and of different projects.

The Community was, in fact, moving forward in economic and monetary integration on two other fronts at the same time that the EMU Project was conceived at the Hague Summit in December 1969. The first of these initiatives had grown out of the Barre Report, submitted in February. The strengthening of procedures for co-ordinating short- and medium-term economic policy proposed in that document had already been approved by the Council on 17 July 1969, but the recommendations for instituting short and medium-term mutual assistance systems had still to be adopted, although an agreement in principle had been achieved on the former in July. That the enactment of the Commission's suggestions should have been so long delayed was perhaps the first real indication of the fundamental differences among the member states on the key issues of economic and monetary affairs.

The German authorities, who would have been the principal providers of assistance, were opposed to the introduction of a new, Community mechanism on both doctrinal and practical grounds. They argued that it was unnecessary, that it would have the effect of increasing what they regarded as an already excessive volume of international liquidity, and that it could prove damaging if it impaired co-operation at the world level. Moreover, it would commit a substantial part of their reserves to a system which, because of its limited membership, make the money potentially illiquid[6]. The Commission, with the support of the French government in particular, took the opposite position and championed the proposed system[7]. The differences between the French and German positions made agreement extremely difficult, and at its session of 17 July the Council had had to refer the question of medium-term assistance back to the Monetary Committee for further study. A compromise was, however, reached on introducing a short-term monetary support mechanism by limiting the size of its resources. It took a further six months to work out the details, but the establishment of a short-term monetary support system was finally approved on 26 January 1970 and the necessary legislation enacted on 9 February 1970*. In the meantime, the Monetary Committee had submitted an interim report, dated 17 January 1970, on instituting a system of medium-term financial assistance, and at its session of 26 January, the Council committed itself to introducing such a mechanism by the end of June.

Thus, less than two months after the Community had set EMU as its goal, it had taken two significant steps towards achieving this. Although these initiatives were formally distinct from the EMU Project – because they had grown out of the proposals of the Barre Report, and hence were based on the need to safeguard the customs union and CAP, rather than a commitment to economic and monetary unification – that they should follow so closely the decision to intensify the economic and monetary integration of the member states was more than just coincidence. The desire to complement the commitment to EMU with concrete action is clearly evident, illustrating the interdependence of the various projects in this field.

The same Council session that had approved the short-term monetary support system and had agreed to introduce a similar mechanism for

---

* The total amount of aid that could be provided was set at $1000 million although this could be increased by a further $1000 million by unanimous decision of the Committee of Central Bank Governors, which was to administer the system. Although the amounts involved might appear impressive at first glance, the amount actually available as aid was much less than it might appear. The sum of all the quotas might be $1000 million but each country could draw only a fraction of this, at most $300 million. Compared with speculative movements of several billion dollars, these resources were pitifully inadequate. Still, the machinery for providing mutual assistance within the Community had been set in place.

medium-term assistance witnessed progress on another front as well. On 26 January 1970 the finance and economics ministers of the Six specified that the Third Medium Term Plan, to be drawn up for the period 1971–75, should contain 'numerical guidelines' that the member states were to follow in formulating their economic policies[8]. Although the new procedure was a retrograde step in that the plan was to be prepared on a country-by-country basis rather than by considering the requirements of the Community as a whole, the setting of quantitative targets represented an important advance: the plan would at least potentially deal with substantive issues in medium-term planning and hence more effectively foster co-ordination of the six national policies.

The advances on the mutual assistance and medium-term planning fronts had moved the Community nearer to its final goal. An initial exchange of views on the Hague Summit in the Council on 26 January made it clear, however, that there were fundamental differences of opinion on the agreement reached by the heads of state and particularly on the project to which they had given their approval. Before any headway could be made in preparing the plan for EMU called for by the summit, it was essential that the finance ministers agree on a common definition of economic and monetary union. But this they were unable to do.

The finance ministers continued their discussions in Paris on 23–24 February 1970, but far from reaching accord, they succeeded only in making the difference in national stands clearer. Although each member state had a distinct position, the Six were basically divided into two camps holding diametrically opposed views. The two different positions were most clearly brought out in rival plans prepared in late February and early March. In the Schiller Plan, the German government set forth its proposals for EMU, which attracted the support of Italy and the Netherlands. The Commission presented its recommendations in the Barre Plan, which was broadly endorsed by the French, Belgian and Luxembourg governments. The contents of these reports will be examined in detail in subsequent sections. Suffice it to say here that the strategies advanced were antithetical.

The Werner Committee: conflict of national conceptions

The Council considered these two contradictory plans when it examined the issue of EMU for a third time on 6 March 1970. It soon became clear that differences in the national positions precluded agreement on a definition of economic and monetary union and that drawing up 'a plan by stages . . . during 1970 with a view to the creation of an economic and monetary union'[9] as mandated by the Summit would be a long and arduous undertaking. It was therefore decided to confer the task of preparing 'a report containing an analysis of the different suggestions and making it possible to identify the basic issues for a realization by stages of economic and monetary union in the Community' on a committee composed of the chairmen of the Central Bank Governors, Short and Medium Term Economic Policy, Monetary, and Budgetary Policy Committees, together with a representative of the Commission, under the chairmanship of the Luxembourg Prime Minister and Finance Minister, Pierre Werner[10]. Better known as the Werner Committee, it was this group that had the herculean task of transforming the vague declarations made by the heads of state into a detailed plan for EMU acceptable to all the member states. It had to do nothing less than resolve the conflict between the national governments so as to formulate a course of action that would realistically lead the Six to their ultimate goal.

It may at first appear that in charging the Werner Committee with the preparation of a plan for EMU, the council was referring the issues to an impartial body which would judge the various alternatives on their merits and recommend the best strategy. However, the picture changes radically if one examines the official positions of the members rather than the Community capacities in which they were appointed: the group included one senior official from each country plus the Commission's Director-General for Economic Affairs. As well as providing a valuable insight into the apportionment of positions within the Community, it makes clear that the Committee was not a body of independent experts. Rather it was an assemblage of national officials who, while not formally representing their governments nevertheless did put forward their national positions. From the start it was clear that the Werner Committee was not conducting a theoretical study of EMU but rather attempting to assess the feasibility of various alternatives with the aim of preparing a realistic plan acceptable to all member states. Thus, while the group's efforts to work out a compromise were not formal negotiations and there was no guarantee that the national governments would accept their proposals, the committee's attempt to formulate a consensual approach to EMU can best be examined in the analytical framework of intergovernmental bargaining.

The differences in national positions which had prevented any progress in the Council rapidly re-surfaced in the Werner Committee. Despite the dissimilar national conceptions of EMU, however, the Committee was able to reach accord on the fundamenal characteristics of economic and monetary union. All the member states accepted that it entailed unrestricted convertibility of currencies, irrevocably fixed exchange rates, and the elimination of fluctuations about parity; effectively, it implied the introduction of a common currency. A common monetary policy would be formulated: interest rates, the growth of the money supply and credit conditions would be determined at the Community level. The six currencies would move as a bloc against third currencies, exchange reserves would be pooled, and the Six would act as a unit in international monetary affairs.

There would, in the words of the French authorities, be 'une véritable intégration monétaire à base de décisions communautaires et de responsabilités communes'[11].

The national governments were further in agreement that economic and monetary union entailed the co-ordination of economic policies. Medium-term objectives would be set in common, the broad outlines of conjunctural policy and particularly the general orientation of national budgets would be determined at the Community level, and structural and sectoral policies would be conducted on the basis of uniform norms. In addition, EMU was taken to imply a certain amount of harmonization in tax systems, particularly in the area of value added taxes; a single European capital market; and a European regional policy 'an der sich die Gemeinschaft bei fortschreitender Verwirklichung der Wirtschafts – und Währungsunion finanziell beteiligen konnte'[12]. This was not regarded as an exhaustive list of the attributes of an economic and monetary union but rather as the minimum necessary 'to realize an area within which goods and services, people and capital will circulate freely and without competitive distortions, without thereby giving rise to structural or regional disequilibrium'[13]. It was on this limited objective that the Werner Committee concentrated, but it stressed that this should be regarded as the basis for further integration in response to the needs and opportunities presented by future situations.

This definition of economic and monetary union was minimalist not only in its objectives but also in the level of consensus it represented. Although all of the member states accepted that every one of these characteristics was essential to EMU, they disagreed fundamentally on the relative importance and precise nature of each. The French authorities, for example, placed great stress on the introduction of a Community currency, the pooling of exchange reserves and the adoption of a common position in international monetary affairs. On the other hand, they had grave reservations about common policy-making. While recognizing that it was indispensable that certain decisions be made at the Community level, they saw this as a means to the end of having a common currency, not a goal in itself, and consequently maintained that policy co-ordination should be limited to the minimum in both scope and form[14]. For the authorities in Paris, acting 'in common' meant making decisions in a very restricted set of areas on the basis of unanimous agreement among national governments. They opposed the transfer of authority to Community institutions, not only because of a doctrinal antipathy to supranationalism, but also because of pragmatic determination to maintain the greatest possible national freedom of action.

In complete contrast, the co-ordination of economic policies was to the German government the central element of EMU, an end in itself. The introduction of a common currency was of secondary importance, a step that was necessary but not sufficient for the free movement of goods, services and the factors of production. It was the forging of a single economic unit that was the essence of EMU; to the authorities in Bonn, this meant common policy-making on the overall conduct of economic affairs. Intergovernmental co-operation was not regarded as sufficient, for in an economic and monetary union, it was essential that the economic policies of the participants be so effectively co-ordinated to prevent substantial divergences in national performance, and this, as the German experience with the Länder in the Konjunkturrat had demonstrated, could be achieved only through the transer of authority to central institutions[15]. The German government consequently took the position that the broad lines of economic policy must be set by supranational bodies, and that the attainment of EMU entailed 'unzweifelhaft eine Übertragung von wesentlichen politischen Hoheitsrechten auf die Gemeinschaft'[16]. To the French objections, the German authorities inflexibly responded that the maintenance of national freedom of action was incompatible with economic and monetary union.

Given the distance between the French and German positions, there appeared little chance of compromise, and under the circumstances the Werner Committee agreed with its chairman that it would be best to put the question of the detailed characteristics of the final goal aside for the present. Such subjects as the making of economic policy at the Community level obviously raised political issues, and in attempting to deal with these, the Committee could easily become mired in the conflict over the transfer of authority. Moreover because the specific structures needed in EMU would become apparent as the Community progressed towards this goal it seemed unnecessary to settle these points immediately. Rather than trying to spell out the institutional implications at the start, Werner preferred to proceed on a pragmatic basis, arguing 'l'union économique et monétaire ne présuppose pas une union politique accomplie, comme d'aucuns l'affirment, mais qu'elle est un processus dynamique qui noue lien après lien'[17].

By confining itself to defining the minimum set of elements to be present in the 'final stage', the Werner Committee was able to reach accord on the ultimate objective and then to achieve consensus on the principles that were to govern the EMU Project. First, progress towards the final goal was to be gradual. Second, although the final goal would be specified at the start, the actual path by which it would be attained was not to be fixed in advance. Instead, the Community's approach was to be flexible and pragmatic, taking advantage of opportunities and responding to needs as they developed. Third, each advance was to be based on the active support of all the member states. Even though the process of integration was regarded as irreversible and the national governments would have to commit themselves at the start to achieving the final goal, there was to be no question of trying to proceed without the approval of all the Community countries. The significance of these principles lay not so much in their representing a crucial decision by the member states as in their explicitly setting forth the conditions under which progress would be made; they reflected rather than shaped the political environment.

In so doing, they revealed an inherent contradiction between the very nature of EMU and the positions of the member states. While it was indisputable that progress towards EMU would have to be on a step-by-step basis at the start, final achievement of this goal could not occur gradually. The irrevocable fixation of the parities between Community currencies could not be progressively introduced: either national authorities were able to modify the exchange rate or they were not. At some point the power to change parities had to pass from the hands of national governments, and however much steps to reduce exchange rate movements might facilitate this transition, in the last analysis, this change could not come about gradually. The same situation applied in the other significant aspects of EMU, suggesting that whatever progress might be achieved in economic and monetary unification by proceeding through a series of stages, the attainment of the final goal would require a 'leap of faith'. This, however, was ignored by the Werner Committee, and it was the principles of gradualism, pragmatism and consensus which permeated the Werner Report and the EMU Project.

By early May the Werner Committee had reached these agreements on the basic characteristics and on the principles to govern the EMU Project, but because this progress had been achieved largely by papering over the disagreements among the member states, there was little scope for further advance. The Committee was soon stalemated when it attempted to reach agreement on the strategy the Community should use in proceeding towards EMU. That all of the elements of EMU would have to be present by the end of the final stage was not disputed; it was rather the point at which and the degree to which they should be introduced which was contested. The French government asserted that priority must be given to the fixation of exchange rates, while the German authorities maintained that the co-ordination of economic policies must take precedence. That the differences were ones of emphasis and timing should not suggest that they were not basic or significant: the two approaches were fundamentally dissimilar, indeed mutually incompatible. Each was a logical and coherent method for proceeding towards the final goal, and each aroused the implacable opposition of three member states. It was to overcoming this impasse and formulating a common strategy acceptable to all that the Werner Committee directed its efforts for the next six months.

The monetarist strategy

The first of these two antithetical approaches is the 'monetarist' strategy, whose chief proponent was the French government, usually with the support of the Belgian and Luxembourg authorities. These countries accepted that in moving towards EMU the member states would

> 's'engagent dans le processus d'une unification de leurs économies en acceptant de soumettre progressivement à l'interêt commun la conduite de leurs politiques en matière de budget, de monnaie, de crédit, et de change, qui relevaient exclusivement jusqu'alors des responsabilités nationales'[18]

but argued that since the central element of EMU was the introduction of a common currency, the initiatives in economic and monetary unification should be directed specifically towards this end. Such a strategy of concentrating exclusively on actions in the monetary field would have the advantages of focusing on the most salient, symbolic and politically attractive aspect of EMU. Moreover, there would be clear targets at each stage, for the reduction of exchange rate fluctuations or the pooling of reserves could be quantitatively measured, and consequently progress could be easily assessed and hence readily grasped by the public. The 'monetarist' strategy would, therefore, permit the Community to advance by means of a series of well-defined steps and avoid the quagmire in which it would be trapped if it tried to move forward by initiatives in the field of policy co-ordination, where the objectives could not be precisely formulated. Such co-ordination as was indispensable to EMU would become evident as integration proceeded and could be instituted then, in forms appropriate to the particular circumstances. Indeed, it was argued that specific initiatives to bring about policy co-ordination would be unnecessary because the need to maintain fixed exchange rates would exert pressure on the member states to make their economic policies compatible at the Community level. In addition, the durability of the exchange rate relationships and the soundness of national payments positions would furnish standards for evaluating the Community's overall success in economic and monetary unification.

The 'monetarist' stategy finds its fullest expression in the Second Barre Plan, published by the Commission on 4 March 1970, although the Commission added certain recommendations, specifically for the harmonization of indirect taxation and for the Commission to play an active role in co-ordinating economic policy that were not part of the 'monetarist' position. According to the Barre plan, the Community is to proceed towards EMU in three stages. Only the first of these is described in detail. During this initial period, the Six would lay the foundations for a common currency by making a start in pooling their reserves, reducing exchange rate fluctuations, adopting a common position in international monetary discussions, and trying to avoid parity changes. Substantive progress in these areas would be small; however, the institutions required in each field would be established, at least in embryo form, and valuable experience for later stages would be obtained.

Specifically, the Barre Plan proposed that a European monetary co-operation fund, a nascent Community central bank, be created. A portion of the countries' reserves were to be pooled in this fund and would be used to finance the interventions required to reduce the size of fluctuations between Community currencies. The fund would also administer the short-term monetary assistance system approved by the Council in February 1970, the medium-term mechanism once this was set up, and in due course the swap arrangements between member states and third countries[19]. Finally, the plan recommended that the aid available under these programmes, especially the former, be greatly increased so that it corresponded realistically to the needs of the member states.

At first glance it might seem illogical that efforts should be directed towards reducing day-by-day fluctuations about parity of at most 3% before parity changes, which could amount to 10% or more, had been ruled out. Clearly such parity adjustments, which in the postwar period have tended to be in the same direction for any given European currency and hence to have a cumulative effect, represented a much more formidable obstacle to monetary unification than mere oscillations: this was not only because of their size, but also because they were a manifestation of divergences in national cost and price trends which would have to be removed if EMU were not to bring about serious imbalances within the Community. The reason for this apparent anomaly was simple: ruling out exchange rate modifications could not be a gradual process. Economic policy co-ordination, mutual assistance mechanisms, and interregional transfer systems would undeniably facilitate the maintenance of unchanging parities, but revaluation and devaluation could only have been excluded when governments had renounced them as a policy tool. This was an all-or-nothing step. And it could come only at the end of the integrative process; the nation states of 1970 might promise to strive to avoid parity changes, but they were obviously not prepared to commit themselves irrevocably to the maintaining of a specific exchange rate.

In the context of the late 1960s, the Barre Plan's approach did not appear as misguided as it now may, for it must be remembered that in the previous ten years exchange rate adjustments had been rare and had amounted to not more than 1% per year when discounted over time. It was therefore not implausible to believe that, in the wake of the 1969 adjustments, there would probably be no further modifications for several years. That national governments retained the ability to adjust parities thus appeared to be more a safety clause than a potential danger. From this perspective, it seemed reasonable to concentrate on reducing the size of fluctuations about parity. These oscillations, after all, accounted for the daily movement in exchange rates, and while they tended to cancel out over time, they were clearly a perturbing factor: under the terms of the European Monetary Agreement, one Community currency could move by as much as 3% against the others, and fluctuations of this magnitude disrupted the functioning of the Common Agricultural Policy as well as hampering trade.

Although the Barre Plan did not specify whether the interventions to reduce fluctuations among Community currencies would be made in dollars or the monies of the member states, the 'monetarist' position was clear: the dollar might currently be the intervention currency for all the Six, but whatever the practical disadvantages, intra-Community parity bands were to be defended through interventions in Community currencies. Aside from the political merit of not using the American currency as the instrument for European integration, this method offered an opportunity for the monetary authorities to develop and practise techniques of multi-currency intervention, which could be vital if a greater degree of flexibility was introduced into the international monetary system, and to set up an intra-Community settlement system which might evolve into the interregional payments network of a European central bank.

Although establishing the institutional framework for a common currency was an important part of the first stage in the 'monetarist' approach, it should be stressed that the Belgian, French and Luxembourg governments were not advocating supranational bodies. The measures they proposed were limited to setting up the procedures necessary for a single currency area and did not entail a transfer of authority to Brussels[20]. In this respect, their position differed from that of the Commission, for the Barre Plan implied that major economic decisions would have to be made at the Community level – and not on the basis of unanimous governmental approval. To this, as to the proposals for initiatives to strengthen policy co-ordination, the 'monetarist' bloc was strenuously opposed. For these countries, particularly France, efforts to arrive at common policy formulation had no place in a plan for EMU.

The French government's stance reflected considerations of national interest as well as a doctrinal preference: common policy-making was seen as disadvantagous because it would limit national freedom of action[21], while the maintenance of fixed and unchanging parities would satisfy a precondition for the smooth operation of the CAP, of which France was a major beneficiary. Moreover, a formal commitment to maintaining existing exchange rates would increase confidence in the franc, as would the pooling of reserves by creating the impression of German reserves standing behind the franc. Should mistrust of the French currency develop, these two elements would be of tangible as well as psychological value, for they would ensure that support from the other member states was forthcoming. Nevertheless, any scenario of France being able to continue on a course of rapid growth, with the high rates of inflation traditionally associated with it, and avoid a devaluation by means of Community assistance was recognized as improbable. If France got into fundamental balance of payments difficulties, it would have to resolve them itself.

Under the circumstances and given the French government's determination to retain the greatest possible freedom of action specifically so that it could keep on its course of economic expansion, it might seem surprising that it should place such emphasis on introducing a common currency because the obligation to maintain a specific parity might force the authorities to adopt a deflationary course. This position, however, reflected a careful calculation of national interest. Many of the specific steps taken in the direction of a common currency, such as reserve pooling, would benefit France, while it was most unrealistic to assume that integration would rapidly progress to the point where exchange rates had to be irrevocably fixed. In other words, the gains from this aspect of economic and monetary unification would come well before the costs. Furthermore, the French government was confident that even if advances on the exchange rate front did come to require the co-ordination of economic policies, this would not compel it to modify its actions significantly: the Community targets for growth and price stability would almost certainly be in line with French aims, since the former generally fell in the middle of the range of targets set by the member states. Thus, national interest coincided with theoretical considerations to result in the 'monetarist' position that the Community should proceed towards economic and monetary union by means of initiatives directed specifically towards the introduction of a common currency.

The economist strategy

The 'economist' strategy was the antithesis of the 'monetarist' approach. It was based on the premise that economic and monetary union could be achieved only through efforts concentrating primarily on the co-ordination of economic policies. Its proponents, principally Germany and the Netherlands, frequently supported by Italy, accepted that a common currency was an important part of economic and monetary unification but rejected the idea that it could be the dynamic element in the integrative process. To attempt to permanently fix exchange rates while six governments autonomously made economic policy decisions was regarded as an exercise doomed to failure since

> 'the reduction of the margins and the harmonization of the exchange rate policy of the member countries will in effect have a solid foundation only if they are secured by a greater convergence of the member countries' economic and monetary evolution. If major divergences were to reappear in the development of wages, prices, balances of payments, etc., such as were recorded in past years, the exchange rate relationship between member countries could inevitably again become strained, despite the reduction in margins, and would possibly require a parity change.'[22]

The maintenance of fixed and unchanging exchange rates had to be based on the convergence of national economic trends, and this, the 'economist' bloc stressed, could be achieved only by closely co-ordinating the economic policies of the member states[23]. Furthermore, they flatly rejected the 'monetarist' assertion that the introduction of a common currency would induce necessary concertation:

> 'Weder gemeinsame Kreditmechanismen oder Reservefonds, noch die vorzeitige Zerrentierung der gegenseitigen Wechselkursrelationen vermögen von sich aus solchen Divergenzen, insbesondere auf dem Gebeit der Preis und Kostenentwicklung, entgegenzuwirken. Die Illusion dass von solchen Mechanismen eine Art "Sachzwang" auf eine harmonisierte Entwicklung der Löhne und Preise ausgehen werde, muss angesichts der Erfahrungen gerade der letzten Jahre begraben werden.'[24]

Initiatives to strengthen policy co-ordination would therefore have to be an essential part of economic and monetary unification. They would have to be aimed at instituting a system of common policy-making, and they would have to precede any attempts to restrict exchange rate movements.

The 'economist' strategy was embodied in the Schiller Plan, which the German government submitted to the Council in March 1970. The plan's description of the final stage bore the unmistakable imprint of the German concept of EMU: the Community was to become one economic unit, characterized by a single, integrated market and common policies determined centrally on the basis of Community objectives, among which price stability was to have as high a priority as growth or full employment. Moreover, not only were these policies to be made by supranational institutions, but the central monetary authority like the Bundesbank, was to be independent of political control, even at the Community level[25].

Furthermore, the Schiller Plan asserted that there could be no stopping and no turning back before this final goal had been achieved. Once the Community had embarked on this endeavour, it would have to continue it to completion. While acknowledging the advantages of a pragmatic approach, especially in the early stages, the Schiller Plan therefore required that the member states commit themselves at the outset to the attainment of this final goal and to a specific set of steps to reach it. This commitment was to be made at the highest political level and in full awareness that it would in time entail the transfer of authority over economic policy to central institutions.

The plan divided progress towards EMU into four stages. First, the existing procedures for consultation on conjunctural, medium-term and monetary policies were to be strengthened so that national policies were in fact co-ordinated, although the specific steps to be taken were not descrbed. At the same time, a system of conditional short-term monetary assistance was to be established. During the second stage, divergences in national economic trends were to be eliminated. Building on the achievements of the first stage, policy co-ordination was to be intensified, with an increasing number of major decisions being made by the Council, albeit still on the basis of unanimous agreement. This would be complemented by the introduction of a system of conditional medium-term assistance. The third stage was to be a transition period from national to supranational control of economic affairs. Common policy-making in the Council would be extended: the broad lines of economic policy would be laid down at Community level on the basis of majority voting. It was at this point that the Schiller Plan envisaged the permanent fixation of parities and the elimination of fluctuations. Simultaneously, foreign exchange reserves would be gradually pooled and the volume of medium-term assistance would be increased as national safeguards disappeared and a single capital market emerged. At the institutional level, a Community central bank and Community bodies responsible for the making of economic policy would be established. Finally, in the fourth stage, a common European currency would be introduced and control of economic and monetary affairs fully vested in Community institutions, responsible to the European Parliament.

The contrast with the Barre Plan is striking, in terms of form as well as strategy. The Schiller Plan describes the final stage in great detail, explores the political and institutional implications of EMU, and presents the route to be followed all the way to the achievement of the ultimate goal; the Barre Plan is vague on the precise attributes of the final stage, skirts the political and institutional questions, and specifies only the measures to be taken during the first stage. Furthermore, while the Barre Plan places great emphasis in the first stage on laying the institutional foundations for subsequent steps, the Schiller Plan calls for substantive progress in intensifying policy co-ordination and rejects the idea of creating new structures since

> 'entscheidend ist . . . nicht, dass wir eine Fassade von neuen Institutionen und Kreditmechanismen oder von wohlklingenden Koordinierungsversprechungen der Mitgliedstaaten errichten [sondern] ob die einzelnen Mitgliedstaaten den Willen und die Fähigkeit besitzen . . . aus der Gemeinschaft eine Stabilitätsgemeinschaft zu machen'[26].

The task of the Six was first to make effective use of the existing structures and procedures to promote economic convergence and only then to embark on institutional innovation and initiatives in the exchange rate field. Finally, the Schiller Plan made clear that EMU would require a fundamental transformation of the relationships among the member states, political as well as economic and concentrated on bringing about the necessary changes, which 'von einer bestimmten Stufe ab sicher nicht ohne eine sehr wesentliche Ergänzung des Vertrags von Rom . . . durchgeführt werden können'[27].

However, there was at least one point of similarity between the two approaches. Both reflected practical considerations of national interest as well a particular conception of EMU and a specific view of economic reality. Just as the French authorities resisted commitments to common policy formulation that would restrict their freedom of action, so their counterparts in Bonn were opposed to initiatives leading to the introduction of a common currency at an early stage, although they accepted the pooling of reserves, the maintenance of fixed and immutable parities and unconditional mutual assistance in the context of a single economic area pursuing common policies[28]. With the largest foreign exchange reserves and the strongest currency in the Community, the German authorities recognized they would have to make the largest contribution in any pooling of reserves and would be the least likely to derive any direct benefit. Supported by the Italian and Dutch governments, they consequently rejected the proposals for reserve pooling. The 'economist' states furthermore disputed the claim that the member states could gradually pool their reserves as they advanced to EMU. Realistically, the amount of reserve pooling that could be contemplated in the initial stages was too small to create an effective fund at the Community level but would deprive certain member states of badly needed assets.

As to setting up mutual assistance systems, the German government remained opposed, just as it had been to the proposals of the Barre Report, arguing that many initiatives were unnecessary and potentially counterproductive. Even were some form of Community assistance desirable, this should not take the form of an institutionalized system that would be relatively inflexible and would impose financial obligations which might, in certain circumstances, be onerous for a given country. Above all, the German authorities were opposed to creating an actual fund, as against a set of commitments, since this was regarded as almost inevitably generating a self-justifying demand for credit. Furthermore, when combined with efforts to limit exchange rate movements, a mutual assistance system was perceived as particularly inimical to German interests. In the absence of effective policy co-ordination, this could result in the Federal Republic having to finance in part the payments imbalances of its less inflation conscious partners, thereby sustaining demand levels which were putting upward pressure on German prices as well as causing a transfer of real resources[29].

In examining the 'monetarist' and the 'economist' strategies, particular attention has been given to the positions of the French and German governments because they were the protagonists in this conflict, being both the principal proponents of these contrasting plans and the major economic and political powers of the Community. The attitudes of the other member states, however, merit consideration in order to present a more complete picture of the situation within the Werner Committee, for the 'economist' and the 'monetarist' blocs were not in fact monolithic. Within the 'economist' camp, the Dutch government carried the institutional implications of EMU to their logical conclusion and called for the basic decisions in economic policy to be made by a federal government as was done in the United States. The

Italian authorities shared the concern of the other 'economists' about introducing a common currency before a high degree of economic convergence had been achieved, but for different reasons: as a country with a chronically weak balance of payments, Italy was loath to enter into commitments that might force the adoption of deflationary measures. The Italian government therefore insisted that the creation of a regional fund to reduce the structural differences among the six economies, as well as the introduction of an unrestricted mutual assistance system, were preconditions for action to reduce exchange rate movements[30].

Likewise, among the 'monetarist' countries the Belgian government envisaged a much greater degree of policy co-ordination than the French and maintained that this would have to accompany progress in the exchange rate field from the start, a stand which in part reflected the openness of the Belgian economy and its consequent vulnerability to external forces[31]. Even though Luxembourg rarely took a strong independent stand because of its relative economic insignificance and its special monetary relationship with Belgium, there was one point on which its government was adamant: the integration process was not to transfer authority to institutions on which they, by virtue of the Belgo–Luxembourg Economic Union, were not represented.

These differences within each bloc on particular issues resulted in a multiplicity of views within the Werner Committee. If we look at the 'monetarist' or 'economist' position or focus primarily on the actions of their principal proponents, France and Germany, this is not because these differences were unimportant but because there was a fundamental similarity in the outlook, goals and approach of each group. These make it both appropriate and analytically useful to study the proceedings of the Werner Committee in terms of a conflict between two factions and to pay special attention to the two protagonists, always remembering that the picture obtained requires significant qualifications on specific issues.

The Werner Plan: the strategy of 'parallelism'

Despite the fundamental differences between the 'monetarist' and 'economist' positions, the Werner Committee had been able to agree relatively quickly on the minimum elements that were to be present in the final stage and on the principles that were to govern the project. In addition, the group agreed that EMU could be attained by the end of the decade, 'provided the political will of the Member States to realize this objective, solemnly declared at the Conference of the Hague, is present'[32]. This limited consensus formed the basis of the Committee's interim report, dated 20 May

1970. Because of the conflict over the strategy that should be followed, the report presented no specific proposals for the first stage, much less an overall plan. The co-ordination of short- and medium-term policies was discussed in general terms, but no new recommendations were made except for proposing that budgetary policy be regularly examined by the Council: the call for member states not to increase the size of fluctuations about parity allowed between Community currencies echoed the Commission's February 1968 memorandum, while the Council decision of 15 April 1964 already provided for Community five year plans[33].

The Werner Committee had been able to reach accord on the interim report by deferring the contentious issues, but the differences between the 'economists' and the 'monetarists' re-surfaced when the finance ministers considered it in Venice at the end of May. There was a particularly heated exchange between the French and German ministers, which made it clear that there was little prospect of agreement in any of the areas of dispute; nevertheless, the finance ministers regarded most of the report as uncontroversial and endorsed it including, significantly, the target of 1980 for the achievement of economic and monetary union[34]. The Council of [Foreign] Ministers, meeting in Luxembourg on 9 June 1970, was even less successful in arriving at a consensus. It too accepted the goal of EMU by 1980, as well as the report's definition of the final stage and the principles that were to govern the project. It also agreed that whatever decisions were reached in the IMF, the size of Community parity bands would not be increased. The Council even concurred in the first stage starting on 1 January 1971, and lasting for three years. But beyond saying that there should be efforts to promote economic policy co-ordination and exchange rate concertation, the ministers could not agree on the actions to be taken during the first stage, let alone on a strategy for EMU. This question was referred back to the Werner Committee.

While the Werner Committee and the finance and foreign ministers were deadlocked over the issue of strategy, the Council in July 1970 approved in principle the Community medium-term financial assistance system, first proposed in the Barre Report of February 1969. Despite differences among the member states, the Monetary Committee had submitted its report on 11 April 1970, and on the basis of these recommendations, the Commission had, immediately after the Luxembourg Council meeting, formally proposed the creation of a $2000 million fund, structured like its short-term counterpart, to provide loans for between two and five years at interest rates and on terms to be fixed by the Council. Disagreement over the size and terms of the credits, however, held up formal approval of the scheme with the result that it was caught up in, and indeed confused with, the formally separate proposals emanating from the Werner Committee. Ironically, it was enacted on 22 March 1971 at the same Council meeting that approved the Werner Report.

The progress in setting up a medium-term financial assistance system was, however, the only bright spot in economic and monetary integration in summer 1970. The conflict in the Werner Committee over the strategy to be followed remained unresolved, blocking further advance. Compromise was impossible, for the 'economist' and 'monetarist' approaches were mutually exclusive. To adopt one necessarily implied rejecting the other: pieces of one could not be combined with parts of the other because the elements of each strategy formed interconnected, indeed indivisible, wholes. If agreement were to be achieved, either the 'economists' or the 'monetarists' would have to give way.

But neither group was prepared to yield, even on minor issues, for to concede any substantive point was to jeopardize the entire strategy, and each bloc regarded it as essential that its approach prevail. The 'economist' countries were firmly convinced that making any concessions, especially by allowing initiatives in the monetary field before effective policy co-ordination had been achieved, would result in economic disaster and political disintegration[35]. The 'monetarists' were equally determined not to give any ground, for they saw the 'economist' strategy as leading to an inflexible process of forced economic policy harmonization bound to produce an economic catasprophe and a political debacle[36]. Quite simply, each government felt that too much was at stake for it to show any flexibility on the issue of strategy.

Because this was the crucial issue, the Werner Committee remained deadlocked until late summer, when a breakthrough was achieved. Although the basic conflict remained unresolved, the Committee was able to reach accord on the actions to be taken during the first stage. The key to this agreement was the fact that, as already mentioned, the introduction of a common currency and the institution of common policy-making are discontinuous processes because at some single point national sovereignty has to be surrendered; this cannot occur gradually. This rather inconvenient circumstance, which had hampered attempts to formulate plans for EMU, now ironically provided a way out of the impasse caused by the conflict between the 'economists' and the 'monetarists'. Both groups recognized that neither a common currency nor common policy-making could be achieved during the first stage. All that could be done was to lay the foundations. Thus, the Barre Plan envisaged some progress in reducing fluctuations, in pooling reserves, in acting in concert at the world level and in eliminating parity changes, as well as in creating new institutions, while the Schiller Plan called for the intensification of policy co-ordination by strengthening and extending consultation procedures. The essential point is that, with minor qualifications, none of these actions would commit the Community to a particular strategy, for the obvious reason that in no case had a decisive step been taken.

The approach actually adopted would depend on the way in which these targets were translated into action during the first stage, not on the targets themselves. Consequently, including elements from the opposite position among the set of goals for the first stage would not endanger the adoption of one's own strategy. The 'monetarists' were therefore prepared to accept that during this initial period policy co-ordination should be 'intensified' and new procedures introduced, while the 'economists' were willing to accept an 'experimental' reduction in parity bands, a greater degree of co-operation in monetary affairs at the world level, and perhaps the establishment of certain institutions, such as a European monetary co-operation fund. On the basis of this compromise, the Werner Committee was at last able to reach accord on the nature of the first stage and resume progress in preparing a plan for economic and monetary unification.

It is conventional to describe the compromise formula as the strategy of 'parallelism', in which progress in policy co-ordination parallels advances in exchange rate concertation. This is certainly a convenient and useful conceptual framework in which to view the Committee's plan for the first stage. Indeed, 'parallelism' is cited in the Council resolution of 22 March 1971 as one of the principles that should govern economic and monetary unification[37]. Yet is is also a potentially misleading term, for it seems to suggest that 'parallelism' resulted from combining the 'monetarist' approach, defined as according priority to monetary measures, with the 'economist' strategy, defined as giving precedence to policy co-ordination, and implies that the two blocs had agreed on the method to be followed in economic and monetary integration. This is not only gross oversimplification; it is also inaccurate. 'Parallelism' was not a synthesis of the two approaches, for the 'monetarist' and 'economist' strategies remained totally incompatible; moreover, the compromise was superficial, for 'parallelism' was interpreted in six different ways. Like EMU itself, the compromise formula was acceptable precisely because it was vague enough to mean whatever the user intended.

The conflict between the 'economists' and the 'monetarists' had not been resolved. Agreement had been achieved on a specific set of proposals for the first stage only by exploiting to the full the flexibility inherent in each position. 'Parallelism' merely concealed the irreconcilable differences among the member states. It was at best a temporary expedient.

Yet the acceptance of 'parallelism' did enable the Six to start on the path to EMU. On the basis of this admittedly imperfect consensus, the Werner Committee was able to agree on the actions to be taken during the first stage, which were presented in its final report, published 8 October 1970. In the field of policy co-ordination, the major initiative was to be the introduction of new consultation procedures. The Council was to meet three times a year to examine the economic situation in the Community, and, as the 'central organ for decisions', to lay down the broad lines of economic policy at the Community level. Other Community institutions, in particular the Committee of Central Bank Governors, were to promote co-ordination in their respective areas. These consultations were to 'have a preliminary and obligatory character', i.e. they were to be held without fail and in advance of governmental decision-making, but significantly the decisions that were reached would not be binding on the member states.

In the field of budgetary policy, the Werner Committee recommended additionally several specific steps to promote co-ordination. Fiscal policy instruments were to be harmonized, financial years synchronized, and the effects of similar policy changes in different countries compared. Most importantly, the principal elements of budgetary policy, and especially revenue, expenditure and financing, were to be discussed at the Community level and guidelines for each member state drawn up by the Council.

Besides these initiatives intended to intensify policy co-ordination, the Werner Committee proposed a series of specific actions designed to integrate further the six economies. The rates of value added tax and the categories of goods and services subject to it were to be aligned throughout the Community. Among the Six, capital controls and discrimination against foreign issues in capital markets were to be gradually eliminated. A common set of regulations for banks and insurance companies was to be formulated so that they could operate in all member states. Statistical procedures were to be improved and standardized to provide the meaningful data at the Community level requisite to the intelligent making of economic policy. Finally, progress was to be made in achieving common industrial, transport, and competition policies so that the Community would move towards the common market envisaged in the Treaty of Rome.

To parallel the progress in policy co-ordination, the Werner Committee recommended that the central banks

> 'from the beginning of the first stage, restrict on an experimental basis the fluctuations of rates between Community currencies within narrower bands than those resulting from the application of the margins in force in relation to the dollar. This objective would be achieved by concerted action in relation to the dollar.'[38]

Were the results of this initial attempt to reduce the size of parity bands satisfactory, the Committee envisaged the possibility of proceeding from a *de facto* to a *de jure* system. This decision, however, would have to be made at a later date 'according to circumstances and to the results achieved in the standardization of economic policies'[39].

Two conclusions emerge from this consideration of the Werner Report. First, progress in policy co-ordination was to counterbalance advances in the monetary field. Second, all the important decisions had been postponed. This was, of course, the price of approval: since the Six could not agree on a strategy, they had to proceed without one. The scope for progress on this basis, however, was limited. Even if national economic trends converged spontaneously, the Six would have to decide by the end of the first stage on whether to concentrate on exchange rate concertation or on policy co-ordination. This was because the Community would have to lay down the specific steps to be taken during the second and subsequent stages and begin the process of amending the Treaty of Rome in order to 'establish the necessary legal bases for the transition to the complete realization of economic and monetary union and the implementation of the essential institutional reforms implied by the latter'[40]. The Community might be able to straddle both paths at the start; but the two routes would soon diverge, and the member states would have to agree on one or the other.

By 1970 this agreement was far from having been achieved. Nevertheless, the Werner Committee could take satisfaction in its accomplishments. The goal of economic and monetary union set by the heads of state at the Hague, had been given a definite form, even if the details had had to be left vague, and the actions that were to be taken during the first stage had been proposed. That this agreement had been reached only by avoiding those issues where the conflict between the 'economists' and the 'monetarists' precluded any chance of accord did not detract from the essential achievement: progress towards EMU could start. Even though the Werner Report did not really constitute 'a plan by stages [for] the creation of economic and monetary union'[41], it did illuminate the problems, identify the significant issues and reveal governmental attitudes. Both directly through its proposals for the first stage and indirectly through the principles it enunciated, the Werner Report was to have an enormous influence on the subsequent course of European economic integration.

The Council resolution of 22 March 1971

The Commission generally endorsed the analysis, conclusions, and proposals of the Werner Report in its memorandum to the Council of 30 October 1970, but it made two significant changes. The Werner Report envisaged the creation of two new Community institutions in the final stage, a 'centre of decision for economic policy and a Community system for the central banks', which 'could be based on organisms of the type of the Federal Reserve System' in the United States[42]. The idea of central control over economic policy was, of course, unacceptable to the French government which opposed any transfer of authority to supranational bodies, especially in a system copied from the United States and allowing the monetary authorities too much independence from political control. In view of the French attitude, the Commission omitted any mention of institutional arrangements in its memorandum and limited itself to stating that the realization of economic and monetary union would require that certain decisions of economic policy be made 'at the Community level', a formula intentionally vague on both the extent and the form of such policy co-ordination. In contrast, the Commission's other modification served to clarify the relation of regional policy to the EMU Project. The Werner Report proposed no initiatives in this field during the first stage, although it did assert that economic and monetary union implied the existence of Community regional and structural policies. Under pressure from the Italian government in particular, the Commission, however, included 'action in the structural and regional fields' among the measures it proposed for the initial period[43].

Although of the two departures from the Werner Report one had been made in deference to the objections of a 'monetarist' state and the other in response to the demands of an 'economist' country, it was clear that the net effect of these changes had been to move the proposed approach closer to the 'monetarist' position. Consequently, when the Council met on 23 November 1970 to consider the Commission's memorandum, the Dutch and German representatives insisted that the supranational elements in the Werner Report be restored. The French delegation, on the other hand, maintained that the Commission's proposals still went too far in the direction of common policy-making[44]. Once again, the irreconcilable differences between the 'economists' and the 'monetarists' had surfaced, and while the Council was able to achieve an informal consensus on the measures to be taken during the first stage at its meeting of 14 and 15 December 1970, the issue of supranationalism prevented final agreement. Consequently, the Council was deadlocked as the year 1971 began.

Although the conflict between the two blocs remained unresolved, the Council, like the Werner Committee, was able to circumvent this difficulty by concentrating on the areas in which a consensus had been reached and deferring the contentious issues. Thus, after achieving a tentative agreement at the session of 8 and 9 February 1971, the Council finally reached accord on a series of measures setting the EMU Project in motion during its meeting of 22 March 1971. The resolution of the Council and the representatives of the governments of the member states 'concerning the realization by stages of economic and monetary union within the Community' is the formal charter for Community activity in this field. In it, the Six affirm 'leur volonté politique de mettre en place, au cours des dix prochaines années, une union économique et monétaire selon un plan par étapes débutant le 1er janvier 1971'[45], and set as their final goal a Community in which there is free movement of goods and services, people and capital; in which there is unrestricted interconvertibility of currencies at fixed, immutable and non-fluctuating exchange rates; and in which the Community

> 'détienne dans le domaine économique et monétaire les compétences et responsabilités permettant à ses institutions d'assurer la gestion de l'union. A cette fin, les décisions sont prises au niveau communautaire et

les pouvoirs nécessaires sont attribués aux institutions de la Communauté.'[46]

This definition of EMU spells out the consensus that had been achieved among the member states. And it clearly indicates the limits of agreement, for while it implicitly recognizes that there will have to be some degree of central control of economic policy, and identifies five areas – domestic monetary policy, international monetary policy, capital market regulations, budgetary policy and structural and regional policies – that would be involved, it does not specify the nature or scope of the institutional arrangements. Decisions are to be made 'au niveau communautaire' and authority transferred to 'institutions de la Communauté', formulas vague enough to be acceptable to both the 'monetarist' and 'economist' blocs. As to the powers that are to be transferred to the Community, the resolution stipulates that

> 'la répartition des compétences et responsabilités entre les institutions de la Communauté d'une part, et les États membres, d'autre part, s'effectue en fonction de ce qui est nécessaire à la cohésion de l'union et à l'efficacité de l'action communautaire.'[47]

That is, to say the least, a masterful compromise, skilfully interweaving elements of the two antithetical positions.

By stating that the degree of economic policy co-ordination would in effect depend on the needs that developed, however, the Council had adopted an approach much closer to the 'monetarist' position than either the Werner Report or the Commission's memorandum. The German government therefore made its approval contingent on the insertion of a safeguard clause, according to which

> 'la validité des dispositions de caractère monétaire . . . et la durée d'application du mécanisme de concours financier a moyen terme sont de cinq ans à partir du début de la première étape. Après accord pour le passage à la deuxième étape, les dispositions mentionnées ci-dessus restent en vigeur.'[48]

Unless the detailed characteristics of the final stage, and specifically the institutional arrangements, were specificied by the end of the first stage, as the resolution provided, the experimental reduction in fluctuations and the medium-term assistance mechanism would lapse on 1 January 1976. The authorities in the Federal Republic were not about to allow the Community to slide into a 'monetarist' strategy.

The Council resolution of 22 March 1971 represents therefore an even lower level of consensus and provides for an even more tentative series of steps during the first stage than the Werner Report. It is a juxtaposition of elements from the two different strategies, not the expression of a single coherent approach. However imperfect this consensus might be, it nevertheless provided the basis for the Council to take the first steps towards EMU. The initiatives approved by the ministers were to come on four broad fronts. In the field of policy co-ordination, the resolution itself provides for the Committee of Central Bank Governors and the Monetary Committee to more closely co-ordinate the monetary policies of the member states and to promote the harmonization of national policy tools. Furthermore, a separate Council decision on 'the strengthening of the co-ordination of short-term economic policy among the member states of the Community' institutes the consultation procedures proposed by the Werner Committee[49]. In the exchange rate sphere, the resolution 'invites' the central banks to reduce on an experimental basis the size of day-to-day fluctuations about parity. Under the rubric of regional policy, the Council commits itself to taking action to reduce regional and structural disparities, in particular by making resources available at the Community level for this purpose. Finally, in the area of liberalizing trade and factor movements, the member states are to take a number of steps, such as harmonizing indirect taxation and standardizing the regulations governing securities. Significantly, however, the Council resolution only mandates these measures; it does not actually enact them. The actions called for in the policy co-ordination and exchange rate concertation fields were in fact implemented at the same time, but the creation of a regional fund was approved only in 1974, while the measures in the last category have still not been enacted.

In addition to approving these proposals emanating from the Werner Committee, the Council took two further steps towards EMU. It endorsed the draft of the Community's Third Medium-Term Plan and authorized the creation of a medium-term assistance system which mirrored its short-term counterpart in all essentials except that the amount of aid was set at $2000 million with no *rallonge* and the provisions of funds was conditional[50]. That these two measures should have been enacted at the same Council session that formally set the Community on the road to EMU was more than just coincidence. These two steps were themselves complementary at least in political terms; more importantly, they formed part of a larger compromise between the 'monetarist' and the 'economist' countries extending beyond the EMU Project to encompass the entire field of economic and monetary affairs: the various initiatives in this area may have been formally distinct, but they were nevertheless perceived by the Six as different aspects of the same endeavour. It was therefore fitting and logical that the various strands in the process of economic and monetary integration should come together at this crucial moment. It was also necessary, for the unresolved conflict among the member states made it indispensable that progress take place on the basis of carefully balanced advances along both the 'monetarist' and 'economist' routes.

The set of decisions adopted by the Council of Ministers on 22 March 1971 marked the birth of the EMU Project. Fifteen months after the Hague Summit had first laid the basis for this endeavour, the vague commitment made by the heads of state had been transformed into a formal agreement setting 1980 as the target date for the achievement of economic and monetary union, whose principal characteristics had now been established. The conflict between the 'monetarist' and the 'economist' blocs still remained unresolved, and the Community therefore still lacked a strategy; agreement had frequently proven possible only by using vague formulas that covered up the fundamental differences, and decisions on important issues had too often had to be postponed. Yet despite the imperfect and limited nature of the consensus, the Six had achieved agreement on the general nature of the final goal, on the principles that were to govern the project, and on the set of steps that were to be taken during the first stage. Moreover, in full awareness of the difficulties involved, the member states had reaffirmed their commitment to the objective set at the Hague and manifested their determination to advance towards full economic and monetary integration. Most importantly, they had demonstrated the political will to work towards their ultimate goal by taking the first steps towards economic and monetary union.

1 *Final Communiqué of the Conference of the Heads of State or Government on 1 and 2 December 1969 at the Hague* [hereafter cited as the *Hague Communiqué*]. In *Report to the Council and the Commission on the realization by stages of Economic and Monetary Union in the Community* [hereafter cited as *Werner Report*]. In *Bulletin of the European Communities*, Supplement, November 1970, p.31
2 *Hague Communiqué*, Para. 13, p.33
3 Guy de Carmoy, 'Monetary Problems of the EEC', *Banker*, 120(527), January 1970, pp.24–25 and Roger Broad and R. J. Jarrett, *Community Europe Today*, Oswald Wolff, London, 1972, pp.138–140
4 *Hague Communiqué*, Para. 8, p.32
5 See Chap. 2, pp.16–19
6 Karl Klasen, 'Die Verwirklichung der Wirtschafts- und Währungsunion aus der Sicht der Deutschen Bundesbank', *Europa–Archiv*, **XXV**, 1970, pp.453–458
7 Communautés européenes, Comité monétaire, Onzième Rapport d'Activité, 1968, [hereafter cited as *Monetary Committee 1968*], pp.14–16

8 *Journal officiel des Communautes européenes* [hereafter cited as *Journal officiel*]**L49**, 1 March 1971, p.5
9 *Hague Communiqué*, Para. 8, p.33
10 *Decision of the Council of 6 March 1970 Regarding the Procedure in the Matter of Economic and Monetary Cooperation*. In *Werner Report*, p.35
11 Banque de France, *Compte rendu* (Exercice 1969) [hereafter cited as *Compte rendu*] p.21
12 *Jahreswirtschaftsbericht 1971 der Bundesregierung* [hereafter cited as *Jahreswirtschaftsbericht*] p.32
13 *Werner Report*, p.9
14 *Compte rendu*, 1970, p.20
15 Klasen, 'Die Verwirklichung der Wirtschafts- und Währungsunion aus der Sicht der Deutschen Bundesbank', pp.453–457
16 Klasen, 'Die Verwirklichung der Wirtschafts- und Währungsunion aus der Sicht der Deutschen Bundesbank', p.453
17 Pierre Werner, 'De l'Union économique et monétaire à l'union politique', *Europe Documents*, 1 March 1972, p.656
18 *Compte rendu*, 1970, p.20

The birth of the EMU Project

19 Rinaldo Ossola, *Towards New Monetary Relationships*, pp.15–20
20 Michel Garibal, 'Une Europe à tempérament', *Revue politique et parlementaire*, April 1971
21 Carmoy, 'Monetary Problems of the EEC', pp.23–25
22 *Geschäftsbericht der Deutschen Bundesbank für das Jahr 1970* [hereafter cited as *Geschäftsbericht*], p.42
23 Klasen, 'Die Verwirklichung der Wirtschafts- und Währungsunion aus der Sicht der Deutschen Bundesbank', pp.453–458
24 *Geschäftsbericht*, 1969, p.47
25 Klasen, 'Die Verwirklichung der Wirtschafts- und Währungsunion aus der Sicht der Deutschen Bundesbank', pp.449–453. The need for strengthening democratic control as the Community institutions acquire greater powers is also discussed in 'Interview: Raymond Barre', *Banker*, 121(539) January 1971, pp.122–131 and Werner, 'De l'Union économique et monétaire à l'Union politique'
26 Klasen, 'Die Verwirklichung der Wirtschafts- und Währungsunion aus der Sicht der Deutschen Bundesbank', p.458
27 Klasen, 'Die Verwirklichung der Wirtschafts- und Währungsunion aus der Sicht der Deutschen Bundesbank', p.450
28 *Jahreswirtschaftsbericht*, 1970, p.29 and *Geschäftsbericht*, 1971, pp.39–40
29 Garibal, 'Une Europe à temperament'
30 Hans Tietmeyer, 'Europäische Wirtschafts- und Währungsunion – eine politische Herausforderung', *Europa-Archiv*, **XXVI**, 1971, pp.415–420
31 Banque Nationale de Belgique, *Annual Report 1968*, pp.11–16
32 *Werner Report*, p.14
33 *Journal officiel*, **C94**, 23 July 1970, p.8
34 Peter Coffey and John R. Presley, *European monetary integration*, Macmillan, London, 1971, pp.43–48
35 Tietmeyer, 'Europäische Wirtschafts- und Währungsunion – eine politische Herausforderung', pp.418–420
36 Garibal, 'Une Europe à tempérament'
37 *Journal officiel*, **C28**, 27 March 1971, p.3
38 *Werner Report*, p.22
39 *Werner Report*, p.28
40 *Werner Report*, p.24
41 *Hague Communiqué*, Para. 8, p.33
42 *Werner Report*, pp.12–13
43 *Bulletin* (of the European Communities), Supplement, November 1970, pp.10–21
44 Tietmeyer, 'Europäische Wirtschafts- und Währungsunion – eine politische Herausforderung', pp.415–419
45 *Journal officiel*, **C28**, 27 March 1971, p.2
46 *Journal officiel*, **C28**, 27 March 1971, p.2
47 *Journal officiel*, **C28**, 27 March 1971, p.2
48 *Journal officiel*, **C28**, 27 March 1971, p.4
49 *Journal officiel*, **L73**, 27 March 1971, p.12
50 *Journal officiel*, **L73**, 27 March 1971, p.13

CHAPTER FIVE
Exchange Rate Concertation: First Faltering Steps

The decisions made by the Council at its session of 22 March 1971, which formally launched the EMU Project, not only committed the member states to the creation of an economic and monetary union by the end of the decade but also specified the actions that were to be taken during the first stage, which was to last three years. The Six were to advance towards the final objective on four fronts. First, exchange rate stability within the Community was to be promoted by reducing the size of fluctuations about parity. Second, the co-ordination of economic policies was to be fostered by intensifying the consultation procedures. Third, structural differences among the six economies were to be reduced by introducing Community policies. Fourth, the movement of goods, services and the factors of production was to be liberalized by a series of measures in the tax and securities fields.

Progress on each of these fronts was obviously interdependent – economically, because the degree of success in harmonizing economic trends among the six countries would clearly have an effect on the feasibility of exchange rate concertation, and politically, because proceeding on the basis of 'parallelism' meant that a step in the 'monetarist' direction had to be balanced by a corresponding advance along the 'economist' route. Initiatives in these different areas were therefore part of a single unified process of economic and monetary integration that indeed extended beyond the EMU Project to encompass endeavours occurring in a number of formally distinct contexts. It is against this background that individual elements must be seen to obtain a comprehensive picture of the Community's actions in this field.

Nevertheless, it appears advisable to separate the strands which have up to this point been considered together and examine progress on each of these four fronts independently. Although such an approach may not bring out the interrelationships, it does offer the advantage of conceptual clarity: advances in one particular area can be studied without distraction from developments in other fields. As the number of initiatives grows during the first stage, it will become increasingly important to focus on one specific aspect of EMU in order to discern the significant trends and developments that might otherwise pass unnoticed. At the same time, any loss in overall understanding caused by such an approach is reduced, for the linkages, both political and economic, between progress in different fields were loose and diffuse, rather than rigid and specific during the first stage. With political agreement on the nature of the steps to be taken, advances on different fronts could take place more or less independently for a couple of years, until the major decisions on the characteristics of the next stage had to be made, while the interconnections in economic terms between these initiatives would be relatively insignificant. In Chapters 5–8, therefore, we shall examine the advances in exchange rate concertation, in liberalizing factor and product movements, in instituting a system of interregional transfers, and in co-ordinating economic policies in turn. The reader is asked to bear in mind throughout that these developments were not taking place in isolation but formed part of a single endeavour to create an economic and monetary union.

It is only appropriate that in examining the progress made on these four fronts during the first stage, we should turn first to advances in the field of exchange rate concertation. Of the substantive decisions made on 22 March 1971, the agreement to reduce the size of fluctuations among Community currencies was the most visible and dramatic. It was also the one offering the largest direct benefits to the public, which had obvious political implications. More important, the maintenance of exchange rate stability was central to EMU: it was the sole characteristic of the final stage on which the member states were fully in accord. Furthermore, it was in this one area that most of the developments in economic and monetary integration were concentrated during the first stage. Indeed, this aspect may justly lay claim to primacy on the grounds of progress during this period, for if the Community's achievements here were modest, they nevertheless dwarfed its accomplishments in other fields. For all these reasons, then, exchange rate concertation was truly the number one initiative taken during the first stage.

In examining developments in exchange rate concertation during the first stage, it is useful to divide this period into three parts. This will reduce the material to be considered in Chapter 5–7 to a more manageable size and more importantly emphasize the three distinct phases through which the international monetary system and concomitantly the Community currency relationships would pass. The first period (discussed in Chapter 5), roughly from March 1971 to end March 1972, is generally a time of international crisis and uncertainty caused primarily by the problems connected with the dollar and resolved temporarily by the Smithsonian Accords. At the European level, it is marked by the failure of the first attempts at exchange rate concertation but also by the approval of a new set of initiatives as it draws to a close. The second interval (described in Chapter 6), from April 1972 to March 1973, is largely one of calm and stability in monetary affairs, though this eventually gives way to crisis with renewed attacks on the dollar. It witnesses the birth of the snake in the tunnel and ultimately the disappearance of the confining membrane. This is followed by a final phase (described in Chapter 7) characterized by flotation but overshadowed by the oil crisis; this is the age of the snake, from the beginning of the joint float in March 1973 to the departure of the franc in January 1974. By so dividing the first stage, the three different phases in the development of exchange rate concertation are clearly brought out. It should be stressed, however, that the Community did not proceed smoothly from one level of concertation to the next. Rather, progress occurred in spasms and was frequently punctuated by setbacks.

That the course of European economic and monetary unification was one of fitful advances and repeated reversals is demonstrated by events in the 12 months following the Council's launching of the EMU Project. This period begins at a peak in the efforts to achieve EMU. The ambitious proposals contained in the Werner Report had been endorsed by the Commission and approved by the Council; the member states had set themselves the target of completing this project by 1980. Although it was recognized that this would be a formidable task requiring a strong political will, there was a degree of confidence that the Six would achieve EMU – and on schedule – that is rather surprising in retrospect. This optimism was symbolized in the April 1971 decision of the governors of the Community central banks to reduce the size of fluctuations among the currencies of the member states from the 3% allowed in the European Monetary Union to under 2½%. This was to be accomplished by reducing the size of parity bands against the dollar from ±1.5% to ±1.2%[1]. This first step in exchange rate concertation was to be taken by 15 June and appeared to herald a new era in European monetary affairs.

The May 1971 crisis

Although the Community appeared poised to make a major advance towards EMU, developments at the world level were rapidly moving to frustrate the attempts to tighten the monetary relationships among the Six. The Bretton Woods system, in which the dollar was the key currency to which all other currencies were linked by fixed, but adjustable parities, was being threatened by the growing imbalance in the American payments position. After a long period of surpluses in the immediate postwar period, the United States payments position had deteriorated steadily throughout the 1960s, largely as a result of the combination of the Vietnam War and large-scale investment by American firms abroad. By 1968 the American basic balance was in deficit by more than $2300 million. Although the official settlements balance remained comfortably in surplus throughout 1968 and 1969 due to substantial surpluses on the short-term capital account, the shift to an expansionary policy in the middle of 1970 produced a sharp turn round, with the official settlements balance* registering a deficit of more than $10 000 million in the year 1970 (exclusive of the allocation of SDRs). By the late 1960s, dollar holdings of foreign central banks had assumed disturbing proportions, and the conversion of dollars into gold, one of the central elements in the Bretton Woods system, had had to be restricted to official reserves. Growing concern among foreign governments about the position of the dollar was accompanied by an ebb in confidence in the American currency on the exchange markets, resulting in a further deterioration in the United States's reserve position. By early 1971, it had come to be widely accepted that the dollar was overvalued, and the flows of funds across the Atlantic that had originally been induced by interest differentials assumed more and more a speculative character[2]. All the ingredients for an international monetary crisis were present; only a spark was required.

At the end of April, the five German economic research institutes released a report stating that the mark was undervalued. The movement out of dollars, largely into marks, rapidly assumed huge proportions, with some DM 8000 million flooding into Germany in the first three business days of May, almost half of which was concentrated in the first two hours of trading on May 5[3]. In the face of this massive, literally unprecedented, wave of speculation, the German authorities resorted to the traditional response to a monetary crisis and closed the exchange markets. This took the immediate pressure off the mark, but only by transferring it to other currencies. Within the Community, the Dutch experienced an inflow of almost $250 million in the short interval before they too closed the official exchange market, and although France and Italy, because of the relative unattractiveness of their currencies, and Belgium, because of exchange controls which had been strengthened in March, were better insulated from the capital flows, most of these countries followed suit and temporarily suspended official interventions.

Besides the inevitable disruption of international trade and finance, the monetary crisis created two special problems for the Community: both the Common Agricultural Policy and the reduction in parity bands scheduled to begin in about six weeks presupposed the maintenance of fixed exchange rates among the member states. These were major considerations as the Monetary Committee met on 6 May to examine the alternatives available to the national authorities[4]†. Since it was clear that the capital movements would continue

---

* The official settlements balance is the amount by which the official foreign exchange reserves increase or decrease. Official reserves, generally held by the central bank, include gold, SDRs, and foreign currencies as well as the country's net position in the International Monetary Fund.

† Significantly, this was the first time the Six had held policy consultations during a monetary crisis, and even if the decision to close the exchanges had already been made, the discussions did take place before the member states had settled on the courses of action they would finally adopt.

continue unless action were taken, the member states had essentially two alternatives. They could take administrative steps to prevent further inflows or they could modify the exchange rates.

Taking administrative action to prevent the inflow of funds, by such means as imposing exchange controls or prohibiting the payment of interest on non-resident bank accounts, had the advantage of not necessitating any modifications in CAP or the EMU Project because it would leave existing exchange rates unaltered, although it would restrict the movement of capital within the Community unless the new measures were limited to third countries. On the other hand, a modification of exchange rates would not impair capital movements but would entail corresponding changes in intervention prices under CAP. If the relationships among the Community currencies were not affected, which would be the case for a common revaluation or a joint float, this would be a purely formal adjustment; otherwise, this would entail a change in the prices of farm products in at least some of the member states, which would almost certainly give rise to pressure for special derogations or a renegotiation of intervention levels. Recourse to individual floating would present even greater problems for the operation of the Common Agricultural Policy, and, moreover, would rule out progress on the exchange rate front of EMU. It is therefore significant that the Six agreed in the Monetary Committee that they should make a common response, although they were divided on what this should be. The German authorities maintained that the member states should jointly float their currencies against the dollar, while the French government asserted that they should introduce more rigorous exchange controls. Like the Werner Committee, the Monetary Committee was not able to reach accord on the strategy the Community should follow; the finance ministers were left to find a solution acceptable to all.

Interestingly, the division in the Council of Ministers when it met on 8 and 9 May to consider the course the Community should adopt parallelled the split in the Werner Committee between the 'monetarists' and the 'economists', with the Netherlands supporting the German position, Belgium and Luxembourg aligning themselves with France, and Italy torn between theoretical preferences and practical considerations. And once again, it was Germany and the Commission that advanced the two alternative sets of proposals. That the cleavage among the member states should once again be along these lines appears coincidental more than anything, for it is difficult to find any connection between the positions on the EMU Project and those on the actions to be taken during the crisis. Rather, the alignment seems to have been determined by the economic situations in the individual countries.

In Germany, the authorities regarded the flotation of the mark as essential in order to restore internal and external balance. The situation was, indeed, very similar to that in 1968–69. The trade, current and official settlements balances were in surplus by large amounts; the economy was showing clear signs of excess demand; prices were beginning to rise more rapidly; and the success of official action to reduce inflationary pressures was limited by the inflows of capital. The influx had begun as early as April 1970, as first relatively high interest rates and then the prospect of a revaluation had attracted capital[5]. A 30% reserve requirement on the increase in non-residents' bank deposits, introduced on 1 April 1970, provided some defence against the inflow, but as it was estimated to have the effect of only a 1% reduction in interest rates, it afforded the Bundesbank little room for manoeuvre[6]. Even after a reduction in the discount rate on 16 July, German interest rates remained attractive and continued to draw foreign funds. Recognizing that monetary stringency would be self-defeating since higher interest rates would merely stimulate greater inflows, the Bundesbank adopted a course of relative monetary ease, even though 'die gegenwärtige binnenwirtschaftliche Entwicklung, insbesondere die Preisentwicklung, eine Lockerung seiner kreditpolitischen Linie nicht rechtfertigen wurde'[7]; at least this strategy would moderate the imbalance in the payments position. Consequently, the discount rate was lowered on 17 November and 2 December 1970, and again on 31 March 1971 to compensate for the fall in Eurodollar rates[8]. Even this, however, failed to prevent huge capital inflows in spring 1971.

Quite obviously, the mark was displaying the classic symptoms of undervaluation. The danger of provoking a massive influx of short-term capital effectively rendered not only monetary but also fiscal policy impotent, for contractionary measures in the budgetary field would further increase the balance of payments surpluses, both on the current and, by stimulating expectations of a revaluation, the capital accounts. Indeed, the 10% income tax surcharge in July 1970 was partly offset by the growth in domestic liquidity[9]. As long as the possibility of capital inflows remained, contractionary measures would have to be that much stronger and hence politically unpalatable, especially because the main reason for the imbalance between supply and demand was not domestic absorption. Consequently, controlling the external flows was of the highest priority, indeed essentially a precondition for reducing the inflationary pressures which had already resulted in producer prices rising at the (for Germany) unprecedented rate of 7% per annum during the six months to April 1971[10]. The Government, however, rejected the use of exchange controls, principally for three reasons. First, direct administrative interference with the operation of the market mechanism was unacceptable on doctrinal grounds[11]. Second, introducing the necessary procedures would not only take time but also be technically difficult given the large number and heterogeneous nature of the participants in the official exchange markets[12]. Third, even if it were fully effective, a system of exchange control would only prevent future inflows; it would not lead to the repatriation of the approximately DM 46 000 million which the which the Bundesbank estimated had entered the country between January 1970 and May 1971[13].

By rejecting administrative controls, the German authorities had effectively opted for an appreciation of the mark. Such a course of action was especially attractive because it would directly contribute to combating inflation by reducing the prices of imports and increasing aggregate supply. Moreover, a deterioration of the trade account would move Germany towards balance on the overall current account, trade and invisibles. It was, of course, recognized that an appreciation of the mark might present problems for particular sectors, but this would be remedied by special assistance[14]. As to the form the appreciation should take, the German government preferred a joint float of the Community currencies, because an independent float would inevitably cause the mark to rise against other European monies[15]. This was seen as both undesirable for German trade and unnecessary, granting the premise that it was the exchange rate relationships with the dollar, not within the Community, which needed adjustment.

In contrast, the French government was totally opposed to an appreciation of the franc and hence to any proposals for floating, either jointly or individually. Unlike the situation in Germany, the balance of payments surpluses in France did not conflict with or weaken government policy. On the contrary, the current account surpluses of FFr 300 million and FFr 750 million in the first two quarters of 1971 respectively bolstered the reserves and strengthened the franc while the concomitant growth in the money supply conformed with the generally expansionary stance of the Banque de France in early 1971[16, 17]. True, the monetary authorities had moved in April to tighten credit by imposing a 0.25% reserve requirement on credits to 'éviter un développement trop rapide des liquidités', but this was aimed specifically at the high rate of domestic credit expansion which was financing a level of private consumption that threatened to divert resources away from exports and investment'[18]. Capital inflows were not restricted and interest rates were maintained at relatively attractive levels: for it was a fundamental tenet of the government's economic strategy that nothing should be done to endanger the country's payments position, for this would jeopardize the plans for economic growth[19]. With an appreciation of the franc consequently ruled out from the start, exchange controls were the only instrument available to the French authorities in responding to the crisis. Because France traditionally had strict regulations governing capital movements, this aroused no doctrinal or practical objections. On the contrary, it was regarded as allowing the authorities more discretion in controlling the flow of funds than would changing the exchange rate.

The Netherlands, which like Germany was experiencing large, unwanted capital inflows and inflationary pressures caused by excess demand, also advocated a common Community float. Even though the Dutch current account was in deficit, the authorities were in favour of an appreciation of the guilder, because this would allow the economy to achieve better balance internally, both by increasing aggregate supply and by enabling the government to take effective action to contract demand. Furthermore, exchange controls were ruled out on the same doctrinal and practical grounds as in the Federal Republic[20].

Belgium, on the other hand, preferred exchange controls, as it was going through a period of economic stagnation caused by the deflationary policies its major trading partners had adopted in trying to combat inflation. With the growth in exports slowing drastically in value terms and an increasing degree of slack becoming apparent[21], the Belgian authorities were opposed to an appreciation of the franc despite sizeable surpluses on both trade and capital accounts.

The most interesting case, however, was that of Italy, which like France had begun 1971 with a significant underutilization of resources and had consequently assumed an expansionary policy stance. Although the authorities were apprehensive of the practical effects allowing the lira to appreciate would have on the export sector, one of the few dynamic parts of the economy, the Banca d'Italia was favourably disposed towards a joint float on theoretical grounds: as early as 1968 it had advocated introducing a substantial degree of flexibility into the exchange rate relationship between the United States and Europe, with maintaining fixed parities within each of these groupings[22]. In the event, considerations of national interest triumphed over doctrinal preferences, and the Government opted for exchange controls.

Thus, the economic situation and objectives of policy in each country resulted in positions reproducing the divisions in the Werner Committee in depth as well as in configuration. Even though the two courses of action proposed in May were not mutually exclusive, the proponents of one categorically rejected the other. The German authorities were prepared to make concessions to the countries opposed to a common float of the Community currencies and specifically 'die Bundesregierung hat dazu . . . ihren monetären Beistand für das Intervenieren in Gemeinschaftswährungen angeboten'[23] – an unprecedented step that had been rejected by the government on all previous occasions – but they absolutely ruled out the introduction of exchange controls in the Federal Republic. Similarly, the Commission's proposal was flexible on the types of controls on short-term capital movements to be introduced but totally rejected a modification of exchange rates. The Commission maintained that the existing freedom of capital movements from official control was a key factor in causing the crisis. While admitting that the Eurodollar market had been beneficial in conferring many of the advantages of a single European capital market, the Commission nevertheless proposed to restrict movements of capital between the Community and third countries by constructing an exchange control wall around the Six. It argued that this would not only provide a defence against monetary disorders but also facilitate the liberalization of intra-Community capital movements and hence the creation of a truly 'European' capital market. As in the Werner Committee, there was little common ground, and although the Council continued to meet throughout the weekend in the hope of reaching accord, it became clear that the differences were too fundamental to permit agreement.

Adopting the traditional Community formula when accord proved unattainable, the Council agreed to differ on 9 May. The member states approved a resolution in which they stressed the importance of fixed and stable exchange rates to the functioning of the Community, emphasized that neither the present situation nor foreseeable developments justified any modification of the existing parities, and stated their determination to maintain the current exchange rate relationships. In view of the problems created by capital inflows of unprecedented magnitude in certain countries, the Six did, however, accept 'dass in gewissen Fällen die betreffenden Länder für eine begrenzte Zeit die Schwankungsbreiten der Wechselkurse ihrer Währungen im Vergleich zu ihren augenblicklichen Paritäten erweitern können'[24]. At the same time, the Council undertook to consider, by 1 July 1971, measures to reduce the size and limit the disruptive effects of short-term capital movements. In other words, the member states, unable to decide on a common response to the crisis, agreed to approve both approaches and allow each government to choose the strategy it preferred.

The differences among the Six were strikingly revealed in the dissimilar national measures adopted to resolve the immediate crisis. The German mark and the Dutch guilder were allowed to float individually, with effect from 10 May, although the German government emphasized that the float, or more accurately the suspension of official intervention, was only a temporary measure in exceptional circumstances and that 'an upward revaluation [was] not contemplates'[25]. The Belgian government intensified the segregation of its exchange markets on 11 May by prohibiting the purchase of foreign currencies for commerical purposes on the free (unregulated) market and the conversion of capital imports on the regulated market. The French and Italian authorities took no specific action, relying on the maintenance of relatively low interest rates, and, in the case of the latter, early repayment of official borrowing abroad to limit capital inflows. This divergent set of responses at the national level may have resolved the May crisis, but it represented a severe reversal for economic and monetary integration. It graphically demonstrated that the member states did not possess the political will to act together in circumstances where each felt its national interests were at stake.

It constituted a setback for European integration in more practical terms as well: the floating of the mark and the guilder endangered the Common Agricultural Policy as the intervention prices expressed in national currencies would no longer be equal throughout the Community. And the German authorities were not prepared to adjust the support levels in marks to reflect the exchange rate movements because they were determined that 'die währungspolitische Massnahme vom 9. Mai wird nicht auf dem Rucken unserer Bauern ausgetragen werden'[26]. Consequently, a complicated system of border taxes and rebates, varying over time to reflect currency movements, had to be introduced. The common market in farm products remained in theory, but these measures made a mockery of it in practice, demonstrating yet again the importance of EMU to the successful operation of the Community.

Far from stimulating greater efforts, however, the May 1971 crisis brought the EMU Project to a halt. The flotation of the mark and the guilder precluded any attempt to reduce the size of fluctuations among Community currencies. The experiment in concerted interventions scheduled to begin on 15 June had therefore to be abandoned, and the French authorities reacted by ceasing to take part in the other initiatives, particularly the harmonization of monetary policy instruments and the co-ordination of medium-term planning[27]. Barely two months after the EMU Project had been launched, the plans for the first stage were in ruins, and the Community, instead of having taken the initial steps towards the final goal, had in fact retrogressed.

Amidst the wreckage of the initiatives so confidently planned in March, the only element of progress was the commitment to consider measures to reduce the size of short-term capital movements and their disruptive effects on national economies. In June the Commission submitted its proposals, which included introducing administrative controls to regulate capital flows, limiting foreign borrowing and restricting the activities of non-residents in the money market. Although the Council accepted in principle the Commissions's recommendations on 2 July – remarkably rapid progress by Community standards – this did not indicate a sense of urgency, for formal approval of these measures, much weakened, did not come until March 1972. However, on 13 June, the governors of the Community central banks at least agreed not to increase their deposits in the Eurodollar market[28]. The Community's dismal performance on even this minor initiative meant that the record of the first months of the EMU Project was an uninterrupted series of reversals, all too clearly demonstrating that the member states were still far from having overcome their differences in economic and monetary affairs. Thus, it was as six individual countries that the Community faced a second and more serious challenge in summer 1971.

The August 1971 crisis

A new flight from the dollar set in towards the end of July, as the latest developments in the American balance of payments gave renewed signs that the dollar was overvalued. The trade account had gone into deficit for the first time in the postwar period in April 1971, while the official settlements deficit had swollen to some $ 11 000 million in the first half of 1971 alone. With Germany and the Netherlands effectively protected from the capital inflows behind their floating exchange rates, France and Belgium were the principal Community targets for these funds. The net foreign reserves of the Banque de France, which had grown by only $ 66 million in May and $ 27 million in June, increased by almost $ 500 million in July[29], and the foreign currency assets of the Banque Nationale de Belgique rose almost $300 million in the first eight months of the year, most of this concentrated in July and early August[30]. The Banque de France, disturbed by the rate of monetary expansion and its implications for private consumption, tried to limit the capital inflows by keeping rates on the money market well below the corresponding Eurodollar rates. Such disincentives proved, however, of little value as the expectations of a revaluation came to overshadow interest rate differentials. Increases in the reserve requirements on both bank liabilities and on the growth in lending, occurring with effect from 27 July and again from 5 August, while moderating the expansion in bank liquidity, were consequently of little use in stemming the inflow and the concomitant growth in the money supply[31]. Nor, in Belgium, did the non-payment of interest on non-resident accounts meet with any greater success.

The flight from the dollar received further impetus at the start of August from the announcement of a deficit on the American trade balance for second quarter 1971 and reports of a Congressional sub-committee recommendation that the dollar be floated[32]. Despite additional measures to discourage the entry of foreign funds, capital from abroad continued to pour into Europe, as the speculative fever came to feed on itself. In France, the authorities prohibited banks from increasing their net foreign liabilities in francs on 3 August, and recommended on 5 August that no interest be paid on non-resident accounts with maturities of less than 90 days, but foreign exchange reserves still rose by over $ 1000 million in August, virtually all of it during the first two weeks[33]. By the middle of the month, the outflow from the United States had assumed alarming proportions, and it was obvious that the international monetary system was in the throes of its second crisis in three months.

The crisis came to a head when President Nixon announced the suspension of the convertibility of the dollar on 15 August 1971. The immediate reason for this action was the loss of reserves in preceding weeks. On an official settlements basis, the American payments deficit was some $ 12 000 million for third quarter 1971, the overwhelming part of which had occurred by the middle of August. Moreover, the gold reserve was reaching the strategic minimum of $ 10 000 million, and only $ 600 million of the IMF gold tranche remained[34]. In a more fundamental sense, however, the measures announced on 15 August represented an attempt to achieve independence from the external constraints which hampered the attainment of domestic objectives of policy; they indicated the triumph of nationalism over internationalism in American economic policy[35].

Quite simply, the American authorities were no longer willing to accept the effects on the United States's economy of the obligation to maintain the convertibility of the dollar. The rules of the Bretton Woods system had not been a major constraint on American policy formulation 25 years earlier, but this situation had changed as the growth of foreign dollar holdings and the decline in the gold reserves in Fort Knox had made the maintenance of convertibility practically contingent on the achievement of overall equilibrium in the balance of payments. At the same time, the predominance of devaluations over revaluations had, the United States asserted, impaired the competitiveness of its exports while the policies of foreign powers, such as CAP, discriminated against American products[36]. The United States government contended that these two developments placed it in an untenable position. To maintain dollar convertibility it had to maintain balance in its payments position but the same rules prevented the United States from using conventional instruments to do so. In other words, it was supposed to achieve payments equilibrium without being able to modify its exchange rate, effectively placing the adjustment burden squarely on domestic demand. The announcement of 15 August served notice that the United States was not prepared to accept this situation. The American government would contribute to the orderly functioning of the international monetary system by maintaining a healthy domestic economy, but unless there were fundamental changes in the system, it would not commit itself to guaranteeing the convertibility of the dollar.

This announcement presented, in effect, an ultimatum to foreign governments at two levels. In immediate practical terms, the suspension of convertibility forced countries to choose between continuing to absorb large quantities of dollars redeemable neither in gold, nor, potentially, in other currencies or taking steps, either by imposing exchange controls or by altering the exchange rate, to restore balance to the American payments position. More fundamentally, foreign governments were faced with the alternatives of allowing the United States to continue to run a deficit on its balance of payments, representing as it did a transfer of real resources, or accepting a reduction in their national payments surpluses, with the consequent effects on their exports, production and employment. The basic issues were not new – the weakness of the dollar and the sickness of the American balance of payments had been discernible for years – but the American ultimatum raised them with a directness and immediateness that was unprecedented. It compelled foreign governments to address themselves to the fundamental questions concerning the international monetary system, and the 10% import surcharge and the 10% reduction in foreign aid except to Latin America, as well as the suspension of convertibility, created a strong incentive for them to do so sooner rather than later.

The challenge issued by the American authorities offered the Six an opportunity to demonstrate their unity by adopting a common position. Acting as a bloc would not only represent an important step forward in economic and monetary integration; it would also enable the member states to exert a much more effective influence on the outcome of the crisis. Individually the six countries were dwarfed by the American colossus; collectively, they accounted for a substantial percentage of the foreign trade of the United States as well as a large share of its capital inflows and outflows. Yet the member states were unable to reach accord on the position they should take on either the immediate or the more fundamental issues. The same disagreements that had prevented a common response in May ruled out a Community answer to the American challenge in August.

When the Council met on 19 August to consider the immediate problem of the massive capital inflows, France still categorically rejected an appreciation of the franc, while the German and the Dutch governments were still unalterably opposed to the Commission's proposals for the introduction of a two-tier exchange system[37]. Only Belgium had significantly changed its position; with the Netherlands she proposed that the Six float their currencies jointly[38]. This initiative, which was primarily a response to the difficulties fluctuating exchange rates and border taxes on agricultural products had created in the context of the Benelux arrangements, foundered on French objections. That the national governments assumed the same stances as in May, even though the capital inflow was directed towards different countries demonstrated that the positions reflected basic doctrinal views and considerations of national interest, not the relative magnitude of the inflow. Recognizing that these fundamental and irreconcilable differences precluded the achievement of a consensus, the Council once again agreed to differ, authorizing the member states to temporarily float their currencies or introduce exchange controls as they saw fit[39].

The consequences of the Community's inability to agree on a common response to the American challenge were, if anything, more damaging for economic and monetary integration than the failure to reach accord itself, for the disunity of the Six was graphically demonstrated in their dissimilar approaches to the problem of capital inflows. Germany continued its individual float, a solution which was also adopted by Italy. France introduced a two-tier exchange rate system, whereby the official parity with respect to the dollar was used for commercial transactions ('commercial franc'), while the exchange rate for financial transactions ('financial franc') was allowed to float in response to market forces. The Benelux countries floated their currencies together, limiting the variation between the Belgian franc and the guilder to 1½% of the pre-May parity by means of interventions in these two currencies, while allowing their value in terms of other currencies to be determined by market forces.

The true magnitude of the setback occasioned by each country resorting to the defence it preferred is, however, only apparent when the effect on the exchange rate relationships among the member states is examined. Whereas the exchange rates among Community currencies could vary only within limits of ±1½% up to May 1971, in the following three months the mark and the guilder floated against the rest – and each other – while after 15 August, the mark, the lira, the commercial benelux franc–guilder, and the financial (French and Belgian) francs all moved independently against each other and third currencies. In other words, when the foreign exchange markets re-opened on 23 August, there were no fixed exchange rated within the Community except for the Benelux arrangement. As a consequence, a complicated system of border taxes and rebates, varying from week to week, had to be put in place for the Common Agricultural Policy. This outcome not only substantiated the Barre Report's assertion that without fixed and stable exchange rates the common market would be jeopardized; it also ruled out any progress on the EMU Project along the lines envisaged in March. More important, the divergent actions of the member states meant that the Community was considerably further from the goal of fixed and immutable exchange rates than it was before the EMU Project was launched.

The same basic differences among the member states emerged as the Community attempted to formulate a common position on the more fundamental issue of the means by which the American payments deficit should be corrected. On the one hand, the French government argued that the American payments deficit was essentially attributable to excessive investment abroad, not to an unfavourable trade balance, since the American trade account had in fact been in surplus until April and the subsequent deficit reflected primariy the cyclical conditions of strong demand in the United States. The proper remedy was, therefore, for the United States to apply more stringent controls on overseas investments by American firms. Given that the United States had instead left it for other countries to take the initiative, the Community's response should be to introduce a system of capital controls, either individually or collectively[40]. This position was not only in line with the traditional French view that imbalances on the capital account should be corrected by exchange controls while exchange rate changes should be reserved for disequilibrium on the current account; it also reflected the government's total rejection of an appreciation of the franc, on both practical and doctrinal grounds:

'Le refus de la réévaluation du franc traduit la volonté de ne pas supporter en termes de croissance et d'emploi les conséquences d'une crise dans laquelle la France considère qu'elle n'a pas de responsabilité. La fixation de la parité d'une monnaie doit résulter d'une appréciation objective de la situation économique du pays: *un tel examen conduit à ne pas modifier la parité du franc.*'[41]

The German government, on the other hand, maintained that the American payments imbalance could best be corrected by a relative depreciation of the dollar. Unlike the French authorities, it had no doctrinal objections to modifying exchange rates to resolve problems on the capital account, because it viewed the exchange rate as an instrument to equilibrate all of a country's transactions with foreigners. Moreover, a devaluation of the dollar would be of practical benefit to Germany, as it would reduce inflationary pressures in the Federal Republic by decreasing the volume of exports and perhaps by limiting the inflow of capital that helped finance private consumption and investment. The German representatives therefore asserted that the Community's response to the American challenge should be a concerted float. Given these conflicting positions, the Council was deadlocked, with the French indicting the German government for acceding too readily to the wishes of the United States and for displaying insufficient Community spirit[42], while Finance Minister Schiller countered that the policies of the Federal Republic were part of 'eine europäische Antwort auf eine Politik des "benign neglect", der dortigen Zahlungbilanzdefizits'[43] Following its usual practice in such situations, the Council deferred further consideration of this subject, adopting a vacuous resolution on the need for reform of the international monetary system.

The disagreement among the member states over the way in which the American deficit should be dealt with persisted throughout the summer. Nevertheless, at the Council meeting of 13 September 1971, the Six were able to reach accord on at least a partial answer to the fundamental questions raised by the American challenge, as they tried to prepare a common position on the reform of the international monetary system for the Group of Ten and IMF meetings later in the month. All the member states agreed that the role of the dollar as a reserve asset should be reduced, that its convertibility should be restored, that efforts should be made to limit speculative capital movements, perhaps by increasing the width of parity bands and that the international monetary system should be based on fixed but adjustable parities. In addition to this consensus on the principles that should govern the monetary relationship between the United States and Europe, the Six were also united in demanding that the American surcharge on imports be lifted.

The emergence of a Community position

These elements of consensus formed the basis of the common 'European' position that emerged during the meeting of the Group of Ten in London in the middle of September. While the American authorities espoused flexible rates, and during the annual meeting of the IMF later that month offered to remove the import surcharge in return for the major industrial countries allowing their currencies to float freely against the dollar[44], the European bloc were united in the view that the resolution of the crisis must be based on a return to fixed parities and convertibility. However, on one important point they remained divided. Although all the other governments accepted that their currencies would have to appreciate against the dollar and even though they had, in deference to the French authorities, laid down that this realignment of exchange rates would have to take the form of a formal devaluation of the dollar, the Government in Paris categorically rejected an appreciation of the franc and made it clear that in the event of a devaluation, the franc would follow the dollar. The French stance provided a valuable insight into the nature of the common 'European' position, for it demonstrated that this new-found unity was the product of a marriage of convenience contracted in response to a threat from a common enemy and based on a very limited convergence of interests. It was only as perceptions of national interest shifted in autumn 1971 that the Six were able to make progress in formulating a Community response to the American challenge. The disagreement over the proper remedy for the American payments imbalance persisted, but both sides showed a growing willingness to compromise as they came to realize that the present stalemate was imposing substantial economic costs.

Initially, all the member states had been satisfied with their individual responses to the May and August crises. In Germany, for instance, the authorities credited the decision to float the mark in May with having protected the Federal Republic from the second wave of speculation in July and August and with having enabled them to take effective action to reduce the high level of domestic liquidity and demand. The Bundesbank neutralized most of the DM 8000 million which had flowed in during May by a DM 5000 million increase in reserve requirements and dollar sales on the free market starting 3 June. At the same time the federal government cut government expenditure by DM 1000 million at the Bund level and DM 800 million at the Land level for the remainder of 1971, froze budgetary surpluses of up to DM 1700 million in an anticyclical reserve at the Bundesbank, and lowered the borrowing limits of both levels of government to correspond with the reduced spending[45]. These efforts to reduce inflationary pressures were directly furthered by the mark's appreciation, which restrained the demand for exports and limited producers' scope for raising prices.

By September, these efforts were beginning to show results. True, consumer demand remained strong throughout the summer and unemployment low, and retail prices continued to rise at a disturbing rate. However, the appreciation of the mark was reflected in a slight decrease in exports, and the rate of producer price increases slowed. Although the Bundesbank was optimistic that inflation had at last been brought under control, it stressed that the economy still showed signs of overheating, particularly in the labour market, and that the restrictive policy stance, anchored on the flotation of the mark, would have to continue[46].

By the end of October, however, market forces had pushed the mark's value 10% higher than in May in terms of the dollar and 6½% on average in terms of its trading partners, far greater than was justified by international cost differentials. Apprehensive that this appreciation might result in the permanent loss of export markets and, sensitive to the criticism that the flotation was responsible for the slowdown in economic growth in the fall, the Bundesbank moved to bring the value of the mark down to more realistic levels. On 1 October it reduced the discount rate and with effect from 1 November 1971, it lowered the reserve requirement on residents' deposits 10%, despite its being opposed to easing its restrictive stance on domestic grounds, pointing out that the labour market was still tight and that consumer demand was still growing strongly[47].

The perception that capital movements were forcing the exchange rate up to objectively unjustified levels led to a growing disenchantment with floating which was accompanied by an increasing interest in defences against capital inflows, especially exchange controls. At the start of November, the President of the Bundesbank stated that adjustment of the exchange rate was not by itself an adequate tool for conducting foreign economic policy, as without the means of directly regulating inflows and outflows of capital, the authorities were limited in their ability to maintain the exchange rate at levels appropriate for commercial transactions[48]. Consequently, despite their traditional antipathy towards interference with the free operation of the market mechanism, the authorities had come to the conclusion by the end of 1971 that controls on capital movements would have to be introduced. This shift in official policy represents a significant step in the direction of the French position. It must, however, be seen in its proper perspective: if the German authorities had become dissatisfied with the operation of a floating exchange rate, they also recognized its merit as the one system that could effectively insulate Germany from capital movements and provide sufficient freedom of manoeuvre for the pursuit of the government's economic policy.

Similarly, the French authorities had been satisfied initially with the two-tiered exchange system and the concomitant regulations introduced on 20 August, the most important of which limited the delay in paying for imports to three months. These measures effectively stopped the surge of funds into France: after rising by over $ 1000 million in August, official reserves declined by more than $ 300 million in September and an additional $ 50 million in October. Moreover, this was accomplished without jeopardizing growth or employment, for exports exceeded imports and the economy expanded strongly in the third quarter, with industrial production rising at a seasonally adjusted rate of 2.4%. Indeed, the French economy showed signs of overheating. Retail prices increased at an annual rate of almost 10% in the nine months to end September 1971 under the impetus of strong demand conditions plus rising costs for raw materials[49]. Determined to curb this upward pressure on prices, the Government reinstituted price controls in the autumn, 'inviting' manufacturers to sign contracts limiting price increases to 1½% until March 1972, freezing profit margins in the service sector and holding administered prices fixed[50].

With the passage of time, however, the satisfaction with the two-tiered exchange system changed into disenchantment, as it became clear that this only imperfectly insulated the French economy from international capital movements. As long as there was no large upward pressure on the franc, the division of the exchange markets worked well, but when, as in late October and early November, a wave of speculation pushed the financial franc well above the commercial franc, the controls could not prevent a sizeable capital inflow via the regulated market that in this case forced the Banque de France to buy over $200 million. The government tried to ease the strain on the two-tiered system by modifying the exchange control regulations so as to increase the supply of francs on the free market. The investment dollar system was abolished in late October, allowing residents to purchase foreign currency on the free market for portfolio investment abroad, and with effect from mid-November, non-residents were permitted to use the free market to convert the proceeds from selling their franc-denominated securities[51]. These measures did not, however, staunch the flow between the two markets. As expectations of a revaluation grew towards the end of November, the leakage into the regulated market became much more serious, forcing the authorities to take the drastic step of declaring non-resident accounts inconvertible on 3 December, as well as relaxing the conditions governing the granting of franc-denominated loans to non-residents. Yet even these measures failed to stop the inflow of funds via the regulated market, demonstrating that while the two-tiered exchange system acted as a barrier to capital movements, it was not watertight[52].

Dissatisfaction with the existing arrangements also arose because of the decline in the level of economic activity in the closing months of 1971. The deflationary policies pursued in certain countries, the American import surcharge and the problems caused by floating exchange rates had resulted in a downturn in exports, which acted to depress the economy. Industrial production grew at a markedly lower rate in October and November, and this slowdown began to be reflected in the labour market towards the end of 1971. Even with the rise in unemployment, however, consumer prices rose 1½% in the last quarter. The authorities did take some steps to support demand, lowering the discount rate at the end of October, announcing a reduction in reserve requirements with effect from 21 December, and orienting the budget proposals for 1972 towards maintaining a satisfactory level of activity. However, they were reluctant to go much further in replacing foreign with domestic demand, in view of the inflationary situation and the aim of achieving a surplus of at least FFr 1000 million on the trade account[53, 54]. In addition to these macroeconomic problems, the system of border taxes and rebates designed to compensate for exchange rate movements was hampering the functioning of CAP, of which France was the main beneficiary[55].

These three considerations all militated for the French government to accept an adjustment of the parities of all the major currencies, including the franc. The proper functioning of the Common Agricultural Policy required fixed exchange rates within the Community, but it was clear that the monetary authorities of certain member states were not prepared to resume official interventions at the existing parities. Likewise, removal of the American surcharge on imports was clearly conditional on international agreement on a new set of exchange rate relationships that could realistically be expected to permit a turn round in the United States's payments position. Finally, the upward pressure on the franc could be eliminated only by an appreciation of the franc. The French authorities were still averse to revaluing the franc in late autumn 1971, but they realized this was the price they would have to pay to protect their national interests.

Thus, by early November, a compromise on a common Community response became possible. All the member states recognized that it was in their interests to achieve a speedy resolution of the crisis, so as to hasten the elimination of the American surcharge and the return to fixed rates and hence were prepared to yield on some points. Talks between French and German representatives hammered out the broad outline of a common position. The Community was to press for the restoration of fixed exchange rates, the repeal of the American surcharge and the resumption of convertibility. In return, the Six would accept the appreciation of their currencies against the dollar on two conditions, namely that the dollar be formally devalued and that the imbalance in the American payments position not be corrected by an improvement on the trade account alone[56]. On the basis of this agreement, the Six were able to present a united front against the United States at the Group of Ten meeting in Rome on 30 November 1971. The advantages of acting as a bloc were rapidly demonstrated as the European countries blocked the American proposals for resolving the crisis, which were predicted on a $ 9000 million improvement in the United States's balance of payments[57].

Yet if the Community Governments had achieved a consensus on the way in which the crisis would have to be resolved, they could not agree on the level at which individual exchange rates should be set, for here the interests of the member states were directly opposed. Moreover, the formulation of a new set of exchange rates acceptable to all the member states was a difficult task in economic as well as political terms. That three very different exchange systems coexisted within the Community presented significant problems in determining the level of equilibrium rates and made the use of existing rates a dubious enterprise. Although the rates for the mark and the lira were ostensibly determined by supply and demand, in practice there was a certain amount of official intervention, and in any case, given the substantial capital flows, the value of these currencies over the past six months would not have been a reliable guide to the rates needed to achieve balance on either the current or official settlements accounts. As to the Belgian franc and the guilder, the situation was further complicated by the fact that they floated together, with one currency influencing the movement of the other and giving rise to bilateral imbalances that had reached 1460 million guilders during the half-year of this arrangement; moreover, for the Belgian franc, only commercial transactions were included in this system. Finally, neither the commercial French franc – pegged to the dollar and hence floating with it – nor the financial franc provided a useful basis for comparison. Added to these technical difficulties was the problem that each government had a different balance of payments goal and a different conceptualization of the exchange rate and its function.

In the last analysis, however, the complexity of determining equilibrium rates was a relatively minor problem, for the fixing of exchange rates was basically a political decision. With national interests so directly involved, it took lengthy and involved discussions to overcome the differences among the member states, a process which demonstrated once again that the Community constituted a monetary unit in terms of neither economic conditions, objectives and requirements nor the political will of its members to act together. Nevertheless, in the end, the Six plus Britain did reach agreement on the structure of exchange rates among their currencies and the level at which the value of the dollar should be fixed. The crucial franc–mark parity, the pivotal element in Community exchange rate relationships, was set by Brandt and Pompidou in Paris on 4–5 December, and with this fixed, the remaining rates rapidly fell into place[58]. Consequently, the French President was able to negotiate with President Nixon on the basis of a firm European position when they met in the Azores on 13 and 14 December. Accord was achieved at this summit on the main elements of the settlement that would resolve the international monetary crisis, but it would be a fundamental misperception to regard this as a case of bilateral bargaining between the United States and a united Europe.

The Azores meeting was significant because the Six spoke with a single voice and because the American President travelled halfway across the Atlantic to discuss and to compromise with its representative. But whatever its symbolic importance, it was not a summit between the leaders of two major economic entities. President Pompidou could speak with the full weight of Europe behind him, but only as long as he adhered to the common position that had been agreed in advance – a consensus that had been achieved only after protracted discussions and even then represented a veneer of accord barely concealing deep and fundamental differences. The 'European unity' at the Azores was merely a convergence of interest in certain specific areas among several independent states, who chose to act together to further their individual goals.

The Smithsonian Accords

The agreement reached at the Azores formed the basis of the accords concluded by the Group of Ten in Washington on 19 December 1971. Known as the Smithsonian Accords, these measures represented a careful compromise between the American and European positions which provided an interim settlement of the issues raised by the United States in August pending their definitive resolution in the context of the efforts to reform the international monetary system. In terms of immediate practical actions to end the crisis that had impaired world trade and finance for half a year, the United States agreed to abolish the 10% surcharge on imports, while the other countries accepted an effective depreciation of the dollar of about 9%, which in deference to the French authorities was largely accomplished by a 7.89% devaluation of the dollar. The value of the franc and the pound remained unchanged in terms of gold and effectively unaltered with respect to the currencies of their major trading partners. The other Community currencies rose or fell by varying amounts in relation to gold, the mark gaining 4.61% and the Belgian franc/Dutch guilder 2.76%, while the lira declined 1%[59].

As to the more fundamental questions concerning the functioning of the international monetary system, the Ten agreed that it should continue to be based on fixed but adjustable parities. But they decided that the width of the parity bands should be increased from 1% (or ¾% in the case of the European Monetary Union) to 2¼% to allow greater flexibility and to discourage short-term capital movements by increasing the exchange risk. The convertibility of the dollar was not restored, as this was regarded as impracticable in the existing circumstances, and there was no commitment to doing to in the future. Nevertheless, the intent of the measures adopted was clearly to strengthen the American balance of payments with a view to the eventual resumption of convertibility. Similarly, while the dollar's privileged position as a reserve currency was not abolished, it was evident that the financing of American deficits through the involuntary accretion of foreign dollar holdings was to end[60]. The sickness of the dollar was, in other words, to be cured by the combination of the American authorities accepting the responsibility to maintain a balanced payments position at a fixed exchange rate and of the other governments facilitating this by allowing their currencies to appreciate.

The Smithsonian Accords had three direct economic consequences of great importance to the Community: aggregate demand increased, trade and financial flows shifted and the size of the fluctuations in exchange rates grew. The abolition of the American import surtax, together with the return to fixed exchange rates on 20 December, brought about a significant increase in the demand for exports in the last week of 1971 and into first quarter 1972. Moreover, as the business outlook improved, investment showed signs of reviving. That some of this upturn, particularly in the first weeks, was a result of a resurgence of confidence and to the placing of orders that had been temporarily delayed rather than to a change in basic economic conditions does not diminish its significance, for uncertainty was a very real cost of the six months' experiment with floating exchange rates. Furthermore, the growth in exports continued into the second quarter in most Community countries, suggesting that the collective appreciation of their currencies against the dollar and many third currencies was not significantly reducing demand for their products in world markets[61, 62].

At the same time that the Smithsonian Accords stimulated a general resurgence of economic activity in the Community, they had a differential effect on the flow of goods, services and capital between individual countries. Although the value of the French franc was effectively unchanged in terms of its major trading partners, the mark had appreciated by about 6½%, and the effects of this rise in the price of German exports were soon reflected in the balance of payments. The trade account surplus remained essentially constant at about DM 1500 million per month for first half 1972, but this concealed an appreciable decline in real terms because the terms of trade had shifted in Germany's favour by about 7½%. In addition, there was a substantial outflow of capital from the Six as speculators realized their exchange gains. In France the exodus of funds, which started the last week of December, was reflected in the trade surplus (on a payments basis) of almost $ 500 million recorded in last quarter 1971 being transformed into a deficit of almost $ 150 million in first quarter 1972, as funds that had entered the country through the regulated market (by means of leads and lags in foreign trade payments) left by the same route[63]. In Germany, which had been insulated since May by a floating exchange rate, the restoration of fixed exchange rates resulted in a deficit of almost DM 7000 million on the short-term capital account for first quarter 1972[64, 65].

In contrast to these two generally positive consequences of the Smithsonian Accords, the increase in the size of fluctuations was detrimental for the Community. Fluctuations within the pre-May limits had caused problems for the Common Agricultural Policy; the new parity bands, three times larger, would render it unworkable because price levels would be able to diverge by as much as 4½% between countries. Nor was this the only difficulty confronting CAP. The common market in farm products was also jeopardized by the system of border taxes that had been introduced in May to offset the effects of exchange rate movements. Although the intervention prices expressed in terms of national currencies should have been modified to reflect the exchange rate adjustments, individual national governments were not prepared to do so as in the cases of Belgium, Germany and the Netherlands this would have resulted in a corresponding decline in farmers' incomes[66, 67]. Consequently, the border taxes were retained. To complicate this situation, the French demands that these 'temporary' arrangements be ended touched off a conflict with other member states which raised the spectre of intervention levels having to be renegotiated. Whatever their macroeconomic benefits for the member states, the changes in intra-Community exchange rates and the enlargement of the parity bands were clearly inimical to CAP.

And to the EMU Project as well. While the reintroduction of fixed exchange rates allowed the Community to resume its efforts to reduce the size of fluctuations, the moves in the direction of greater flexibility, specifically the enlargement of parity bands, meant that it had much further to go than it had nine months previously. The Smithsonian Accords consequently represented a considerable and highly visible setback in the attempt to achieve the greater exchange rate stability. They dealt an even more serious blow to the cause of economic and monetary unification by demonstrating that the six Governments lacked the political will to act together when confronted by a crisis in which each perceived its own interests threatened. Instead, they resorted to a set of heterogeneous national responses and were able to present a united front only after much effort – and even then on the basis of a limited convergence of national interests. The increase in the size of fluctuations seems therefore an appropriate event to symbolize the course of economic and monetary unification in the year 1971.

The relaunching of exchange rate concertation

Paradoxically, the enlargement of the parity bands is a particularly fitting symbol for the first 12 months of the EMU Project as well, because it calls to mind not only the failures and disappointments of 1971 but also the attempt to begin again in the first months of 1972. Precisely because the increase in the size of fluctuations in intra-Community exchange rates represented such a serious setback for economic and monetary integration and jeopardized the common market,

> 'l'idée a fini par s'imposer qu'il n'était pas possible, sans risque pour la Communauté, de laisser les monnaies des pays membres accuser entre elles des variations dont l'ampleur était inconciliable avec l'existence des marchés communs agricole et industriel.'[68]

Taking advantage of this consensus, the Commission advanced a set of proposals on 12 January 1972 designed to re-launch the EMU Project. As well as recommending that intra-Community exchange rates not diverge by more than 2% from parity, the Commission called for the creation of a European monetary co-operation fund to administer the Community's short and medium-term mutual assistance mechanisms and to operate the multilateral intervention system which would be required to keep the five currencies within their tighter limits. In addition, it requested that the Council approve the draft common policy on controlling short-term capital movements, on which agreement should have been reached by 1 July 1971[69]. None of these proposals were new. In fact, they were considerably less ambitious than the initiatives envisaged in March 1971. Nevertheless, if approved, they would set the Community back on the road to economic and monetary union.

At first, it may appear that January 1972 was a singularly unpropitious time to re-launch the EMU Project. After all, the events of the previous year had not only revealed the fundamental differences, both economic and political, among the member states that prevented them from pursuing a common set of monetary and fiscal policies, they had also culminated in the utter failure of the initiatives agreed upon in March. But the developments of 1971 had also demonstrated the need for EMU and created an environment favourable to this endeavour. Although the crises of May and August had brought out the conflicts of interest among the member states, they had also shown that the economic policies of the United States, determined as they were almost exclusively by domestic considerations, could at time be inappropriate for European countries. Moreover, the anomalies of a situation in which the monetary relationships between individual currencies and the dollar were tighter than those within a community that was trying to operate a Common Agricultural Policy had become evident. The Community had therefore come to recognize that it needed a framework in which it could more effectively control European economic conditions and maintain stable exchange rates, and that this could best be achieved by creating an economic and monetary union independent of the United States.

Just as the experience of 1971 had strengthened the case for EMU, so it had promoted co-operation among the member states in the monetary field. Although the first half of the year had ended on a note of discord, this had given way to a certain amount of concerted action among Community countries as they perceived the numerous interests they had in common and the advantages of acting in concert. This practice in working together was particularly valuable as it included the British government, which had been an active partner in the discussions culminating in the agreements reached in London in September and in the Azores in December, and which had taken part in the work of the various specialized committees dealing with economic and monetary affairs from late 1971[70]. This involvement of the prospective members of the Community in the formulation of common positions and other aspects of the integration process not only would facilitate subsequent progress in economic and monetary unification but had already added greater weight to the 'European' stand and made a 'European' monetary alternative more credible than had it been limited to the Six. The mere fact that co-operation was, for the first time, taking place within the Community in the monetary field was, however, even more significant than the number of countries taking part, for it meant that the Commission proposals of 1972 were launched in an environment of successful collaboration among the member states.

In addition to these general factors, there were two specific aspects of the situation in early 1972 which enhanced the prospects of success for this initiative. First, and generally ignored amidst the setbacks of 1971, there had been one notable success in achieving exchange rate stability: the Benelux arrangements limiting the fluctuations between the franc and the guilder to 1½% had survived the turmoil of the second half of 1971 intact, preserving the franc–guilder rate unchanged. With the restoration of fixed rates in December, these special arrangements were retained, although both of these currencies were revalued by 2.8%. Although this was obviously a special case in view of the size and relative homogeneity of the areas as well as the heritage of co-operation in the context of the Benelux agreements, it nevertheless demonstrated that a system of fixed rates and restricted fluctuations could work given the political will.

Second, attitudes towards exchange controls had shifted markedly in the Netherlands and in Germany. In order to prevent capital movements that could put pressure on the relationship with the Belgian franc in the context of the joint float, the Dutch authorities instituted a 'closed circuit' system for transactions in guilder-denominated securities. Under these arrangements, purchases of Dutch securities by non-residents could be made only with funds coming from sales by non-residents. This segregation of part of the exchange market resulted in two, different floating rates of exchange between the guilder and non-Benelux currencies – parallelling to some extent the split market in Belgium[71]. In Germany the Bundestag amended the Foreign Trade and Payments Law on 10 December 1971 to empower the Bundesbank to impose a special cash deposit (Bardepot) requirement on foreign borrowing except for trade credits and to authorize the federal government to take administrative action to stop other forms of capital inflows. Nevertheless, the German aversion to interfering with the free operation of market forces persisted, and is manifest in this law. It was only an enabling Act, its provisions were only to be applied temporarily under dire circumstances, and it would in any case not affect the vast majority of German firms or individuals directly or indirectly. Even so, it aroused a large amount of opposition because it was allegedly an example of *dirigisme*. There had been a significant change in German policy, but it was limited. Split markets were still unthinkable in the Federal Republic[72].

There was one final factor acting to favour progress in economic and monetary integration in early 1972: the Community hd not made any significant advances in the year since it had launched the EMU Project. If the commitment to Economic and Monetary Union, and particularly the target of 1980 for its realization, were to remain credible, it was indispensable that the Six rapidly begin to move towards that goal. This recognition that the initiatives abandoned in May had to be re-launched without delay in order to maintain the momentum imparted by the Hague Summit and the Werner Plan lay behind the Commission's proposals of 12 January 1972. As on previous occasions the initiative was a blend of necessity and aspiration.

That there were numerous factors militating in favour of re-launching the EMU Project in January did not, however, mean that the Commission's proposals received unhesitating support from the member states, for each of the Six was opposed to certain aspects of the recommendations. The idea of creating a European monetary co-operation fund drew fire from both sides. Adhering to their earlier positions, the German and Dutch authorities still maintained that institutional innovations were inappropriate at this stage, while the French Government objected to the supranational element in the proposals. The draft common policy on controlling short-term capital movements encountered opposition, especially from the German authorities, who were concerned by the degree of interference with market forces. Yet it was the proposals for a reduction in the size of fluctuations in intra-Community exchange rates which produced the most pronounced disagreement. Although there was a consensus that movements of 9% in the value of one Community currency against another, theoretically possible under the Smithsonian Accords, were unacceptable, the size to which the bands of fluctuation should be limited and the means by which this should be accomplished were areas of dissension.

Interventions could be made either individually or multilaterally and in either dollars or Community currencies. Moreover, because all the member states ruled out individual action exclusively in dollars, whichever method was chosen would result in central banks accumulating claims and liabilities against each other, and the Six disagreed on the procedures for settling these balances. The technical complexities meant that there were numerous possibilities, and it is hardly surprising that each Government adopted a different position. As usual, however, the critical conflict was between Germany, which, as a potential creditor, wanted settlements to be made in convertible assets, such as gold or SDRs, and France, which argued they should be made in dollars. Correspondingly, the German authorities advocated intervention in Community currencies while Italy in particular, wanted to use dollars[73, 74]. In view of these differences, the Council was unable to reach agreement when it considered the Commission's proposals during its sessions of 31 January–1 February and 28 February 1972.

As on previous occasions, the key to agreement lay in avoiding the areas of conflict and exploiting the flexibility inherent in each position. On this basis, the Council reached accord on 21 March 1972. In the future fluctuations in intra-Community exchange rates were to be limited to a maximum of 2¼% on each side of parity by means of multilateral interventions in Community currencies. The choice of 2¼% had symbolic importance, for it meant that exchange rate movements within the Community would not exceed those against the dollar. The resulting claims and liabilities were to be settled monthly, with the composition of the debtors' reserves, determining the percentage of the payments to be made in each type of asset. The size of these very short-term credits was unlimited, but they were covered by an exchange rate guarantee, subject to interest at the mean of the discount rates of the five central banks, and financed direclty by the central banks, without a Community intermediary[75]. Finally, within the framework of the Community arrangements, the Benelux countries were allowed to maintain the closer relationship between their currencies. In graphic terms, inside the tunnel formed by the intervention limits with respect to the dollar, the Community currencies appeared as a snake, within which was the Benelux worm.

This system struck a careful balance between the conflicting positions. Yet it itself was part of a larger compromise between the member states which permitted the re-launching of the EMU Project. As one year before, the Council laid down in its resolution of 21 March 1972, that progress was to occur 'dans le respect du parallélisme entre le développement de l'unification monetaire, d'une part, la convergence des politiques economiques et le développement d'actions communes dans les domaines régional, structurel et social, d'autre part'[76]. In concrete terms, the bargain concluded on 21 March was composed of five main elements: (i) the reduction in the size of intra-Community exchange rate fluctuations; (ii) a closer co-ordination of economic policies, specifically by creating a high level group with a restricted membership of one representative from each country to facilitate the exchange of information on national economic strategies; (iii) agreement in principle on the creation of a regional fund or other appropriate structure to channel Community assistance to areas lagging behind in economic development, with part of the FEOGA budget to be used in the interim for this purpose[77]; (iv) the approval of a directive aimed at establishing a common policy on controlling short-term capital movements by ensuring that the authorities in each country had at their disposal certain basic policy instruments, specifically, the ability to regulate the inflow of funds by controlling access to the money market, the level of interest payable on non-resident accounts, and the conditions governing non-commercial loans and borrowing abroad, and to neutralize the undesirable effects of such capital flows by limiting the foreign position of the banking sector and by imposing special reserve requirements on non-resident deposits; and (v) the Council committed itself to making a decision on the creation of a European monetary co-operation fund, on which agreement had proven unattainable, by the end of the year.

The major significance of the March 1972 resolution is clearly that it represented a renewed commitment by the Six to economic and monetary unification. Despite the reversals of 1971 the member states explicitly reaffirmed their determination to proceed towards the ultimate goal of forging a single economic unit. The specific measures they had agreed upon, appearances to the contrary, did not constitute real progress towards this objective. The directive on capital controls was a step forward, but because in all cases the relevant national authorities already possessed the specified powers, it was really just a formalization of existing arrangements. Moreover, each member state would still determine the action it would take in a specific situation, and the controls imposed would affect intra-Community as well as external capital movements. The other initiatives had already been approved almost precisely one year before, and if the commitments in the areas of policy co-ordination and regional policy were slightly more specific, there had been a serious regression on the front of exchange rate concertation. Even when the 'snake in the tunnel' arrangements became fully operative, the limits on fluctuations in intra-Community exchange rates would be 50% larger than previously. That this was primarily attributable to developments at the world level does not exonerate the Community countries. They could have decided not to make full use of the flexibility allowed by the IMF, as they had done through the European Monetary Union, as the Commission had repeatedly suggested, and indeed as the Council resolution of 22 March 1971 stipulated. Yet even if it only represented 'progress' when viewed against the dissolution of the international monetary system, the 'snake in the tunnel' system was important because it involved the monetary authorities of the Community in close co-operation and provided a symbol of the renewed efforts in economic and monetary unification. The significance of the Council resolution of 21 March 1972 lies, therefore, not so much in the specific measures it approved but in the reaffirmation of the commitment to economic and monetary union it represented.

1 Michel Albert, 'La désunion monétaire européene', *Revue Francaise de Science Politique*, XXII, 2 April 1972, pp.382–390
2 Communautés européenes, Comité Monétaire, *Treizième Rapport d'Activité*, [hereafter cited as *Monetary Committee*] 1970/71, pp.5–7
3 *Monatsberichte der Deutschen Bundesbank* [hereafter cited as *Monatsberichte*] June 1971, pp.7–8 and Banca d'Italia, *Abridged version of the Report for the Year 1971* [hereafter cited as *Banca d'Italia Report 1971*] p.10
4 *Monetary Committee 1970/71*, pp.16–18
5 *Geschäftsbericht der Deutschen Bundesbank für das Jahr 1970*, [hereafter cited as *Geschäftsbericht*] pp.14–22, 44–50
6 *Monatsberichte*, September 1970, pp.10–13
7 *Monatsberichte*, April 1971, p.5
8 *Monatsberichte*, December 1970, pp.5–7
9 OECD, *Economic Surveys, Germany*, 1970, pp.21–32
10 *Monatsberichte*, June 1971, pp.5–6
11 *Reden zur Wirtschaftspolitik*, September 1971, pp.45–49
12 *Geschäftsbericht*, 1971, pp.34–38
13 *Monatsberichte*, June 1971, pp.6–7
14 *Jahreswirtschaftsbericht 1971 der Bundesregierung*, [hereafter cited as *Jahreswirtschaftsbericht*] pp.36–37
15 *Monatsberichte*, November 1971, pp.5–10
16 Banque de France, *Compte rendu* (Exercise 1971) [hereafter cited as *Compte rendu*] pp.31–42
17 OECD, *Economic Surveys, France*, 1971, pp.25–47
18 Banque de France, *Bulletin trimestriel*, [hereafter cited as *Bulletin trimestriel*] No. 1, November 1971, p.13

19 'Le rapport économique et financier' (du Projet de Loi de Finances pour 1972) [hereafter cited as 'Le rapport économique et financier'] in *Statistiques et Etudes Financières*, **XXIII**, October 1971, pp.5–6
20 De Nederlandsche Bank, *Report for the year 1971* [hereafter cited as *Nederlandsche Bank*], p.105
21 Belgium Ministère des Affaires Economiques, *l'Economie belge en 1971*, **pp.ix–xxiv**, 201–206, 398–399
22 *Banca d'Italia Report 1971*, p.173
23 *Reden zur Wirtschaftspolitik*, September 1971, p.45
24 *Journal officiel des Communautés européenes*, [hereafter cited as *Journal officiel*] **XIV:C58**, 10 June 1971, p.1
25 Federal Republic of Germany, Press and Information Office, *The European Community: From the Summit Conference at the Hague to the Europe of the Ten*, pp.91–92
26 *Reden zur Wirtschaftspolitik*, September 1971, p.49
27 *Nederlandsche Bank*, 1971, p.106
28 Belgium, Ministère des Affaires Economiques, *l'Economie belge en 1971*, p.17
29 *Le Rapport Annuel du Conseil National du Crédit 1971* [hereafter cited as *CNC 1971*], pp.13–27
30 Belgium, Ministère des Affaires Economiques, *l'Économie belge en 1971*, p.386
31 *Compte rendu* 1971, pp.44–53
32 *Monetary Committee 1970/71*, pp.7–9
33 *Bulletin trimestriel*, No. 1, November 1971, pp.10–12
34 Susan Strange, 'The Dollar Crisis 1971', *International Affairs*, **XLVIII** (2), April 1972, pp.203–206
35 Edward L. Morse, 'La Politique Américaine de Manipulation de la Crise', *Revue Francaise de Science Politique*, **XXI**(2), April 1972, pp.359–376
36 *Economic Report of the President*, January 1972, pp.142–164
37 'Le rapport économique et financier', 1972, p.24 and David Blake, 'Europe's Unhelpful Role', *Banker*, **122**, (551), January 1972, pp.20–27,
38 *Nederlandsche Bank* 1971, p.106
39 *Monetary Committee 1970/71*, pp.18–19
40 *Compte rendu* 1971, pp.5–14
41 'Le rapport économique et financier', 1972, p.24
42 Albert, 'La désunion monétaire européene, pp.388–390

43 *Reden zur Wirtschaftspolitik*, September 1971, pp.50–51
44 Hans Roeper, 'Erste Schritte zu einen neuen Währungsystem', *Frankfurter Allgemeine Zeitung*, 18 September 1971
45 *Jahreswirtschaftsbericht*, 1972, pp.6–7 and *Monatsberichte*, September 1971, pp.8–10
46 *Monatsberichte*, September 1971, pp.5–8
47 *Monatsberichte*, December 1971, pp.5–7
48 *Monatsberichte*, November 1971, pp.10–13
49 *Bulletin trimestriel*, No. 1, November 1971, pp.7–11, 21–24
50 France, Ministère de l'Economie et des Finances, Service de l'Information, *Le Point de la Politique Economique et Financière, 1969–1972*, pp.15–19
51 *Compte rendu* 1971, pp.15–20
52 *Geschäftsbericht*, 1971, pp.34–48
53 'Le rapport économique et financier', 1972, pp.5–6
54 France, Commissariat Général du Plan d'Equipment et de la Productivité, *VIe Plan de Développement Economique et Social, 1971–1975*, p.22
55 *Compte rendu* 1971, pp.24–30
56 Guy Berger, 'Le conflit entre l'Europe et les États-Unis, *Revue Francaise de Science Politique*, **XXII** (2), April 1972 pp.354–356
57 Morse, 'La Politique Américaine de Manipulation de la Crise', pp.376–381
58 Strange, 'The Dollar Crisis of 1971', pp.206–209
59 *Monetary Committee 1970/71*, pp.9–10
60 Strange, 'The Dollar Crisis 1971', pp.209–215
61 *Geschäftsbericht*, 1971, pp.24–28
62 OECD, *Economic Surveys*, France, 1972, pp.7–13
63 *Bulletin trimestriel*, No. 4, September 1972, pp.8–9
64 *Monatsberichte*, November 1974, p.70*
65 *Monatsberichte*, June 1972, pp.25–42
66 Reginald Dale, 'A Shock to the EEC's Farm Price System', *Financial Times*, 21 December 1971
67 Ian Davidson, 'Currency Crisis: The Threat to EEC Monetary Union', *Financial Times*, 6 June 1972
68 *Compte rendu* 1971, p.86
69 European Communities Commission, *Fifth General Report on the Activities of the Communities*, 1971, pp.143–144
70 *Monetary Committee 1970/71*, p.19
71 *Nederlandsche Bank*, 1971, p.114

72 *Geschäftsbericht*, 1971, pp. 34–38
73 *Compte rendu*, 1971, pp. 24–30
74 Federal Republic of Germany, Press and Information Office, *The European Community: From the Summit Conference at the Hague to the Europe of the Ten*, pp. 110–118
75 *Abkommen zwischen den Zentralbanken der Mitgliedstaaton der Gemeinschaft vom 10 April 1972 uner die Verringerung der Bendbreiten zwischen den Wehrungen der Gemeinschaft*
76 *Journal officiel*, **XV:C38**, 18 April 1972, p. 3
77 *Jahreswirtschaftsbericht*, 1972, pp. 27–28

CHAPTER SIX 111
Exchange Rate Concertation: the Snake in the Tunnel

The Council resolution of 21 March 1972 provided for the resumption of the efforts on the exchange rate concertation front which had had to be abandoned in the aftermath of the May 1971 international monetary crisis. Although the increased flexibility introduced into monetary relationships as a result of the Smithsonian Accords meant that the specific aim in terms of the maximum movements in exchange rates between Community currencies was much less ambitious than the previous year, the new initiative resembled its predecessor in most other respects. The reduction in the size of fluctuations was to be accomplished by means of multilateral interventions in the currencies of the member states, and the resulting claims and liabilities were to be settled at the end of the following month, with the structure of the debtor's reserves determining the asset composition of the payment[1]. The task of administering this system was conferred on the Committee of Central Bank Governors, which met on 10 April to make the necessary technical arrangements and fixed 24 April as the date to start gradually reducing the magnitude of fluctuations to within the limit of 2¼%, a target which was to be achieved by 1 July 1972.

The snake in the tunnel

As all the intra-Community exchange rates were within 2¼% of their par value on 24 April, the new limits were put into effect immediately. Although the birth of the snake was thus in some sense a non-event, the success of the new initiative was, of course, to be measured not by the magnitude of official interventions but rather by the degree of exchange rate stability achieved, and by this standard the first days of the multilateral intervention system were completely satisfactory. Likewise, the snake's enlargement to include the British and Irish pounds and the Danish kroner on 1 May, followed by the Norwegian kroner on 23 May was accomplished without discernible impact on the exchange markets[2]. So, one year after the debacle of 1971, the Community had made its first advance on the front of exchange rate concertation.

It remained for the new arrangements to be put to the test to see if they would prove durable under fire, and this trial was not long in coming. Pressure on the dollar had been gradually mounting since April, as mistrust of the parities established in December spread. On the one hand, the fundamental problem of the dollar did not seem to have been resolved. The American balance of payments position continued to deteriorate, and although a temporary worsening on the current account was only to be expected in the aftermath of the parity adjustments, the growing deficit on the American trade account gave rise to doubts

> 'ob die anlässlich der Washingtoner Währungsconferenz im Dezember 1971 vereinbarte Abwertung des US-Dollars ausreichen würde, die stark passive Zahlungsbilanz der Vereinigten Staaten längerfristig wieder ins Gleichgewicht zu bringen'[3].

Moreover, the rise in European rates of interest as a result of contractionary action by central banks had induced a flow of capital across the Atlantic aggravating the deficit on official settlements and thereby further eroding confidence in the dollar.

On the other hand, the danger of capital inflows was once again preventing the monetary authorities in Europe from achieving the restrictive monetary conditions called for in their economic circumstances. To be sure, the Smithsonian Accords had been followed by a substantial exodus of funds from the Community as a whole. However, whereas France, Italy and the Benelux countries had experienced sizeable outflows in the early weeks of 1972, the repatriation of capital from Germany had been on a very small scale and indeed had been replaced by appreciable inflows in the new year, despite a reduction in the discount rate on 23 December aimed at bringing interest rates in the Federal Republic down to world levels[4]. By February all the member states were experiencing renewed inflows which they tried to discourage by making investments from abroad less attractive. In Germany, the Bundesbank reduced the discount rate a second time on 4 February even though 'unter rein binnenwirtschaftliche Gesichtspunkten hätte keine Veranlassung bestanden, den Diskontsatz so stark zu senken'[5]. The Banque de France, which had removed most of the restrictions affecting capital inflows within a few days of the parity adjustments in December, started to reimpose controls in February, notably by limiting access to the forward market to commercial transactions, and reduced the discount rate[6]. For their part, the Benelux countries responded by reducing the discount rate, the Banque Nationale de Belgique on 6 January and 3 February and the Nederlandsche Bank on 6 January[7, 8].

All of these measures had only limited success. The entry of foreign capital was most serious in Germany, which had experienced inflows of DM 10 000 million during the first two months of 1972. To exacerbate the situation, the economy was showing signs of overheating and experiencing inflationary pressures. Convinced that they would be unable to restore balance between supply and demand without controls on the movement of capital, the authorities decided to make use of the new powers granted them the previous December and imposed, with effect from 1 March, a 40% reserve requirement (Bardepot) on the proceeds of all non-trade related foreign borrowing by German firms since 1 January in excess of DM 2 million[9]. As almost half of the capital entering the Federal Republic in January and February had come via this route, the introduction of the Bardepot was instrumental in reversing this flow of funds and bringing about a deficit of almost DM 5000 million on the short-term capital account for the three months to end April. As a result, the Bundesbank did not have to intervene on the exchange markets after 10 March. Moreover, the Bardepot directly contributed to internal balance because it reduced the money supply by immobilizing a considerable amount of liquid funds[10].

The very efficacy of the Bardepot, however, caused new problems for the Community, as the flow of funds shifted towards other member states. In France, the dollar fell to its lower limit against the commercial franc and remained there during the first weeks of March, while declining to a discount of more than 4% against the financial franc. The combination of the French government's total rejection of a further appreciation of the franc and the maintenance of relatively unattractive rates of interest were sufficient, however, to discourage the large-scale entry of foreign funds[11]. In contrast, a joint discount rate reduction in Belgium and the Netherlands on 2 March failed to stem the tide, forcing the authorities to introduce more stringent exchange controls. With effect from 9 March, Belgian banks were instructed not to allow their foreign positions to deteriorate, while Dutch banks were prohibited from paying interest on non-resident accounts[12].

These measures stopped the speculative movements for the moment, and by the end of the month the dollar was rising against most European currencies. Nevertheless despite the exchange markets remaining calm throughout April and May, European Governments still found themselves in the same basic predicament. Indeed, the recourse to exchange controls, albeit providing a temporary palliative, revealed openly the authorities' difficulty in maintaining healthy economic conditions domestically while respecting their obligations under the international monetary system.

It was against this background of growing mistrust of the dollar, largely as a consequence of the visible problems facing the European as well as the American economies, that the snake was launched. Ironically, however, the crisis that was to provide the first test of the new Community arrangements centred not on the dollar but on the pound. The attack on sterling that developed in early June can be traced back to the Smithsonian Accords, pursuant to which the pound, like the franc, retained its gold parity and consequently appreciated some 8% against the dollar. Sterling's effective appreciation, however, was less than 1%, which, as the Bank of England observed, was more than offset by the removal of the American import surtax. Although the pound's new dollar parity was slightly higher than its floating level, it was, therefore, accepted by the market, and the performance of sterling broadly parallelled that of other European currencies in early 1972, with a slight outflow of capital being followed by upward pressure on the exchange rate during January and February. Interest rates were maintained at unattractive levels and controls on the use of sterling for foreign investments in Britain and British investments overseas liberalized to prevent the pound from reaching its upper intervention point[13]. Behind these defences, the pound remained relatively stable against the dollar and withstood the speculative wave in early March, a divergence from the behaviour of continental currencies giving the first indication of sterling's underlying weakness. The flight from the dollar temporarily bolstered the position of the pound and focused attention on the American currency, but with the re-establishment of order in exchange markets in late March, the vulnerability of sterling became apparent.

The United Kingdom's surplus on the balance of payments, which had averaged over £ 800 million per quarter in 1971, virtually disappeared in first quarter 1972. As this was primarily due to the expected deterioration on the capital account, it might not have occasioned much concern had the current account not registered a deficit of £ 13 million in contrast to a surplus of approximately £ 270 million in the fourth quarter of 1971[14]. This poor performance prompted doubts about the exchange rate, especially in light of three disturbing developments in the British economy. First, problems in industrial relations, such as the miners' strike, were adversely affecting production, and this would inevitably have negative repercussions on the trade balance. Second, the budget announced in March added an additional 2% of GDP to demand. This was bound to result in an increase in imports, which, in view of the difficulties on the domestic side, might be quite sizeable. Third, inflation, fuelled by wage increase running at an annual rate of almost 10% in the first quarter, was impairing the competitiveness of British products abroad, and the expansionary course adopted in the budget augured ill for a reversal of this trend in the coming months[15]. The resulting mistrust of sterling was not allayed by the Chancellor's statement that 'it is neither necessary nor desirable to distort domestic economies to an unacceptable extent in order to maintain unrealistic parities'[16].

As the signs of trouble in the British balance of payments multiplied in April and May, funds began to leave the country, first in dribbles, then in larger amounts. It took only the prospect of a dock strike to spark a large speculative attack on Thursday, 15 June. The British authorities were compelled to intervene on a substantial scale, both in dollars and, as the pound reached its floor against the Belgian franc, the strongest currency in the snake, in Belgian francs. Simultaneously, the authorities in Brussels automatically entered the markets to support sterling under the snake arrangements, being joined later in the day by the Banque de France. The next day, the pound also had to be defended against the mark and the Norwegian kroner, and subseqently against the guilder as well. Sterling recovered the following Monday, but the attack recommenced on Tuesday. By Thursday evening, 22 June, continental central banks had acquired just over £ 1000 million under the multilateral intervention mechanism; Germany had the largest share, some 1500 million units of account, while France held just under 500 million[17, 18, 19]. Faced with a claim on their reserves of this magnitude, on top of the £ 1000 million that had been spent supporting the pound in London, the British authorities decided that night to cease further intervention and to close the exchange markets.

Although by suspending interventions the authorities had indicated their inability to maintain the value of the pound at its official parity in the face of this speculative attack, the Chancellor emphasized that 'there was nothing in the objective facts of our balances of payments position or the level of our reserves to justify these movements[20]. He ruled out a devaluation, especially as it was only six months since the parity adjustments in Washington; and asserted that given the degree of spare capacity in the economy, 'it is not necessary, or indeed desirable, to introduce restrictive measures'[21]. Yet it was clear that either deflation or depreciation would have to be accepted, as strengthening the exchange controls by limiting the scheduled territories (those countries to which funds could be transferred without restriction) to the United Kingdom and Ireland had not sufficed to stem the drain on the reserves. The Government consequently decided to allow temporarily the value of the pound to float in response to market forces as from June 27, thus effectively electing depreciation.

The flotation of the pound necessarily entailed its withdrawal from the snake. Although the Government reaffirmed its commitment to fixed exchange rates and its intention to return to the Smithsonian parity and to the snake as soon as possible, the decision to float constituted a severe setback for economic and monetary unification. The Chancellor might argue that Britain had fulfilled its Community obligations since the 'experiment in exchange rate concertation was never intended to deal with an exceptional situation like this'[22], but the fact remained that the attempt to achieve exchange rate stability among the currencies of the 'enlarged' Community had failed. Moreover, the departure of the premier European currency raised serious questions about the viability of the remaining group as a monetary unit.

More fundamentally, the crisis demonstrated that although the multilateral intervention system functioned smoothly, co-operation among the countries taking part in this initiative did not extend beyond this formal level. Continental central banks were prepared to purchase vast quantities of pounds, but only as agents of the Bank of England. The resulting sterling balances were presented for conversion into gold and dollars at the end of the following month – and at the official parity, placing the entire burden of the exchange loss on the British authorities[23]. Furthermore, no financial assistance was extended to the government in London; after all, the United Kingdom was not a member of the Community, and hence not eligible to benefit from the mutual assistance system. However, the Six not only did not make assistance available on a bilateral basis but also refused to make a public statement declaring their preparedness to back sterling with their reserves, this despite an assurance from the British government that they would not be called upon to do so.

In this way, the sterling crisis illuminated the basic weakness of the snake, for the special relationship between the Community currencies would be maintained only so long as the member states possessed the means and the determination to defend a particular exchange rate. The arrangements among the central banks merely created the machinery to enable the system to function; they did not provide the will to make it work. Except for the mutual assistance systems, there was no provision for monetary support or for the concertation of national economic policies. Far from being an instrument of economic and monetary unification as the 'monetarists' had argued, the snake was a gauge of the degree of integration that already existed. Moreover, given the weakness of the official commitment to immutable exchange rates, it was clear that its survival was contingent on the existing monetary relationships remaining compatible with the attainment of national economic objectives.

That the achievement of national economic aims took precedence over the initiative in exchange rate concertation was clearly demonstrated in the aftermath of the sterling crisis. Just as the British government had opted out of the snake system when the maintenance of sterling at the official parity became incompatible with the efforts to reflate the economy, so the Danish and Italian governments asserted that they could not remain in the snake as it was presently constituted when speculative attention focused on the kroner and the lira after the pound's flotation. The lira continued to participate in the system because the Six amended the regulations to allow the Banca d'Italia to settle its intervention debts exclusively in dollars. However, excusing the Italian authorities from making payments in gold and SDRs, which comprised a major part of their reserves, not only frustrated the attempt to harmonize the reserve structure of the member states but also acknowledged that Italy could not continue to take part in the snake without special dispensations. As similar concessions were not offered to the Danish authorities, the kroner dropped out[24].

Thus, the snake emerged from its first test severely mutilated. The experiment in exchange rate concertation comprising eight currencies that had begun so auspiciously barely two months previously, was now a battered remnant of five currencies and one hanger-on. Yet economic and monetary integration had suffered an even more serious setback, as the crisis had shown again that, when put to the test, the member states put their short-term economic interests before the imperatives of the EMU Project.

The dollar crisis: summer 1972

Once the sterling crisis had been resolved by the flotation of the pound, the latent mistrust of the American currency which had developed over the previous six months came to the surface. Conditions on both sides of the Atlantic suggested that the Smithsonian Accords had solved neither the fundamental problems of the dollar nor the dilemma of European monetary authorities. A massive flight from the dollar set in the last week of June. As in 1971, European countries, especially Germany and Switzerland, were the principal targets for these speculative funds. And once again, the governments reacted by closing the exchange markets, in this case with effect from June 26. Of course, this was at best an interim measure, providing a little time for national authorities to decide on a response to this latest crisis. Ironically, the waves of speculative funds surging across the Atlantic presented a much more serious challenge to the snake than the sterling crisis, for while the latter directly affected one set of exchange rates between the participants, the former affected all the member states – in dissimilar ways – raising the spectre of each country resorting to different safeguards.

At first glance, it might appear that the dollar crisis of June 1972 was bound to destroy the snake just as the crisis of May 1971 had aborted the earlier initiative in exchange rate concertation. The magnitude of the inflow varied greatly among the participants in the snake system: for the three months ending 30 June 1972 the change in national reserves was $ 3000 million in Germany; $ 262 million in France; $ 176 million in Belgium; $ 27 million in the Netherlands; and $ 223 million in Italy[25]. Since these capital movements were superimposed onto existing differences in domestic economic conditions, they posed dissimilar problems in each country, and, it seemed, therefore, a foregone conclusion that the national authorities would respond in nine dissimilar ways.

As on previous occasions, Germany sustained the largest inflows, which bloated domestic liquidity and exacerbated inflationary pressures. Clearly, it was indispensable to the restoration of internal balance that the entry of foreign funds be stopped, but the experience with the Bardepot had confirmed the Bundesbank's assertion that exchange controls were an inadequate defence for Germany[26]: despite the Bardepot, some DM 8500 million in foreign currency entered the Federal Republic between 15 June and 23 June, of which almost DM 3000 million was concentrated in the morning of 23 June, and official rserves at the end of the month were approximately DM 14 000 million higher than six months before[27]. The Bardepot had, in fact, proven effective in restraining the inflow of capital in the form of loans from abroad, but it had been easily circumvented: the Bundesbank calculated that over DM 10 000 million had entered the country in the latter part of June through purchases of bonds and money market paper[28]*. Consequently, while the government did not rule out the introduction of further controls on short-term capital movements, it appeared likely to opt for an appreciation of the mark, either by revaluation or, more probably, by floating, as a means of resolving the crisis.

The French authorities, in contrast, rejected an appreciation of the franc, arguing that it had already risen by almost 8% against the dollar, far more than was justified by changes in relative prices. As it was, the government was concerned about the competitive position of French industry, especially in view of the resurgence of inflation and the shrinking surplus on current account. Moreover, the two-tiered exchange system, together with interest rates about 1½% below Eurodollar levels, had kept the inflows during the June and July crises to modest dimensions of 'quelque U.C.E. (European Units of Account) 1200 millions de devises'[30] (compared with some U.A. 10 000 million in Germany[31]) and this did not seriously conflict with national policy aims[32]. An appreciation consequently appeared both ill-advised and unnecessary to the French government, an attitude that was shared by the Italian and Belgian authorities. The former had had to intervene on a 'massive' scale to *support* the lira during the eight days of the sterling crisis, while the latter had, like France, been able to prevent capital inflows on a scale potentially endangering its national objectives by holding interest rates down to unattractive levels and retaining the system of split markets[33, 34]. Belgium's partner in the worm, the Netherlands, did not have such an elaborate system of exchange controls, but was nevertheless able to effectively exclude foreign capital by adopting a similar policy of monetary ease. In any event, the Netherlands was predisposed against an appreciation of the guilder as this would shatter the Benelux arrangements[35].

On first examination, it might look as if a conflict of fundamental national interests would once again prevent the Community from agreeing on a common response to an international monetary crisis and that each country would resort to a different set of unilateral safeguards, with the obvious consequences for the snake and the EMU Project. Against the divergence of national economic conditions, theoretical constructs and objects of policy, the only integrating factor appeared to be the commitment of the Six to the EMU Project and specifically exchange rate stability, and after the sterling crisis this looked a very frail reed indeed. Yet the snake survived. That it passed the test of the dollar crisis was a significant success for the EMU Project. But it did not indicate that the spirit of integration had triumphed

---

* Since the information available about the size and particularly the sources of speculative capital is extremely limited, it may be of interest to note that of the DM 3500 million that flowed into Germany in the form of purchases of fixed interest securities, DM 1 100 million came from Belgium (Luxembourg), DM 600 million from the United Kingdom, DM 400 million from the Netherlands, DM 400 million from France and DM 300 million from Switzerland. It must, however, be emphasized that these are the countries where the transactions originated and are not necessarily the real source of the funds[29].

over national interests. The outcome primarily reflected the determination of each of the seven governments, for its own reasons, to maintain the parities set in Washington the previous December.

This consensus against modifying the existing exchange rate relationships was based in part on the belief that doing so barely six months after the parities of the European currencies had been realigned would set a dangerous precedent. Furthermore, reaching accord on a new set of rates would be a political nightmare. More importantly, the opinions of speculators notwithstanding, it was regarded as still too early to assess whether the Smithsonian parities were realistic and appropriate. After all, it would take a number of months for the effects of the changes to work through to international patterns of trade and investment. Yet in the last analysis it was considerations of national interest which caused the rejection of exchange rate modifications.

With the French and Italian governments totally opposed to an appreciation of their currencies, and the Benelux countries not particularly favourably disposed either, the German authorities were faced with a situation in which the only alternative to defending the existing parity was to allow the mark to rise in value against not only the dollar but also the other snake currencies. This they were not prepared to do. Since September 1969 the mark had appreciated 14–20% in terms of the currencies of its trading partners, and exporters were finding it increasingly difficult to compete in foreign markets. Moreover, there was no indication that the German payments position was in fundamental disequilibrium. The current account had been slightly in deficit for the first half of the year, and the large surplus in terms of official settlements was, according to the Bundesbank, almost entirely attributable to speculation. This rejection of a unilateral float of the mark was the key factor permitting agreement to be achieved within the Community.

With the government decided against an appreciation of the mark, 'the only adequate instrument for guarding against external pressures is measures to reduce capital inflow from abroad'[36]. Consequently, with effect from 29 June, purchases of domestic bonds by non-residents, which had accounted for the bulk of the inflow since April, required prior authorization from the Bundesbank. To complement this, the Bardepot imposed on non-trade-related foreign borrowing by German firms was increased from 40% on borrowings in excess of DM 2 million to 50% on amounts above DM 500 000. Furthermore, with effect from 1 July, reserve requirements on non-residents' bank deposits were raised to 40% on the total amount plus 60% on any increases above October 1971 levels so that new deposits were subject to a 100% requirement. With the external flank thus protected, the authorities acted to reduce the level of domestic liquidity, raising reserve requirements on residents' deposits and reducing discount quotas by 10% on

1 July and again on 1 August. All told, over DM 15 000 million was removed from bank liquidity[37].

Given the decision not to float the mark, the parities among Community currencies were unchanged, and the snake, albeit reduced to seven members, remained alive. This was a significant accomplishment both in itself, and also in preventing a halt in progress towards EMU. Even though the survival of the snake might be primarily attributable to factors other than a commitment to economic and monetary integration, the crucial decision of the German government was not uninfluenced by an unwillingness for the Federal Republic to appear to have twice frustrated progress on the EMU Project[38]. As it was, the initiative launched in March could proceed, and in view of the recent satisfactory results, further steps along the same lines could be envisaged.

That the tighter exchange rate relationships within the snake survived was all the more significant because the exchange markets did not immediately accept that parity adjustments were not necessary. Mistrust of the dollar persisted, and speculative capital movements resumed when the official markets re-opened on 28 June. Despite maintaining low interest rates and strengthening their controls over short-term capital movements, France, Belgium and the Netherlands experienced increases in their official reserves during July of almost FFr 2500 million (U.A. 450 million), BFr 10 000 million (U.A. 250 million), and $ 550 million (U.A. 500 million) respectively[39]. As on previous occasions, it was Germany, however, that was the principal target for speculative funds: the Bundesbank had to purchase the equivalent of about DM 2500 million on 3–4 July, another DM 4000 million on 13–14 July, and an even larger sum on 17 July, for a total of some DM 27 000 million (U.A. 7500 million) during the first 17 days of July[40]. The influx of capital and the corresponding increase in domestic liquidity presented severe problems for the authorities in each country, but the Governments persevered in their determination to maintain the existing parities, entering the exchange markets to the extent necessary to accomplish this. Eventually, as their resolution became evident, and especially after the finance ministers of the Community formally committed themselves on 17 July to defending the Smithsonian parities, the market acknowledged that there would be no exchange rate adjustments and the speculative wave subsided, with no interventions to support the dollar being required after the end of July.

With the restoration of stability in the exchange markets, national authorities were able – for the first time in about six months – to effectively pursue monetary policies aimed at combating the general resurgence of inflation throughout the Community. The Bundesbank increased reserve requirements by 10%, with effect from 1 August[41]. The Banque Nationale de Belgique reduced discount quotas by 1/9 and called for BFr 10 000 million in voluntary supplementary deposits, with effect from 26 July. And the Banque de France raised the level of reserve requirements by 2% on 21 July and, after the banking system had ignored repeated warnings about the expansion of credit, imposed a 15% reserve requirement on lending above the level of 5 April 1972[43].

As in the negotiations leading to the Smithsonian Accords, concerted action had produced results none of the member states acting individually could have achieved. On balance, therefore, it would seem that the crises of June 1972 had advanced economic and monetary unification, at least in terms of the attempt to promote exchange rate stability. The snake system had passed its first major trials. True, Denmark and the United Kingdom were no longer taking part in these arrangements. However, this could be attributed to their not being members of the Community. In any event, both Governments had committed themselves to rejoining the snake in the near future, a conceivable move as both currencies remained firm against the dollar from the middle of July. True also, the normal settlement procedures had had to be relaxed for the Italian authorities, but the lira was still included in the snake. This was the essential point: whatever qualifications had to be added, the initiative in exchange rate concertation had survived the crises, and progress had been made in forging closer monetary relationships.

Yet if the outcome of the June crises was a success in terms of the snake, it represented another setback for economic and monetary unification. The sterling crisis had all too graphically demonstrated the low level of co-operation among the countries participating in the snake. And while the Six had maintained the existing exchange rate structure in the face of the challenge presented by the dollar crisis, the price had been the extension of exchange controls. As the Bundesbank ruefully commented, in so doing, 'passte sich die Bundesrepublik einer internationalen Entwicklung an, die, für sich betrachtet, sicher nich befriedigt, die aber ein einzelnes Land nicht ändern kann'[44]. Significantly, as the new regulations applied to capital movements among member states as well as those involving third countries, they were a step backwards on the road to economic and monetary union. Furthermore, they confirmed the 'economist' argument that initiatives in the field of exchange rate concertation would not spontaneously result in the convergence of national wage and price trends which was a precondition for exchange rate stability. In other words, these two crises had shown that the maintenance of fixed and immutable exchange rates among the countries of the enlarged Community would lead to serious payments imbalances and that national governments were not prepared to sacrifice national interests to economic and monetary integration. This had profound implications for the EMU Project. It meant that regardless of any transient successes that might be achieved on particular initiatives, the attempt to create an economic and monetary union was doomed unless these two fundamental conditions changed.

The Paris summit

Whatever the fundamental problems in economic and monetary integration, the EMU Project appeared to have advanced considerably in the first six months since its re-launching in March 1972, and it was against this background of progress that the finance ministers of the enlarged Community assembled in Rome on 12 September 1972 to discuss the next series of steps to be taken. The principal item on the agenda was the creation of a European monetary co-operation fund on which the Council had been unable to agree in March. According to the resolution of 21 March 1972, the Monetary Committee and the Committee of Central Bank Governors were to have submitted reports on this matter by 30 June so that the Council could take action by the end of the year, but in typical Community fashion, they had missed this deadline by several months; the Monetary Committee did not present its findings until 5 September. Although it had achieved a consensus that the fund should administer the multilateral intervention system, use a European unit of account to record the resulting claims and liabilities and organize settlements on a multilateral basis, the same conflict over pooling national reserves and placing the mutual assistance mechanisms within the Fécom framework that had prevented accord in March blocked agreement in the Monetary Committee[45]. Once again, an issue that had deadlocked the Werner Committee divided the Six along the familiar lines of 'economists' v. 'monetarists'.

The same pattern repeated itself in the Council of Ministers. The Dutch and German representatives reiterated their opposition to creating a monetary co-operation fund at this early stage, arguing, as in March, that until significant progress had been made in the co-ordination of economic policies and the concertation of exchange rates, the fund would have no real function to perform and that the Community should concentrate instead on achieving a higher degree of co-operation. They further pointed out that the events of the previous six months had shown that the existing arrangements were adequate from a technical point of view and that the problems that had arisen could best be resolved by taking steps to bring about a convergence of national economic trends, particularly by a reduction of inflation rates throughout the Community. France, supported by Belgium, drew a diametrically opposed conclusion from the success of the snake, asserting that this confirmed the 'monetarist' view that advances towards EMU should come on this front. They were, therefore, strong proponents of a monetary co-operation fund, which they saw as making an important contribution to tightening the monetary relationships among the member states by formalizing the existing arrangements and by centralizing operations in an incipient Community central bank. However, the French authorities, while regarding the creation of such a fund as a step towards a *de jure* as opposed to a *de facto* exchange rate concertation system, did not envisage abjuring recourse to parity adjustments. Instead they maintained that until the final stage national governments would have to be able to take emergency action, a view with which the British government, concerned about protecting the level of employment, strongly concurred. Furthermore, the French were clear that the fund was to be an intergovernmental –not supranational – body[46].

As in March, there seemed little common ground, but by using the now familiar method of deferring the contentious issues and formulating an uncontroversial compromise on the rest, the finance ministers were able to reach accord during the September meeting. Once again, progress was to be based on the strategy of parallelism, with modest and carefully balanced advances on the fronts of exchange rate concertation, economic policy co-ordination and regional policy. Specifically, the finance ministers agreed in principle to the creation of a European monetary co-operation fund, which was to co-ordinate the interventions of the central banks under the snake arrangements, organize settlements on a multilateral basis, conduct transactions in a Community unit of account, and administer the short-term monetary support mechanisms[47]. As all of these functions were already performed by the Committee of Central Bank Governors, the practical import of this change would be nil. Symbolically, however, it established a link between the multilateral intervention system and the short-term monetary support mechanism. This was a gesture in the direction of increasing the amount of aid available under the latter so that it corresponded to the size of the liabilities incurred under the former. But it was largely an empty one because the substantive decisions on integrating the mutual assistance system into the snake arrangements and on pooling reserves were put off because the agreement in principle did not commit the member states to specific action in the future.

The steps to be taken on the other two fronts were equally insignificant and tentative. There was to be a new initiative in the field of economic policy co-ordination, but since the existing institutional arrangements were regarded as adequate, it called merely for greater co-operation among the member states, especially in efforts to reduce inflation. Similarly, the principle of a European regional fund was accepted, but its size and function were unspecified. That the agreement attained by the ministers in September represented such a small advance beyond what had been decided in March reflected at one level the problems in having to maintain parallelism between progress on each front, for difficulties in one area prevented forward movement in all the others. More fundamentally, however, it was also a manifestation of the limitations of the strategy of parallelism. While it might be possible for the Community to proceed on the basis of simultaneous advances along the 'economist' and 'monetarist' paths in the early stages of the EMU Project, the incompatibility of these two antithetical strategies would eventually render such a course impracticable and compel the member states to choose one alternative or the other. Yet it had been necessary to resort to a 'parallel' approach precisely because the national governments were not prepared to yield in any meaningful sense on this issue.

The Community had not yet reached the limits of parallelism in the autumn of 1972, but already there were signs of the impasse looming ahead. Decisions on pooling reserves, on modifying the mutual assistance mechanism to provide automatic financing for debts incurred under the multilateral intervention system, and on endowing the snake arrangements with a binding as opposed to an experimental character, as well as on going beyond voluntary co-operation in economic policy-making, had to be postponed because they would have committed the Community either to the 'monetarist' or the 'economist' approach. In short, any issue raising the basic issue of strategy had to be left unresolved.

It was the progress that had been made on the initiatives launched in March, however, that was the dominant theme of the Paris Summit of 19–21 October 1972. The heads of state of the enlarged Community reaffirmed their commitment to creating an economic and monetary union, reiterated their determination to complete this project on the scheduled date of 1 January 1980, and undertook to proceed to the second stage, as planned, at the beginning of 1974[48]. Yet the significance of the Paris Summit in terms of economic and monetary integration was much more in that it endorsed the course on which the Community had embarked or even that it resulted in a renewed commitment to EMU at the highest level despite the setbacks and failures of the first two years. The crucial point was rather that the three future members, Britain, Ireland and Denmark, had committed themselves to the attainment of economic and monetary union[49].

The heads of state manifested their determination to proceed towards economic and monetary union in deeds as well as in words, agreeing on a series of measures designed to prepare for the transition to the second stage at the end of the following year. They approved in principle the creation of a monetary co-operation fund, with the functions outlined by the finance ministers. They also laid down that the Council, on the basis of reports to be submitted by the Commission, the Monetary Committee, and the Committee of Central Bank Governors, was to examine the question of changes in the short-term monetary support system by 30 September 1973 and the more contentious issue of reserve pooling by 31 December 1973. Moreover, they decreed that a regional fund was to be established by 31 December 1973, and that the finance and economics ministers were to decide on a set of measures to combat inflation at the Community level at the Council meeting of 30–31 October 1972. Finally, the heads of state agreed to adopt a common position in the discussions on the reform of the international monetary system based on the principles advanced by the European countries during autumn 1971.

The new elements in the agreements reached in Paris thus consisted largely of imposing deadlines, and although this was not without its importance in a Community which habitually postponed decisions on controversial issues, these time limits had either effectively already been laid down by the Council resolution of 22 March 1971, or involved a commitment to study a particular question without necessarily coming to any specific conclusion. That the initiatives approved at the Paris Summit represented a very small advance towards EMU is, however, of secondary importance, for the essential fact is that the political leaders, by deciding on a new set of measures in economic and monetary integration demonstrated their confidence in the plan for achieving EMU and their commitment to attaining this goal.

The dollar crisis: February–March 1973

The Paris Summit ended exactly seven months after the Council had re-launched the EMU Project; precisely seven months after the British Government had decided to float the pound in the aftermath of a massive speculative attack on sterling, the Italian Government had decided, under similar circumstances, to float the financial lira. With uncanny regularity, three months and two days after the ringing declarations of commitment to EMU and the confident inauguration of new initiaives, the Community found itself in the throes of an international monetary crisis which put the resolution of the member states to maintain the closer monetary relationship among themselves to the test and found them wanting. That this challenge should have come at such uniform intervals was coincidental. That it came was not.

As in spring 1971 and early 1972, the environment in autumn 1972 seemed at first glance favourable to progress in economic and monetary integration. The initiative in exchange rate concertation had withstood the trials of the previous summer, and the snake countries had been kept within their tighter limits with only minimal intervention since the resolution of the sterling and dollar crises in the middle of the summer. Moreover, the Danish kroner had rejoined the snake on 10 October, and the British chancellor had declared his commitment to putting the pound back on a fixed parity by the end of the year if at all possible[50]. At the world level, the dollar had recovered from its weakness of June and July and stayed within its parity bands without central bank support, rising to a slight premium against the commercial French franc by the end of the year[51].

With the immediate threat of large-scale transatlantic capital movements eliminated and interest rates following a generally upward trend, the authorities in all the Community countries had, moreover, been able to effectively pursue increasingly restrictive monetary policies aimed at reducing the accelerating rate of inflation. The Bundesbank raised the discount rate from 3 to 5% in a series of ½% steps between 9 October and 12 January 1973, while the Banque Nationale de Belgique implemented an increase of 1% between 23 November and 21 December 1972[52, 53]. The French authorities not only allowed day-to-day rates to rise 2% on the money market during the fourth quarter, but also introduced, with effect from 21 November, a 33% reserve requirement on the growth in bank lending above the level it had been in April. When even these measures failed to reduce the disturbing rate of credit expansion, a system of penal reserves was imposed under which increases in loans above a normative annual rate of increase, set at 10% for 3 April 1973 and 17% for 3 July, were subject to special reserves calculated at the rate of $(0.3 + 0.1X)X\%$, where X is the percentage by which the bank exceeded the norm on the monthly reference date[54]. Even if such measures did not end the conditions of excess demand, the authorities were at least able to follow a course consistent with the requirements of their national economies, a considerable improvement on the situation earlier in the year.

Yet beneath the surface the situation was anything but favourable for further advances in economic and monetary unification. Once again another attack on the dollar was taking shape. Despite the July 1972 declaration by European finance ministers of their commitment to maintaining the present set of parities and the recovery of the dollar in the following months, confidence in the American currency had never really been restored, and when the United States balance of payments position worsened at the end of the year, mistrust again set in. Although it was recognized that there might be a considerable lag before the competitive advantage conferred by the depreciation of the dollar was reflected in an improvement on the trade account, the steady growth of the current account deficit, reaching a record annual total of almost $ 10 000 million in 1972, gave rise to concern that the dollar might still be overvalued. These doubts were strengthened by the announcement of a deterioration in the American reserve position of similar magnitude, in spite of the repatriation of speculative capital after the Smithsonian parity changes and the relatively attractive rates of interest prevailing in the United States. At the beginning of 1973 a flight from the dollar had not yet developed but all the ingredients were already present.

Ironically, the disturbance that unleashed the attack on the dollar once again had its origins within the Community. On 22 January 1973, in an attempt to stem the drain on their reserves that had been gathering momentum since the beginning of the year, the Italian authorities introduced a two-tiered exchange system, intervening only in the official market, which was restricted to transactions on the current account. The following day, the Swiss Government floated the franc in response to enormous inflows of funds, in large part from Italy[55]. Although these developments did not directly concern the dollar, it was nevertheless indirectly involved as a vehicle currency: the flow of, initially, primarily Italian funds into Switzerland had gone through the intermediary of the dollar, resulting in pressure on the dollar–franc parity, and with the floating of the franc, there was a sharp fall in the dollar rate. The dollar's weakness against the Swiss franc aroused the latent mistrust of the American currency, and this, agravated by injudicious remarks by representatives Mills and Reuss as well as by fears that other European countries might follow the Swiss example precipitated a flight from the dollar in the closing days of January [56]. Some $ 8500 million left the United States in the three weeks to 9 February[57], for which Germany, as on previous occasions, was the principal target, attracting approximately $ 6000 million in the first two weeks of February[58]. France, on the other hand, was shielded by the prospect of Presidential elections as well as a relatively high rate of inflation and experienced only minor inflows, while the Benelux countries absorbed some $ 1500 million[59].

The initial response of the European countries was to resort to the measures usually taken to combat capital inflows. In addition to tightening exchange controls, the Banque de France forbade the payment of interest on non-residents' accounts having initial maturities of less than 180 days and imposed a 100% reserve requirement on the increase in non-resident deposits from 4 January 1973[60]. The German authorities took even more drastic action. On February 5 borrowings abroad in excess of DM 50 000, transfers of more than DM 50 000 by international businesses to their German subsidiaries, all purchases of securities denominated in marks by non-residents and all delays in payment for imports beyond the usual trade practices were made to require prior authorization from the Government. Moreover, legislative approval was sought to raise the Bardepot rate to 100%, the threshold having already been lowered to DM 50 000 at the start of the year[61].

Following an all too familiar pattern, these proved unequal to containing the pressures created by the flight from the dollar, as was demonstrated by the entry of more than $ 1500 million into the Federal Republic on 6 February alone. Consequently, as the crisis entered its second week and the flow of capital towards the European countries continued to increase, it became clear that member states were once again faced with a choice between continuing to absorb vast quantities of dollars through attempting to defend existing parities or allowing their currencies to appreciate, either through floating or exchange rate adjustments.

As in July, the Finance Ministers of the enlarged Community maintained that the dollar was not overvalued and opposed a modification of exchange rates on principle. They recognized, however, that to resist a relative depreciation of the dollar was to commit themselves to absorbing funds from abroad on a vast scale because the speculative pressures were far greater than they had been even seven months before and had given rise to capital movements of unprecedented size. Despite stringent capital controls, the Bundesbank had had to purchase more than DM 5000 million in foreign currency on each of two consecutive days in the second week of February, and total purchases were over DM 18 000 million for the first ten days of the month. By way of comparison, the total increase in reserves was less than DM 8000 million during the May 1971 crisis and about DM 8500 million in June 1972[62, 63].

Tolerating inflows of such dimensions was clearly out of the question, as it would result in an explosion of liquidity and hence credit that would greatly exacerbate the problem of inflation, which was much more serious throughout the Community than seven months previously[64, 65]. The Finance Ministers therefore concluded that they had no practical alternative but to allow their currencies to appreciate against the dollar. As to the form the adjustment should take, they were united in rejecting flotation against the dollar, in part because they did not want to repeat the experience of 1971 with its deleterious effects on their economies and in part because the German authorities categorically refused to float the mark independently while the other member states ruled out a joint float in which their currencies would be dragged up by the mark. Consequently, the only remaining course of action was a formal devaluation of the dollar. Despite their preference for flotation, the American authorities accepted this solution after talks with the major financial powers during the weekend of 10–11 February. With effect from 12 February 1973, the dollar was devalued by 10%.

In terms of the EMU Project, the outcome of the February 1973 crisis displays many similarities with that of the June 1972 crisis. Except for Italy, which announced on 13 February that, because of the persistent drain on its reserves, it was floating the 'commercial' as well as the 'financial' lira, the exchange rate relationships between the member states remained unaltered when the exchange markets re-opened on 14 February. Once again the snake had survived, though dismembered. The departure of the lira revealed anew the vulnerability of the snake system, for however successfully it functioned at the technical level, it could not provide the assistance the Italian authorities would realistically have needed to keep the lira in the snake[66]. This demonstration of the shortcomings in the existing system was particularly significant because the Italian Government, unlike the British in June 1972, would have been eligible for assistance under the Community mutual aid mechanisms. It could, of course, be argued that the lira was a casualty of the dollar crisis, but the fact was that the strains between the lira and the other five countries had been building up for months. Moreover, while Italy had admittedly always been the weak sister of the Six, the EMU Project was designed to forge a single economic unit out of the *entire* Community.

Of the ten countries that had formed the snake at its inception in spring 1972, three had already dropped out because they were not prepared to pay the price, in terms of the consequences on their domestic economies, of continued participation*. This was the crucial flaw in the initiative in

---

* In addition, the Norwegian kroner had left the snake in November 1972 following the unfavourable result of the 26 September referendum on membership in the Community.

exchange rate concertation: the survival of the snake depended on the member states maintaining a specific set of exchange rates. But governments made economic policy decisions, which ultimately determined whether a given parity could or would be defended, on the basis of a multitude of considerations, among which the imperatives of economic and monetary unification were among the least important. Both in the summer and in the winter of 1973 the snake participants did present a united front, but this was due more to the fortuitous convergence of their individual national interests rather than to a commitment to concerted action. Just as they had agreed to maintain the existing parity relationships in July because each had rejected, for its own reasons, a modification of exchange rates, so they were in accord on a devaluation of the dollar in February because they had all independently ruled out the other alternatives.

Nevertheless, as in September, it was the survival of the snake and the resolution of the crisis rather than the setback in economic and monetary unification signified by the intensification of exchange controls and the weakness of the commitment to EMU which set the tone for the Council meeting of 14 February 1973. This satisfaction at the accomplishments on the exchange rate concertation front was reflected in the Finance Ministers' decision to advance the deadline for the submission of reports on modifying the short-term mutual assistance system and on reserve pooling by three and six months respectively to 30 June 1973[67]. At first this optimism seemed justified. With the dollar's devaluation, the flight of capital from the United States had stopped and indeed a modest return of funds had set in, with the Bundesbank being able to sell almost $ 3000 million by the end of February[68]. At the same time, the creation of a European monetary co-operation fund was moving slowly forward as the Committee of Central Bank Governors and the Monetary Committee proceeded to hammer out the organizational details.

As on previous occasions, however, the confident expectations of further progress towards EMU were soon abruptly shattered. The underlying mistrust of the American currency had not been completely removed, despite the 12 February devaluation, and as early as 22 February there was a new flurry of speculation prompted by the gradual upward movement of the Swiss franc and rumours of a European float against the dollar. Official interventions quickly quelled this disturbance, but the attack on the dollar resumed on 1 March. Although the pattern of capital movements resembled that of the previous month, the amounts involved were much larger. On 1 March alone the Bundesbank absorbed almost $ 3000 million, while in the space of a couple of days the Dutch authorities acquired over $ 750 million, almost twice as much as during the February crisis[69]. Faced anew with large-scale speculative inflows, the member states, true to form, closed the exchange markets with effect from 2 March. For the second time in less than a month, European monetary authorities were confronted with the unattractive alternatives of either allowing their currencies to appreciate against the dollar or continuing to absorb vast amounts of foreign capital. As in February, tightening exchange controls was not a real option because since recent experience had

> 'made it abundantly clear that even stronger administrative action against capital flows from foreign countries, such as was taken by the Federal Government with effect from 5 February 1973, does not suffice when speculative expectations run particularly high'[70].

Neither appreciation nor capital inflows had much appeal. The Community countries opposed yet another appreciation against the dollar, as this would further impair the competitiveness of their products in world markets. But because it was regarded as absolutely indispensable that the present influx of funds be stemmed in view of its totally unacceptable consequences on their booming economies, the Community countries had little choice but to contemplate an upward movement in the value of their currencies. As to the form the adjustment should take, the snake participants unanimously rejected a formal parity change for essentially the same reasons as in June and July 1972. Moreover, there was no guarantee that a second dollar devaluation would be accepted by the markets or resolve the crisis any more successfully than its predecessor in February. Finally, the member states were loath to give this movement in exchange rates the official sanction a parity change would imply because they maintained that the dollar was not overvalued[71, 72].

By this process of elimination, the snake participants had effectively opted for flotation. It only remained for them to decide whether to float their currencies jointly or individually. Here agreement proved difficult to achieve. As on the two previous occasions, the German authorities were not prepared to envisage the unilateral flotation of the mark. The French Government continued to rule out placing the franc in a joint float including the mark[73]. The Dutch authorities, for their part, advocated a joint Benelux–German float, while the Italian Government was determined to continue with the independent float of the lira. The British Government indicated that it was willing to consider rejoining the snake and participating in a joint float but, even after having depressed the exchange rate by massive sales of sterling, only with a guarantee of support from the other members and particularly Germany. However, the Federal Republic refused to commit its reserves to the defence of other currencies[74, 75]. As in May 1971 it appeared inevitable that the Community would fail to agree and that each country would adopt a different course of action.

Yet agreement was achieved, albeit only among the countries participating in the snake. The breakthrough came when a compromise between France and Germany was achieved: the franc would take part in a joint float, while the mark would be slightly revalued. The Benelux and Danish governments quickly indicated their approval of these arrangements, and the Council, at its meeting of 11 March, ratified the decision of Belgium, Denmark, France, Germany, Luxembourg and the Netherlands to float collectively their currencies against the dollar while continuing to maintain the reduced level of fluctuations among themselves[76]. Thus, once again, the initiative in exchange rate concertation appeared to have passed the test of an international monetary crisis, for the parity relationships were unchanged when the exchange markets re-opened on 19 March – except for a 3% revaluation of the mark – and the snake survived intact.

The outcome of the March crisis clearly constituted a success for the snake. The closer exchange relationships among the member states assumed a new importance with the abandonment of fixed parities in relation to the dollar, because they became the only fixed point of reference in the members' monetary relations with other countries. Symbolically, the emergence of the snake from the tunnel reinforced the Community's identity in monetary affairs. Technically, it raised the level of co-operation as the central banks had to develop procedures for multilateral intervention in the absence of a constant standard. Yet the emergence from the tunnel, like the birth of the snake itself, appears as progress in terms of exchange rate stability only against the background of developments at the world level, where the Bretton Woods system of fixed rates was giving way to a new set of more flexible arrangements. The relationships between the Community currencies did not become any closer as a result of the March crisis; their links with third currencies merely became less tight.

In a more fundamental sense as well, the outcome of the March crisis represented another setback for economic and montary integration. Once again the lack of the political will to work towards EMU was starkly revealed. Britain and Italy both decided to remain outside the snake. While they were formally committed to returning, that the pound had depreciated 15% against the other Community currencies in less than nine months and the lira 7% in just one month raised serious doubts about either being able to stay within the prescribed limits, let alone at the official parity, for a prolonged period of time[77]. Even within the snake, the revaluation of the mark had been a precondition for the participation of the franc. National interests, in other words, continued to take precedence over the cause of economic and monetary unification. Even when they coincided, as they did for the German authorities, the advocacy of a float of all eight currencies emanated more from a desire to prevent a relative appreciation of the mark than from a commitment to exchange rate stability, while the acceptance of a small revaluation reflected primarily a calculation of economic advantage.

Whatever the implications of this lack of political commitment for the future of economic and monetary integration in the Community, the March crisis resulted in a much more immediate and serious reversal for the EMU Project: the snake ceased to be a visible means for working towards economic and monetary union because it was no longer an instrument for promoting the integration of the *Community*. Not only were three of the member states not involved in this attempt to forge closer monetary relationships, but two non-members joined the multilateral intervention systems on 19 March. True, Norway and Sweden were not eligible to participate in the mutual assistance system and settled any claims and liabilities on a bilateral basis, but their currencies participated in the joint float just like those of member states*.

This dealt the final blow to the hopes that the snake arrangements would serve as the means for introducing a single Community currency. Whether the new grouping of eight countries formed a more homogeneous and sensible unit than the Nine in economic or even political terms, whether the snake conferred sizeable benefits on its participants, indeed whether other countries linked their currencies to the joint float – even without formal agreement, as did Austria and later Switzerland – are all secondary issues. The essential point is that the entry of the Norwegian and Swedish kroners, in conjunction with the departure of the lira and the pound, transformed the character of the snake system so that it was no longer a Community institution. In so doing, it exploded the fiction of the initiative in exchange rate concertation fostering an integrative process among the member states and revealed the snake as it was – a collection of national currencies whose only common characteristic was the ability and the will to maintain a set of fixed exchange rates. In other words, in terms of neither membership nor function were the efforts on the exchange rate front of the EMU Project any longer acting to forge a single economic unit out of the Community, and whatever advances or successes there might be in these endeavours, they would not necessarily bring the member states any nearer to their final goal.

This fundamental change was not, however, recognized by national governments or even by the Commission, for they had come to equate the snake with the EMU Project, its survival with progress towards the final objective and, indeed, participation in it with fulfilling one's Community obligations. The outcome of the March 1973 crisis was thus perceived as representing considerable progress in the attempt to create an economic and monetary union. After all, the snake had survived intact, evidence that the efforts to forge closer monetary relationships among the members had prevailed over the strains produced by the international monetary crisis. It had emerged from the tunnel, replacing the link with the dollar as the central element in the members' exchange rate relationships. Finally, it had attracted two new participants, indicating the advantages it conferred on its members

---

* Strictly speaking, Norway and Sweden were not members of the snake system, but associates. In this book, the term 'snake participants' will be used to include Norway and Sweden as well as the 'snake members, i.e. the Community countries taking part in the multilateral intervention system.

by providing a stable framework of fixed parities among them. The Governments were confident that in launching the joint float they had taken a decisive step towards creating a distinct and independent European monetary area, and that in so doing they had made a large stride in the direction of establishing an economic and monetary union.

The second phase of the initial stage of the EMU Project thus ends on a note of unresolved contradictions. At one level, the member states appeared to have made a substantial advance in economic and monetary unification. The initiative in exchange rate concertation had proved successful in reducing the size of fluctuations, and the closer monetary relationships among its participants had generally weathered the storms of three international monetary crises. Yet in a more fundamental sense, the member states had failed because they had not achieved the political will to work towards economic and monetary union. National interest still took precedence over the imperatives of economic and monetary integration. In practical terms, this had been reflected in the departure of three currencies from the multilateral intervention system. In doctrinal terms, this was manifested in the unresolved conflict between the 'economists' and the 'monetarists'. Thus, the twelve months since the re-launching of the EMU Project had been characterized paradoxically by considerable progress on specific elements of this project and at the same time by the failure of the member states to come any closer to attaining their final goal.

1 *Abkomen zwischen den Zentralbanken der Mitgliedstaaten der Gemeinschaft vom 10. April 1972 über die Verringerung der Bandbreiten zwischen den Wahrungen der Gemeinschaft*
2 *Bank of England Quarterly Bulletin*, XII(2), June 1972, pp.165–170
3 *Geschäftsbericht der Deutschen Bundesbank für das Jahr 1972* [hereafter cited as *Geschaftsbericht*] p.81
4 *Geschaftsbericht*, 1971, pp.54–59
5 *Monatsberichte der Deutschen Bundesbank* [hereafter cited as *Monatsberichte*] March 1972, p.7
6 Banque de France, *Bulletin trimestrial* [hereafter cited as *Bulletin trimestriel*]No. 3, May 1972, pp.17–21
7 Belgium, Ministère des Affaires Economiques, *l'Economie belge en 1972*, pp.217–219
8 De Nederlandsche Bank, *Report for the Year 1971* [hereafter cited as *Nederlandsche Bank*] pp.111, 119
9 *Monatsberichte*, March 1972, pp.5–7
10 *Monatsberichte*, June 1972, pp.5–7, 35–42
11 *Bulletin trimestriel*, No. 3, May 1972, pp.5–10
12 Belgium, Ministère des Affaires Economiques, *l'Economie belge en 1972*, pp.218–221
13 *Bank of England Quarterly Bulletin*, XII(1), March 1972, pp.3–9
14 Bank of England, *Statistical Abstract No. 2*, 1975, p.129
15 OECD, *Economic Surveys, United Kingdom*, 1972, pp.5–15
16 *Hansard*, Vol. 833, Col. 1354, 21 March 1972
17 *Bank of England Quarterly Bulletin*, XII(3), September 1972, pp.310–316
18 *Monatsberichte*, September 1972, pp.10–12
19 *Bulletin trimestriel*, No. 4, September 1972, pp.8–10
20 *Hansard*, Vol. 839, Col. 878, 26 June 1972
21 *Hansard*, Vol. 839, Col. 879, 26 June 1972

22 *Hansard*, Vol. 839, Col. 886, 26 June 1972
23 *Bank of England Quarterly Bulletin*, XII(3), September 1972, pp.306–309
24 *Bulletin trimestriel*, No. 4, September 1972, pp.8–10
25 IMF, *International Financial Statistics*, XXV(12) December 1972
26 *Jahreswirtschaftsbericht 1972 der Bundesregierung* [hereafter cited as *Jahreswirtschaftsericht*] pp.9–11
27 *Monatsberichte*, July 1972, pp.5–7
28 *Geschäftsbericht 1972*, p.10
29 *Monatsberichte*, June 1972, pp.39–41
30 Banque de France, *Compte rendu* (Exercice 1972) [hereafter cited as *Compte rendu*] p.38
31 *Monatsberichte*, September 1972, pp.10–12
32 *Compte rendu*, 1972, pp.37–40
33 Banca d'Italia, *Abridged version of the Report for the Year 1972*, pp.87–89, 199
34 Belgium, Ministère des Affaires Economiques, *l'Economie belge en 1972*, pp.217–222
35 *Nederlandsche Bank*, 1972, pp.111–115
36 *Monatsberichte*, July 1972, p.7
37 *Geschäftsbericht*, 1972, pp.16–23
38 Federal Republic of Germany, Press and Information Office, *The European Community: From the Summit Conference at the Hague to the Europe of the Ten*, 1972, pp.91–92, 103–112
39 *Bulletin trimestriel*, No. 4, September 1972, pp.19–24
40 *Monatsberichte*, August 1972, pp.5–7
41 *Monatsberichte*, August 1972, pp.5–6
42 Belgium, Ministère des Affaires Economiques, *l'Economie belge en 1972*, pp.217–223
43 *Bulletin trimestriel*, No. 4, September 1972, pp.11–14
44 *Monatsberichte*, July 1972, p.9
45 European Communities, Monetary Committee, *Avis au Conseil et à la Commission*, in *Quatorzième Rapport d'Activite* [hereafter cited as *Monetary Committee 1972*] 1972, pp.34–38
46 'Le rapport économique et financier' (du Project de Loi de Finances pour 1973) in *Statistiques et Etudes Financières*, XXIV(286), October 1972, p.19
47 *Monetary Committee 1972*, p.10
48 *Schlusserklarung der Konferenz der Staats- bzw. Regierungschefs der Mitgliedslander der erweiterten Gemeinschaft vom 19, 20 und 21 Oktober 1972 in Paris*. In European Communities, Monetary Committee, *Kompendium von Gemeinschaftstexten in Bereich der Währungspolitik*, pp.26–27
49 *Hansard*, Vol. 843, Col. 791–809, 23 October 1972
50 *Hansard*, Vol. 843, Col. 81–135, 17 October 1972
51 *Bulletin trimestriel*, No. 6, February 1973, pp.9–10
52 *Geschäftsbericht*, 1972, pp.21–23
53 Belgium, Ministère des Affaires Economiques, *l'Economie belge en 1972*, pp.217–223
54 *Bulletin trimestriel*, No. 6, February 1973, pp.10–19
55 *Monatsberichte*, February 1973, pp.5–7
56 *Bulletin trimestriel*, No. 7, May 1973, pp.10–12
57 *Bank of England Quarterly Bulletin*, XIII(2), June 1973, pp.127–131
58 *Monatsberichte*, February 1973, pp.32–33
59 *Nederlandsche Bank*, 1973, p.115
60 *Bulletin trimestriel*, No. 7, May 1973, pp.10–12
61 *Monatsberichte*, February 1973, pp.32–33
62 *Monatsberichte*, September 1972, pp.10–12
63 *Monatsberichte*, February 1973, pp.32–33
64 OECD, *Economic Surveys, Germany*, 1972, pp.13–22
65 OECD, *Economic Surveys, France*, 1972, pp.15–25
66 Banca d'Italia, *Abridged version of the Report for the Year 1972*, pp.69–70, 202–205, 222
67 European Communities Commission, *Seventh General Report on the Activities of the Communities*, p.176
68 *Geschäftsbericht*, 1972, p.17
69 *Monatsberichte*, June 1973, pp.10–12
70 *Monatsberichte*, March 1973, p.5
71 *Geschäftsbericht*, 1972, pp.23–25, 31–35
72 'Le rapport économique et financier', 1974, p.23
73 *The Economist*, 246 (6759), 10 March 1973, pp.59–60, 98–100
74 *Bank of England Quarterly Bulletin*, XIII(2), June 1973, pp.127–131, 137–140
75 *The Economist*, 246 (6758), 3 March 1973, p.75
76 *Erklärung des Rates vom 12 March 1973*. In European Communities, Monetary Committee, *Kompendium von Gemeinschaftstexten in Bereich der Währungspolitik*, p.61
77 Bank of England, *Statistical Abstract No. 2*, 1975, pp.162–163

CHAPTER SEVEN
Exchange Rate Concertation: the Snake

The contradictions between the significant accomplishments in certain areas of the EMU Project, such as the progress in fostering closer monetary relationships within the Community that the snake system represented, and the failure of the member states to find the political will to work towards economic and monetary integration were resolved during the final period of the first stage. Two series of developments, independent yet interrelated, impelled the Nine towards the moment of truth that would decide the fate of economic and monetary unification in the Community. On the one hand, the emergence of payments imbalances and tensions within the snake demonstrated the inherent incompatibility of national autonomy in economic policy-making with the maintenance of fixed parities and reduced fluctuations among Community currencies. On the other hand, the need to decide on the steps to be taken during the second stage brought to a climax the conflict over the approach the Community should adopt in the EMU Project. If the Nine were to advance to the next stage, in which the experimental and non-binding steps of the three preceding years were to be replaced by major, irreversible progress towards the final objective, now only seven years distant, they would have to agree on a strategy. At least the conflict between the 'economist' and the 'monetarist' states that persisted beneath the veneer of accord or 'parallelism' would have to be resolved. As in spring 1971, so too in the winter of 1973–74, the practical economic and the fundamental political strands of the EMU Project came together at a critical juncture when the member states determined the future course of economic and monetary integration.

The Commission's proposals for the second stage

The basic pattern of crisis, survival of the snake, launching of new initiatives in economic and monetary integration, and renewed challenge to the closer exchange rate relationships among the member states has become familiar from Chapter 6. This cycle was to repeat itself once more before giving way to a momentous series of events which resulted in the abandonment of the EMU Project. The emergence of the snake from the crises of February and March, followed by the Commission's proposals in April and June for the second stage and then in June and July yet another speculative attack on the intra-Community exchange rate structure bear many similarities to earlier episodes, but they also contain harbingers of the impending catastrophe. The decision to free the snake from the confinement of the tunnel is not accompanied by the usual declarations of commitment to economic and monetary unification; the Commission's recommendations for the second stage do not produce agreement in the Council; and the strains within the snake, if temporarily relieved by the revaluation of the mark, recur intermittently throughout the summer.

In spring 1973, however, confidence and optimism surrounded the EMU Project. The snake had survived the recent crises, losing a member but growing in importance with the severence of its link with the dollar, and conditions in the aftermath of the launching of the joint float appeared propitious to further progress in economic integration. When the exchange markets re-opened on 19 March, there was little upward pressure on any of the European currencies, and the dollar in fact remained within the limits set in February until the middle of May[1]. Within the snake, little intervention was required to maintain the reduced fluctuations among the seven currencies for the remainder of March and virtually none in April.

Moreover, with the massive capital inflows of past weeks now eliminated, national authorities could at last effectively pursue a deflationary course in line with the requirements of domestic conditions. Central banks in all the snake countries moved rapidly to take advantage of this situation. The Bundesbank reduced discount quotas by 10% on 1 April, raised the discount rate 1% on 4 May and 1 June, and kept reserve requirements at the high levels imposed during the March crisis as well as allowing domestic liquidity to be reduced by an outflow of DM 2500 million in April prompted by market forces[2]. Similarly, the Banque Nationale de Belgique called for an increase of approximately 50% in the voluntary supplementary reserves held for March, April and May and raised the discount rate on 10 May[3], while the Banque de France restrained domestic credit expansion through its system of penal reserves on banks exceeding norms on the growth of lending, lowering the targets from 19% in March to less than 15% in the autumn[4]. As a result, interest rates rose steadily throughout the spring, with overnight money in Germany fetching as much as 30% during April. The reduction in the growth of the money supply and tightening of credit conditions made a valuable contribution to the efforts to combat inflation, but it rapidly became clear that action on the monetary front would not be sufficient to restore balance between supply and demand. Because high levels of demand were primarily responsible for the inflationary pressures, reliance solely on monetary policy would have required a degree of monetary stringency no country was prepared to accept. Moreover, because of the high level of liquidity during the early months of 1973, most sectors started from strong financial positions, a situation which caused a delay in the effect official action had on expenditures[5]. Even in France, where the direct regulation of credit resulted in a much quicker transmission of the contractionary impulse, the money supply continued to grow apace during the second quarter, and the Banque de France warned that to take the drastic action that could alone end this expansion would be to endanger 'les objectifs d'expansion et de lutte contre le chômage'[6].

Consequently, most of the countries participating in the snake moved to complement the monetary measures with fiscal ones during the late spring and early summer. The German government, in its second stability programme of 9 May 1973, imposed an 11% tax on investment, an increased tax on hydrocarbons, and a 10% surcharge on income tax for one year beginning 1 July; suspended accelerated depreciation for tax purposes on most forms of investment; and further reduced government spending for the second half year[7, 8]. The Belgian Government limited spending on non-priority investment in the first half of the year to 37½% of the total amount for 1973, with corresponding ceilings for most of the second half, abolished all general investment incentives, and deferred the payment of subsidies for housing construction[9]. Even with these measures, the battle against inflation had still to be won in the early summer, but that national authorities could, for the first time in several months, take effective action to restrain the rise in prices was a significant accomplishment – and one which was largely attributable to the joint float. Moreover, as with the 1971 float, the appreciation of the snake currencies acted directly to reduce inflation by moderating the increases in the cost of raw materials, as well as gradually altering trade patterns so as to enlarge aggregate supply. These beneficient effects of the joint float redounded to the credit of the EMU Project, while confidence in the snake was further strengthened by the broadly similar courses pursued by all the snake participants, a development which seemed to confirm the monetarist view of exchange rate concertation as an integrative process.

The Council's decision on 3 April 1973 to create a European Monetary Co-operation Fund was another indication that the EMU Project was progressing satisfactorily. True, the finance ministers failed to meet the 1 April deadline laid down by the Paris Summit, but to have come within two days was, by Community standards, a notable achievement, especially as the crises of February and March had prevented earlier consideration of the proposals submitted by the Commission on 24 January. Although the establishment of the fund had been agreed upon in principle at the Paris Summit the previous October, so expeditious a decision would nevertheless have proven impossible had the Council not excluded the contentious issues of pooling reserves and of integrating the short-term mutual assistance system with the multilateral intervention mechanism, which were being studied separately by the relevant Community institutions. In this way, agreement was achieved on a fund which would administer the snake intervention system, organize the settlement of the resulting claims on a multilateral basis, conduct transactions in a Community unit of account, and manage the short-term monetary support mechanism. Significantly, the Commission's recommendations that Fécom be endowed with a substantial capital of its own and that it be run, under the supervision of the central bank governors, by a director-general were rejected as they were unacceptable to both the 'monetarist' and the 'economist' states for the same reasons as they had been in autumn 1972[10, 11].

The creation of Fécom, which was to start functioning on 1 June, undoubtedly constituted a step forward on the EMU Project, but it had virtually no practical significance. Its sole consequence was that certain operations formerly performed by the Committee of Central Bank Governors would be taken over by Fécom, whose Council of Administration had exactly the same membership as – and met immediately after, or indeed on occasion in the middle of – the governors committee. As Fécom had no capital, it was a fund without money. Its accounts consisted of entries reported to it by central banks, and the assets and liabilities recorded on its books had no physical counterparts. It was, in other words, purely a book-keeping operation, totally dependent on the governors, even for defraying its running expenses.

Of course, the significance of establishing Fécom was in terms not of the present, but of the future, for it was seen as developing into a Community central bank, and its charter had been carefully drafted to allow an expansion of its responsibilities as monetary unification progressed. Nevertheless, it is hard to regard the creation of Fécom as a major departure in European monetary affairs, because it is difficult to imagine a Community central bank growing out of an institution whose council met routinely, albeit for sound practical reasons, in Basel, whose day-to-day business was conducted by its agent, the Bank for International Settlements and whose only physical presence in the Community, despite the Council decision of 24 July fixing Luxembourg as Fécom's 'provisional' seat[12], consisted of a post office box.

However slight its real significance, the creation of Fécom representd the fulfilment of one of the objectives set at the Paris Summit and hence seemed to confirm the view that economic and monetary integration was progressing well. Thus, it appeared that the time was ripe for the Community to take a new set of steps towards EMU, especially as the Council resolution of 22 March 1971 specified that the first stage was to end on 31 December 1973, and stipulated that the Commission was to submit by 1 May

> 'd'une part, une communication faisant le bilan des progrès accomplis au cours de la première etape [et] . . . d'autre part, un rapport, établi en collaboration avec les comités consultatifs intéressés, sur la répartition des compétences et des responsabilités entre les institutions de la Communauté et les Etats membres qui est nécessaire, en particulier dans les

domaines de la politique conjoncturelle, de la politique de la monnaie et du crédit, et de la politique budgétaire, au bon fonctionnement d'une union économique et monétaire',

so that

'Le Conseil et, le cas échéant, les représentants des gouvernements des Etats membres, arrêtent, sur proposition de la Commission, avant la fin de la première étape d'une durée de trois années, les mesures conduisant, après le passage à la deuxieme étape, à la réalisation complète de l'union économique et monétaire.'[13]

Arguing that 'il n'était guère possible de dissocier le bilan de l'action passée des propositions pour l'avenir'[14], the Commission combined the examination of all these topics into a single 'Communication au Conseil' which was submitted on 19 April 1973.

The Commission's communication concentrates primarily on two of these subjects, the assessment of the progress that had been achieved and the measures to be adopted in order to proceed to the second stage. In both areas the imprint of the optimism surrounding the EMU Project in spring 1973 is unmistakable. The Commission acknowledged the enormity of the task and the fact that advances during the first stage had been disappointingly slow and small, with the letter rather than the spirit of the March 1971 resolution being respected. But it argued that significant progress had been made despite unforeseen problems – largely connected with the breakdown of the international monetary system – and that given the necessary political will the goal of completing the project by 1980 could be achieved. Its proposals for the second stage had, therefore, been formulated to enable the Community to meet its target, and while admitting that the specific measures envisaged were ambitious, the Commission stressed that it would be failing in its duty if it attempted to disguise the effort required.

Like its previous recommendations, the Commission's proposals for the second stage were based on the strategy of parallelism. The limits on the size of fluctuations 'pourront être réduites progressivement au cours de la deuxième étape, dans la mesure où le fonctionnement du marché des changes et la convergence des politiques économiques et structurelles le permettront'[15] and would be conducted on a *de jure* rather than on an experimental basis because the safeguard clause would expire with the transition to the second stage. This advance, which reflected the 'monetarist' strategy was to be counter-balanced by progress in the co-ordination of economic policies. The Council would prepare a series of annually revised five-year plans to guide national authorities in formulating both short- and medium-term policies. Budgetary policy, in particular, would be tightly co-ordinated, with special attention being given to the method of financing deficits and the harmonization of policy instruments. In the field of monetary policy, the Community would set targets for the growth of the money supply, interest rates and credit conditions, while the return of the lira and the pound to the snake would foster unity in exchange rate policy. These initiatives were to be complemented by action to reduce the structural differences between Community countries: recognizing that a common unemployment insurance system could be introduced only in the final stage, the Commission advocated a step in this direction by making Community funds available for retraining programmes. Furthermore, as agreed at the Paris Summit, a regional fund was to be established. Finally, systems of indirect taxation were to be harmonized and levels of direct taxation aligned in an attempt to make up for the signal lack of progress in this area during the first stage, while capital markets were to be unified behind a Community exchange control system.

The most striking characteristic of the Commission's proposals for the second stage was not their ambitious nature but the vagueness of the objectives and the diffidence in proposing specific measures. The absence of detailed recommendations in the field of structural policies was understandable because these were being considered separately, but the initiatives in economic policy co-ordination were left equally indefinite. The Commission called for national monetary policies to be concerted by fixing common goals but did not describe how these targets would be set or, more importantly, how they would be operationalized; the report contains only the unhelpful statement that 'en cas de déviation par rapport à ces normes, la situation du pays considéré serait examinée. Si nécessaire, des mesures communes ou coordonnées seraient adoptées'[16]. Likewise, it called for the co-ordination of fiscal policies to be intensified but did not suggest the procedures by which this was to be achieved. In part, this lack of precision could be attributed to the Commission's report taking the form of a communication rather than a set of proposals. But its explicit purpose was to set forth the specific actions that would have to be taken in order to proceed to the second stage, and the relevant section was entitled 'propositions concrètes'. In part, the absence of detailed plans could be ascribed to the difficulty in laying down in advance precise norms for co-ordination. However, several pages earlier the communication had unequivocally stated that the experience of the previous two years had shown that co-ordination 'ne permettait d'arriver qu'à des résultats insuffisants et que l'emprise sur les décisions nationales était faible', and consequently that for the second stage, 'dans certains domaines importants, le stade de la simple coordination des politiques économiques doit être dépassé et des responsabilités effectives doivent être exercées au niveau communautaire'[17].

Yet the report did not address the issue of transferring authority over certain aspects of economic policy to Community institutions. Indeed it scrupulously avoided any discussion of the institutional aspects of economic and monetary unification and hence did not include the recommendations on the division of responsibilities and authority between the member states and the Community for which the March 1971 resolution had called. The Commission justified this omission on the grounds that the proper framework in which to consider these issues was the report about the creation of a European Union that the Paris Summit had decreed was to be prepared by end 1975. Although this argument may well have been sound, and this would certainly not have been the first time a deadline set by the Council had not been met, the Commission must have realized that a decision on the attributes of the final stage could not be postponed without deleterious consequences for the EMU Project. The Dutch and German governments had made it abundantly clear in 1971 that under no circumstances would they be prepared to embark upon the second stage until the detailed characteristics of the final stage had been specified and the member states had irrevocably committed themselves to attaining this objective. There was no indication that this situation had changed in 1973[18, 19]. In other words, the Community could not advance to the second stage until the institutional issues had been settled. However the Commission did not even broach this subject. It did not because it could not, for to have done so would have forced it to abandon the strategy of parallelism.

The Community had at last reached the limits of parallelism. Up to this point, it had been possible to proceed on the basis of simultaneous and carefully balanced advances along the 'monetarist' and 'economist' paths. With the raising of institutional questions, however, this artificial 'compromise' between two fundamentally incompatible strategies broke down. The decision on the detailed attributes of the final stage, and specifically on the extent to which authority was to be transferred from the national to the Community level would necessarily commit the member states to one approach or the other. But the six Governments were no more able in 1973 to overcome their differences and agree on a common approach to economic and monetary unification than they had been in 1971. On the contrary, the experiences of the first stage had hardened national positions, and there were now nine member states. Quite simply, the Community was in a situation where further advance was impossible without agreement on a strategy, but the member states were unable to resolve the conflict between the 'economist' and 'monetarist' blocs. The EMU Project was deadlocked.

In carefully avoiding the institutional issues the Commission had adopted the approach that had been followed since the drafting of the Werner Report: contentious issues were simply deferred. By so doing it had avoided provoking a battle potentially fatal to the EMU Project, but it was clear that there was little scope for progress because at least two member states would block the transition to the second stage scheduled to take place in little more than six months unless the institutional questions were resolved.

The failure of the Commission to meet the 1 May deadline for preparing a report on the division of responsibilities and authority between the

Community and the member states was only one indication of the problems facing the EMU Project. Including Norwegian and Swedish representatives on the panels of experts connected with the snake provided yet another sign of that system's bankruptcy in terms of economic and monetary unification in the Community. True, the governors of the central banks of these two countries did not sit on Fécom's Council of Administration. But their close informal contacts with the other snake central banks and the presence of their subordinates on the committees of technical specialists, which not only monitored the functioning of the multilateral intervention arrangements but also studied possible innovations, enabled them to exert considerable influence. This demonstrated yet again that the joint float, far from being a means of fostering the monetary integration of the Community countries, was instead a co-operative venture comprising those countries having the will and ability to maintain a particular set of exchange rates. A third portent of potential danger for the EMU Project were the adjustments made to CAP on 30 April 1973 to take account of the developments in the exchange rate field[20]. This step suggested that the restoration of fixed rates among all the Community currencies was not expected for some time. More importantly, it showed that CAP could continue to function, albeit with difficulty, in conditions of unstable exchange rates, thereby effectively exploding one of the major arguments for economic and monetary unification in the Community.

Despite these signs of the forces gathering to prevent further progress on the EMU Project, the Commission remained confident that the target of 1980 could be met and in this spirit on 27 June submitted to the Council an ambitious set of proposals for modifying the short-term financial support system and for pooling reserves. Although these represented the Commission's suggestions for dealing with the two contentious issues which had been put aside when Fécom was created in April, they were presented as a single, coherent initiative designed to endow Fécom with real powers and responsibilities from the beginning of the second stage. The idea of granting the fund a capital of U.A. 500 million, rejected in April, was resurrected. More important, the Commission proposed that the member states pool 20% of their reserves, approximately U.A. 11 000 million in Fécom[21]*. With these new financial capabilities of its own, Fécom would directly fund the short-term financial support system, the quotas for which the Commission proposed to increase sixfold while extending the maximum duration of credits to 18 months.

These changes, the Commission argued, were necessary not only to ensure that Fécom's development proceeded at a rate consistent with achieving

---

* It was envisaged that the remaining 80% would be surrendered against corresponding credit balances in units of account, in four equal instalments at 18-month intervals so that the process was completed by 1 January 1980.

economic and monetary union by the end of the 1970s but also to overcome certain difficulties that had recently appeared in the functioning of the multilateral settlements arrangements. The agreement of 10 April 1972, establishing the snake system, specified that payments were to be made in a mix of assets the same as in the debtor's reserves, but with the price of gold on the free market well above $ 150/oz., central banks were understandably reluctant to engage in transactions at the official rate of about $ 42/oz. A special procedure had therefore been instituted under which a country's gold claims and liabilities were entered in a separate 'gold account' on which interest was paid at half the rate for very short-term credit. For the expense of this extra book-keeping, the problem was resolved by allowing the debtor bank to retain possession of its bullion and presumably dispose of it eventually at an attractive price.

A second difficulty, however, had arisen in the middle of May, when the exchange rate between the dollar and snake currencies came to diverge by more than 2¼% from the official parities. A number of reserve assets, notably SDRs, were valued in terms of gold but according to IMF rule O-3 could be transferred only at their official dollar price. Monetary authorities were therefore loath to cede these assets because they had become undervalued as a consequence of the depreciation of the dollar against the snake. Unwilling to add to the complexities of the settlements system by establishing yet another special account, the central banks simply postponed transactions in SDRs and other gold-based assets, but this situation was regarded as unsatisfactory by all the participants.

Both of these problems, the Commission asserted, would be eliminated by the measures it proposed because all claims and liabilities would be settled directly with Fécom in units of account, with the fund assuming the exchange risk on the assets it acquired[22, 23]. In fact, however, the new procedure merely substituted one difficulty for another. As national experts were quick to point out, the problems associated with the use of gold in current transactions might be circumvented, but in their place would be the difficulty in setting the value at which gold contributed by the member states would be converted into units of account.

It was not, however, on the flaws in the Commission's reasoning that national opposition centred, but on the specific measures envisaged themselves. If the Commission regarded the recommendations as constituting a coherent whole, in which the monetarist elements of pooling national reserves and expanding the short-term financial support system were balanced by provisions calling for a stricter co-ordination of monetary policy and a greater Community involvement in the making of national exchange rate policies, the member states examined the individual elements separately and found each of them unacceptable. The Dutch and German governments rejected both an increase in the size of mutual assistance of the order suggested and the pooling of reserves, for the same reasons as on previous occasions.

The remaining countries, particularly Britain, France and Italy, were generally in favour of these proposals, provided a satisfactory solution could be found to the myriad technical questions, especially those concerning the valuation of gold, but they in turn objected to Community involvement in the formulation of monetary and especially exchange rate policy, even though the Council declaration of 8 May 1964 specified that parity changes should be regarded as a matter of common concern. The fundamental differences in national interests and doctrines once again prevented the member states from reaching agreement, and following the customary procedure in such circumstances, the Council referred these issues back to the Monetary and Central Bank Governors Committees for further study at its meeting of 28 June 1973.

Juxtaposed against the tacit refusal of the Council to approve the Commission's proposals, which provided yet another indication that the Nine could proceed no further in economic and monetary integration on the basis of 'parallelism', was the significant success for the EMU Project at a more practical level represented by the granting of assistance to Italy under the short-term financial support system. The lira had come under growing pressure in June, and even with the Banca d'Italia having raised the discount rate by 2%, there had been a serious fall in reserves. The Italian authorities were consequently trying both to restore confidence and to bolster their reserves by marshalling support from abroad. Yet the importance of the Italian request for funds was far greater for the Community than for Italy, as this was the first time a member state had asked for assistance under the mutual aid system instituted in 1970. It was therefore vital to the EMU Project that the Community provide rapid and substantial assistance, especially as the American authorities had already granted Italy a $ 1 250 million line of credit.

Influenced as much by political as by economic considerations, the Community agreed at the end of June to make available to Italy – for a period of six months initially – over U.A. 1500 million, of which U.A. 200 million represented the Italian quota and the balance the *rallonge* granted on the basis of unanimous accord[24]. Furnishing this assistance, which, not coincidentally, was larger than that from the United States, was clearly a positive step in terms of the EMU Project, but it constituted progress only in a very superficial sense, because it was not motivated to any significant extent by considerations of economic and monetary unification. True, the mutual assistance mechanism was used as the vehicle for providing funds. However, credit would have been made available even without this mechanism, as co-operation among central banks was an established feature of international monetary relations. Significantly, the aid was to be channelled through national institutions, with Fécom involved only in a formal sense, and indeed was supplemented in the case of Germany by a direct loan secured by gold. Like so many developments in the first half of 1973, the response to the Italian request appeared on the surface to mark an advance on the EMU Project, but on closer examination, this proved to be illusory.

Strains within the snake: the mark and the guilder revalued

The survival of the snake and the maintenance of the reduced limits of fluctuation without substantial interventions, the ability of national authorities to pursue cyclically appropriate policies, the submission of the Commission's proposals for the second stage and the extension of credits to Italy had fostered a confidence that the EMU Project was progressing satisfactorily in the aftermath of the March 1973 crisis and that conditions were propitious for further advances towards the final goal. However, all this was abruptly shattered just three months after the launching of the joint float, when, at the end of June, the Community found itself once again in the throes of a speculative crisis which challenged the determination of the member states to maintain the existing exchange rates.

After two months of calm on the foreign exchange markets, the snake arrangements had come under pressure in early May. At first it had been the mark, as a consequence of its recent revaluation, and the guilder, because of the low level of Dutch interest rates, which had had to be supported, primarily against the franc, but by early June the situation had changed, with the mark pushing its upper limit in the snake[25]. The upward pressure on the mark increased in the second half of June, and under the multilateral intervention arrangements the Bundesbank had to purchase slightly more than U.A. 500 million worth of foreign currencies, principally guilders. The speculative attack came to a head on 29 June, when the German authorities had to buy over U.A. 700 million in various Community currencies. Although only a fraction of the inflows the Federal Republic had experienced in previous crises, these capital movements were more serious for the snake because they were among participants in the joint float rather than with the United States as in the three preceding speculative disorders. While the influx of capital did not pose insuperable problems for the German authorities, the corresponding outflow of funds was resulting in a serious drain on the reserves of certain member states. Unless this was stopped, there was a very real danger that some of the participants – and not necessarily those that had been most severely affected by the capital movements – might decide that they were no longer able to remain in the joint float[26].

The most disturbing element of the crisis was not that some of the countries might cease to participate in the snake system but that this challenge to the intra-Community exchange rate relationships arose at all, for barely three months previously the parities of the currencies in the snake had been adjusted, the mark appreciating by 3% in this re-alignment. That the mark should be straining against its upper limit just one hundred days after it had been revalued clearly raised serious questions about the feasibility of any attempt to maintain stable exchange rates among this group. This was especially true because they were all in the same general phase of the economic cycle and France, Germany and the Netherlands in particular were pursuing similar policies of demand restraint.

That the capital movements had their origins in the contractionary policies of the Bundesbank, which had resulted in German interest rates rising several points above levels in other snake countries, and in the stringency of the German stabilization programme, rather than the actual German balance of payments position, served to confirm, not controvert, this disturbing weakness of the snake[27]: it demonstrated that the national authorities were not prepared to alter their policies for the sake of the snake system. Interest rates were allowed to diverge appreciably, even after it had become apparent that the resulting differentials were inducing unwanted capital movements. Similarly, the German Government persisted in pursuing stringent anti-inflationary policies which were bound sooner or later to introduce tensions into the joint float. Economic policies, in other words, were still set at the national level on the basis of the individual interests of the eight countries.

The June crisis must be considered against this background. It was clear that certain countries would have left the joint float rather than accept the changes in their policies that maintaining the existing exchange rate structure would have entailed. Paradoxically, however, the snake's very weakness enabled it to survive this crisis intact. The German authorities, unwilling to sacrifice their anti-inflation policies to the cause of EMU, yet equally opposed to floating the mark independently, revalued the mark by 5½%, with effect from 29 June 1973. This revaluation, of course, directly affected only currencies in the snake. For other currencies, the effect was to produce a slight appreciation of the mark, which had already floated upwards under the speculative pressure, and generally a slight depreciation of the remaining snake currencies[28]. With the parity adjustments, the Federal Republic's inflow rapidly subsided, and although there was some speculation on a revaluation of the guilder or even the franc in the following days interventions under the snake arrangements soon dwindled to minute proportions[29]. Once again, the efforts to achieve a closer monetary relationship among the Community countries had prevailed over a challenge in the form of speculative capital movements, but only at the price of a revaluation.

No sooner had these internal problems been resolved than the snake encountered difficulties on the external front. Until 14 May, the dollar had remained within the 2¼% band around its February parity, but hurt by an unfavourable interest rate differential, it declined steadily against the snake currencies in the following weeks. The revaluation of the mark, together with a worsening in the American trade balance, further eroded confidence in – and hence intensified the flight from – the dollar. For the snake participants, protected by the joint float from the capital inflows of previous crises, this speculative pressure was manifested in a persistent appreciation of their currencies against a dollar which had, as in late 1971, 'atteint des niveaux nettement inférieurs à sa valeur fondée sur les données de l'économie réelle'[30]. On 18 July the mark had risen over 40% above its Smithsonian level, while even the weaker snake currencies were about 25% higher[31]. Once again, European countries were faced with the familiar choice between absorbing vast amounts of dollars or allowing their currencies to appreciate, in this case even more than they already had. Because the snake members regarded a further rise of their currencies against the dollar as unacceptable, they had little option but to enter the exchange markets in order to reduce the upward pressure on the snake, acquiring in the process substantial volumes of dollars.

It only remained for the participants to select the framework in which these interventions would be carried out. On the one hand, the authorities were loath to commit themselves to defending a fixed exchange rate against the dollar. On the other, they were determined to maintain the snake system for it was recognized that these arrangements had provided an, albeit limited, island of exchange rate stability and that no currency had been dragged upwards because of its participation. The eight countries therefore agreed on 9 July to continue the joint float but to enter the exchange markets to limit currency gyrations[32]. Although this course of action entailed the practical inconvenience of consultations among as many as eight central banks to determine whether and to what extent intervention was appropriate, it had the merit of conferring a large degree of flexibility. The American authorities, for their part, indicated that they were prepared to take steps along the same lines, and on 18 July it was officially announced that the Federal Reserve and European central banks would on occasion be undertaking co-ordinated interventions to steady the dollar's rate, and that in their opinion its value was unrealistically low[33].

The announcement had the desired effect. The combination of a more realistic assessment of the value of the dollar, an improvement in the United States's trade balance, a rise in American interest rates and a certain amount of intervention resulted in a steady recovery of the dollar on European exchanges throughout the remainder of the third quarter[34]. Yet, as in June, the resolution of this crisis was followed almost immediately by the emergence of new problems for the snake. Just as the revaluation of the mark in June had prompted a further attack on the dollar, so the reappraisal of the value of the dollar in July led to a more critical assessment of the strength of each of the snake currencies. Whereas the upward pressure on the joint float had been general, the recovery of the dollar proceeded on a selective basis. The strength of its resurgence varied considerably, reflecting forecasts of the different prospects for individual currencies, thereby causing tensions to begin to appear inside the snake[35].

The first signs of trouble came at the end of July when there was a sizeable movement out of francs and guilders into marks. As in June, this flow was largely interest rate-induced, and interest rate increases in France and the Netherlands – reflected in discount rises of 1 and ½% respectively – were enough to reduce it to a trickle by the first week of August[36]. Within a month, however, the exchange rate relationships among the snake currencies were once again under severe strain, this time as a result of a growing movement of capital towards the Netherlands. Dutch interest rates had been rising gradually since the beginning of the summer, as the authorities first allowed the outflow of funds in June and July to reduce liquidity but then directly tightened monetary conditions by limiting borrowings from the central banks under the discount facility. By September, the price of day-to-day money had reached German levels and was attracting substantial inflows of funds[37]. This flow of capital rapidly increased and assumed a speculative character as the underlying strength of the Dutch balance of payments and hence of the guilder became recognized. By the end of the second week of September, the Nederlandsche Bank had acquired more than U.A. 200 million worth of foreign currencies, primarily francs, under the multilateral intervention system, most of it concentrated in the last five days.

Unlike the situation in June, the September crisis was a threat to the joint float not only because of the drain on some of the participants' reserves but also because the influx of capital was seriously impairing the Dutch authorities' ability to pursue a contractionary course[38]. Essentially, the Dutch Government was faced with a choice between allowing the guilder to appreciate, inside or outside the snake, or easing monetary conditions, either voluntarily through policy changes or involuntarily through the entry of large amounts of foreign funds. Because a shift in the present contractionary course was ruled out and a unilateral float rejected for the same reasons as earlier in the year, the authorities decided to revalue the guilder by 5%, with effect from 17 September 1973[39]. Thus, for the second time in the six months since the launching of the joint float – itself preceded by the revaluation of the mark – strains within the snake had necessitated an adjustment of the exchange rate relationships.

The fragility of the snake was further demonstrated in the next few days, as rumours of an impending revaluation of the mark or the Belgian franc resulted in yet another assault on existing parities. In the week following the revaluation of the guilder, the Banque de France incurred liabilities of over U.A. 1500 million to Fécom, representing purchases made on its behalf by the Belgian and German authorities. In addition, the Bundesbank purchased approximately DM 1000 million worth of non-snake currencies, largely dollars, in an attempt to depress the mark's exchange rate[40, 41]. It was particularly disturbing that much of this pressure on exchange rate relationships within the joint float came from outside the Community, for this indicated that the attempt to achieve exchange rate stability within the

Community was vulnerable to external forces as well. In other words, although the joint float could prevent the inflows associated with a generalized flight from the dollar, albeit at the price of appreciation, it did not provide a defence against an attack on one or two particular currencies. While the float could be managed so as to ensure that the group as a whole experienced no inflow, selective pressure on specific currencies from outside would, by pushing these against their limits with respect to other snake currencies, put a strain on the exchange rate relationships within the snake which could be offset only by central bank interventions of corresponding magnitude.

As it happened, the speculative pressures on the mark and the Belgian franc did not result in the abandonment of the existing set of exchange rates. The resolution of the German and Belgian Governments in rejecting a revaluation, together with a 1½% rise in the French discount rate, sufficed to dispel the expectations of parity alterations, and by the end of September, interventions had declined to insignificant amounts. As in June 1972 the snake members had successfully resisted the forces pushing for a change in exchange rates, but it is noteworthy that in September 1973 the repatriation of funds that ensued was of a much smaller magnitude than the inflows. The existing parity structure might have withstood the challenge, but there was little confidence that it would prove durable.

Thus, the events of the first six months after the snake's emergence from the tunnel provided clear evidence of its vulnerability to pressures from both within and outside the Community. As long as national economic trends continued to diverge and policy objectives differed, it was inevitable that strains developed in the exchange rate relationships among the snake participants. And given the precedence accorded to national interests over the cause of economic and monetary integration, it was clear that such pressures would be relieved by giving ground in the efforts to achieve exchange rate stability rather than by altering the course of national policy. In other words, it was already clear by the end of the third quarter that the attempt to maintain a stable set of exchange rates among the Community countries was doomed to failure.

The oil crisis

On 16 October 1973 the major Middle Eastern oil producers imposed limits on petroleum production and placed an embargo on exports to certain countries, including the United States, in an attempt to pressure the western powers to push for a resolution of the conflict between Israel and her neighbours favourable to Arab interests. The resulting oil crisis had a profound effect throughout the world, since, by curtailing the supply and drastically raising the price of the world's main source of energy, it fundamentally altered the environment in which economies operated. The ramifications of these developments extended to all facets of economic life and are still being felt today. The oil crisis affected European economies and monetary unification in two principal ways: by changing the parameters of the system in which Community countries functioned, it necessitated the reappraisal of national economic strategies and the formulation of new policies, and by causing major shifts in the international flow of funds, it drastically altered the balance of payments positions of the member states. These developments had important consequences for the EMU Project, and especially for the initiative in exchange rate concertation, dependent as it was on the maintenance of a particular set of exchange rates.

Yet it must be stressed that the oil crisis acted to intensify forces that were already present; it did not create them. Progress on the transition to the second stage was already stalemated because of the irreconcilable differences over the strategy that should be adopted. The snake had already lost certain essential attributes of its identity as a Community creature and survived as a currency bloc composed of a dwindling number of member states linked by fixed but very adjustable exchange rates. If the oil crisis was a major factor in the withdrawal in January 1974 of the French franc from the joint float, an event examplifying the demise of the snake as an institution capable of fostering the monetary integration of the member states, it contributed to this result by illuminating and magnifying pre-existing differences among the snake countries, not introducing new ones.

In this context, it is of prime importance that the effect of the oil crisis was basically the same for all the member states. Arab embargoes of specific countries notwithstanding, reductions in the supply of oil and increases in price were generally uniform throughout the Community; exceptions to this pattern, such as the relatively low price and restricted availability in Belgium, were a result of national action[42]. Moreover, the changes in price and supply had broadly similar effects on the snake countries. As *Table 7.1* shows, the degree of dependence on oil as a source of energy varied remarkably little within this group – with the exception of Denmark. For the Community as a whole, the differences were greater, but in part these can be attributed to dissimilarities in national industrial structures, with countries with large iron and steel sectors consuming proportionately less oil. Furthermore, in each of the snake participants, the increases in the cost of oil were estimated to add about 2–3% to the level of retail prices[43, 44, 45]. Similarly, as is clear from *Table 7.2*, the projected deterioration in national current accounts attributable to the oil crisis, as a percentage of GNP, varies quite modestly, especially in comparison with the existing differences in national payments positions. Obviously, the effects of the oil crisis did vary from country to country, even among the members of the joint float, but the essential point is

Table 7.1 *Degree of dependence on oil as an energy source*

Country	Percentage of oil in total raw energy consumption
Netherlands	50
Germany	55
Belgium–Luxembourg	60
France	67
Denmark	95
United Kingdom†	50
Ireland†	69
Italy†	74

† Non-snake country
Source: European Communities, Commission, *Crise Petrolière et Problèmes Economiques liés à l'Equilibre Extérieur à Moyen Terme des Pays de la Communauté* (Document of the Commission II/130/74 of 8 March 1974).

that these differences were ones of degree, and not very significant at that. In contrast to the fundamental shift in the economic balance between the United States and Europe it engendered, the oil crisis did not introduce strains into the monetary relationships among the member states but rather intensified ones that were already there[46].

Just as important, the oil crisis injected an element of uncertainty into

Table 7.2 *Effects of the oil crisis on the balance of payments of the member states*

Country	Estimated change in current account for 1974 as a result of the increase in oil price, including secondary effects US $ billion	percentage of GNP	Pre-oil crisis estimate of current account for 1974 (percentage of GNP)
Germany	−5.8	−1.6	+3.1
France	−5.3	−2.1	−0.3
Belgium-Luxembourg	−1.2	−2.5	+3.5
Netherlands	−0.9	−1.5	+2.4
Denmark	−0.9	−2.8	−1.2
United Kingdom	−4.7	−2.7	−1.1
Italy	−4.2	−3.0	−3.3
Ireland	−0.2	−3.3	−7.1

Source: As for *Table 7.1*.

economic affairs[47]. Initially, the obscurity cloaking the actual level of oil exports from Arab producers, let alone their intentions for the future, prompted fears about supplies in individual countries. When it subsequently became clear that the availability of oil was not going to be a major constraint on economic activity, the question of the price of oil became the major concern. Finally, the use the producers would make of the massive revenues accruing to them added a third element of uncertainty. It is worth stressing that this situation did not arise because of deliberate attempts to maintain secrecy or to foster confusion. Uncertainty was unavoidale in circumstances where decisions affecting the future had not been made because they themselves depended on other factors that could not be accurately assessed in advance. Nor should it be assumed that the ambiguities inherent in this state of affairs were necessarily undesirable, for the haze shrouding the size of shipments allowed the oil companies to distribute oil on a more equitable basis than might otherwise have been possible.

Uncertainty was without doubt the dominant note on the exchange markets in the immediate aftermath of the Yom Kippur war. This was manifested largely in erratic behaviour, with the dollar first rising, then falling, then rising again against the snake currencies, while these latter oscillated from the top to the bottom of the joint float. Once the effects of the oil crisis on individual economies became clear, however, the market was ready to translate this information into decisive exchange rate movements. When the significance of the United States's relatively low dependence on imported oil came to be recognized in the last days of October, the dollar started to climb steadily against all the snake currencies. Its recovery was most pronounced against the mark and the guilder, for the technical reason that because these currencies had been pushed up most by speculative forces in preceding months, they were most vulnerable to downward pressure. The decline of the mark and guilder relative to the other snake currencies necessitated limited interventions throughout November, but, otherwise, there was no strain on the parity rates within the joint float until early December, when the guilder came under considerable attack for several weeks, largely as a consequence of the embargo on oil supplies to the Netherlands imposed by the Arab states[48]. In other words, after two months the oil crisis had not yet resulted in a fundamental reappraisal of the strengths of individual snake currencies.

Uncertainty was also the main element the oil crisis initially introduced into the domestic economic situation in the first weeks after the wielding of the 'oil weapon'. Sales in the automobile industry slumped dramatically in the fourth quarter of 1973 because of fears of limited and expensive petrol, even though there was no shortage of fuel at the time. In contrast, speculative buying, stimulated by apprehension about the future availability and price of goods and uncertainty about future trends in income, increased demand in some other sectors, especially consumer durables. Industrial production continued to rise in most countries but at a slightly slower rate, reflecting a certain hesitancy on the part of business to expand until the prospects of demand became clearer. In retrospect, it is obvious that there was no constraint on production because of an energy shortage[49, 50]. Government policies, however, were formulated on the basis of official views at the time, and although the national authorities recognized that given the level of oil stocks and of deliveries, economic activity was not likely to be limited by a lack of fuel before the end of the year, there seemed to be a very real danger of a serious shortage of energy developing in 1974.

Besides the plans for sharing oil internationally and reducing consumption, as well as developing alternative sources of energy, which were prepared during this early period when the oil crisis was perceived as being a problem primarily in terms of the shortage of fuel, national governments also prepared to change course in economic affairs to respond to the new conditions. The most important effect of the oil crisis on economic policy-making was that it was believed to have imposed a constraint on output. A fall in production would necessarily depress real gross national product and therefore real incomes. At the least, this could mean short-time working, a drastic fall in profits and a decline in the standard of living; if the shortage of energy were particularly severe, substantial unemployment. numerous bankruptcies and privation could result. National authorities, however, could do little in the way of economic policy to ameliorate this situation, for the usual remedy, stimulation, would not only prove ineffective in the face of this external constraint but would exacerbate inflation, which had already received further impetus from the increase in oil prices. Instead, it appeared that the best strategy was to try to keep demand in line with the reduced supply of goods and services[51].

In the case of the snake countries, this implied continuing to follow the deflationary courses adopted earlier in 1973. The Bundesbank tried to preserve the tight monetary conditions established during the summer, moving to counter the capital inflows of September by lowering on 1 October the reference level used in calculating the increase in foreign liabilities, which were subject to a special reserve requirement. In addition, it reduced discount quotas for the larger banks on 4 October and raised the reserve requirements on sight and time deposits by 3%, with effect from 1 November. However, when capital outflows drove the rate for day-to-day money to over 20% during November, it enlarged discount quotas and made special credits available in order to avoid an overly restrictive course[52]. The Belgian and Dutch central banks raised their discount rates ½% in the first half of October in an attempt to tighten credit conditions, especially after the inflows of previous weeks, as well as to conform to a world movement towards higher rates. The Banque Nationale de Belgique took the additional step of reducing discount quotas at the end of November[53, 54].

Even though all the snake members were pursuing deflationary policies, the degree of monetary stringency and the severity of fiscal restraint varied substantially, with some governments reducing or blocking expenditures while others exceeded their original spending projections [55, 56]. Under these circumstances, there was naturally a marked contrast between the performance of various economies. The French retail price index, for example, rose about 2½% in the third quarter while the German cost of living index increased by less than ½% over the same period and results for the fourth quarter presented essentially the same picture[57, 58]. It must be stressed that these differences in national economic policies and trends antedated the events of October: the oil crisis did not produce them but merely intensified and highlighted them.

The role of the oil crisis as a catalyst in revealing the disunity of the snake participants was forcefully demonstrated as the crisis moved into a second phase in December, when it was recognized that the price, not the supply, of oil was the basic problem. The drastic rise in the cost of oil affected the Community economies in two principal ways: it gave further impetus to the upward movement in prices, and it entailed a large transfer of funds to the oil-exporting countries. Although here again the effects on individual member states were very much alike, the situations from which economies started differed appreciably in terms of inflation and the balance of payments so that Governments found themselves operating in dissimilar environments as they tried to plan for 1974.

Although the Community countries had a greater freedom of manoeuvre than they would have done in the case of a rigid limit on production imposed by a shortage in the supply of energy, the virtual tripling in the price of oil nevertheless imposed an external constraint, in terms of the balance of payments, on the courses they could adopt. While the severity of this constraint depended on the country's payments and reserve positions, there were only a small number of steps any individual country could take to ease it. It could try to strengthen the current balance, but because the overall level of imports into the oil producing countries would be relatively uninfluenced by actions taken abroad, it realistically could only export more at the expense of other countries, most likely other major industrialized states, which could be expected to offer stiff resistance and possibly retaliate if the bounds of acceptable competition were exceeded. In order to guard against a repetition of the competitive devaluations of the interwar period, there was a tacit agreement among the major western countries that they would not pursue beggar-my-neighbor policies. In the context of the Community, the Council adopted a resolution on 29 October reaffirming the commitment of the member states to prior consultations on actions in the exchange rate field. With the scope for improvement on the current account limited, governments could attempt to borrow, but the availability of credit was inversely proportional to the need for it, as the larger the deficit to be financed, the worse the repayment prospects, *ipso facto*. Thus, in the last analysis,

Governments had little option but to tailor their economic policies to fit the constraints the oil crisis had imposed on them.

Given the differences in economic situations, as well as objectives, it was inevitable that each Government would opt for a different approach. In Germany, the increased cost of oil imports did not impose a serious constraint on the formulation of economic policy, as the Federal Republic had, in terms of its balance of payments

> 'vorerst keine unmittelbaren Schwierigkeiten zu befürchten. Die auf rund 17 Mrd DM jährlich geschätze Mehrbelastung der Bundesrepublik kann voraussichtlich getragen werden, ohne dass es notwendigerweise zu Defizite der Leistungsbilanz kommt'[59].

It was rather the inflationary effect of the oil crisis that was the major consideration in formulating the official course of action. Already before the oil crisis, the upward movement in wages and prices had been gaining speed, and the increased cost of oil was estimated to add a further 2% to consumer prices in 1974[60]. If inflation was to be held to its 1973 rate, let alone reduced – as had been envisaged before the outbreak of the war in the Middle East – it was clearly imperative that there be no upward pressure on the price level from the demand side[61]. The economic policy measures announced by the federal government on 19 December were therefore designed to bolster the stringent monetary and fiscal policies already in effect, notably the 10% surcharge on both individual and corporate income taxes. At the same time, however, the funds for regional policy which had been frozen earlier in the year as part of the stabilization programme were released and a further DM 900 million appropriated in January to provide special aid for those sectors and regions most severely affected by the oil crisis. In addition, the 11% tax on investment imposed in May was lifted and accelerated depreciation restored for tax purposes in an attempt to counteract the decline in investment[62, 63]. The authorities recognized that this restrictive strategy would result in an appreciable decline in economic growth and, potentially, employment but accepted this as the price of attaining their foremost objective, bringing inflation under control.

As in Germany, the increased cost of oil did not pose a balance of payments problem for either Belgium or the Netherlands, since both countries enjoyed current account surpluses more than sufficient to cover the estimated increase in the import bill. Once again it was the domestic situation, especially in terms of inflation, that was the decisive factor in shaping economic policy. However, unlike their German counterparts, the Benelux authorities were unwilling to adopt strategies that would restrain demand because of the implications in terms of economic activity and unemployment, this even though their economies remained robust and indeed, according to first indications, consumer spending had increased considerably in the fourth quarter of 1973[64]. Consequently, these two governments decided to combat inflation by intensifying price control through requiring prior notification of increases and strengthening surveillance to ensure that there was real competition, and by maintaining a moderately contractionary stance in monetary and fiscal policy. Although credit conditions were tightened in both countries at the end of the year, this reflected developments at the world level, not a change of course. Indeed, the Dutch Government slightly reduced taxes and marginally increased public spending to offset the deflationary effect of the oil crisis[65, 66]. In part, the decisions essentially to continue with the existing policy orientation reflected the uncertainty created by the oil crisis, for the Governments were reluctant to revise their strategies until the situation became clearer. That firmer action was not taken to reduce inflation was, however, mainly an indication that the priorities were different from those in Germany.

The French Government was faced with a much more severe constraint than the German or Benelux authorities as France already had a sizeable current account deficit. Balance of payments considerations consequently assumed much greater importance in determining the strategy to be adopted in economic affairs. The Banque de France actively tried to encourage the inflow of foreign funds, specifically into non-residents' bank accounts, by allowing the payment of interest, eliminating the special reserve requirements on new deposits, and, on 21 October, reducing regular reserve requirements, which were subsequently abolished, with effect from 15 January[67]. The Government however ruled out a course of depressing economic activity in order to strengthen the current account. But it was equally determined to prevent conditions of excess demand from developing because reducing the rate of inflation was a vital element in its strategy, essential to achieving domestic objectives as well as strengthening the balance of payments by keeping French products competitive[68]. Consequently, when demand rose to dangerously high levels at the end of the year as a result of speculative purchases, the authorities acted rapidly to bring it back into line with supply, tightening the terms for buying on credit, increasing the personal income tax instalment due in February from one-third to 43% of the total liability, advancing the first corporate tax payment to February and raising it from ⅕ to ⅓ of the total amount due, making minor reductions in government expenditures, and deferring 60% of public investment until the second half of the year. Interest rates were increased in December to encourage saving, in view both of the immediate need to reduce private consumption and the longer-range imperative of freeing resources for investment or possibly increased exports. Price controls were extended to cover items previously exempt, such as those facing international competition, and made more stringent, with profit margins on many consumer items, including food, being frozen, and increases in rents and utility bills, except for energy, being blocked[69, 70].

It is important to stress that the programme announced in December was

It is important to stress that the programme announced in December was a response to a particular situation and did not indicate a shift to a more restrictive stance. Significantly, it was designed to defer rather than permanently reduce demand. This stance reflected the same aversion to depressing the level of economic activity that has been constant throughout the history of French economic policy. In the view of the French government, allowing the economy to operate with a significant degree of slack would not help to reduce the rate of inflation since this was primarily due to structural factors, but it would result in an appreciable underutilization of resources, characterized by a fall in output, earnings, and thereby investment, which was needed to modernize the economic structure so as to reduce permanently the rate of inflation[71]. The course charted by the French authorities was therefore one of striving for as high a level of economic activity as possible – by means of official support, if necessary – while avoiding conditions of excess demand. Whether this strategy would prove feasible in view of the external constraint imposed by the oil crisis would be revealed by the subsequent course of events.

By the end of 1973, then, the snake members had decided to follow essentially three different strategies in economic affairs. There were, of course, many common elements. All six governments intended to increase their exports, especially to the oil producing countries, to maintain interest rates at internationally competitive levels, to reduce inflation rates, to prevent large-scale unemployment, and to safeguard the more vulnerable parts of the economy from the direct or indirect effects of the energy crisis on costs and demand. The differences were, in fact, ones of degree rather than direction. The policies adopted by the German authorities were designed to keep demand well within the bounds of a reduced supply; those of the Benelux countries and Denmark to reduce the rate of inflation without depressing the level of economic activity; and those of France to maintain the highest possible levels of production and employment consistent with avoiding upward pressure on the price level from the demand side. The courses chosen by the snake members thus reflected the relative importance assigned to price stability in contrast to economic growth and full employment.

That the differences in policy orientations arose from dissimilar rankings of the same basic objectives did not make them any the less significant or fundamental. These differences in priorities had already resulted in considerable variation in the performance of these eight economies, even though they began 1973 in essentially the same phase of the economic cycle. While the growth of aggregate demand was slowing slightly in Germany during the fourth quarter and continuing at about the same rate in the Benelux countries, it was accelerating in France. Moreover, on top of this dissimilarity in economic conditions would be superimposed the differences in national strategies. Under these circumstances, it was inevitable that strains emerged within the joint float. Exchange rate relationships in the snake had already come under pressure on several occasions in previous months. The even more pronounced differences in national economic situations resulting from the oil crisis would, three months and three days after the wielding of the 'oil weapon', make these rates untenable. Under the impetus of events in the Middle East, developments in the area of exchange rate concertation were racing towards the disastrous conclusion, foreordained long before, that would deliver the *coup de grâce* to the EMU Project.

The limits of parallelism: deadlock over the second stage

At the same time that dissimilar national priorities were inexorably pushing the Community towards failure on the exchange rate concertation front, they were also preventing agreement on a strategy for the EMU Project, thereby producing a stalemate in the efforts to formulate the steps to be taken in the next stage of economic and monetary unification. Because the plans for the second stage encompassed all the facets of the EMU Project it will be necessary at times to focus on developments outside the exchange rate field: the initiatives foreseen on different fronts formed part of – and hence must be examined as – a single, coherent programme, for decisions on one aspect of the project influenced the outcome of others.

That further progress in economic and monetary unification was already blocked had become clear at the Council session of 28 June. There the Finance Ministers had been unable to reach agreement on the Commission's proposals for pooling reserves, increasing short-term financial assistance and taking other measures connected with the transition to the second stage. They had referred them for further study to the various Community committees concerned with monetary affairs. The representatives of the Nine had no greater success in achieving a consensus at this level, however, as the fundamental differences between national positions remained unresolved. Consequently, a stalemate developed: the committees were reluctant to make decisions on substantive issues, which they regarded as the preserve of the Council, while the Ministers were not prepared to commit themselves to any specific steps because of the uncertainty about future developments introduced by the oil crisis.

Nevertheless it was imperative that agreement be rapidly reached on these measures if the transition to the second stage were to occur on schedule by the end of the year. Despite the inauspicious climate, the Commission therefore submitted to the Council on 15 November a set of five draft decisions embodying its proposals for the next series of steps to be taken[72]. These were essentially elaborations of the suggestions made six months previously, despite objections which member states had raised at the time. The absence of a new approach was attributable first to the relatively short period of time that had elapsed; this would have presented not inconsiderable practical difficulties for the Commission in coming up with a fundamentally different set of proposals. Secondly, it was attributable to the Commission's reluctance to make any major change in its approach until its initial set of recommendations had been clearly rejected, persistence having on previous occasions usually been rewarded by eventual success as in the case of Fécom. And thirdly it reflected the fact that the Commission lacked any real alternative, for only by following its strategy of parallelism and steering clear of contentious issues could it avoid bringing the conflict between the economists and monetarists to the surface, thereby bringing progress to a halt.

The draft decisions therefore contained few new ideas, and scrupulously avoided institutional issues in terms of both the second and the final stages. The 'Project de résolution du Conseil concernant la réalisation de la deuxième étape de l'union economique et monétaire dans la Communauté', for example, is virtually identical with the proposals advanced in the Commission's memorandum of 30 April 1973, except that 10 rather than 20% of the member states' reserves were to be pooled on 1 January 1974, and that 31 December 1974 was set as a deadline for the harmonization of company income taxes, securities taxes, and that portion of VAT accruing to the Community, as well as the enlargement of travellers' tax-free allowances.

The four other texts, which detailed the steps to be taken to implement the provisions of the resolution, also followed along the lines of the Commission's earlier reports. The draft decision 'on the attainment of a high degree of convergence of the economic policies of the member states' reproduced the recommendation, advanced in April, that the Council prepare a series of five-year plans, revised annually, to guide the national governments in formulating their short- and medium-term economic policies. Indeed it contained a provision, suggested in the Werner Report and already incorporated into the Council resolution of 22 March 1971, that the Council examine conditions throughout the Community monthly and devote three sessions a year to considering the economic situation and laying down guidelines for the member states. In contrast, the proposals for requiring formal consultations and the written opinion of the Monetary Committee or the Council before any parity changes were new, though obviously logical extensions of earlier suggestions. As usual, the question of the transfer of authority was carefully avoided: the text stated that the basic direction of policy was to be set by the Council but specified neither the method by which decisions would be made nor, more important, the means by which they would be made operational.

The attempt to foster policy co-ordination by strengthening the consultative procedures was also manifest in the draft decision establishing an economic policy committee, but here too these efforts were weakened by the failure to clarify the institutional issues. Although it was obvious that the existing system of a multiplicity of committees each concerned with a particular aspect of economic policy had resulted in considerable confusion and, more importantly, in the loss of an integrated view of economic policy as a whole, merging the short and medium-term policy and budgetary policy committees into a new economic policy committee did not appear sufficient to remedy these shortcomings because broadening the mandate of the Community bodies was only half the answer. To succeed in achieving a global approach, a fundamentally different body, composed of the very senior officials responsible for actually *setting* economic policy, i.e. for deciding on the strategy a given country would follow, would have been necessary, and this would have been too big an advance on the 'economist' front for the Commission to propose.

The draft directive on stability, growth and full employment was intended to promote the co-ordination of economic policy in another way, by harmonizing policy instruments. According to its provisions, national governments were to ensure that within one year the monetary authorities in all nine countries had the authority to impose reserve requirements on both bank deposits and lending, to undertake open market operations, to impose and vary discount quotas, to regulate the rates of interest at savings institutions as well as banks, to set the terms for instalment credit and, if necessary, to impose quantitative limits on lending. Governments were to have the power to regulate the rate of disbursement of public funds, to effect minor adjustments in the levels of direct and indirect taxation and to impose taxes on, or reduce the incentives normally provided for, investment – all this effectively without prior specific legislative approval as the draft texts stipulated that the authorities were to be able to act within 30 days. In addition, national governments were to be able to exert control over the budgets and especially the borrowing requirements of lower levels of government. Finally, the central banks and the government were to establish procedures for joint action to sterilize excess revenues or the proceeds of certain loans so that these could be swiftly implemented should the need materialize. The practical significance of the proposals was, however, extremely limited because the provisions relating to monetary policy had already been enacted in the Council decision of 5 December 1972 on combating inflation, and in any case, the relevant authorities in most countries already possessed all the tools mentioned[73].

The same pattern of avoiding the critical issue of transferring authority to the Community was discernible on the exchange rate concertation front. The draft resolution on the second stage affirmed that 'la suppression des marges et la fixité des parités constituent l'objectif final à atteindre pour l'année 1980', but as to the actions to be taken in this field, these were left for the Council to decide 'sur la base des résultats obtenus dans le domaine de la coordination des politiques economiques'[74]. Indeed, the most important advance, namely that the limitation of fluctuations would assume a *de jure* character because the

The limits of parallelism: deadlock over the second stage 161

safeguard clause would lapse with the transition to the second stage, was not explicitly mentioned. In view of the experience over the past two years of countries unilaterally leaving the snake, this change could not, however, be regarded as having an enormous effect on the exchange rate concertation system. A draft regulation to strengthen Fécom, the fifth element in the package submitted to the Council essentially reproduced the modest proposals contained in the Commission report of 27 June 1973. The exceptions were that 10 rather than 20% of the reserves were to be pooled, and the amount of short-term financial support was to be increased eight – rather than six – fold, and its term extended up to a maximum of two years, albeit with ever more stringent examinations of the situation in the debtor country. Thus, the Commission had carefully balanced the minute advances it proposed on the policy co-ordination front with minimal progress in the exchange rate concertation area.

Since the Commission's formal proposals for the second stage followed essentially along the same lines as its recommendations earlier in the year, it is hardly surprising that the response of individual Governments paralleled their reaction to the reports of the previous spring or that the Council session of 3–4 December was in many ways reminiscent of that of 28 June. When the Finance Ministers met less than a month before the end of the first stage, their attention was once again focused on the proposals for strengthening Fécom, this time in the context of the opinions submitted by the Monetary and Central Bank Governors committees. And once again the Council decided to consider the various elements in the Commission's package independently, specifically by separating the issue of reserve pooling from that of increasing the amount of aid available under the short-term financial support mechanism[75].

Although this decision may seem a minor procedural point, it effectively meant that the Council had rejected the Commission's assertion that the proposals formed a logical whole and hence had to be considered together. More importantly, it demolished one of the major arguments for reserve pooling: the Finance Ministers had decided that the question of increasing short-term monetary support was not really contingent on that of communalizing foreign reserves, although the latter might affect the way in which the former was provided. On a more practical level, they regarded the existing mutual assistance arrangements as having functioned satisfactorily without Fécom having real resources at its disposal. Furthermore, as in June, the Ministers rejected the Commission's claim that adoption of its proposals would improve the functioning of the multilateral settlements system, for the vexing question of the value at which gold would be converted into units of accounts still remained. The Commission envisaged the official rate being used, with any gains subsequently arising being distributed among the member states in proportion to their gold contributions, but this was in essence the same expedient as the existing 'gold account' arrangements. Consequently, even before the Council began to consider the substantive issues, the Commission's package for strengthening Fécom was already in peril, especially the proposal for reserve pooling.

To concentrate on the fate of the Commission's proposals is, however, to examine the real issues at one remove, for the draft decisions merely supplied the framework in which the fundamental issues involved were discussed. At this more general level, the prospects for success did not appear bright in view of the irreconcilable differences between the member states. As on previous occasions, the conflicting views of the Governments ruled out any agreement on pooling reserves. The Council once again decided to refer this matter back to the Monetary and the Central Bank Governors Committees for further study, and although it pledged to reconsider this issue by 30 June 1974, this commitment signified little as it was the traditional formula adopted to conceal the failure to reach accord, even on rejecting a proposal. On the other hand, while certain member states categorically rejected the eightfold increase in the size of the short-term financial support system proposed by the Commission, it did not appear inconceivable that a compromise could be worked out on this point in the context of a larger agreement on the EMU Project. As to the remaining elements of the Commission's proposal, the member states did achieve a consensus but of a purely negative character. Just as earlier in the year, the Nine were united in ruling out, albeit for contradictory reasons, the authorization of even a small amount of capital for Fécom, the appointment of a director-general and the creation of a permanent committee to govern Fécom. Thus, by the time the Council adjourned on 4 December, it was clear that the Commission's ambitious proposals for strengthening Fécom were a dead letter.

The day of reckoning for the remaining elements of the Commission's set of proposals for the second stage was not long in coming. On 17 December, the Council met to consider the other four draft texts. In contrast to the previous session, three of the texts were approved in principle, with only a few changes[76]. However, this was a hollow accomplishment: the few alterations that had been made had completely vitiated the texts, as every provision of real significance had been excised. Just two modifications were made in the decision on achieving a high degree of convergence, but these eliminated the requirement of obtaining a written opinion before any change of parity and the provision for the Council to take legislative action if necessary 'dans le cas où un État membre menerait des politiques economiques, monétaires, et budgétaires s'écartant des orientations définies par le Conseil ou presentant des risques économiques pour l'ensemble de la Communauté'[77].

Likewise, the directive on growth, stability and full employment was weakened by the single change of extending from 30 to 90 days the period within which governments were to be able to take action in the tax and expenditure fields. This meant it would no longer be necessary for governments to have discretionary authority, because there would be ample time for specific legislative approval to be secured*. Finally, the decision on creating an economic policy committee was accepted as proposed, except for an inconsequential change in defining what constituted a quorum, but then as discussed earlier, it was already devoid of real substance.

Once again, the unresolved conflict among the member states had prevented further progress on the EMU Project. At one level, this was reflected in the inability of the national governments to agree on the specific initiatives, resulting in the Commission's proposals for the second stage being rejected. In excising the provisions that represented the major initiatives in the Commission's plans, the Council demonstrated that the Community simply could not advance to the second stage on the basis of parallelism. Yet at a much deeper level, the differences among the Nine precluded not only agreement on the Commission's proposals but any further progress in economic and monetary unification at all. Whatever the approach adopted by the Commission, the outcome would have been the same, for there was no set of measures that would have been acceptable to all the national governments. There was no common ground between the German position that

'für die zweite Stufe der Wirtschafts- und Währungsunion und den weiteren Ausbau hält die Bundesregierung es für notwendig, von Anfang an zu verbindlicheren Formen der Koordinierung und Harmonisierung der Wirtschaftspolitiken der Mitgliedstaaten zu kommen'[78]

and the French Government's categorical rejection of common decision-making. The flexibility in these two basically incompatible approaches, which had allowed the EMU Project to progress so far, had finally been exhausted.

At last, the Community had reached the point where the gap between the economist and monetarist paths could no longer be bridged. With the start of the second stage, the basic decisions about the nature of the final stage, the transfer of authority and the relationship of policy co-ordination to exchange rate concertation had to be made because now substantive progress towards common policy-making was essential if policy co-ordination were to precede or even parallel advances on the exchange rate concertation front. Yet in 1973, as in 1970, the nine Governments could not agree on a common strategy. The EMU Project was at a dead stop.

The blow delivered by the Council on 17 December had consequences much graver than ruling out the transition to the second stage. It inflicted a mortal wound on the EMU Project. That the member states lacked the

---

*A second change included wage and price controls as tools that national administrations should have at their disposal.

political will to proceed any further towards the final goal irretrievably doomed the attempt to create that economic and monetary union in the European Community which had been conceived at the Hague Summit, taken shape in the womb of the Werner Committee and been born in the Council resolution of 22 March 1971. Not only was the 1980 target now unattainable, but the route chosen by the Community had proven a dead end. The strategy of parallelism had allowed the Nine to make a limited advance in the direction of EMU, but it had failed in its critical task of bringing about the fundamental changes in the relationships among the member states that were indispensable for economic and monetary unification. The inability in December 1973 of the Community to advance any further towards its avowed objective was a clear manifestation of the failure to alter a situation in which immediate national interests overruled advances in economic and monetary integration. This lack of political will has been a recurrent theme throughout the life of the EMU Project and is in the last analysis the fundamental reason for its failure. When, in December 1973, the member states had to choose between EMU and their perceived short-term economic interest, they decided against further progress in economic and monetary integration; this effectively constituted the abandonment of the EMU Project.

However the Council's actions had a second and equally important consequence. The decisions adopted on 17 December might have marked the end of the EMU Project, but they also indicated that the Nine did not intend to abandon the progress of the past three years. While the experience of the previous six years had revealed the problems and difficulties in the Community's trying to act as a unit in monetary affairs, it had also demonstrated the advantages. The benefits of presenting a common front at the world level, of the system of mutual financial assistance, of the joint float and of the regular exchange of information on economic conditions and strategies had not been lost on the member states. These they were determined to retain. It is in this context that the full significance of the decisions adopted on 17 December becomes evident. Precisely because they are restatements of agreements that had previously been concluded and undertakings that had already been made, they are a forceful reaffirmation of the will of the nine countries to work together

> 'to promote throughout the Community a harmonious development of economic activities, a continuous and balanced expansion, an increase in stability, an accelerated raising of the standard of living and closer relations between the States belonging to it.'[79]

If the Nine could not agree on advancing to *the* second stage envisaged in the Werner Report, they were nevertheless in accord on proceeding to *a* second stage, which was to be essentially a prolongation of the first. Although described as 'an opportunity for catching up on the delays incurred in the first stage'[80], or, even more optimistically, as a period in which 'nicht nur Versäumtes nachgeholt, sondern auch die politisch-institutionelle Weiterentwicklung ernsthaft vorangetrieben wird'[81], this second stage was in reality to be a period of suspended animation, during which, as measures accepted by the Council made clear, there would be no major initiatives.

Even if no progress in economic and monetary integration occurred during this second stage, the decision to maintain the status quo was nevertheless extremely important, not only because of its direct implications for the relationships among the member states but also because it preserved the achievements of the past three years as a base for any future advance. Even though officially the Community was still committed to achieving economic and monetary union by 1980, however, the problems in securing formal approval of even the weakened texts about the second stage brought home the reality that the resumption of movement towards EMU was not on the cards for the time being. Although the Council had agreed in principle to the draft decisions on 17 December, the representatives of Italy and the United Kingdom refused to give their assent unless there was a definite commitment to create a regional fund. Arguing not completely ingenuously that because it had been agreed at the Paris Summit of October 1972 that a regional fund was to be established by 31 December 1973 and that 'dieser wird von Beginn der zweiten Phase der Wirtschafts und Währungsunion an aus Eigeneinahmen der Gemeinschaft . . . finanziert'[82], they asserted they could not formally approve the transition to the second stage or any of its components until such a fund, from which they expected to be major beneficiaries, had been set up. Not surprisingly, the principle reason for the delay in creating the fund had been disagreement over its size. While the Nine were not able to reach accord on this point for many more months, Britain and then Italy were persuaded to lift their vetoes in early 1974. As a result, the decisions concerning the harmonization of policy instruments, the procedures for economic policy co-ordination and the establishment of an economic policy committee were formally approved by the Council on 18 February 1974, and with this, the Community passed into a second stage of economic and monetary unification.

The departure of the franc

The failure of the member states to manifest the political will to proceed further towards EMU was parallelled at a more practical level by their failure to follow the economic policies necessary to maintain the exchange rates among the currencies in the snake. Like the EMU Project itself, the snake was intended to bring about closer monetary relationships among the member states by getting them to work more and more tightly together as they progressed through a series of steps which had been laid down in advance on the basis of the commitment to achieving fixed and non-fluctuating exchange rates among Community currencies. However there had been growing signs over the past two years that the initiative in exchange rate concertation had not been leading to the economic and monetary integration of the nine countries. As a result of the withdrawal of three member states and of the repeated parity changes among the remaining participants, the snake could no longer be realistically regarded as preparing the ground for the introduction of a common currency because it neither included all the Community countries nor entailed the maintenance of stable exchange rates.

We have argued that the snake ceased to be a feasible instrument for the economic and monetary unification of the nine Community countries as early as March 1973. Just as it had taken the failure to agree on the transition to the second stage to drive home the incontrovertible fact that the member states lacked the political will to proceed any further in economic and monetary integration and resulted, in effect, in the abandonment of the EMU Project, so it required the withdrawal of the franc in January 1974 to drive home the reality that the snake was not a route to the introduction of a common currency and result in the demise of the snake as a Community endeavour. In both cases the process by which progress towards EMU actually came to a stop was a gradual one that defies precise dating. The departure of the franc was simply the event that, coming as it did, as the culmination of developments over the two previous years, forced recognition of the fact that the snake was not furthering the economic and monetary integration of the member states; the significance of this event must be seen in this perspective, for there was nothing inherent in the franc's departure *per se* making this the necessary or inevitable outcome.

In a very real sense, the series of events leading up to the franc's departure from the joint float began in December 1973 with the French Government's decision on the course it would pursue in the aftermath of the oil crisis. For the first half of that month, the franc had been the strongest currency in the snake, resulting in the Banque de France having to purchase over U.A. 300 million worth of foreign currencies, primarily marks and guilders, which remained depressed for technical reasons. By the end of the month, however, the franc had fallen to its floor within the joint float, in part because interest rates in Germany and especially the Netherlands were allowed to rise in line with the restrictive monetary policies being pursued in both countries[83, 84]. With the start of the new year, the authorities had to enter the markets on several occasions to support the franc to a slight extent, and in an attempt to stem the outflow of funds, the Banque de France let the rate for day-to-day money rise 2% in the first week of January. This action restrained but did not stop the exodus of capital, which in fact gathered momentum on subsequent days as it assumed an increasingly speculative character[85]. The initially interest rate-induced outflow had focused attention on the franc, and given the nervous and unsettled conditions on the exchange markets, it required only the impression of weakness to precipitate a massive attack on the franc.

Although the effect of the oil crisis on the French economy, in terms of supply, prices and the balance of payments was broadly comparable to that in other countries, there was ample reason for concern about the future strength of the franc. The country's payments position was weak, with the current account already in deficit, and the reserves, which stood at approximately $ 8000 million at year-end 1973, could cover the increased cost of imports, estimated at $ 5500 million in 1974, for less than 18 months[86, 87]. More seriously, the policies being pursued by the Government seemed to imply relatively higher levels of demand and inflation than in other snake countries, with obvious implications for the balance of payments. Against the resulting mistrust of the franc, monetary measures were of little avail, and thus, despite a 2% increase in reserve requirements announced on 15 January, the flight out of the franc continued to snowball. By 18 January, the Banque de France had incurred liabilities of almost U.A. 300 million under the multilateral intervention arrangements. This was in addition to having sold over U.A. 350 million worth of dollars in an attempt to support the franc against the American currency[88]. Once again a crisis had developed that challenged the determination of the snake countries to maintain the existing exchange rate relationships.

The French authorities had essentially three alternatives in responding to the attack on the franc. They could continue on their present course, defending the parity of the franc within the snake through the use of the reserves; they could change their economic policies; or they could adjust the exchange rate. Even though the decline in the Banque de France's net foreign assets had so far been relatively small, the Government ruled out the first alternative because it could entail a substantial drain on the reserves, which the authorities were loath to allow in the face of the increased bill for imports; moreover, it was not certain that a resolute defence of the franc would restore confidence[89]. The Government also rejected a change in its economic policies: its tightening of credit conditions had failed to stem the attack on the franc and made it clear that a large deflation of demand would be required to restore confidence in the currency. This far it was not prepared to go[90]. In other words, the Government was not willing to accept the consequences in terms of growth, investment and unemployment of committing itself to defending the existing set of parities. By the process of elimination, the authorities had effectively decided on a modification of the exchange rate.

It remained only for the Government to choose between devaluing the franc within the snake or withdrawing it from the joint float altogether. From the point of view of the French authorities, there were two powerful arguments in favour of the latter alternative. First, an independent float would allow a greater freedom of action, in terms not only of exchange rates and hence the use of the reserves, but also of monetary policy and demand management. Such flexibility was regarded as extremely valuable in the conditions of uncertainty created by the oil crisis, which placed a premium on the ability to react quickly and decisively to unforeseen developments. Second, an independent float would allow a depreciation of the franc without the problems and inconveniences of a formal devaluation. Although the French current account deficit was growing rapidly, this situation was common to most industrialized countries in the aftermath of the oil crisis. A devaluation of the franc of the magnitude needed to restore the current account to equilibrium would, therefore, have been difficult to justify and might have invited retaliation. Leaving the snake would, of course, have a certain political cost, both domestically and at the Community level, for the French Government had, after all, been the most ardent advocate of the initiative in exchange rate concertation, but compared with the practical advantages, this was not a real deterrent. Consequently, the French Government announced on 19 January that the franc was temporarily being allowed to float against the other European currencies. The authorities emphasized that the situation would be re-examined in six months and that they remained committed to the maintenance of fixed exchange rates within the Community. These declarations did not, however, alter the import of this decision: the franc had left the snake.

The departure of the franc was the *coup de grâce* which removed whatever pretence remained of the snake being a means of proceeding towards the introduction of a common currency. The decision of the French authorities was but another indication that national interest still took precedence over the imperatives of economic and monetary unification. The implications of this for the viability of any system of fixed rates among the member states were unmistakable: as long as the strategies and performance of the member states in economic affairs continued to differ, such an endeavour was doomed to fail. It is therefore important to stress that neither the divergence in national economic policies nor consequently the withdrawal of the franc was caused in any fundamental sense by the oil crisis, although it may have precipitated events. The tensions inside the joint float had been evident for months and had already forced an adjustment of parities on two previous occasions. It was precisely because the floating of the franc was the product not of special circumstances but of the dissimilarity in national economic policies which had been evident for years that it demonstrated so conclusively that the snake was not leading to exchange rate stability within the Community.

Of course, that parity changes occurred or even that they were happening more frequently did not necessarily indicate that the snake was not a feasible route for the introduction of a common currency. The Werner Report and the Council resolution of 22 March 1971 had recognized that there would be problems at the start in maintaining a set of fixed exchange rates among the member states and had explicitly provided for parity changes during the initial three-year period. It was rather the lack of the political will to achieve exchange rate stability manifest in the French decision to leave the snake altogether that showed that the initiative in exchange rate concertation had failed in its quintessential task of establishing EMU as an important objective not to be thrust aside by short-term national interests.

At another level, the decision to float the franc made it clear that the snake had ceased to be a tool for bringing about the economic and monetary unification of the Community countries because it no longer included all the member states. This did not, of course, necessarily indicate that it was not leading to an integrative process in the Community, for the absence of a given currency might be temporary. The experience of the previous two years suggested, however, that this was not the case, for with the exception of the special case of Denmark in 1972, none of the currencies that had left the snake had returned to it, and although the French franc would rejoin the snake in July 1975, it would withdraw again only eight months later. That four of the member states had withdrawn from the snake demonstrated conclusively – and more forcefully than the parity adjustments – that the initiative in exchange rate concertation was not leading to the economic and monetary integration of the nine Community countries.

While the flotation of the franc at last dispelled the illusion that the initiative in exchange rate concertation was leading to a common currency, the snake itself survived and emerged as it had from previous crises – dismembered but alive. The snake that made its appearance on the exchange markets on 21 January 1974* was nevertheless, a very different animal from the creature that had begun life on 24 April 1972. It had lost its original *raison d'être* but in the process had acquired another. Quite simply, it had been transformed gradually, almost imperceptibly, from an initiative preparing the ground for the introduction of a common currency into a currency bloc providing a limited degree of exchange rate stability among its members. With the departure of the franc, it became only too obvious that the snake had assumed an existence separate from that of the EMU Project and, indeed, the Community.

The snake that emerged after the withdrawal of the franc had lost its identity as a Community creature at two levels. Institutionally, the altered character of the joint float was symbolized by the decision of the five member states still participating in what was now called the 'minisnake' to conduct the discussions on exchange rate strategy outside the Community framework. Ever since the launching of the initiative in exchange rate concertation, it had been a cardinal principle that policy issues should be considered in the Committee of Central Bank Governors or the Council, so that all the member states, including those that had 'temporarily' withdrawn from the snake

---

*Its participants were Belgium, Denmark, Germany, Luxembourg and the Netherlands, with Norway and Sweden as associates and Austria and Switzerland informally linking their currencies to it.

arrangements, could take part. But when the Finance Ministers of the minisnake members met on 21 January 1974 to chart their future course of action, they met alone[91]. The import of this development was unmistakable: while Fécom would continue to administer the multilateral intervention system and payments arrangements, major policy decisions about the conduct of the joint float would be made by the participants alone. Obviously, the symbolic importance of this change was far greater than its practical significance, as the snake system had always really been run by those directly concerned; the new procedures merely made this explicit. Nevertheless, excluding the non-minisnake countries and the Commission (as well as the non-Community associates) did have real consequences, for it meant that these four member states were no longer able to participate in the decision-making process, express their views, listen to the arguments of other countries and monitor developments at first hand. Henceforth, they would be outsiders, and this effectively shattered the illusion of the snake as a Community institution.

In a more fundamental sense, the snake lost its Community character because it ceased to be an identifiably Community grouping. So long as France took part, the joint float had a Community flavour, but with the departure of the franc, it appeared as little more than an enlarged DM-bloc. The snake's new character as a loose grouping of currencies centred on Germany became even more apparent if one included the four non-Community states associated, officially or unofficially, with the joint float. True, none of these were eligible to participate in the activities of Fécom, particularly the mutual assistance system, and only two, Norway and Sweden, were included in the multilateral intervention system. However, the essential characteristic of the snake was, after all, not the consultations and co-ordination supposed to take place in Fécom, not the multilateral payments arrangements or even the joint intervention system, which were merely means to an end, but the maintenance of fixed exchange rates among the participants – and in this respect, the four non-menbers were indistinguishable from the Community countries.

Thus, the events of January 1974 resulted in the initiative in exchange rate concertation diverging from the EMU Project in terms both of membership and of function. The joint float might now correspond to a grouping of countries much more homogeneous in terms of their economic conditions, objectives and performances than the Nine or even the Six had ever been and might have become more resilient as a result of the more flexible and pragmatic approach to exchange rates that now prevailed, but it was no longer an instrument of economic and monetary integration. It existed rather as a means to maintain fixed exchange rates within a group of countries sharing, at any given time, the ability and the will to do so. This transformation in the essential nature of exchange rate concertation was symbolized by the severance of the snake from the EMU Project.

The loss of the snake as part of the EMU Project dealt the *coup de grâce* to the attempt to create an economic and monetary union in the Community which had been conceived at the Hague five years previously. The snake had in a very real sense been the heart of the efforts to forge a single economic unit out of the nine economies. It had been not only the symbol but also the central element of the EMU Project. It severance from this endeavour therefore inflicted a wound as fatal as the blow delivered by the Council three weeks before, and brought home with a force the more recondite events in the Council could not the fact that the EMU Project had been abandoned. But more importantly it signalled the beginning of a new phase in monetary affairs in the Community. The age of the snake as an instrument of economic and monetary integration was over. A new era of the snake as a means of promoting the individual national interests of the member states had dawned. Henceforth, the monetary relationships among the Community countries would evolve, not on the basis of a common commitment to a specific plan for achieving economic and monetary union, but under the impetus of a pragmatic commitment to the further integration of the nine economies.

1 De Nederlandsche Bank, *Report for the year 1973* [hereafter cited as *Nederlandsche Bank*]p.115
2 *Geschäftsbericht der Deutschen Bundesbank für das Jahr 1973* [hereafter cited as *Geschäftsbericht*] pp.4–9
3 Belgium, Ministère des Affaires Economiques, *l'économie belge en 1973*, pp.223–226
4 Banque de France, *Bulletin trimestriel* [hereafter cited as *Bulletin trimestriel*] No. 8, September 1973, pp.11–21
5 *Geschäftsbericht 1973*, pp.8–12
6 Banque de France, *Compte rendu*, (Exercice 1973) [hereafter cited as *Compte rendu*] pp.13–15, 42
7 *Geschäftsbericht 1973*, pp.15–20
8 OECD, *Economic Surveys, Germany*, 1972, pp.53–56
9 Belgium, Ministère des Affaires Economiques, *l'économie belge en 1973*, pp.227–230
10 *Journal officiel des Communautés européenes* [hereafter cited as *Journal officiel*] XVI(L89), 5 April 1973, pp.2–5
11 *Nederlandsche Bank*, 1973, p.110
12 *Journal officiel*, XVI(L207), 28 July 1973, p.46
13 *Journal officiel*, XIV(C28), 27 March 1971, p.4
14 *Bulletin* (of the European Communities), Supplement, May 1973, p.5
15 *Bulletin*, Supplement, May 1973, p.13
16 *Bulletin*, Supplement, May 1973, p.15
17 *Bulletin*, Supplement, May 1973, p.10
18 *Nederlandsche Bank 1973*, pp.108–109
19 *Jahreswirtschaftsbericht 1973 der Bundesregierung* [hereafter cited as *Jahreswirtschaftsbericht*] pp.9–10
20 *Journal officiel*, XVI(L114) 30 April 1973, p.4
21 European Communities Commission, *Bericht der Kommission an den Rat* (uber die Umgestaltung des Kurzfristigen Währungsbeistandes und die Bedingungen einer Vergemeinschaftung der Reserven) (Document of the Commission 1099 dated 27 June 1973) pp.2–8
22 European Communities, Committee of Central Bank Governors, *Rapport Preliminaire sur les Problèmes soulevés par le Rapport de la Commission au Conseil concernant l'Aménagment du Monétaire à court-terme et les conditions de la mise en commun progressive des réserves* [Document of the Commission 1099 dated 27 June 1973] (Report #16 of the Théron Group [of Experts] dated 5 September 1973)
23 European Communities, Monetary Committee, *Rapport du Comité sur le problème de l'Or* (Document of the Commission II/202/74 dated 8 April 1974)
24 Banca d'Italia, *Abridged Version of the Report for the Year 1973* [hereafter cited as *Banca d'Italia*] p.79

25 *Bulletin trimestriel*, No. 7, May 1973, pp.10–12, *Monatsberichte*, June 1975, pp.34–39 and *Nederlandsche Bank 1973*, pp.111–116
26 *Geschäftsbericht*, 1973, pp.47–49
27 *Monatsberichte*, September 1973, pp.8–12, 35–36
28 *Nederlandsche Bank*, 1973, pp.114–118 and Statistical Annex, pp.67–68
29 *Monatsberichte*, September 1973, pp.11–14
30 *Compte rendu* 1973, p.29
31 *Geschäftsbericht* 1973, pp.21–23
32 'Le rapport économique et financier' (du Projet de Loi de Finances pour 1974) [hereafter cited as 'Le rapport économique et financier']. In *Statistiques et Etudes Financières*, **XXV**(298), October 1973, pp.9–10
33 *Compte rendu*, 1973, p.29
34 *Monatsberichte*, September 1973, pp.35–36
35 *Bulletin trimestriel*, No. 9, November 1973, pp.8–11
36 *Geschäftsbericht*, 1973, pp.20–22
37 *Nederlandsche Bank*, 1973, pp.111–117, 120–122
38 *Bulletin trimestriel*, No. 10, February 1974, pp.11–13
39 *Nederlandsche Bank*, 1973, pp.12–17, 68–70, 112–117
40 *Bulletin trimestriel*, No. 9, November 1973, pp.8–11
41 *Monatsberichte*, October 1973, pp.5–7
42 European Communities Commission, *Aspects économiques à moyen terme de la crise de l'énergie pour la Communauté*, (Document of the Commission II/43/74 dated 8 February 1974)
43 *Compte rendu*, 1973, pp.103–105
44 OECD, *Economic Surveys, Germany*, 1973, pp.34–38
45 *Jahreswirtschaftsbericht*, 1974, pp.5–6
46 European Communities, Commission, *Crise Petrolière et Problèmes liés à l'Equilibre Extérieur à moyen terme des Pays de la Communauté*, pp.8–9, 11–14 (Document of the Commission II/130/74 dated 8 March 1974)
47 Germany, Sachverständigenrat zur Begutachtung der gesamtwirtschaftlichen Entwicklung, 'Zu der Gesamtwirtschaftlichen Auswirkungen der Olkrise' (Sondergutachten vom 17 December 1973) [hereafter cited as Sachverständigenrat] in *Vollbeschäftigung für morgen* (Jahresgutachen 1974/75), pp.183–184

48 *Monatsberichte*, December 1973, pp.19–25
49 *Bulletin trimestriel*, No. 10, February 1974, pp.5–11
50 OECD, *Economic Surveys, Germany*, 1973, pp.34–44
51 Sachverständigenrat, pp.183–198
52 *Monatsberichte*, December 1973, pp.29–33
53 Belgium, Ministère des Affaires Economiques, *l'Economie belge en 1973*, pp.223–226
54 *Nederlandsche Bank*, 1973, pp.111–114
55 OECD, *Economic Surveys, France*, 1973, pp.20–23
56 OECD, *Economic Surveys, Germany*, 1973, pp.5–12
57 *Bulletin trimestriel*, No. 9, November 1973, pp.5–8
58 *Monatsberichte*, December 1974, p.67*
59 *Geschäftsbericht*, 1973, p.52
60 *Geschäftsbericht*, 1973, pp.39–45
61 *Monatsberichte*, December 1973, pp.5–16
62 Sachverständigenrat, pp.193–198
63 *Jahreswirtschaftsbericht*, 1974, pp.5–8
64 European Communities Commission, *Crise Petrolière et Problèmes liés à l'Equilibre Extérieur à moyen terme des pays de la Communauté*, pp.8–9
65 Belgium, Ministère des Affaires Economiques, *l'Economie belge en 1973*, pp.xv–xxii, 227–238
66 *Nederlandsche Bank*, 1973, pp.17–22, 74–78
67 *Bulletin trimestriel*, No. 9, November 1973, pp.18–23
68 'Le rapport économique et financier', 1974, pp.35–41
69 *Bulletin trimestriel*, No. 10, February 1974, pp.5–11, 21–33
70 OECD, *Economic Surveys, France*, 1973, pp.20–23
71 See Chap. 3, pp.50–51
72 *Journal officiel*, **XVI**(C114), 27 December 1973, pp.33–45
73 See Chap. 8, pp.189–191
74 *Journal officiel*, **XVI** (C114), 27 December, 1973, p.34
75 European Communities Council, *Relevé des décisions prises par le Conseil lors de sa 266 ème session tenue les 3 et 4 decembre 1973*. (Document of the Council R/3263/75 (FIN 846) dated 20 December 1973)
76 European Communities Council, *21st Review of the Council's Work*, 1973, p.35
77 *Journal Officiel*, **XVI** (C114), 27 December 1973, p.40

78 *Jahreswirtschaftsbericht*, 1973, p.10
79 *Traité instituant la Communauté économique européene*, in *Traités instituant les Communautés européenes*, (Art. 2), p.179
80 *Nederlandsche Bank*, 1973, p.109
81 *Jahreswirtschaftsbericht*, 1974, p.9
82 *Schlüsserklärung der Konferenz der Staats- bzw. Regierungschefs der Mitgliedstaaten der erweiterten Gemeinschaft vom 19, 20 und 21 Oktober 1972 in Paris*, in European Communities, Monetary Committee, *Kompendium von Gemeinschaftstexten in Bereich der Währungspolitik*, pp.26–27
83 *Monatsberichte*, February 1974, pp.10–15
84 *Nederlandsche Bank*, 1973, pp.111–114
85 *Bulletin trimestriel*, No. 10, February 1974, pp.11–18
86 *Compte rendu*, 1973, p.114
87 European Communities, Commission, *Crise Petrolière et Problèmes liés à l'Equilibre Extérieur à moyen terme des pays de la Communauté*, p.2
88 *Bulletin trimestriel*, No. 10, February 1974, pp.21–33
89 France, Ministère de l'Economie et des Finances, Service de l'Information, *Les Nouvelles Mesures Monétaires*, pp.3–6. (Allocution prononcée par le Ministre de l'Economie et des Finances devant l'Assemblée Nationale, 22 Jannuary 1974).
90 'Le rapport économique et financier', 1974, pp.16–25
91 *Vereinigte Wirtschaftsdienst Europa*, No. 48/74, 8 March 1974, pp.1–3

CHAPTER EIGHT
Completion of the Common Market, Interregional Transfers, and Economic Policy Co-ordination

Chapters 5–7 have been concerned with one aspect of the attempt to create an economic and monetary union in the European Community, namely the initiative in exchange rate concertation designed to prepare the ground for the introduction of a common currency, and have concentrated on the monetary relationships among the member states. The resulting picture of the process of economic and monetary unification during the period from the launching of the EMU Project on 22 March 1971 to its abandonment three years later has therefore been incomplete. Consequently it is necessary to turn to the three remaining facets of economic and monetary unification, the establishment of a real common market, the institution of a system of interregional transfers and the co-ordination of economic policies. As in previous chapters, progress on each of these fronts will be considered separately; it is, therefore, especially important to bear in mind that these efforts were not taking place in isolation but occurred against the background of developments on other fronts of the EMU Project which both economically and especially politically exerted an influence on all the various aspects of this endeavour.

Because of this interconnection between advances on the different fronts of the EMU Project, particularly in reaching agreements on the specific steps to be taken, the preceding chapters have made mention, admittedly cursory, of developments in all fields of economic and monetary unification. This procedure will not be repeated here, for to do so would be not only redundant but also impractical because the limited number of events in these three areas constitutes an inadequate framework for analysing advances on the project as a whole. It is, therefore, all the more vital that the material presented here be seen in the context of the developments described in Chapters 5–7 so that it appears in proper perspective.

Completion of the Common Market

Unlike the initiatives on the exchange rate concertation front, the efforts to complete the establishment of the common market did not represent a new field of activity for the Community. The Treaty of Rome specifically provided for the free and unrestricted movement of goods, services and the factors of production and the co-ordination of certain policies to prevent the distortion of product or factor markets. Consequently, while the Werner Report and the Council resolution of 22 March 1971 both stressed that the transformation of the Community into a common market was an essential part of economic and monetary unification, the EMU Project contained only two initiatives on this front. Most of the attempts to promote factor mobility occurred outside the framework of the EMU Project, but it must be emphasized that this was a reflection of historical and organizational factors and in no sense indicated that advances on this front were regarded as unimportant or peripheral to economic and monetary unification.

The two initiatives that were incorporated into the EMU Project represented advances beyond the creation of a common market and hence had not been mandated in the Treaty of Rome: they provided for national taxation systems and capital market regulations to be harmonized in order to facilitate product and factor movements. Specifically, the Council resolution of 22 March 1971 stated that the member states were to work towards establishing a set of uniform rates for and a common 'basket' of articles liable to value added tax, to align the rates of corporation tax, to increase gradually the value of goods travellers could take from one country to another without incurring tax, to develop consistent policies on the taxation of interest and dividend income and to modify regulations governing access to national capital markets so that issues from all member states were on equal footing[1]. Translating this commitment into action proved, however, to be a very slow and difficult process. As the Commission tactfully put it in 1973 in assessing the achievements of the first stage, 'les résultats ne sont pas aussi satisfaisants que l'on avait pu l'imaginer lors de l'etablissement du plan par étapes'[2]. In fact, the only accomplishment in terms of taxation had been a small increase in travellers' tax-free allowances*. Likewise, 'la libération des mouvements de capitaux et la coordination des politiques des États membres à l'égard des marchés financières n'ont marqué aucun progrès au cours des dernières années.'[4] Indeed, the introduction of more or less stringent controls on capital movements, which applied to intra-Community flows as well as those with third countries, was a considerable step backwards. There was, however, one trace of progress: at the end of June 1973 the Council reached accord on a series of measures which essentially allowed banks in one member state to provide services to customers in all other member states so long as they did not conduct any operations there[5].

The same picture of desultory progress emerges from an examination of the efforts made outside the framework of the EMU Project to increase

---

* Of course, the system of value added taxation had been introduced in all nine member states by 1 April 1973; however, the Council decision of 9 February 1967 had set 1 January 1970 as the deadline, and in any case the individual modes of application varied greatly[3].

factor mobility. According to the Treaty of Rome, all barriers to the free movement of goods, services, labour, entrepreneurship, and most forms of capital were to have been eliminated by the end of the transition period, which occurred on 1 July 1968, but in 1971 the Community was still far from having accomplished this. Tariffs had been completely abolished among the Six and considerable strides made in harmonizing standards and regulations. Nevertheless, free trade was still hampered by customs formalities, border taxes on products included in the Common Agricultural Policy, value added tax rebates and levies and a host of non-tariff barriers, such as public procurement policies and safety requirements. Similarly, substantial advances had been made in ending discrimination against workers from other member states, but labour mobility was still impaired by the lack of a Community social security system and the difference in the national regulations with which workers had to comply. The Community in 1971 was even further from constituting a common market as far as professionals were concerned, for national governments still refused to recognize qualifications from other member states.

Over the next three years, the Community advanced little further towards establishing the free movement of goods, services and the factors of production. Some progress was made in agreeing on common standards in certain areas, but this was a very slow process. In those fields where the member states were trying to move beyond merely eliminating existing barriers and to take positive action to facilitate factor mobility, the advances were even more modest. To cite only the most obvious, the Community of 1974 still lacked a common industrial policy, a uniform company law and, despite important advances in establishing the rights of Community nationals working in other member states, a European social policy. Across the wide range of areas in which the Community was trying to liberalize trade and factor movements, the picture was thus one of relatively little progress during the first stage, and most of this represented steps which, according to the Treaty of Rome, should have been taken years before[6].

Although it is questionable whether any realistic course of action could have resulted in the Community becoming a common market in fact as well as in name, given the fundamental differences among these countries in language, social structure and business organization, the essential point is that in 1974 the member states had not advanced very far towards this destination, despite the initiatives, inside the EMU Project and more importantly outside as well, taken during the first stage. Indeed, it was questionable whether the Community in 1974 even constituted an area in which there was free trade in the fullest sense of the word. After three years of the EMU Project, in short, the member states had not even come close to achieving the common market, which was to have been completed five years previously, let alone made progress beyond that towards establishing an economic union.

The institution of interregional transfers

Although the redistribution of welfare gains was an established part of the Community system, the introduction of a system of interregional transfers represented an extension of Community activity into a new field. Nevertheless, the initiatives on this front of economic and monetary unification did not form part of the EMU Project because they fell instead into the domain of regional policy, and for this reason while the March 1971 Council resolution emphasizes the need for instituting a transfer mechanism in order to prevent the emergence of tensions and imbalances within the Community, it does not specify the actual steps to be taken. As has been previously described, the heads of state agreed in principle to the creation of a regional fund at the Paris Summit of October 1972. Despite the British and Italian attempt to make formal approval of the decisions concerning the second stage contingent on the establishment of a regional fund of satisfactory size, however, the fund was approved only months later on 10 December 1974[7].

Strictly speaking, therefore, there was no substantive progress on this front during the first stage. Even if the temporal limitation is removed, the conclusion is not markedly altered, as the fund was to be endowed with a mere U.A. 1300 million over three years, less than the FFr 6400 million spent in just 1974 on investment incentives alone by the two French agencies primarily concerned with regional development[8]. Even Belgium in the late 1960s was spending about U.A. 500 million every three years on investment incentives for development areas plus some U.A. 1000 million annually on infrastructural investments[9,10]. Of course, the real significance of creating a regional fund, as that of setting up Fécom, was that it instituted a mechanism which would be needed at some later stage in economic and monetary unification. Moreover, substantial interregional transfers *were* taking place, though through such institutions as FEOGA rather than a regional fund, which was a particularly transparent and hence politically unattractive vehicle. Precisely because the regional fund was merely a means to the end of establishing a redistribution system, the vital question is whether a single Community welfare function, the practical prerequisite to such a system, existed, and the experience of the first stage, in terms of the battles over the Community budget and the self-seeking economic policies of the member states, suggests that it did not. Instead, there were nine individual welfare calculuses, indicating that on this front of economic and monetary unification, the Community had made little real progress.

Economic policy co-ordination

Perhaps even more striking than the absence of progress on these two fronts of economic and monetary integration is the lack of activity. This is largely attributable to the Community concentrating primarily on initiatives in the fields of exchange rate concertation and economic policy co-ordination. It is to the series of developments on this latter and fourth aspect of the EMU Project that we now turn. This is in a very real sense the other half of the narrative presented in Chapters 5–7, for the initiatives in economic policy co-ordination were the counterpart of the efforts to introduce a common currency, in both economic and political terms.

The initiatives on the exchange rate concertation and economic policy co-ordination fronts complemented each other in terms not only of the strategies they represented but also of their nature. Whereas the former extended Community activity into a new field, the latter did not. Efforts intended to foster common policy-making may have begun only with the EMU Project, but the member states had been working together in the area of economic policy for years. The Treaty of Rome recognized that a certain amount of co-ordination of national economic policies was requisite to the smooth functioning of the common market and provided for the institution of consultation procedures. In the course of the first decade of the Community's existence, five committees had been established to promote co-operation in economic affairs. Consequently, initiatives on this front of the EMU Project were designed to intensify co-ordination within the existing institutional framework rather than create new bodies such as Fécom[11, 12].

A second contrast between the initiatives of these two fronts is that whereas the route to the introduction of a common currency is quite straightforward, that towards common policy-making is anything but obvious. From the start of the deliberations in the Werner Committee it had been agreed that progress in this latter area would have to be based on the voluntary co-ordination of national policies, but the member states had recognized that this approach had the drawbacks that it would be possible neither to set precise targets for each stage of the integrative process nor to work directly towards the final objective. Progress on this front would instead have to come through measures designed to promote co-ordination indirectly by creating an environment conducive to consultations and by fostering the political will to conduct economic policies in concert[13]. As there were a number of ways in which the Community could proceed and the member states were unable to settle on any one of them, it was decided, in typical fashion, to try several different methods during the first stage. These can be grouped under the three general headings of strengthening consultative procedures within the Community, trying to reach agreement on the basic objectives of economic policy and harmonizing the policy instruments available to national authorities.

Before examining in turn these three ways in which the Community tried to promote economic policy co-ordination it should be made clear they all fit together to produce a single, coherent set of efforts. Consequently while it is advantageous for analytical purpose to separate those steps designed to introduce and intensify consultations among the member states from those aimed at setting common objectives or harmonizing the policy instruments available to national authorities, and to consider each individually, this has the disadvantage that the Commission's proposals, which mix elements of all three approaches, have to be cut apart. Previous chapters have, of course, already broadly described the various Commission proposals and Council decisions in their entirety, and it is important that the reader bear in mind the basic pattern of developments presented there so as to obtain a complete picture of developments on this front and to place them in their proper perspective in terms of the EMU Project.

Consultative procedures

The initiatives in the field of economic policy co-ordination that were mandated by the Council resolution of 22 March 1971 fell largely into the category of measures designed to intensify consultations among the member states. Although it had been decided that the Community should concentrate on strengthening existing procedures for co-ordination rather than institutional innovation, the system of five committees, each concerned with a particular aspect of economic affairs, had serious shortcomings because they had grown up in response to specific needs over the previous 12 years and did not constitute a coherent set of institutions covering the whole of economic affairs[14]. First, there was a considerable amount of overlap, with, for example, both the Committee of Central Bank Governors and the Monetary Committee directly concerned with monetary policy*. Second, the specialized nature of the committees tended to be reflected in their membership, making them excellent fora for the exchange of information and the discussion of problems at a technical level but generally poor places for the actual co-ordination of policies, which required close consultation among those directly involved in decision-making.

---

* In part the multiplicity of committees concerned with a single topic reflected the considerable differences among the member states in the institutions responsible for making policy in particular areas. For example, although the central bank was charged with conducting monetary policy in all nine countries, its areas of jurisdiction and, more important its relationship to the government differed significantly in each case. The Bundesbank and the Banca d'Italia, for instance, enjoyed a large degree of autonomy, while the Banque de France was virtually an extension of the Ministère des Finances et Affaires Economiques[15]. For this reason the Monetary Committee included representatives of both central banks and finance ministries. However, along with the Monetary Committee there was the Committee of Central Bank Governors, organized along institutional rather than functional lines, which provided a forum for dealing with those, usually more technical, matters that were the exclusive responsibility of central banks. In practice, the distinction between the competence of these two committees was blurred, with the Council of (Finance) Ministers, itself in some sense the counterpart of the governors' committee – but obviously very, very different – routinely referring issues concerning EMU, such as reserve pooling, to both bodies for study.

Despite the problems in the existing structures fulfilling the tasks assigned to them in the Werner Report, the Council resolution of 22 March 1971 provided for no institutional changes during the first stage and indeed, beyond calling for an intensification of consultations, provided for no major alteration in the functioning of the five existing committees[16]. It proposed rather to overcome the compartmentalization and lack of authority of the present system by making the Council of Ministers the 'central organ of decision for general economic policy'[17]. The vital innovation was to involve the Council directly in the process of co-ordinating economic policies by stipulating that it 'lay down, on the proposal of the Commission, the broad lines of economic policy at Community level and quantitative guidelines for the principal elements of the whole of public budgets'[18]. According to the decision on strengthening the co-ordination of short-term economic policies, the Council was to meet at least three times a year to consider the economic situation and the orientation of national policies. During the first quarter, it would examine the results of the previous year and make any necessary modifications to the plan for the year in progress; during the second quarter, it would review the policies being pursued and set guidelines for national budgets for the following year, especially in terms of surpluses or deficits and their financial implications; and during the third quarter, it would decide on the course to be followed for the coming year[19]. In so doing, the Council was to concern itself with substantive issues as well as general orientations as it was to set guidelines 'in a specific and detailed manner'[20] for the making of national policies.

In terms of its membership, the Council was unquestionably the ideal body for the co-ordination of economic policy in terms of its membership, but there were insurmountable difficulties in other respects to its fulfilling this role. The Council of Finance and Economic Ministers was responsible not only for economic and monetary affairs but also for the Community budget, both revenues and expenditures, and by extension the financial implications of any project on which the Community embarked. Meeting generally only once a month because of the extremely tight schedules of its members, the Council could hardly be the forum for conducting a leisurely discussion of economic conditions throughout the Community. The Council, in its legislative capacity, considered and made the final decisions on the actual steps to be taken in the EMU Project, but otherwise it simply had no time available for routine consultations on economic affairs.

Despite this crucial flaw in the consultation procedures envisaged by the Council resolution of 22 March 1971, and despite the international monetary disorders in May 1971 that temporarily delayed the application of the resolution's other provisions, this first set of steps on the policy co-ordination front was implemented on schedule. The first set of guidelines was drawn up by the Commission on 14 September 1971 and approved by the Council on 26 October[21]. Thereafter the cycle of consultations occurred as specified in the

Economic policy co-ordination

Werner Plan. Yet the question remains whether the Six were actually engaged in a process of policy co-ordination, for the introduction of consultative procedures was a necessary but not a sufficient condition.

Any attempt to determine whether the introduction of these consultative procedures actually had an influence on policy-making at the national level and resulted in concertation, not just an interchange of ideas and information, falters on the insurmountable problems inherent in trying to assess the importance of various factors in influencing decision-making. However, that the Council sessions devoted to setting guidelines took place after national governments had decided on the general orientation of the course they would pursue does establish beyond a reasonable doubt that whatever these meetings accomplished, they did not result in co-ordination. As *Table 8.1* shows, throughout the first stage national budget proposals were consistently submitted to Parliament before the Council met to set the norms that were ostensibly to guide policy formulation for the following year. It is perhaps well to emphasize that by the time the budget was officially presented, the decision-making process was already over because the government's proposals were invariably approved virtually unaltered.

The basic decisions on the macroeconomic course to be followed in the budget were, moreover, made months before its presentation to Parliament, generally at the start of the year, although the precise orientation of budgetary policy was not determined until summer, principally because it was only then that the rough amounts of money allotted to individual departments was known. In France and Germany, at least, the overall size of the budget, the magnitude of any surplus or deficit, and the financial arrangements were fixed by the government by the end of the summer; the intervening period until the draft budget was submitted weeks later was taken up by political bargaining over the detailed allocation of funds. The implication is clear: neither the guidelines laid down by the Council, nor the recommendations of the Commission, nor even the second set of annual consultations, all of which were ostensibly intended to set norms for the formulation of national budgets for the following year, could conceivably have influenced the course of budgetary policy. Of course, this does not necessarily imply that policy co-ordination was not occurring; the member states could have been working together in another framework. However, there is no evidence of any other set of meetings in which the member states were attempting to concert their budgetary policies. Moreover, to assume that the Six were co-ordinating their policies not through the consultation procedures established for that express purpose and which they claimed they were using but instead through another set of arrangements does not seem overly plausible.

The assessment that the efforts to intensify consultations were not resulting in economic policy co-ordination is further substantiated by examining the major shifts in national policies that occurred during the first stage. In many respects, the changes of course that took place in the aftermath of key

Table 8.1 Timing of national budgetary preparation compared with submission and approval of community guidelines

Annual report on economic situation in the Community (EEC guidelines)		Main lines of budgetary policy decided by national government			Presentation of national budgets to Parliament			
Submitted by the Commission	Approved by the Council	France	Germany★	Belgium	France	Italy	Netherlands
14 September 1971	26 October	n.a.	10 September 1971	October	mid-September	end July	September
8 September 1972	31 October	end July	6 September 1972	September	15 September	31 July	22 September
18 September 1973	9 November	mid-June	5 September 1973	3 October	mid-September	31 July	13 September

★ In the case of Germany, the adoption by the Federal Government of the main lines of budgetary policy is tantamount to the approval of the budget project that will subsequently be submitted to the Bundestag and the Bundesrat.

Sources: Economic Situation in the Community
Jahresgutachten des Sachverstandigenrates
Keesing's Contemporary Archives
Année Politique, Economique, Sociale

developments at the national or international level were more interesting, significant, and revealing than, for example, the annual preparation of budgets, which generally was an expression of the existing strategy. It was, after all, at these critical junctures, such as France in late spring and summer 1969, that economic policies were reviewed, new approaches chosen, and the course that the country would follow until the next crisis determined[22]. The decisions made at such turning points did not always exercise so lasting an influence on the subsequent conduct of economic affairs, especially during the three years of the first stage when unsettled conditions necessitated frequent adjustments of course, but this in no way lessened their significance as they remained the crux of economic policy-making.

Apart from the advantages for the Community as well as for individual member states of all nine countries acting in concert in a crisis situation, it was therefore particularly important in terms of economic policy co-ordination for national governments to work together at these critical junctures which offered an excellent opportunity for influencing in a formative period the national strategies that would determine the future conduct of economic affairs. Yet all the available information suggests that each government charted its economic policy course independently and without consultations. The policies adopted in response to the oil crisis, for example, were decided upon during the last quarter of 1973, and while there were frequent meetings among national officials during this period, there is no evidence of a co-ordination of economic policies beyond the agreement to hold consultations prior to any changes of parity.

'Den vielen Aktivitäten der Kommission der Europäischen Gemeinschaften und den anspruchsvollen Beschlüssen des Ministerrats im Jahresverlauf fehlte die Entsprechung im konkreten Handeln der Gemeinschaftsländer . . . .
   Die Partnerstaaten hatten sich zwar am 18. Februar 1974 auf stabilisierungspolitische Richtlinien und solche Bestimmungen geeinigt, die "einen hohen Grad an Konvergenz der Wirtschaftspolitik" herbeiführen sollten, doch haben weder diese Beschlüsse noch die Anpassung der wirtschaftspolitischen Leitlinien an die neuen Bedingungen in Juli 1974 zu einem gemeinsamen Konzept in der Konjunkturpolitik geführt.'[23]

In part, of course, this lack of co-ordination could be ascribed to the absence of appropriate consultation procedures since the arrangements for meeting at regular intervals were ill-suited to crisis situations. However, the Council resolution of 21 March 1972 provided that special sessions of the Council could be called in the event of any member state contemplating measures that would entail a departure from the guidelines laid down by the

Council[24]. As in the case of budgetary policy, the conclusion must be that although a framework had been created in which the member states could have concerted their actions, they continued to decide unilaterally on the courses they would follow without consulting the other Community countries.

Even in the field of exchange rate policy, where the member states were committed to acting in concert as a result of the initiatives in exchange rate concertation as well as the efforts on the policy co-ordination front, the key decisions – to revalue, devalue or float – were invariably made independently by national authorities, with the Community being, at best, informed after the fact. There was, of course, a premium on rapid and decisive action, but it would be difficult to argue that time constraints precluded consultations, for at least as early as 1972 all the Community central banks were linked by a special telecommunication network installed in connection with the multilateral intervention system. It was rather the absence of the political will to conduct exchange rate policies in concert which lay at the root of this lack of co-ordination. This attitude was clearly revealed in the refusal of the Nine to commit themselves, as part of the transition to the second stage, to obtaining the written opinion of the Council or the Monetary Committee in advance of any major changes of exchange rate policy. Because the Council had laid down on 8 May 1964 that consultations were to be held 'préalablement à toute modification de la parité de change de la monnaie d'un ou de plusieurs États membres'[25], it would be an understatement to say that the efforts to foster policy co-ordination had produced very little progress in the exchange rate field. Nor had the Community advanced any further in terms of co-ordinating exchange control, interest rate or indeed monetary policies as a whole, as became obvious in previous chapters.

Under such circumstances, it is evident that the political will to co-ordinate economic policies simply did not exist. The consultative procedures instituted by the Community were, therefore, a hollow achievement. The Council did meet three times a year at more or less the prescribed times to examine the economic situation, and guidelines were laid down. But the critical policy decisions were still made unilaterally on the basis of individual national interests. That the new procedures failed to result in the common formulation of economic policies was not due to any inherent defects, for the consultative arrangements could have worked had there been, for instance, relatively small changes in the schedule of budgetary preparation; this had actually been envisaged in the Council resolution of 22 March 1971 which specified that the member states were to 'rapprocher les calendriers des procédures budgétaires nationales'[26]. The problem was rather that co-ordination by its very nature could not be brought about by legislation. Even had the consultative process preceded the making of policy decisions, there still would have been no guarantee that co-ordination would have resulted, for the concertation of economic policies would have occurred only if the

Community countries had manifested the political will to do so. That national strategies were determined before consultation took place or indeed without them demonstrated clearly that the member states lacked this commitment to policy co-ordination and that the procedures introduced during the first stage had not resulted in progress on this front of economic and monetary unification.

Harmonization of economic goals

That the member states lacked the political will to co-ordinate their economic policies was also demonstrated by the failure of the attempt at formulating a common set of economic objectives. Here too, the proposals advanced by the Commission were approved by the Council and duly implemented by the Community countries, and here too, these instituted a process that could have led to policy co-ordination. Yet, once again, the initiatives failed to produce any real progress on this front of the EMU Project because governments continued to make decisions unilaterally and on the basis of their individual and dissimilar national interests.

Initiatives aimed at harmonizing economic goals, in contrast to measures to strengthen consultative procedures, were not contained in the Werner Plan or the Council resolution of 22 March 1971 primarily because the Community was already making efforts in this direction. Ever since 1964 the member states had been trying to formulate common objectives in the context of preparing medium-term plans. Since the Community had opted to work within the existing institutional framework, the focus of endeavours in this aspect of policy co-ordination was the medium-term planning system. Even though, strictly speaking, this was not part of the EMU Project, the formulation of a common set of objectives for the medium-term plan was, therefore, regarded as an integral part of the efforts to foster common policy-making, especially as the Community guidelines discussed earlier were to be based on these targets.

As it happened, the Third Medium-Term Plan, covering the period 1970–75, was being prepared at precisely the time that the Werner Report was being drafted, and, in fact, the plan was approved on 9 February 1970 at the same Council session that agreed in principle on the set of initiatives to be taken during the first stage. This fortuitous conjunction of events offered the member states the chance to demonstrate their commitment to economic policy co-ordination at the moment they were formally embarking on the road to economic and monetary union. Yet the Third Medium-Term Plan remained, like its predecessors, a mere recapitulation of the goals national governments had already set for themselves independently. As *Table 8.2* shows, the third plan's objectives for the Community were essentially a

Table 8.2 *Medium-term economic targets 1970/75: National objectives and Community goals compared*

	Target (per cent per annum)					
	Germany	France	Italy	Netherlands	Belgium	Luxembourg
Real increase in GNP						
National targets	4.5	5.6	6.0	4.7	4.8	3.5
Community targets	4.3–4.8	5.4–5.9	5.7–6.2	4.5–5.0	4.3–4.8	3.0–3.5
Consumer price index						
National targets	1.9	2.8	2.5	3.3	3.7	2.5
Community targets	1.2–1.8	2.5–3.0	2.5–3.0	2.8–3.5	2.8–3.3	2.3–2.8
Unemployment in 1975						
National targets	0.7	1.3	2.7	1.3	1.5	0
Community targets	0.8	1.5	3.0	1.3	1.7	nil
Current account surplus as percentage of GNP						
National targets	0.2	0.1	0.8	0.8	0.1	0
Community targets	0.2	0.1	0.8	0.8	0.1	0

Source: 'Troisième programme de politique économique à moyen terme'. *Journal officiel*, XIV(L19) (1 March 1971).

juxtaposition of national targets, even though these divergent national policy orientations were incompatible with the avowed intent of fostering a convergence of the six economies. Quite clearly the national governments were unwilling to compromise on the targets they had set for their countries.

Moreover, although the plan approved by the Council was essentially a verbatim restatement of national targets, even this did not ensure that it was respected. On the contrary, for none of the five years covered by the plan did the official targets for the rise in consumer prices in the French and German annual economic reports ever fall within the specified range, and actual performance diverged from the guidelines even more. As *Table 8.3* shows, the record was little better in terms of unemployment, with France never meeting its target and Germany only in 1971. Indeed with just one or two exceptions, the objectives of the German government, which because of its strong commitment to economic policy co-ordination would have been expected to make a considerable effort to conform to the plan, deviated significantly from the plan's targets for real growth, unemployment and current account surplus as well as price increases throughout this period. Of course, the increasing divergence over time from the course laid down in the plan could partly be attributed to changes in economic conditions that could not have been foreseen in 1971, notably the oil crisis. Yet national targets moved further away not only from those specified in the plan but also from each other, and

Table 8.3 *Comparison of French and German annual economic targets and performance*

		1968	1969	1970	1971	1972	1973	1974*	Targets contained in third medium-term plan
Real increase in GDP									
France:	Targets	5	7.1	4.0	5.7	5.2	5.8	5.5	5.4–5.9
	Performance	3.4	8.6	6.2	5.6	5.6	6.6	4.7	
Germany:	Targets	4.0	4.5	4–5	3–4	2–3	4–5	0–2	4.3–4.8
	Performance	6.8	8.2	5.9	2.6	3.0	5.5	0.5	
Increase in consumer prices									
France:	Targets	3	4	4.9	3.7	4.3	5.6	7.2	2.5–3.0
	Performance	4.9	6.9	5.5	5.6	5.9	7.2	14	
Germany:	Targets	2.5	2	3	3	4.5	5.5–6	8–9	1.2–1.8
	Performance	2.0	2.5	3.6	5.2	5.7	7.2	7.0	
Unemployment									
France:	Targets	na	na	na	na	na	na	na	1.5
	Performance	1.7	1.8	1.6	2.0	2.2	1.9	na	
Germany:	Targets	1.4	1.0	1–	1–	1+	1–	~2	0.8
	Performance	1.5	0.8	0.7	0.8	1.1	1.2	3.5	
Current account surplus as percentage of GNP									
France:**	Targets	na	na	1	1	0.5	1	0.5	0.1
	Performance	±0	±0	0.5	0.5	1	1	−1.5	
Germany:	Targets	2.8	2	1.5–2	1.5–2	1.5–2	1.5	1.5–2	0.2
	Performance	3.4	2.4	1.6	1.5	1.7	2.9	2.4	

* For France, pre-oil crisis targets
** Surplus on goods and services account
Sources: Jahreswirtschaftsbericht der Bundesregierung, 'Le rapport économique et financier'

this reflected the dissimilar priorities accorded to basic economic goals by individual governments.

The basic problem was 'dass die Länder in den Grundfragen der Wirtschaftspolitik, die den Rang der wichtigsten Ziele betreffen, nicht übereinstimmen'[27]. If in 1970 the differences in national price stability objectives were cause for concern, as

'ce sont en effet des écarts de cet ordre, se traduisant par une différence de 5 à 10% sue une période de cinq ans, qui ont largement contribué à la détérioration des équilibres extérieures at aux perturbations monétaires récentes'[28],

by 1974 the situation had become much more serious as the rate of price increases in France had become significantly 'supérieures à celles des Pays-Bas, des États-Unis et surtout de l'Allemagne, notre principal partenaire commercial. Un tel décalage-il y a près de 8 points d'écart entre les deux pays-ne peut se prolonger sans danger'[29], not only for the French economy but also for stable exchange rates within the Community. Yet, as is evident from a glance at *Table 8.3*, the targets set by the Governments in the two most economically important countries in the Community continued to diverge throughout the first stage. Quite simply, the member states were not prepared to compromise in order to achieve a single Community set of objectives. The exercise in medium-term planning had, in other words, failed to result in progress in economic policy co-ordination.

The Community itself tacitly concurred in this verdict by changing its approach. Instead of working through medium-term planning, which dealt with all four basic economic objectives, the Council decided to concentrate on only one, namely price stability, and at its meeting of 26 June 1972 launched a new initiative calling on the member states to take co-ordinated action with the aim of reducing the rate of inflation to 3.5% by the end of 1973[30]. Inflation had become an international phenomenon in the early 1970s in part as a result of simultaneous boom conditions throughout the world and increases in the cost of raw materials. All six Governments had come to regard it as the major economic challenge facing the Community, and since it was recognized that collective action was required to deal effectively with this problem, discussions of how to bring the upward price spiral under control came to dominate the sessions of the Council devoted to economic affairs. There was also a political motivation for mounting a campaign at the Community level against inflation: such concerted action would constitute a step towards the Stabilitätsgemeinschaft envisaged by the German Government, counterbalancing the initiatives on the monetary front and specifically the creation of Fécom. The agreement that the restoration of price stability was to be the paramount objective of the member states in economic affairs and that the ministers were to decide on 'gezielte Massnahmen auf den verschiedenen Gebieten ... die sich für eine wirksame und realistische kurzfristige Aktion zur Erreichung dieser Ziele eignen'[31], was therefore an important element in the compromise reached at the Paris Summit of October 1972.

Disagreements, primarily over the target rate of inflation, prevented the Council from meeting the deadline of 31 October set by the Summit, but the resolution 'sur les actions à mener contre l'inflation' was approved on 5 December 1972[32]. Although largely a paraphrase of the second report on the economic situation in the Community, which the Council had ratified on 31 October, the resolution nevertheless was a significant new initiative in economic policy co-ordination. For the first time on this front of the EMU Project, a precise target had been set and specific measures adopted to ensure that this was met. To be sure, the goal of reducing the increase in consumer prices to 4% for the period from December 1972 to the end of 1973 had already been in the October report on the economic situation, but it had taken the form of a guideline for the member states, not a formal commitment by the Council[33]. Moreover, the resolution imposed clear obligations on the Community countries, since it specified that the rate of growth in the broadly defined money supply, M_3, was to be brought down by the end of 1974 to the rate of real growth in GDP plus the target rate of inflation and that the rate of increase in government spending was to be limited to the rate of nominal growth in GNP. Admittedly there were exceptions for countries experiencing particularly severe unemployment, but these were explicitly described. Furthermore, even though the introduction of price surveillance and a system of employment offices might only be recommended, not required, and even though the national monetary authorities might already have had the authority to set discount rates and quotas, conduct open market operations, impose reserve requirements on bank liabilities and credits and control the international movement of capital by the means outlined in the Council decision of 21 March 1972, the significance of these provisions was that they specified policy instruments the member states could use in order to meet the inflation target. Thus setting a quantitative target the resolution both constituted a step forward in achieving a common set of objectives and also gave a sharp focus and direction to the consultations among the member states.

The target of reducing inflation to 4% provided an unambiguous standard for evaluating the Community's success in implementing the resolution of 5 December 1972. As events turned out, it might have been better to have followed the earlier practice and avoided precise commitments, for by mid March 1973 it was clear that the Community could not possibly attain its objective[34]. To some extent, this failure was a result of problems inherent in setting quantitative goals, for the unforeseen intensification of inflationary pressures from abroad, especially in the form of rising raw material prices, severely handicapped the Community's efforts to reduce the rate of price increases. Yet there was another and more serious reason for the

Community's inability to meet its target: the member states did not take the actions prescribed in the resolution. As *Table 8.4* shows, government spending grew faster than the gross national product in half of the Community countries, and amongst those that managed to stay within these

Table 8.4 *Growth in the money supply, gross national product and government spending in Community countries, 1972–73*

		\multicolumn{5}{c}{Increase over previous year (per cent)}	
Year: Quarter:		1972 IV	1973 I	II	III	IV	1973 Full year
Belgium:	M$_2$	16.5	18.0	17.6	16.5	15.6	
	Real GNP	5.4					6.0
	Government spending						13.9
	Nominal GNP						13.1
Denmark★:	M$_2$	13.3	13.7	13.7	14.3	13.7	
	Real GNP	4.4					5.1
	Government spending						6.7
	Nominal GNP						15.9
Germany:	M$_2$	15.8	18.4	19.7	16.9	16.0	
	Real GNP	3.0	6.0	6.5	5.5	3.5	
	Government spending						9.6
	Nominal GNP						11.7
France:	M$_2$	19.2	15.9	15.7	13.4	13.4	
	Real GNP	5.5					6.1
	Government spending						13.5
	Nominal GNP						13.7
Ireland★:	M$_2$	17.8	22.1	22.3	22.6	25.7	
	Real GNP	3.0					7.0
	Government spending						23.5
	Nominal GNP						20.0
Italy:	M$_2$	18.2	18.6	19.4	21.0	21.0	
	Real GNP	3.2					5.7
	Government spending						36.0
	Nominal GNP						17.1
Netherlands:	M$_2$	11.9	15.5	16.3	16.7	20.7	
	Real GNP	4.7	4.7	4.6	4.5	4.5	
	Government spending						16.0
	Nominal GNP						13.3
United Kingdom★:	M$_2$	24.1	27.8	24.3	27.2	23.7	
	Real GNP	3.0	8.0	5.0	6.1	2.8	
	Government spending						12.5
	Nominal GNP						16.1

★ Budgetary year begins 1 April.
Sources: European Communities, Committee of Central Bank Governors, 'Report on the Development of the Money Supply in the EEC Member Countries' (Bastiaanse Group), 4 March 1974, and Jahresgutachten der Sachverstandigenrat

not very restrictive limits, public spending increased more rapidly than revenue in two states, Britain and France. In the words of the Sachverständigenrat, 'weder spiegeln die tatsächlichen öffentlichen Ausgaben in den Gemeinschaftsländern eine harmonisierte noch gar eine stabilisierungskonforme Entwicklung wider'[35]. The Community was even less successful in implementing its target for the growth of the money supply, for although the rate of monetary expansion did decrease in some countries, it remained far above the rate of growth in real GNP.

This was a serious setback for the EMU Project. Up to this point the member states had always scrupulously respected the letter of the agreements they had made, even if they had subsequently interpreted decisions in ways that completely vitiated their original intent. Although the precise wording of the anti-inflation resolution would have made such tactics more difficult, it did not preclude them. The prescribed limits of increase in both money supply and public spending, for example, were determined by the projected rate of growth in GNP, which according to the resolution, was to be based on 'des hypothèses budgétaires des États membres' and was therefore susceptible to manipulation by national governments[36]. That the Six did not fulfil their obligations was, therefore, a particularly damaging blow to the EMU Project, for as well as setting a dangerous precedent it indicated that they were not prepared to go out of their way to maintain at least the appearance of achieving agreed goals.

The danger for the Community system as a whole as well as for the EMU Project of the member states again failing to comply with the terms of a Council decision, together with the unpleasant experience with the December 1972 resolution ruled out another initiative having quantitative targets and precise obligations. Consequently, the resolution of 14 September 1973 on supplementary measures to fight inflation had as its objective simply to 'ralentir le hausse des prix', and committed the member states merely to pursuing policies 'de manière à obtenir d'ici la fin de l'année 1973, une réduction substantielle du rythme d'expansion de la masse monétaire' and to conducting budgetary policy in line with the rather ambiguous guideline that

> 'Le rythme de l'accroissement des dépenses prévu dans les projets de budget pour 1974 de tous les États membres doit être modéré. En règle générale, il doit être inférieur au taux d'augmentation actuellement prévisible pour 1973 par rapport à celui de l'année précédente. Dans les pays où les dépenses budgétaires ont augmenté au cours des deux dernières années moins rapidement que le produit national brut en valeur, il conviendra que l'accroissement de ces dépenses soit en tout état de cause inférieur à celui actuellement prévue pour le produit national brut en valeur en 1974.'[37]

While it may be overly critical to say that the resolution of 14 September 1973 was little more than a statement of good intentions, it clearly was a step backwards on the path to economic policy co-ordination. The Community had reverted to its previous strategy of employing vague formulas as means of achieving agreement and ensuring compliance among a group of states unable to overcome the fundamental differences separating them.

Neither the anti-inflation resolution of 5 December 1972 nor that of 14 September 1973 had succeeded in getting the Community countries to orient their economic policies towards achieving a common target. There were no further attempts during the first stage to foster economic policy co-ordination by trying to harmonize national policy goals, although as part of the transition to the second stage, the Commission proposed that the member states use the objectives laid down by the Council as guidelines in formulating national policies and that they prepare their five-year plans in conformance with the Community's medium-term plan[38]. Clearly, the Commission had reverted to its earlier strategy, but as before it did not prove possible to make any real progress along this path, for medium-term planning continued to consist of juxtaposing national goals. Despite the efforts made during the first stage, the member states had failed to achieve the political will to put the imperatives of the EMU Project ahead of their immediate national interests and this effectively doomed the attempt to establish a common set of objectives.

Harmonization of policy instruments

The third means by which the Community tried to foster economic policy co-ordination was by attempting to harmonize the policy instruments available to the authorities in each of the nine countries. Unlike the initiatives discussed in the two preceding sections, which were concerned with the process of policy-making, the steps taken in this area bore upon policy implementation and were intended to ensure that when the Community had progressed to the point of having a common set of policies, it would be technically able to apply these in a uniform manner so as to achieve a coherent approach throughout the Community. In other words, this group of initiatives was intended to foster common policy-making by facilitating the use of similar policy instruments in comparable situations.

The steps taken in policy tool harmonization were aimed at building a basic set of instruments common to all the member states, not at instituting a uniform set of instruments. Thus, as described earlier, the anti-inflation resolution of 5 December 1972 stipulated that governments and central banks throughout the Community were to have available certain instruments in budgetary and monetary policy, which the directive on stability, growth and full employment of 18 February 1974 extended to include tools for sterilizing budgetary surpluses as well as limited discretionary powers over taxation and public expenditure[39]. In neither case, however, was there any constraint on the other tools national authorities could have at their disposal or the way in which these were employed. Moreover, as the relevant authorities in each country almost without exception already possessed the instruments mentioned, these initiatives had virtually no practical effect.

The same assessment also applies to the Council directive of 21 March 1972 about regulating international capital flows which specified that the monetary authorities in each country were to have a basic set of instruments, such as exchange controls, available to them[40]. As was discussed in earlier chapters, the tools Community countries used to control capital movements did, in fact, become much more similar during the first stage, but this did not come about as a consequence of the Council directive. On the contrary, the directive reflected changes that had already taken place in response to the altered situations in which governments found themselves as a result of the increased international mobility of capital[41]. As in the case of the anti-inflation resolutions, the member states complied with the provisions of the Council decision in the field of policy instruments, but the result was not progress in harmonizing policy tools, much less an advance towards policy co-ordination.

The limits of co-ordination

The conclusion which emerges from the three preceding sections is that the initiatives in consultative procedures, goal harmonization and policy instrument harmonization did not bring about any real co-ordination of economic policies during the first stage. Consultative procedures were instituted, Community targets were laid down and a common set of basic policy tools was adopted. However, these failed to result in prior consultations, a common set of policy objectives or similar approaches to using policy instruments. Guidelines were regularly drawn up by the Council and from 1971 onwards national budgetary proposals usually mentioned these and invariably contained a statement that 'les recommendations . . . ont été respectées'[42] or 'diese Zielkombination . . . stimmt mit der wirtschaftspolitischen Zielrichtung der Europäischen Gemeinschaft . . . überein'[43]. Indeed, the Community suggestions were frequently implemented and on occasion even cited as a justification for a particularly unpopular policy. But in practical terms, the guidelines had little influence on the decisions made by national governments, for the Community targets were largely a reflection of the intentions of the member states: 'wie bisher spiegeln sich in den wirtschaftspolitischen Empfehlungen der europäischen Organe für die einzelnen Länder vornehmlich die jeweiligen nationalen Vorstellungen und Absichten wider.'[44]

In other words, the member states continued to make decisions principally on the basis of national interest rather than according to the dictates of economic and monetary unification. So long as the Community guidelines were compatible with the course charted by national governments, they were respected. However if they came into conflict with national policies, either because they had failed to evolve with the government's strategy or because they had never accurately reflected official intentions, the member states had no hesitation in disregarding them, as was demonstrated particularly strikingly in the debacle of the 5 December 1972 resolution on inflation.

> 'Zwar wurden, wie auch in früheren Jahren, gemainsame Richtlinien für die Expansion der öffentlichen Haushalte, jedenfalls was die zentralen Budgets angeht, beschlossen. Diese wurden aber bereits durch die Haushaltsansätze in den einzelnen Ländern nicht eingehalten und schliesslich durch die tatsächliche Entwicklung vollends überrollt.'[45]

Quite simply, the Nine would not accept constraints on their conduct of economic affairs. It was this lack of the political will to put economic and monetary unification ahead of short-term national interest that in the last analysis doomed the initiatives aimed at fostering economic policy co-ordination to failure.

Yet while the member states might not be willing to shift their course in economic affairs for the sake of economic and monetary unification, they were prepared to work together and even to modify their policies if this were perceived as promoting the national interest. The best example of this pragmatic co-ordination is the concertation of economic policies that occurred in the context of the snake. The maintenance of a stable set of exchange rates required that the monetary and more generally the economic policies of the participants be closely co-ordinated so as to prevent the emergence of strains and imbalances among them. The influence of the snake on the courses pursued by individual governments was clearly demonstrated in 1975, when 'das enge Kursband zwang die Zentralbanken der Mitgliedsländer zu einer gleichgerichteten monetären Politik, was freilich auch angesichts des Konjunkturgleichschritte nahelag'[46]. Countries where monetary conditions were comparatively relaxed, such as the Netherlands, experienced capital outflows, and

> 'Länder, die in ihren Bemühungen um Stabilität zurückblieben, mussten befürchten, mit dem Wechselkurs ihrer Währung an die untere Bandgrenze zu stossen. Zwar müssen solche Währungen dann gestützt werden. Wie das Beispiel Frankreichs im September zeigte, kann ein Land jedoch infolge des vereinbarten Saldenausgleichs sehr schnell einen erheblichen Anteil seiner Reserven einbüssen. Will es nicht abwerten, kann nur eine Anpassung in der monetären Restriktion verhindern, dass es zu viele Devisen verliert.'[47]

The conclusion was clear: so long as a state wished to participate in the snake system, it had to conduct its monetary and fiscal policies in harmony with those of the other participants.

But only for so long. If the authorities considered that the maintenance of a specific exchange rate and the policies it entailed were not, on balance, in the national interest, they could and indeed on numerous occasions did change them. Yet such was the attraction of membership in the snake that this was a far more potent force in harmonizing the economic policies of the Community countries during the first stage than the various initiatives specifically directed to this end. Whereas national governments generally refused to co-ordinate their economic policies in the interests of economic and monetary unification, certain of them were prepared, for limited periods of time, to act in concert in order to realize the benefits of stable exchange rates with some of their major trading partners.

In a curious way, the monetarist argument had rung true. The initiative in exchange rate concertation had, in fact, resulted in a certain co-ordination of economic policies among the participants. The scope for harmonizing policies within the snake was, however, very limited, for ultimately national governments retained the ability to choose the course they would follow. As long as economic conditions in the snake countries were similar and the policies pursued by their governments basically compatible, as in early 1973, the snake helped promote co-ordination. But when, as at the end of 1973, the courses charted in each member state began to diverge and a conflict arose between perceived national interests and the requirements of staying in the snake, the outcome was invariably the rejection of the exchange rate constraint and a breakdown of co-ordination.

The benefits of co-operation

The conclusion that emerges from the preceding sections is that despite the series of initiatives designed to promote economic policy co-ordination during the first stage, decisions in the field of economic affairs continued to be made independently by the individual Member States on the basis of their national interests. It is easy to presume from this that steps taken failed to result in any progress on this front. One of the principal points made earlier in this chapter, however, was that because of the very nature of policy co-ordination, the initiatives on this front could only indirectly contribute to the attainment of their ultimate objective by creating a favourable environment. In this respect, the measures adopted during the first stage and especially those dealing with consultative procedures did have a significant influence on the relationships among the member states at a practical level, for they required the member states to engage in a more and more intense process of communication. The increased flow of material among the Community countries benefited the authorities by enlarging the amount of information available to them in reaching decisions on matters of economic policy while at the same time the closer contacts instilled the habit of working together, which in the long term could prove one of the most powerful forces for policy co-ordination[48].

National authorities had of course long monitored developments, conditions, policies and likely prospects in foreign countries, particularly where these affected their own economy, in order to formulate policies more intelligently. In addition there had been a considerable interchange of information concerning economic affairs among the member states before the launching of the EMU Project, in the context of international organizations such as the OECD and the IMF as well as through the relevant Community structures, such as the Monetary Committee. However, it was only with the Council decision of 22 March 1971 to strengthen the co-ordination of short-term economic policy that discussions of economic affairs were instituted on a regular basis at the ministerial level. Perhaps more important, the need to draft detailed reports on the economic situation in the Community and to prepare guidelines for each of the member states required a much more intense interaction among national officials than had previously occurred. One of the principal consequences of this increased communication was that knowledge about economic conditions in other Community countries improved greatly. In addition to a greater flow of material, especially statistical, about the performance of individual economies, there was also a better understanding of the precise meaning and significance of the information supplied by each country. Discussions among national officials brought out the subtle but important differences in the definitions used in compiling statistics that persisted despite efforts at standardization, especially under the aegis of the Statistical Office of the European Communities. This exchange of information reached its highest level in the context of the snake system, for here the member states were engaged in an endeavour requiring that each at all times know the exchange rates, balance of payments positions and overall monetary conditions of all the other participants.

The exchange of factual material was, however, only one aspect of the improvement in communications. In their meetings, national officials discussed not only the present situation but also the directions in which individual economies seemed to be evolving, the problems facing specific member states, the efficacy of the policies being pursued, official thinking on the future course of events and the strategic options available to national governments. The governments of the member states were consequently able to make major policy decisions with the benefit of detailed knowledge about the actions their partners were planning to take, and equally to express their views on the policies other governments were pursuing or contemplating, although these admittedly had little influence.

The greater interchange of ideas that developed during the first stage was of less tangible benefit than the increased flow of factual information but it was of vital importance to economic and monetary integration in the longer term, for one of the major obstacles to economic policy co-ordination was the different conceptualization of economic reality held by each of the nine governments. Conceptions of the balance of payments – what it signified, what the objective should be, and what policy tools were appropriate in dealing with it – differed radically among the Nine; so did views on the significance of actions in the monetary field and by implication the role of monetary policy. Each country, in fact, had its own conceptual framework in which it considered economic issues, and while these theoretical constructs did indeed undergo substantial change in the course of the first stage (though more as a result of developments affecting national economies than of the EMU Project) they still constituted a most heterogeneous lot at the end of 1973[49]. If the initiatives in economic policy co-ordination served to clarify rather than change these differing national perspectives, this exchange of ideas nevertheless afforded national authorities the opportunity to profit from the experience of other countries. Given the structural dissimilarities between the nine economies, the lessons learned in one situation might not be directly applicable to another, but at least they identified potential dangers in a particular course of action, provided an idea of its effectiveness and suggested possible alternatives. In this way, national officials, exposed to the techniques and instruments used in other countries and able to discuss their functioning with the bodies directly concerned, were stimulated to apply methods used elsewhere to their own problems, albeit after modification[50].

Perhaps ultimately the most significant aspect of the increased communications engendered by the EMU Project was that the frequent meetings and hence the repeated contacts between national officials accustomed representatives of the Nine to working together in a Community framework. Although the consequences and importance of this greater interaction at a personal level among those responsible for the formulation of economic policy, whether as experts or ministers, are much more difficult to assess than that of the enhanced flow of information, it may well be the former that has the greater effect on economic and monetary integration. For it is only through a change in the attitudes of the nine governments that the political will indispensable to economic policy co-ordination will be achieved.

In view of what has just been said, it would be incorrect to conclude that nothing was accomplished on this front of the EMU Project during the first stage. Yet, in the last analysis, the verdict on the initiatives in this field must be that they failed. They failed to result in prior consultations, in a single, Community set of goals, or in a common set of instruments in the field of economic policy. More fundamentally, they failed to result in the co-ordination of economic policies at the Community level. That the steps taken during the first stage had not fostered the political will to place the cause of economic and monetary unification ahead of immediate national interests is a fatal indictment of the strategy employed. As in the exchange rate field, the Community had attempted to proceed towards economic and monetary union on the basis of the commitment made at the Hague, embodied in the Council resolution of 22 March 1971 and reaffirmed at the Paris Summit of 1972. Once again, this commitment had not proved strong enough to overcome the forces of national interest. As the first stage came to a close and the EMU Project was abandoned, the Community was compelled to acknowledge this fundamental reality and alter its strategy. Henceforth, progress on this front of economic and monetary integration would come, not by taking a series of steps laid down beforehand in a detailed plan, but through a pragmatic co-ordination of economic policies.

1 *Journal officiel des Communautés européenes* [hereafter cited as *Journal officiel*] XIV(C20), 27 March 1971, p.3
2 *Communication [de la Commission] au Conseil relative au bilan des progrès accomplis au cours de la première étape de l'Union économique et monétaire, à la répartition des compétences et des responsabilités entre les institutions de la Communauté et les États membres que nécessite le bon fonctionnement de l'Union économique et monétaire, et aux mesures à adopter au cours de la deuxième étape de cette union* [hereafter cited as *Commission communication of 30 April 1973*]. In *Bulletin* (of the European Communities) Supplement, May 1973, p.7
3 Roger Broad and R. J. Jarrett, *Community Europe Today*, Oswald Wolff, London, 1972, pp.157–159
4 *Commission communication of 30 April 1973*, p.7
5 *Journal officiel*, XVI(L194), 16 July 1973, pp.1–5
6 European Communities Commission, *Report of the Study Group 'Economic and Monetary Union 1980'*, esp. pp.34–35
7 *Journal officiel*, XVIII(L73), 21 March 1975, pp.1–7
8 'La loi de Finances poir 1974' in *Statistiques et Etudes Financières*, XXVI(310), October 1974, pp.198–199
9 Belgium, Ministère des Affaires Economiques, *l'Economie belge en 1968*, pp.211–216
10 Belgium, Ministère des Affaires Economiques, *Balans der Toepassing van de Expansiewetten* (Official document) 1970
11 See Chap. 2, pp.13–19 and Chap. 4, pp.62–70
12 On the institutional aspects of policy co-ordination, see William Wallace (rapporteur), 'The Administrative Implications of Economic and Monetary Union within the European Community', *Journal of Common Market Studies*, XII, 1974, pp.415–430 (A Federal Trust/ UACES Report)
13 See Chap. 4, pp.60–61 and pp.72–73
14 *Report to the Council and the Commission on the realization by stages of Economic and Monetary Union in the Community* [hereafter cited as the *Werner Report*]. In *Bulletin*, Supplement, November 1970, pp.17–18
15 European Communities, Monetary Committee, *La politique monétaire dans les pays de la CEE, passim*
16 *Journal officiel*, XIV(L73), 27 March 1971, p.14
17 *Werner Report*, p.17.
18 *Werner Report*, p.27
19 *Journal officiel*, XIV(L73), 27 March 1971, pp.12–13
20 *Werner Report*, p.16
21 European Communities Commission, *Economic Situation in the Community*, 1971 (3). (From 1971 onwards, this number contains the annual report on the economic situation in the Community adopted by the Council).
22 'Le rapport économique et financier' (du Projet de Loi de Finances pour 1970) [hereafter cited as 'Le rapport économique et financier'] in *Statistiques et Etudes Financières*, XXI(250), October 1969, pp.4–22
23 Germany, Sachverständigenrat zur Begutachtung der gesamtwirtschaftlichen Entwicklung, *Vollbeschäftigung für morgen*, (Jahresgutachten 1974/75) p.37

24 *Journal officiel*, XV(C38), 18 April 1972, p.3
25 *Journal officiel*, 77, 21 May 1964, p.1226
26 *Journal officiel*, XIV(C28), 27 March 1971, p.3
27 Germany, Sachverständigenrat zur Begutachtung der gesamtwirtschaftlichen Entwicklung, *Mut zur Stabilisierung*, (Jahresgutachten 1973/74), p.108
28 *Journal officiel*, XIV(L49), 1 March 1971, p.18 ('Troisième Programme de politique économique à moyen terme')
29 'Le rapport économique et financier', 1975 in *Statistiques et Etudes Financières*, XXVI(310), October 1974, p.28
30 European Communities Commission, *Sixth General Report on the Activities of the Communities*, 1972, p.106
31 *Schlüsserklarung der Konferenz der Staats-bzw. Regierungschefs der Uitgliedsländer der erweiterten Gemeinschaft vom 19, 20 und 21 Oktober 1972 in Paris*, in European Communities, Monetary Committee, *Kompendium von Gemeinschaftstexten in Bereich der Währungspolitik*, p.27
32 *Journal officiel*, XV(C133), 23 December 1972, pp.12–15
33 European Communities Commission, *Economic Situation in the Community*, 1972 (3)
34 European Communities Commission, *Mesures arrêtées à la mi-mars 1973 dans les pays membres en application de la résolution du Conseil du 5 décembre 1972 sur les actions à mener contre l'inflation*, (Document of the Commission II/167/73 undated) p.1
35 Germany, Sachverständigenrat zur Begutachtung der gesamtwirtschaftlichen Entwicklung, *Mut zur Stabilisierung*, (Jahresgutachten 1973/74) p.108
36 *Journal officiel*, XV(C133), 23 December 1972, p.13
37 *Journal officiel*, XVI(C75), 19 September 1973, pp.1–2
38 *Journal officiel*, XVII(L63), 5 March 1974, pp.17–20
39 See Chap. 8, pp.189–190
40 *Journal officiel*, XV(L91), 18 April 1972, p.13
41 See Chap. 5, pp.96–99
42 'Le rapport économique et financier', 1974, in *Statistiques et Etudes Financières*, XXV(298), October 1973, p.26
43 *Jahreswirtschaftsbericht 1973 der Bundesregierung*, p.4
44 Germany, Sachverständigenrat zur Begutachtung der gesamtwirtschaftlichen Entwicklung, *Vollbeschäftigung für morgen*, (Jahresgutachten 1974/75), p.37
45 Germany, Sachverständigenrat zur Begutachtung der gesamtwirtschaftlichen Entwicklung, *Mut zur Stabilisierung*, (Jahresgutachten 1973/74), p.108
46 Germany, Sachverständigenrat zur Begutachtung der gesamtwirtschaftlichen Entwicklung, *Mut zur Stabilisierung*, (Jahresgutachten 1973/74), p.141
47 Germany, Sachverständigenrat zur Begutachtung der gesamtwirtschaftlichen Entwicklung, *Mut zur Stabilisierung*, (Jahresgutachten 1973/74), p.141
48 Leon N. Lindberg and Stuart A. Scheingold, *Europe's Would-Be Policy*, Prentice Hall, Englewood Cliffs, 1970, pp.95–97, 119
49 See Chap. 5, esp. pp. 94–95
50 On the introduction of new techniques of official re-financing in France, see Banque de France, *Compte rendu*, (Exercice 1971), pp.36–42, and *Compte rendu*, (Exercice 1973), pp.53–63

CHAPTER NINE
Conclusions: European Integration and the EMU Project

Chapters 2–8 have traced the saga of the EMU Project over the six-year period from its origins in the monetary upheavals of 1968 to its abandonment in early 1974. They have described the motivations for this endeavour and discussed the formulation of this specific set of initiatives. They have analysed this attempt to forge a single economic unit out of the countries composing the European Community, assessed its achievements and examined its effects on the monetary relationships among the member states. The purpose of this chapter is not to restate these ideas but rather to draw together the various elements of the EMU Project and to suggest some conclusions at a more general level about the attempt to create an economic and monetary union, about the overall strategy that was chosen and about the larger process of European integration.

The results of the EMU Project

The point of departure in drawing conclusions from the experience of the EMU Project is, obviously, an assessment of the results of this endeavour. As has become evident in preceding chapters, the record of these three years has been checkered with advances in one area of economic and monetary integration being offset by stagnation or even regression in others. A system of mutual financial assistance was put in place, and the snake arrangements limited the exchange rate fluctuations among the currencies of certain member states. But the size of the funds available under the mutual aid mechanisms did not correspond to the needs that could develop in an international monetary crisis, and the snake system neither produced exchange rate stability nor included all the Community countries. Communication among national officials had been greatly improved but prior consultations, common objectives and a uniform set of instruments in the field of economic affairs had not been achieved. Progress had been made in harmonizing national standards and safety requirements for manufactured products and in removing the barriers to the free movement of labour within the Community. But trade was still hampered by customs formalities, VAT rebates and assessments and a host of other non-tariff barriers. The common market in agricultural products was obstructed by border taxes and rebates.

Intra-Community capital mobility was impaired by exchange controls which had been intensified during the first stage. And the ability to establish branches or even to provide services in other member states was limited as a result of the failure to formulate Community statutes governing companies, especially in the banking and insurance fields. Sizeable transfers among the member states had occurred, and a regional fund had, albeit after much delay, been established; but the Community was still far from having a single welfare function, and the resources of the regional fund were woefully inadequate.

As is evident from this cursory catalogue of achievements, the EMU Project was clearly not a total loss. The concrete accomplishments of the first stage and equally important the better understanding of the process of economic and monetary unification and what it entailed were very considerable attainments, of benefit to the Community as a whole and to the cause of economic and monetary integration. Yet in answer to the question whether, as a result of the numerous initiatives taken during this three-year period, the Community had moved any closer towards becoming an economic and monetary union, the response must be that it had not. As a committee of experts appointed by the Commission put it in assessing the results of the first stage,

> 'without denying certain progress of a technical nature, notably as regards co-operation between the central banks, the Group is of the opinion that the efforts undertaken since 1969 add up to a failure. The "snake" has exploded and the "narrowing of the margins of fluctuation" no longer exists except between those currencies which are more or less closely linked with the Deutsche Mark; the Monetary Cooperation Fund plays only a minor role in European monetary affairs.
>
> Europe is no nearer to EMU than in 1969. In fact if there has been any movement, it has been backward. The Europe of the 1960s represented a relatively harmonious economic and monetary entity which was undone in the course of recent years; national economic and monetary policies have never in 25 years been more discordant, more divergent, than they are today.'[1]

Exchange rates among Community currencies, even those inside the snake, fluctuated within much larger margins than in 1971; with parity changes more common and floating an official strategy for several currencies the Community was even further from fixed and immutable exchange rates than it had been when the EMU Project was launched. The establishment of the common market had not been completed; whatever advances had been made represented steps long overdue, not any progress beyond the Treaty of Rome. Interregional tansfers, in the sense of a systematic channelling of funds to the less prosperous or dynamic regions of the Community as opposed to compensating individual countries for the adverse effects of particular policies, had not been instituted. Economic policies were not co-ordinated; important decisions were still made on the basis of the individual and divergent interests of the member states. In short, on none of the four fronts of economic and monetary unification had the Community made any real progress. The EMU Project had failed.

The causes of failure

What had gone wrong? The answer to this question is of crucial importance, for it not only identifies the reasons why this attempt at economic and monetary unification failed but also illuminates the motives behind these efforts and the forces that frustrated them; moreover, in probing more deeply into the experience of this one project, one obtains valuable insights into the more general process of European integration. The preceding chapters have suggested two factors acting to prevent progress in economic and monetary unification. First, developments over which the Community countries had little control hindered advances during the first stage. The breakdown of the international monetary system deprived the Community of a framework of fixed and generally stable exchange rates within which to forge the tighter links among the currencies of the member states. The emergence of inflation as a global phenomenon and later the oil crisis presented national governments with problems unprecedented in the postwar period and consequently made it that much more difficult to bring about the co-ordination of economic policies. However – in the words once again of the Study Group –

> 'Like all crises, they could have been the occasion of progress, by provoking a crystallization of latent wills. Great things are almost always done in crises. Those of recent years could have been the occasion for a leap forward.'[2]

But instead of exploiting the opportunities for systems transformation[3], the member states elected to safeguard their immediate national interests, thereby in effect opting to abandon the EMU Project.

This lack of the political will to put economic and monetary unification ahead of short-term national interests was the second and decisive factor that prevented progress towards EMU. Time and time again, when the Community countries had to decide whether to take a specific step in the EMU Project, they chose not to do so. Quite simply, they did not have the determination to translate the commitments made at the Hague into action. It is now time to elucidate more precisely what this lack of political will means and why it doomed the EMU Project to failure. In order to do so, it is essential to examine the overall strategy the Community adopted in its attempt to create an economic and monetary union.

As Chapter 4 made clear, the commitment to economic and monetary unification made at the Hague and reaffirmed in the Council resolution of 22 March 1971 was seen as providing the motor force for this endeavour; the determination to achieve EMU was to be transformed into a series of specific steps in this direction *through national governments acting in their own interests*. The commitment to EMU was therefore vital not because it imposed definite obligations on the Community countries, for given the political realities it was patently unrealistic to compel the member states to act against their will, but because it was seen as an indication that governments perceived economic and monetary unification to be in their national interests. This point is vitally important for all too often some diffuse 'Community spirit' is regarded as the motor force behind European integration. While it is true that to a great extent progress in integration has come through the efforts of dedicated individuals, it must be remembered that, in the last analysis, their actions and those of national governments were largely motivated by the conviction that the construction of a united Europe was in the best interests of each country and the continent as a whole.

The commitment to EMU, however, was never as strong as it seemed. The declaration at the Hague was more a statement of intent than a formal undertaking; moreover, it reflected a consensus based on a very vague conception of economic and monetary union.

> '. . . the decision in 1969 to create an EMU in the course of the next 10 years [was made] without any precise idea of what was being undertaken. At government level, there was no analysis, even approximative, of the conditions to be fulfilled. It was just as if the governments had undertaken the enterprise in the naive belief that it was sufficient to decree the formation of an EMU for this to come about at the end of a few years, without great effort nor difficult and painful economic and political transformation.'[4]

Even the Council resolution of 22 March 1971, drafted with the benefit of the Werner Report's analysis, described the objective in decidedly imprecise terms.

Consequently the Community was trying to advance towards EMU on the basis of a commitment which was both diffuse and insubstantial. This undertaking ostensibly showed that economic and monetary unification coincided with national interests, but in fact, since national governments had not examined, much less promised to take, the actions that the achievement of EMU implied, it did not demonstrate anything of the kind. In fact, as Chapters 5–8 have made clear, the actions that were called for during the first stage were generally perceived as not being in the interests of the Community countries. The commitment to EMU thus proved to have no real foundation and was therefore not strong enough to serve as the basis for progress in this endeavour. It is in this sense that the Community lacked the political will to proceed in economic and monetary unification: national governments were just not sufficiently committed to EMU to take the practical steps required by the EMU Project.

This is the fundamental reason for the failure of the EMU Project. That the member states were not prepared to place the cause of economic and monetary unification ahead of their national interests is emphatically not a criticism of national governments. On the contrary, for them to have conducted economic affairs other than in line with what they perceived as the best interests of their country would have been a betrayal of the trust placed in them by the electorate. Admittedly, the national interest as perceived by the government may not necessarily represent the country's best interests, especially in the area of sovereignty, where the government has its own prerogatives to defend. However, sovereignty was not really an issue in terms of the initiatives during the first stage because neither in the exchange rate nor in the policy co-ordination fields would the steps that were contemplated have deprived national governments of final control over economic affairs. Nor should it be assumed that the national interest as seen by the government diverged from that perceived by the country as a whole in this area. Even though national autonomy in economic affairs was limited, a surrender of sovereignty would have entailed the loss of real powers at the national level that, given the differences in economic structures and objectives, certain nations would have regarded as contrary to their interests. And it would have been contrary to the Community's strategy for achieving EMU for the member states to put economic and monetary unification before their national interests. European integration was not an end in itself; it was a means to an end, namely the amelioration of the conditions of life for the peoples of Europe. The allegation that the EMU Project failed because the member states were lacking in 'Community Spirit'[5] is thus as specious as it is invidious.

In the last analysis, then, the EMU Project failed because economic and monetary integration was not seen as increasing the welfare of the member states. For progress to be made in this endeavour, each of the Community countries had to regard every step, together with any compensation that might be made, as making it better off in terms of its own welfare function based on its individual goals. This condition was not met. Governments did place a high value on exchange rate stability, but they were not prepared to defend established parities under all circumstances. On the contrary, exchange rate adjustments occurred on numerous occasions during the first stage because situations arose in which the authorities regarded this as having the smallest welfare costs of all the alternatives. Similarly, while national governments perceived the provision of financial assistance to other Community countries experiencing payments difficulties to be generally in their national interests, they were not prepared to go beyond the existing level of co-operation; specifically they were not willing to make funds available on an unlimited and/or unconditional basis. As to economic policy co-ordination, the idea of a common monetary policy had never attacted the Community countries. It had not been one of the factors motivating the EMU Project in 1969, and events over the next four years made it abundantly clear that the member states still did not regard it as being in their best interests, even though they recognized that, in spite of the new policy tools adopted in individual countries, they remained limited in their ability to control monetary conditions. In contrast, governments had been and remained keen to exert an influence on the policies of other member states, but few were prepared to accept the corresponding obligation to modify their policies in line with the wishes of other member states. Lastly, although the Community countries agreed that special assistance should be provided to areas adversely affected by measures intended to increase the welfare of the Community as a whole, they saw no welfare gain in instituting interregional transfers merely to reduce structural weaknesses and regional imbalances. In sum, then, contrary to what had been assumed in 1969, progress on the individual elements of economic and monetary unification had not coincided with the interests of the member states as perceived during the first stage.

Moreover, the experience of the first stage demonstrated that, for these four years at least, progress in economic and monetary integration had not been indispensable to safeguarding the Community achievements of the previous decade. Exchange rate movements had presented problems for the functioning of the Common Agricultural Policy, but new arangements, such as border taxes and their lineal descendants, MCAs, allowed it to keep operating, albeit in a much more complicated form which made an even greater mockery of the notion of a common market in farm products. Likewise, while fluctuating currency values had unquestionably made international trade more difficult, exporters and importers had learned to work under the new conditions, and intra-Community trade had continued to expand. Exchange rate movements and particularly the extension of capital controls had interfered with international investment flows, but the adoption of new techniques, such as matching currency assets and liabilities, allowed investors to operate under these conditions. Divergent trends in national economies had engendered strains within the Community, and had on occasion threatened the customs union itself, as when Italy instituted an import deposit system in early 1974[6]. Yet 'free' trade in goods and services, in the sense of the absence of tariff barriers, had survived the challenges, and indeed some advances had been made in liberalizing factor movements. In short, another assumption on which the EMU Project was based turned out to be unfounded.

A third assumption was shattered when it became clear that not only the individual elements of the EMU Project but also economic and monetary unification at the conceptual level was not perceived to be in the interests of the member states. The case, on economic grounds, for economic and monetary integration rested on the premise that it would increase efficiency in the utilization of resources, thereby raising output and increasing the Community's aggregate welfare. Yet factor mobility in the Community was low, and at least in the case of labour, government action could do little to improve the situation because the barriers were primarily cultural, linguistic and social. It was, therefore, questionable that progress in economic and monetary unification would lead to greater efficiency and hence to welfare gains; in other words, it was dubious that the Community constituted an optimal currency area[7]. Moreover the efforts of national governments to direct investment to economically backward areas rather than moving the available labour to job opportunities, for example, seemed to indicate that the member states did not necessarily perceive greater efficiency to be in their national interests; even though the increase in the market value of production might result in substantial welfare gains, the movement of resources from one sector or region to another that this required was regarded as having a social cost not infrequently perceived as outweighing the potential benefits. This had obvious consequences:

> 'It may be hypothesized . . . that this resistance [to the formation of a monetary union] is due to the fact that democratically elected governments reduce substantially their chances for re-election if they are unable to maintain full employment, while the diffuse gains in income associated with currency area formation have very little effect on the chances of re-election.'[8]

Contrary to what had been assumed in 1969, then, the generalized benefits of economic and monetary integration did not predominate over the specific and more immediate costs to particular sectors. Consequently, neither the individual elements of the EMU Project nor, more generally, the process of economic and monetary integration was regarded by the member states as being in their interests and they therefore lacked the political will to translate the commitments made at the Hague into action.

The divergence of national interests

The conclusion that the EMU Project failed in the last analysis because the commitment of the member states was never as strong as it appeared logically raises the question of why progress in economic and monetary unification was regarded as contrary to the interests of the Community countries. Without embarking on a detailed analysis of what and how each member state defined its national interest, it appears, nevertheless, possible to offer a few thoughts on this subject by drawing on the material that has been presented so far. And it seems valuable to do so, not only to provide further insight into the EMU Project but also to identify the areas in which changes will be required if the process of economic and monetary unification is to proceed in the Community.

From previous chapters it seems clear that the principal reason for the conflict *between* progress in economic and monetary unification and the perceived interests of the member states was differences *among* the perceived interests of the member states. In order to advance, the EMU Project required that the Community countries agree – on the steps that should be taken and the policies that were to be followed. However, throughout the first stage each government pursued an independent course in economic affairs, attempting to maximize its own national welfare. Since it was virtually inevitable that the courses charted by individual countries would differ, it was only to be expected that economic and monetary unificatioan would come into conflict with national interests. Of course differences in perceived national interests did not necessarily have to block progress in economic and monetary unification, for individual countries suffering welfare losses as a consequence of steps towards EMU could always be compensated. However, it was very questionable that any country would see itself benefiting sufficiently from economic and monetary unification to be prepared to make the necessary transfer payments. As the first stage repeatedly demonstrated, the sum of the perceived costs to individual countries of aligning national economic policies were greater than the perceived benefits. In other words, if divergent orientations independently maximized national welfare, it was dubious whether progress towards EMU would make most, let alone all, of the states concerned better off in terms of their individual welfare functions.

On the basis of the material that has been presented in previous chapters, there seem to be three main sets of factors that account for the divergence in the interests of member states. First, the ranking of fundamental economic goals differed among countries. All nine governments shared the traditional quartet of objectives – economic growth, full employment, price stability and external payments equilibrium – but their preference functions varied considerably so that under comparable circumstances their perception of the trade-offs and hence their priorities might be quite dissimilar. Germany, for example, placed a relatively greater importance on price stability than most of the other member states, invariably striving for lower rates of inflation than, say, France or Italy, all other things being equal. Naturally, because economic conditions varied both between countries and over time, the underlying value structure can be discerned only by making comparisons among national objectives in relative terms, taking into account the overall situation. That *Table 9.1* shows, for example, that the German goal for the rate of price increases was consistently though not significantly higher in absolute terms than the French for the years 1972–74 does not permit any

Table 9.1 Comparison of French and German official targets and performance

	Increase in consumer prices (per cent)			Increase in real GDP (per cent)			Unemployment (% of labour force)		
	1972	1973	1974*	1972	1973	1974*	1972	1973	1974*
Official targets									
France	4.3	5.6	7.2	5.2	5.8	5.5	n.a.	n.a.	n.a.
Germany	4.5	5.5–6	8–9	2–3	4–5	0–2	1+	1–	±2
Actual performance									
France	5.9	7.2	14	5.6	6.6	4.7	2.2	1.9	n.a.
Germany	5.7	7.2	7.0	3.0	5.5	0.5	1.1	1–2	3.5

* The French economic targets for 1974 are considerably more optimistic than the German in large part because *le rapport économique et financier* is published in October, and hence embodies projections based on assumptions made several months in advance. The German *Jahreswirtschaftsbericht*, in contrast, appears in January and in this case had been corrected to take account of the effects of the oil crisis.

Sources: *Le rapport économique et financier*, 1972–75
Jahreswirtschaftsbericht der Bundesregierung, 1972–75

meaningful inferences. When these figures are seen against the background of the corresponding growth and/or unemployment targets it is clear, however, that Germany did place a relatively greater importance on price stability than France, a view that seems to be confirmed by the actual performance of the two economies. Interestingly, this basic pattern does not appear to have changed in the aftermath of the oil crisis, though specific targets in each country were obviously modified.

While a detailed analysis of the reason for these differences in the ranking of economic objectives would be beyond the scope of this book, it nevertheless seems appropriate to make the obvious and important point that national preferences appear to be rooted at least in part in the historical experience of each country. It is generally accepted, for example, that the attitude towards price stability in Germany was conditioned by the experience of extremely severe inflation in the interwar and immediate postwar periods, which resulted in profound economic, political and social upheavals. Although the imprint of these incidents on national values lessened with the passage of time, the premium on stable prices resulted in an era of very low inflation in the 1950s, which in turn gave rise to expectations of price stability that are now a significant factor influencing popular attitudes and hence policy-making. France, in contrast, has experienced a greater or lesser amount of inflation for at least the past 50 years and has learned to live with, if not to accept, it. Indeed, until very recently, it was a key element in the financing of investment: the rise in prices (in conjunction with considerable printing of money) acted to redistribute income towards business and government and hence served as a substitute for higher taxes, lower public spending or other fiscal action[9, 10]. In fact, it was only with the opening of the French market to foreign competition, culminating in the realization of a full customs union on 1 July 1968, that the control of inflation became a priority objective of economic policy[11]. That national attitudes are founded on past experiences suggests that the ranking of fundamental economic goals changes only very gradually over time. By implication, then, the differences in emphasis between countries are a more or less stable element on the European scene acting to impede economic and monetary unification.

Structural differences among the economies of the Community countries were a second factor accounting for the divergences in national interests. By definition structural characteristics are relatively unchangeable in the short-term and hence these dissimilarities among countries were also an essentially constant factor in Community affairs during the first stage. Perhaps the most striking difference was the contrast in the rates of growth in the labour supply and real productivity in individual member states. Comparing once again the situations in France and Germany, *Table 9.2* shows that although productivity grew at approximately the same rates in these two countries over the period 1968–73, the increase in the total

Table 9.2 *Projected and actual rates of growth of the labour supply and of productivity in France and Germany, 1968–73*

Yearly rates of growth (per cent per annum)

	Official projections					Actual results				
	Labour supply	Employment	Av. no. hours worker	Real GDP man-hour	Real GDP		Labour supply	Employment	Av. no. hours worker	Real GDP man-hour	Real GDP
France										
1968	n.a.	n.a.	n.a.	n.a.	5			n.a.	n.a.	n.a.	5.4
1969	n.a.	n.a.	n.a.	4.7★	7.1			+1.7★	'slight'	5.5★	7.7
1970	+1.1★	−0.9★	4.1★	4			+2.0★	−1.1★	4.9★	6.0
1971	+1.4★	−1.0★	5.6★	5.7			+1.2★	−0.8★	5.5★	5.6
1972	+1.2★	−0.7★	5★	5.2			+1.3★	−0.9★	5.5★	5.6
1973	+1.4★	−0.7★	5.3★	5.8			+~2★	−0.9★	5.7★	6.2
Germany										
1968	−0.5	+0.1	−0.3	4.2	4.0	−0.3	+0.2	+0.1	7.1	7.4
1969	+0	+0.5	−0.5	4.5	4.5	+1.3	+1.6	−0.7	7.3	8.2
1970	+0.5	+0.5	−0.5	4.5	4.5	+1.3	+1.3	−0.2	4.8	5.9
1971	+0.5	+0.5	−0.5	3.5	3.5	+0	−0.0	−1.0	3.7	2.6
1972	−0.5	−1.0	−0.5	4	2.5	−0.6	−0.7	−0.7	4.4	3.0
1973	−0	±0	±0	4.5	4.5	n.a	+0.0	−0.6	6.0	5.5

★ Excludes agricultural sector.
Sources: 'Le rapport économique et financier' and 'Compte prévisionnel de l'année . . . et principles hypothèses économiques pour . . . ', 1968–73
Jahreswirtschaftsbericht . . . der Bundesregierung

number of hours worked in each economy differed significantly. Throughout this period the French domestic labour supply was growing about 1% per annum, as a consequence of the upsurge in births in the immediate postwar years and the increasing numbers of women seeking employment. In addition, approximately 4% of the agricultural workforce was leaving that sector each year[12]. In Germany, in contrast, the size of the domestic labour supply remained essentially static for the period 1968–73 because the modest growth in working-age population was offset by the longer duration of education and earlier retirement; moreover, the agricultural sector was releasing relatively few people since the migration off the farms was largely complete[13].

These structural differences had a significant influence on the orientation of national policies. In France, somewhere in the vicinity of 400 000 new jobs had to be created each year in order to absorb the growth in the labour force. Even though this 1½% increase in non-agricultural employment was offset to some extent by the decline in the average number of hours worked, just keeping the unemployment rate constant implied annual increases in real GNP of the order of 6%[14]. Because it was a basic tenet of French policy that the rate of economic expansion should be sufficient to keep unemployment to politically acceptable levels, it was clear that growth was given a higher priority than in Germany where a static labour force did not require any net creation of jobs. Indeed, because the average length of the work week declined, the total number of hours worked in the Federal Republic actually decreased. A lower rate of economic growth, nearer to 5 than 6%, was thus consistent with maintaining employment levels[15].

Four other structural differences mentioned in previous chapters also help to account for the divergences in national aims among the Community countries. First, the less advanced economies, with relatively old industrial plants and traditional patterns of sectoral activity as well as comparatively low levels of GNP per capita, have tended, as *Table 9.3* demonstrates, to have higher targets for economic growth. This pattern reflects not only their relatively greater potential for increasing output but also their need for a relatively rapid and sustained rate of economic expansion in order to stimulate the modernization of productive facilities and to shift resources into the more dynamic sectors[16]. Second, countries, such as the U.K., in which business or labour had a significant degree of market control and used this to maximize its earnings clearly were subject to added inflationary pressure on the cost side and achieved a lower level of price stability than would otherwise have been the case. These states could be expected to make relatively greater efforts to reduce inflation, but they would still most likely have to tolerate a higher rate of price increases, as well as poorer results in terms of other economic goals, than countries with a greater degree of competition. Third, countries in which the factors of production, particularly labour, were relatively immobile also tended to have greater pressure on

Table 9.3 *Per capita GNP compared with target and actual rates of growth in real GNP in Community countries*

	Belgium	Denmark	France	Germany	Ireland	Italy	Luxembourg	Netherlands	U.K.
	European Units of Account								
Per capita GNP (1970)	2625	3150	2800	3050	1325	1725	3250	2425	2175
	Per cent per annum								
Target rate of growth in real GNP 1970–75	4.8	n.a.	5.6	4.5	n.a.	6.0	3.5	4.7	n.a.
Actual rate of growth in real GNP 1960–70	4.7	5.3	5.8	4.9	n.a.	5.7	3.4	5.0	3.0
Actual rate of growth in real GNP 1968–73	5.3	4.7	5.9	5.3	4.9	4.6	5.5	5.3	2.9

Sources: 'Troisième Programme de Politique à Moyen Terme' Sachverständigenrat zur Begutachtung der gesamtwirtschaftlichen Entwicklung, *Krise der Marktwirtschaft* (Jahresgutachten 1975/76) their price level; this because they were likely to experience shortages and bottlenecks at lower levels of economic activity than countries where factors flowed freely between regions and sectors in response to the demand for them. Fourth, countries that were less vulnerable to the external payments constraint because of large reserves and/or easy access to international capital markets tended to take less drastic action in the event of a balance of payments deficit, the Netherlands in 1973 being a good example[17]. More fundamentally, the responsiveness of the balance of payments to policy actions obviously affected the severity of the measures adopted. Countries with, for example, comparatively low marginal propensities to import and comparatively low import and export demand elasticities had to take more stringent action to achieve a given improvement on the current account. These four factors, of course, could have and almost certainly did act to bring national interests closer together as well as to drive them further apart, but the essential point is that they introduced differences into what were perceived as the interests of the member states.

Dissimilarities in actual economic circumstances were a third set of factors accounting for the differences in the immediate aims of the member states. Countries in different phases of the economic cycle clearly had dissimilar orientations in their economic policies, since greater efforts were likely to be made in the area of economic growth in a period of recession than in a boom. However, these differences in national priorities did not reflect a fundamental divergence of interest. Consequently, while indisputably acting to make economic and monetary unification more difficult, the asynchronization of economic cycles in the Community was not a reason for the failure of the EMU Project in the same sense as dissimilar rankings of economic goals and structural differences.

The material presented in this book suggests, therefore, that the differences in national rankings of fundamental economic goals and in the structural attributes of individual economies were key causes of the divergence in the interests of the member states during the first stage. Because the conflict between individual national interests was itself the reason for the costs of economic and monetary unification being perceived to outweigh the benefits, it follows that for progress to be made towards EMU the differences among the member states must be reduced in such areas as the relative importance attached to the basic economic goals and the structural attributes of their economies.

The process of economic and monetary unification

Having examined the reasons for the failure of the EMU Project, it is now appropriate to make a few general comments on the process of economic and monetary integration which may help to put the material presented in the preceding chapters into perspective. Although the intent is not to suggest the steps that should be taken to work towards EMU, it is inevitable that in drawing conclusions from the experience of the EMU Project a number of inferences about the future course of economic and monetary unification will suggest themselves, and in this sense this section may provide some insight into the route the Community will have to follow if it is to achieve its ultimate goal.

The first and unquestionably the most important conclusion from the experience of the EMU Project is that progress in economic and monetary unification can be achieved only through the member states acting in their own national interests; this is simply a consequence of political realities in the Community. Since the experience of events over the period 1968–73 conclusively demonstrates that the Community countries did not regard progress in this endeavour to be in line with their individual interests, it follows that for the foreseeable future the efforts to create an economic and monetary union in the Community will most productively be directed towards changing the factors responsible for the conflict between perceived national interests and economic and monetary unification.

The crucial assumption, of course, is that the efforts in economic and monetary unification will continue. For this reason the second conclusion is extremely important: national governments continued to regard economic and monetary unification as desirable on political grounds. For the member states it was still an article of faith that European integration was in their national interests, and whatever the lessons of the first stage, they never wavered in their conviction that the creation of a united Europe should be their ultimate objective. It was the prospect of proceeding towards the political unification of the continent through the creation of a single economic unit which had, in the last analysis, been responsible for the birth of the EMU Project at the Hague Summit. That economic and monetary union still remained the goal of the Community in 1974, in spite of all the problems, setbacks and failures of the first stage, demonstrates the tremendous motive power of this political consideration.

While this political commitment provided the vital assurance that efforts in economic and monetary unification would continue, it would be a fundamental misperception to think that the perceived benefits in terms of European integration could offset the substantial practical economic costs associated with EMU. National governments make decisions on the basis of hard calculations of what is best for the country in the short-term, taking a perspective that rarely extends beyond the next election, at most five years distant. In this calculus a commitment to the long-term goal of a united Europe carries little weight. The logical implication of these two conclusions is that the Community can and should proceed by endeavouring to lessen the divergence in the interests of the member states, specifically by reducing the dissimilarities in the economic goals and structures of the nine countries.

This is clearly a long-term process. It requires many years to modify national attitudes, since this occurs only as new experiences are acquired and new generations replace the old. Altering birth or migration patterns, renewing the industrial plant or shifting the sectoral pattern of activity, changing the degree of market control exercised by business and labour, or reducing dependence on imported goods likewise cannot be accomplished overnight. Nothing less than a fundamental transformation of the economy, indeed of the society, is needed, and this simply cannot be achieved in a few years. The inference is clearly that an EMU Project that aims to achieve this final goal in 10 years is a nonsense; for real progress in economic and monetary unification to occur – let alone for EMU to be attained – would require a sustained effort over several decades.

Moreover many of the changes required cannot be brought about directly by government action, whether at the Community or the national level, because attitudes about the economic goals towards which a nation should strive or the use which should be made of a certain degree of market control are not particularly amenable to official influence in a free society. There are nevertheless a number of areas in which national governments can take steps to modify the structural attributes of their economies, and in many of these action is already being taken. These initiatives must, however, be seen in their proper perspective. They are not part of any grand design trying to work directly towards EMU; until the fundamental divergence in national interests is reduced, such efforts are doomed to failure. They are rather an attempt to do the limited amount possible to foster the long-term transformation that is required. Such an approach presupposes a strong commitment to economic and monetary unification over a period of many years and a preparedness to concentrate on the small and unimpressive steps that can be fruitfully taken at the outset.

Some of the steps that could be taken have been suggested earlier in this book. At the Community level, much still remains to be done to remove the barriers that, despite the Treaty of Rome, still impede the free movement of goods, services and factors of production. At the national level, the authorities could try to foster similar rankings of economic goals in the member states through the educational system, though the most powerful force would probably be the passage of time, as the historical experiences of the western European countries gradually grow together. This process might well be speeded by government action to encourage contacts among national officials, especially those concerned with policy-making, such as already are taking place in the context of Community institutions.

In terms of reducing the structural differences among the member states the scope for government action is clearly greater. Governments are already actively engaged in promoting and directing investment, in developing new technologies, in encouraging expansion into dynamic new fields, and in many other activities intended to modernize the economy by renewing the industrial plant and shifting patterns of sectoral activity. It should be borne in mind, however, that these efforts will make the nine economies more advanced, not necessarily more similar. Likewise, the authorities can take significant steps to harmonize the regulations governing monopolies, as they have started to do in the context of the Community's competition policy. Governments can and already are taking action to increase factor mobility, by such means as establishing national employment offices and special retraining facilities. Finally, countries relatively vulnerable to the external payments constraint can take steps to strengthen their position in international trade, such as diversifying into sectors with reasonably high demand elasticities or increasing their commercial representation abroad.

It is important to remember that even at this modest level progress in economic and monetary unification can be achieved only through the member states acting in their national interests. Fortunately, most of the specific steps that can be taken to promote the convergence of national interests incorporate clear welfare benefits, as is evidenced by the fact that national governments are already making efforts in many of these areas. For the beginning at least, the steps that can be productively taken appear to be largely on the front of completing the common market, specifically in the areas of liberalizing factor movements and harmonizing structural characteristics; ironically, initiatives in these fields generally had not been part of and had not been dealt with in the framework of the EMU Project. On the basis of past performance, it is to be expected that these efforts will remain peripheral to the Community's strategy for economic and monetary unification and will be undertaken primarily for the immediate welfare gains they offer, not because of their importance for the larger endeavour.

The concertation of exchange rates and the co-ordination of economic policies will, of course, remain the heart of economic and monetary unification. Little progress can be expected on either of these fronts under present conditions, but the member states have *de facto* decided to maintain a flexible form of co-operation. This will permit certain countries to maintain fixed but adjustable exchange rates among their currencies and allow a certain amount of policy co-ordination when this is felt to be appropriate. The nine Community countries have, in other words, opted to let their economic and monetary relationships develop on a pragmatic basis. Yet the ideal of EMU has not disappeared entirely. It is reasonable to expect that the Community will continue to reaffirm its commitment to EMU and will persist in making grand declarations of its intentions in this field. While such statements always carry the risk of undermining the Community's credibility, as long as the pitfalls of specific objectives are avoided these pronouncements may fulfil the useful function of keeping the ultimate goal in view and arousing support for efforts that at this stage would have a rather lackluster quality.

It is, in fact, vitally important for the goal of EMU to keep on being expressed, for there is no reason to believe the relationships among the member states will necessarily evolve in this direction on a pragmatic basis. In fact, the trend in recent years has been towards co-operation among groups of countries other than the nine member states, which has given rise to some concern that the Community might not be an appropriate unit for economic and monetary integration. These developments must be seen in their proper perspective. The co-operation taking place is no greater than had been achieved during the EMU Project and is unlikely to become so, especially in groupings that include non-members. Of course, it is conceivable that one tier of member states could proceed more rapidly in creating an economic and monetary union among themselves than the Community as a whole because the divergence of interests were less. However, any efforts to achieve faster progress towards EMU among a limited group of countries has, to date, always been regarded as a provisional arrangement until the time when all member states were prepared to participate. As long as the Community countries remain committed to the ideal of a united Europe, the basic thrust of all these efforts will be to work towards the economic and monetary unification of all the member states.

The process of European integration

The conclusions that have been drawn from the EMU Project have so far referred specifically to the process of economic and monetary unification. At this point, however, it seems appropriate to move to a higher level of generality and to focus on the insights that this material affords into the phenomenon of European integration. Many of the points made in this and previous chapters are directly relevant to the integration process in general, particularly those concerning consensus formation and decision-making in the Community. After all, the EMU Project is illustrative of one aspect of the process of European integration, and an understanding of economic and monetary unification enhances one's conception of this more general phenomenon. There are, however, a few conclusions that apply specifically to the process of European integration, and it is to these that we now turn.

The first and most obvious conclusion from the EMU Project is that setting a fixed objective and imposing a deadline do not in themselves constitute a sufficient basis for progress in European integration. The Community had used this approach with success in constructing the customs union and in setting up the Common Agricultural Policy, but it was not suited to a project as conceptually complex as economic and monetary unification. The crucial flaw in the EMU Project was that the commitment made by the heads of state was not based on a full understanding of the final goal, what it entailed or how it was to be achieved; when it came time for the official declarations to be translated into action, the member states found themselves called upon to take steps that turned out in general to conflict with their national interests. In creating a customs union the specific actions required had been clearly understood, but more and more the practical implications of the projects on which the Community is embarking are not immediately obvious. Moreover, although the imposition of deadlines can be useful in overcoming government inertia, putting pressure on the member states to take actions to which they were opposed can be a very dangerous tactic for an institution as vulnerable as the Community, as the experience of the anti-inflation resolution of 5 December 1972 demonstrated.

While the experience of the EMU Project shows that a commitment to a stated objective is not a sufficient basis for progress in European integration, it also demonstrates that it is essential for there to be a definite goal and for each step to be directed towards this final destination. If each specific action is not carefully assessed in terms of the ultimate objective as well as the proximate aim, initiatives can acquire a momentum of their own and cease to further their avowed aim, as in the case of the snake, or even come into conflict with the final goal, as in the case of the common policy on short-term capital movements which erected barriers to capital movements within the Community. This conclusion applies outside the field of economic affairs as well – agricultural policy being an obvious example. As the Community embarks on more complicated projects, it will be increasingly important that each new step be scrutinized to make certain that it does, in fact, contribute to progress towards the final goal of creating an economically and politically united Europe.

The third conclusion suggested by the EMU Project is that European integration has entered a phase in which progress will be achieved on a pragmatic basis. The use of detailed plans laying down in advance the steps to be taken has been abandoned, for as the first stage demonstrated, the actions that could be taken depended on the situation. Instead, the Community has *de facto* adopted a more flexible approach, responding to the opportunities and challenges in each set of circumstances. Already the Commission has become more adept in formulating its proposals to take advantage of the possibilities inherent in each situation, though too often it merely dusts off old ideas, as in the case of mutual assistance in the aftermath of the oil crisis. However in attempting to capitalize on the potential in each set of circumstances, the Community has routinely paid insufficient attention to ensuring that the initiatives furthered the underlying aim of economic and political unification. Maintaining a certain momentum in Community activity is, of course, an important consideration, but if progress in European integration is to be achieved, it is essential that a clear sense of direction be infused into all the initiatives that are taken.

Perhaps most important, the experience of the EMU Project suggests that the gradualist step-by-step approach used with great success in the first decade of the Community's existence is not suited to the projects that are currently being carried out. Many of the goals the Community has set itself entail a transfer of authority, and as the Werner Committee discovered, this cannot be achieved gradually or in stages. There may be many steps that can be taken to foster or promote a shift in the locus of decision-making, but in the last analysis, the transfer of control can occur only at one discrete point in time. The strategy of progressing through a series of stages worked in the case of creating a customs union, but only because the crucial transfer of authority has already taken place, since the Treaty of Rome vested control over tariffs in the Community. In most fields of Community activity today, however, the task is to bring about this cession of national authority. Progress in European integration will therefore depend on the success of practical initiatives in fostering the willingness of the member states to take the momentous step of transferring control over national affairs to Community institutions. The efforts required in the field of economic and monetary unification give some idea of the challenge facing the Community.

The transfer of authority that will be required if the ideal of a united Europe, to which all the member states are committed, is to be attained will come about only if the governments of the nine member states see this as being in their national interests. For this to be the case, the targets, aims and policies of the Community countries in the broadest sense will have to converge so that there is truly a commonality of goals and aspirations. There is little that official action can do to bring this about, but much that can be done to facilitate and encourage the necessary transformation of economic, political and social structures. Which initiatives will be feasible and productive will depend on the particular circumstances, and progress will therefore have to be achieved on a pragmatic basis. There will be little place for detailed plans or grand designs, but it will be essential that the final goal provide a sense of direction and that each step be an advance towards this objective. Such an undertaking will be long and arduous, but if the commitment to European integration proves equal to the test, it will eventually result in the community of nations which will make possible a truly united Europe.

1 European Communities, Commission, Report of the Study Group 'Economic and Monetary Union 1980', 1975, p.1
2 European Communities, Commission, Report of the Study Group 'Economic and Monetary Union 1980', 1975, p.4
3 Leon N. Lindberg, and Stuart A. Scheingold, Europe's Would-be Polity, Prentice-Hall, Englewood Cliffs, 1970, Chap. 4
4 European Communities, Commission, Report of the Study Group 'Economic and Monetary Union 1980', 1975, p.4
5 European Communities Commission, Erklärung zur Lage der Gemeinschaft, passim (Document of the Commission COM (74) 150 dated 31 January 1974)
6 European Communities Commission, Empfehlung gemäss Artikel 108 Ziffer 2 des Vertrags zwecks Billigung einer Richtlinie, mit der Italienischen Republik der gegenseitige Beistand eingeräumt wird, passim (Document of the Commission COM (74) 700 dated 7 May 1974)

7 Robert A. Mundell, 'The Theory of Optimum Currency Areas', *American Economic Review*, **LI**(4), 1961, pp.657–665
8 Herbert G. Grubel, 'The Theory of Optimal Regional Associations'. In H. G. Johnson and Alexander K. Swoboda, (eds.), *The Economics of Common Currencies*, Allen and Unwin, London, 1973, p.110
9 David S. Landes, *The Unbound Prometheus*, Cambridge, Cambridge University Press, 1969, pp.360–380, 404–419, and 490–498
10 France, Commissariat Général du Plan d'Equipement et de la Productivité, *Ve Plan 1966–1970: Rapport Général de la Commission de l'Economie Générale et du Financement*, pp.19–82
11 'Le rapport économique et financier' (du Project de Loi de Finances pour 1969) in *Statistiques et Etudes Financières*, **XX**(239), 1968, p.1167
12 OECD, *Economic Surveys, France*, Paris, 1972, pp.35–64
13 OECD, *Economic Surveys, Germany*, Paris, 1971, pp.33–43
14 France, Commissariat Général du Plan d'Equipement et de la Productivité, *VIe Plan de Développement économique et social*, pp.130–138
15 *Geschäftsbericht der Deutschen Bundesbank für das Jahr 1973*, pp.33–37
16 France, Commissariat Général du Plan d'Equipement et de la Productivité, *VIe Plan de Développement économique et social*, pp.63–68
17 Nederlandsche Bank, *Report for the Year 1973*, pp.68–70, 111–119

CHAPTER TEN

Economic and Monetary Integration after the EMU Project

The EMU Project came to an end with the failure to progress to the second stage and the departure of the franc from the snake in January 1974. The goal of achieving economic and monetary union in the Community remained, however. Efforts in this direction continued over the following years, but they assumed a different form; likewise the external environment changed profoundly in the aftermath of the oil crisis. Just as the sharp deterioration in national payments positions, domestic price stability, economic growth and unemployment caused governments to retreat into policies designed to safeguard their own national interests, so the demise of the EMU Project resulted in the abandonment of the strategy of proceeding through a series of initiatives carefully planned in advance. The different initiatives launched during the first stage remained, of course, but they took on a life of their own. The snake, or 'minisnake' as it was now colloquially called, continued to function, but merely as a grouping of currencies maintaining fixed exchange rates with each other. Likewise, the Community countries strengthened the mutual financial assistance systems, but these now existed without the direct linkage to economic and monetary union. Co-ordination of economic policies persisted and indeed was intensified; here too, however, the commitment to working together was absent: national self interest was the motivating factor, and indeed the participants were frequently not synonymous with the Community countries. Only in the field of facilitating the free interchange of goods and services did the member states continue to work together to advance the aims of the Treaty of Rome, and this activity had been going on long before the EMU Project was begun. In short, the member states found the procedures established during the first stage a useful framework in which to co-operate on these projects of mutual benefit, but these initiatives were no longer considered to be steps leading to economic and monetary unification. Whatever progress would occur, it would come on the basis of pragmatic advances, capitalizing on the opportunities inherent in new situations.

Exchange rate concertation after the departure of the franc

Nowhere is the change in character of the EMU initiatives clearer than in the exchange rate concertation system. With the departure of the French franc in January 1974, the snake, comprising the Belgian franc, the guilder, the

Danish kroner and the mark, had essentially become an enlarged DM-bloc. Although Germany did not dominate the snake, it certainly led it. This was clearly demonstrated in 1974, when the mark, as the strongest currency, led the snake on its upward path against the dollar in the first half of the year and, as the weakest currency, set the course in the decline during the second half. The modest net increase in the Federal Republic's reserves due to purchases and sales of foreign currency in connection with the exchange rate concertation system, totalling only DM 200 million in 1974 as compared with the DM 6800 in 1973, belies the strength of the mark's influence on other currencies in the snake. More revealing is the fact that U.A. 250 million worth of marks was required to keep the German currency within the 2¼% margins when the mark dragged the snake upwards and that purchases of a like magnitude were necessary during the subsequent downward movement[1]. Similarly, it was German policy, albeit representative of majority view, that set the tone of the exchange rate concertation system. Although unlimited support was available through the short-term monetary assistance system to enable countries to defend their currency against temporary speculative attacks, increases in unconditional assistance for longer periods of time were ruled out on the grounds that they would merely serve to delay necessary adjustments in exchange rates or domestic economic policies. Clearly implicit is the view, first formally enunciated in the Schiller Report, that exchange rate relationships could only be fixed permanently if there were real co-ordination of economic policies. Moreover the participants were opposed to relaxing the payments discipline within the system and indeed saw the snake as a step towards establishing a 'Community of (price) stability'.

Although the participants were keen for other member states to rejoin the snake, they were not prepared to make concessions on these points to facilitate the return of the French franc, lira or pound. Consequently, the French Government's proposals of establishing a loose link between the snake and the dollar, lengthening the settlements period and increasing credit facilities, relaxing the requirement that payments be made in the same mixture of assets as the debtor's reserves and changing the 2¼% band so that it represented the maximum distance between any one currency and the weighted average of the rest rather than the strongest/weakest one – which undeniably would have eased the constraints of the snake system – were rejected by the participants in the fall of 1974[2]. The effect of this decision was to delay the return of the franc by some nine months, something that would have been unthinkable as long as the snake remained a creature of the EMU Project.

Whatever its shortcomings as an instrument of economic and monetary integration, the snake did serve to further the national interests of the participants. The German authorities praised the snake system for protecting the country from unwanted inflows of foreign funds such as had disrupted the economy on previous occasions and for helping to promote equilibrium in the balance of payments. Admittedly, they had had to accept a 7% appreciation of the mark over the course of the year, but this was primarily the result of the strength of their currency, not the operation of the snake. Moreover, the mark's appreciation roughly corresponded to the relative price movements over the year, suggesting that it had not impaired the competitiveness of German exports. In contrast to the situation in 1971, export growth in 1974 remained strong, rising some 15% in volume over the previous year, although it did slow down in the second half in response to the weakening of economic activity overseas, and the trade account recorded a DM 56 000 million surplus[3].

Besides making monetary policy freer to respond to the needs of the domestic rather than the external situation, having the mark float together with the other snake currencies against third currencies had practical benefits in terms of price stability: not only did appreciation help restrain the rise in the costs of imports, but it helped dampen increases in the prices of domestic production and, indirectly, of labour. Furthermore, the rise in the value of the mark could be cited as evidence that Germany was doing its part to promote the adjustment in the international flow of goods and services necessitated by the oil crisis. Foreign governments might assert that the German authorities were making their task of achieving payments equilibrium more difficult by keeping demand in the Federal Republic at very moderate levels even after the steps taken in the fourth quarter to ease monetary controls and the enactment of a special DM 1730 million programme to stimulate employment plus a 7.5% grant for investments in plant and equipment made between 30 November 1974 and 1 July 1975. However, the appreciation of the mark could be cited as an attempt to reduce the payments surplus while internally it emphasized the authorities' determination not to allow an increase in inflation[4].

That the authorities did not take stronger steps to stimulate the economy did not mean that Germany was exempt from the high levels of unemployment afflicting other industrial countries. Gross national product expressed in terms of constant prices rose only ½% in 1974 and fell 3.2% the following year. Over one million persons, or almost 5% of the labour force, were out of work by early 1975, and certain groups, such as construction workers, were even more severely affected. In part, the eschewal of strong reflationary measures reflected the traditional preoccupation with price stability. Although the appreciation of the mark moderated the rise in the cost of imported raw materials, prices of industrial products rose 13½% in 1974, in large part in response to wage hikes of approximately the same magnitude. Only as export orders and private investment turned downward in second half 1974 did the decline in the level of economic activity exert a restraining influence on price increases[5].

Yet it was not just concern about inflation which limited reflationary moves. The Bundesbank maintained that stimulatory measures would at best have delayed the recession, citing the experience of other western countries as evidence for its assertion. The rise in oil prices had resulted in a massive shift of purchasing power towards the oil exporting countries, and each sector of the economy had to recognize that a transfer of goods and services was necessary and unavoidable. Attempting to compensate for the immediate effects of this change by taking expansionary actions would merely have encouraged business to pass on increased costs as well as increasing the import bill, thus deferring and possibly making the required adjustment more difficult. Moreover, at least half of the unemployment was due to structural factors, such as lack of skills or regional mobility, and long-term programmes were required to remedy this[6]. As it turned out, industrial product prices stabilized by the end of 1974, and the authorities were confident that the foundations had been laid for a sound and prolonged recovery in late 1975.

Although capital exports of almost DM 25 000 million in 1974 and more than DM 12 000 million in 1975, encouraged by the low rates of interest in the Federal Republic from the second half of 1974 on, acted to reduce the balance of payments surplus and helped restrain the mark's appreciation, Germany nevertheless set an ambitious standard for the other snake members in terms of the strength of its currency as well as the level of inflation. None of the other participants were able to equal its performance in price stability over this period, and except for Denmark, they all experienced a worsening in their current account positions between 1974 and 1975. In a number of cases, such as Denmark, maintenance of the snake parities compelled the Government to adopt stringent fiscal and monetary policies, as well as borrowing abroad on a sizeable scale. Nevertheless these small and open economies had no real alternative. Withdrawing from the exchange concertation system might ease the pressure on their currency, but it would give added impetus to domestic inflationary forces through a rise in import costs. Moreover, it was questionable whether a devaluation would bring about any real improvement in their balance of payments.

French national interests, in contrast, were perceived as being best served by remaining outside the snake because the obligations imposed were incompatible with the Government's short-term objectives. The franc's departure from the snake had been accompanied by a depreciation which had given French products a competitive advantage that had been the basis for a remarkable improvement in the balance of payments. Consequently, despite the undesirable effects on the price level, the authorities preferred to retain flexibility in setting their policies as opposed to accepting the conditions implicit in maintaining a fixed rate. Yet it nevertheless remained an avowed goal of French monetary policy to strengthen the franc so that it would be able to rejoin the snake *at its former parity*. In part this reflected political considerations at both national and international levels. Domestically, the return of the franc to its former parity would be seen as a sign that the Government's economic policies had succeeded and equally importantly as a manifestation of the nation's economic strength. Although 30 years of co-operation in Western European organizations had done much to soften the old Franco–German rivalry, there was nevertheless a certain feeling of national humiliation at the franc bowing before the mark, a disgrace which would be effaced by the resurgence of the franc. Internationally, the re-entry of the franc into the exchange rate concertation system would not only symbolically re-establish the franc amongst Europe's stronger currencies with the attendant prestige, but it would also counterbalance the influence of the mark within the snake.

That the return of the franc would bring the snake closer to being a Community institution was an incidental plus: it was most unrealistic to think this step might pave the way for the reintegration of the other Community currencies into the snake, for far from wanting to ease the discipline within the system it was precisely the rigors that attracted France. Interest in a looser, more flexible system of exchange rates was manifested only when the franc was in a period of weakness. With the robust franc that emerged in early 1975, the object could only be reintegration into the snake on the original terms. In the last analysis, however, it was economic logic which underlay the Government's determination to rejoin the snake. Just as concern lest the country's economic growth be sacrificed to maintain an unrealistic exchange rate had motivated the withdrawal of the franc on 21 January 1974 so concern about the costs of imports and hence the rate of inflation and the competitiveness of French exports was at the root of the desire to rejoin the snake[7].

What had happened between January 1974 and June 1975 to account for this complete reversal in the French government's policy on the snake was that the current account had moved dramatically from deficit into surplus, foreign currency reserves had increased and inflation had begun its descent from its post-oil crisis peak. In large part this represented the delayed effects of the restrictive fiscal and monetary policies adopted by the French authorities in 1973. In December of that year, tax payments had been advanced and credit growth subjected to severe limits. Interest rates had been further raised to ensure a positive differential with Eurodollars and credit growth had been held to 12% in early 1974 in response to speculation on the franc. At first, the high level of existing liquidity cushioned the private sector, but as these sources of capital were exhausted, funds for new investment and stockbuilding became scarce. At the same time the French economy also began to feel the effects of the worldwide slowdown in economic activity, with exports beginning to weaken in the fourth quarter, and private consumption turned downward in the last months of the year as inflation eroded disposable income. These trends were reinforced in June by sharp increases in the discount rate in response to the rapid fall in the value of the franc to 13% below the snake and by surcharges in income taxes – subsequently refundable in the case of individuals – contained in the July budget modifications[8].

Although the sharpest fall in economic activity and the most rapid rise in unemployment occurred in fourth quarter 1974, it was in 1975 that the effect of the Government's restrictive policies was most pronounced. Demand fell 4% in comparison with the previous year, and this figure understates the magnitude of the recession as a recovery set in in the latter part of the year. Exports stagnated; investment declined despite the reintroduction of accelerated depreciation, a 10% tax credit for orders placed between 1 May and 31 December and selective interest subsidies; and inventories continued to be trimmed in response to the lower levels of sales. Unemployment passed the one million mark in October, not including the significant numbers of early retirements or of workers kept on the payroll because of the costs of severance. In response to the worsening situation the Government shifted its budgetary stance during 1975 towards maintaining employment. FFr 6900 million was added to government expenditure in May, and in September FFr 15 900 million in tax concessions were approved for new construction or investment projects, plus FFr 5000 million in individual and FFr 9600 million in corporation tax reductions[9]. Reserve requirements on demand accounts were lowered from 17 to 2%, those on savings and term accounts having been suspended at the beginning of the year. The supplementary reserves imposed for exceeding the normative rate of increase in domestic lending were retained, but since the actual rate of growth at 9.8% was well below the official norm of 12% because of the sluggish demand for funds, these limits were not really a constraint on the availability of credit. Most visibly, with the franc strengthening, interest rates were allowed to decline from 11½% for one-month money in January to 6½% in December[10].

As a result of this loosening of monetary and fiscal policies, private consumption began to recover in the last months of 1975 and imports started to rise. Nevertheless, France recorded a FFr 4000 million trade surplus in 1975, a performance that is especially impressive when viewed against the FFr 21 000 million deficit of 1974. Part of the improvement was due to official efforts to boost sales abroad, such as FFr 4000 million in special credits available for export finance and exemption from the 18% cyclical tax for profits on exports. That exports rose only 2% for the year while imports fell 8% clearly indicate, however, that the major contribution had been made by the depressed level of domestic economic activity. Moreover, much of the FFr 17 200 million increase in reserves in 1975 reflected the efforts taken since January 1974 to strengthen the capital account: long-term capital inflows encouraged by the suspension of controls on non-residents' investments and the abolition of the two-tier market in France together with public sector borrowing in foreign capital markets, provided over FFr 9000 million in the two-year period 1974–75[11]. The clear implication was that despite the significant short-term accomplishments, France still had a considerable distance to go in developing the strong export base requisite to a sound balance of payments position in the long term.

An indispensable element in strengthening their export position, the French authorities recognized, was achieving a lasting reduction in the rate of inflation. The priority attached to restraining prices was manifest in the strategy adopted in early 1974. In addition to the restrictive fiscal and monetary policies which reduced demand pressures on the price level, the Government extended price controls to firms competing on international markets because the depreciation of the franc relaxed the discipline previously imposed by foreign producers, froze the price of all goods and services provided by the public sector except energy for the first quarter of 1974 and limited the increases to 5% for the second; and reduced the VAT on public transportation from 17.6 to 7%. Furthermore, in order to restrain wage increases, which were running in excess of 15%, a special tax was imposed on the growth in companies' turnover. However, as with the balance of payments, it was the recession rather than these official efforts that was the major factor in the subsequent decline in the rate of inflation. Despite the cost burden of underutilizing both plant and labour, producer prices began falling in second half 1974, followed in October by the first significant inflection in the retail price index in over a year. This trend continued in 1975, with the retail price index registering an increase of only 9.6% compared with over 15% in 1974. Producer prices, a more sensitive indicator of demand conditions, started to rise towards the middle of the year in response to the shift in government policy, but the increase was moderated by the franc's appreciation of on average 11% against the dollar, which helped hold down the cost of raw materials[13].

The marked improvement in the balance of payments and the encouraging signs on the inflation front engendered a return of confidence in the franc in early 1975. Starting the year some 5% below its former parity in the snake, the franc moved in parallel with the currencies of the joint float as they appreciated against the dollar during the first quartr. The franc, however, continued to climb upwards in April, and by May the gap between its actual value and the old snake parity was rapidly narrowing. On 9 May the Government decided, in principle, on the franc's return to the snake at its former parity and one week later the franc moved within the 2¼% band, marking its effective return after an absence of about 17 months. One month later, on 16 June, the franc's reintegration into the exchange rate concertation system was made official, with effect from 10 July. At the same time, the regulations within the snake were eased so that the settlement of intervention debts could be postponed three months.

The return of the franc to the snake was undeniably an important step forward in economic and monetary unification. That it was based on considerations of national economic and political interest rather than a commitment to European integration does not detract from its significance. Realistically, a convergence of national interests was a much firmer base on which to build than attachment to an abstract ideal. Yet it can be seriously questioned how similar the snake participants really were in terms of the strength of their currencies, the structure of their economies or their goals in economic affairs. The statements of the Governor of the Banque de France that only by achieving lasting control over inflation could a durable recovery be achieved could have been made by any of his colleagues in the Community, but even as the French Government was deciding on returning to the snake, it was adopting policies that, because of their effects on demand and prices, were incompatible with maintaining the fixed exchange rates within the joint float. As in previous occasions, when faced with trade-offs between employment and price stability, the French authorities consistently placed a lower priority on restraining inflation than the other major economic power in the snake, Germany. Already at the end of 1975 French industrial producer prices were rising at approximately 10%, more than 1½ times as fast as in the Federal Republic, and the comparison between consumer price indices was hardly more favourable to France[14]. Under these circumstances the renewed participation of the franc in the snake could only be a temporary phenomenon and its second withdrawal only a matter of time.

For the moment, French interests happened to coincide with membership in the joint float. The deflationary policies of 1973–74 had made it possible for the franc to return at its old parity without sacrificing growth or employment. True, the authorities carefully maintained interest rates above world levels for the remainder of 1975, but this was not out of line with their overall stance. Price stability remained an important object, especially as it became clear that depreciation was not necessarily a real solution to balance of payments deficits. Yet the inherent tension between the degree of price stability that participation in the snake demanded and that implicit in the expansionary course set by the French Government remained. At some point, the policies effectively imposed by membership in the snake were bound to become too unpalatable to continue and when this occurred, less than 10 months after the franc's return, it became obvious once again how fragile a basis for economic and monetary integration the fortuitous convergence of national interests really was.

The second departure of the franc

The inevitable happened on 15 March 1976 when the French Government withdrew for a second time from the snake system after an attack on the franc the previous week had caused a serious drain on the reserves. The franc

The second departure of the franc

rapidly declined 4–5% against the major currencies and fell a further 5–7% during the summer. Although the severe drought which affected much of the country was a key factor in the summer decline, a marked deterioration in the balance of payments was the primary factor underlying the franc's weakness. After being roughly in balance in 1975, the current account recorded a deficit of FFr 27 500 million in 1976, virtually all of which was attributable to a worsening of the trade account. Although higher oil prices added slightly more than FFr 5000 million to the import bill, the deterioration in the trade balance was mainly the result of the resurgence of domestic economic activity: while the terms of trade remained essentially unchanged, import volumes grew substantially. Larger amounts of oil purchased contributed some FFr 5000 million to the deficit, but the 19% growth in volume terms of non-oil imports added approximately FFr 30 000 million. Exports, in contrast, rose only 9% in real terms. As the Banque de France noted it was certainly normal 'que le redressement de la demande interne pèse sur le commerce extérieur. Le phénomène a été cependant beaucoup plus marqué que l'on ne l'avait généralement prévu'[15]. Even in an environment where the combined deficits of the OECD countries rose from $ 6500 million in 1975 to $ 24 000 million in 1976, the evolution in the French balance of payments attracted attention because of its sharpness and magnitude.

Although it is difficult to isolate all the factors responsible for the deterioration in the French balance of payments, it is clear that the relatively high rate of inflation in France was a key element. In contrast to Germany, where retail prices increased only 3.9% in 1976, the consumer price index in France rose 9.9% for the year as a whole, growing at an annual rate of over 11% in both the first and third quarters. Although the severe drought and the rise in commodity prices accompanying the upturn in world economic activity were significant factors, the fundamental cause was a sharp increase in wage costs, with hourly earnings growing by approximately 15% in 1976. The consequent decline in the competitiveness of French products was clearly reflected in the growth of France's trade deficit with its Community partners from FFr 4000 million in 1975 to FFr 18 000 million in 1976. The authorities recognized that 'la poursuite d'une inflation plus forte que chez nos principaux partenaires commerciaux risquait de déclencher un processus de dépréciation continue du taux de change . . . et rendait aléatoire la possibilité de rétablir . . . l'equilibre des paiements courants'[16], but nevertheless delayed taking effective action until September, when the economic recovery was well under way. Even then, the measures taken – freezing prices until the end of the year, reducing the rate of value added taxes on 1 January, and imposing temporary surcharges on personal and corporate income taxes – lacked the stringency that would have been required to achieve the same degree of price stability as that of the members of the snake. That the authorities set 12.5% as the target for the growth in the broadly defined money supply (M_2)* in 1977, a rate which would essentially acommodate the projected growth in nominal GNP, clearly reflected the orientation of French policy; by way of comparison, the Bundesbank was aiming at 8%[17]. Quite simply, the French Government was not prepared to adopt deflationary policies in order to maintain the value of the franc against the stronger currencies in the Community.

For the countries remaining in the snake, however, withdrawal was not a realistic alternative. Although the Benelux countries abolished the special 1½% limit on fluctuations in the Belgian franc–guilder rate, they and Denmark recognized that they were too small in economic terms for individual floating to be an attractive option, especially as Germany was their main trading partner[18]. Given the openness of their economies, they had to rely on domestic fiscal and monetary policies, not exchange rate adjustments, to foster equilibrium in their balance of payments. Germany, on the other hand, had strong incentives to remain in the snake, as this effectively expanded the 'domestic' market as well as demonstrating a commitment to economic and monetary union in the Community. Consequently, when the withdrawal of the franc led to pressure on parities within the snake, the Scandinavian and to a lesser extent the Benelux countries took action to support their currencies, notably by allowing monetary conditions to tighten with the outflows, and quelled the disturbance. And when despite their basically similar economic policies a second flurry of speculative activity, which sent several billion marks into the Federal Republic, drove home the fact that the economies of the snake countries had evolved in a way that made continued maintenance of the existing parities impractical, the participants manifested the determination to establish a new set of parities that would enable the snake system to keep functioning. Consequently, on 17 October 1976, the Finance Ministers and Central Bank Governors agreed in Frankfurt on a 2% revaluation of the mark against the European Monetary Unit of Account, together with 1% devaluations of the Norwegian and Swedish kroners and a 4% devaluation of the Danish kroner. For the mark this resulted in an effective appreciation of 2½% while the other snake currencies, including the Belgian franc and the Dutch guilder, whose official parities did not change, all depreciated on a trade-weighted basis. A further adjustment was made the following 4 April, when the Danish and Norwegian kroners were devalued an additional 3% and the Swedish kroner another 6% in response to continuing payment imbalances[19].

Two extremely significant conclusions can be drawn from this pattern of parity changes. First, even among countries with fundamentally similar economic structures and a fair degree of policy co-ordination, some measure of flexibility is required during at least the initial stages of exchange rate

---

* In France, this encompasses demand, time and savings deposits of non-banks with banks, the post office giro system, and the Treasury, as well as coin and currency in circulation.

concertation. Second, given that the participants share a commitment to the exchange rate system, it can be made to work, and indeed a surprising degree of exchange rate stability can be achieved: in the three years following the oil embargo of 1973 – a period of sizeable fluctuations in the currency markets – the five remaining members of the snake – Belgium, Denmark, Germany, Luxembourg and the Netherlands – succeeded in maintaining the values of their currencies within 2¼% of the parities set before the oil crisis. Even taking into account the adjustments made in 1973, 1976 and early 1977, the snake system had functioned for more than four years with the maximum movement between its participants being about 15% between the mark and the Danish kroner. Excluding Denmark, which joined the Community only in 1973, the maximum divergence, between the mark and the Belgian/Luxembourg franc shrinks to 7.5%, or less than 2% a year. Clearly the Community was a long way from attaining the fixed and immutable exchange rates called for in the Council resolution of 22 March 1971, but very slowly on a limited scale it was making progress along the lines envisaged six years earlier.

Community initiatives to mobilize national gold reserves

At the same time that it created new challenges and opportunities in the field of exchange rate concertation, the oil crisis also stimulated a series of initiatives on the other fronts of economic and monetary unification designed to facilitate the transformations in the flows of goods and resources the new environment required. These efforts were concentrated in essentially three areas: the role of monetary gold was redefined so that the reserve holdings of gold, sizeable for certain Community countries, could be mobilized for use in international payments; loans and other credit facilities of varying durations were created to permit the necessary adjustments to be carried out in an orderly manner; and principles of conduct in international economic affairs were agreed upon to prevent a series of competitive devaluations accompanied by discriminatory trade barriers. Although all of these issues were global in nature and hence had ultimately to be resolved through organizations such as the IMF, the Community played an important role, both as a means for the member states to present a united front and as a framework within which action could be taken when global solutions proved either unattainable or too slowly achieved.

The importance of mobiizing national gold reserves so that they would be available for use in international payments is evident from *Table 10.1*. Evaluated at the official rate of $ 42.44 per ounce, gold respresented over 25% of the total reserve assets of the Community countries, and for two of them, France and Italy, approximately half of their national reserves. In a situation where the OECD countries were faced with the prospect of a

Table 10.1 *Official reserves of the Community countries as of 31 December 1973*

	Gold*	SDRs	IMF position	Foreign currencies	Total
			Units of Account (Millions)		
Belgium	1 476	626	493	1 560	4 155
Denmark	64	119	119	719	1 021
France	3 532	73	377	3 088	7 070
Germany	4 116	1 388	1 207	21 510	28 221
Ireland	15	32	33	769	849
Italy	2 887	343	296	1 818	5 344
Netherlands	1 902	475	309	2 692	5 378
United Kingdom	735	600	116	3 917	5 368
Total	14 727	3 656	2 950	36 073	57 406

* Converted at the official rate of 1 unit of account = 0.88867088 grams of fine gold
Source: Committee of Governors of the Central Banks of the Member States of the European Economic Community, *Interim Report on the Commission's Proposals Concerning the Pooling of Reserves*: March 1974

$ 22 000 million current account deficit for 1974, re-establishing gold as a means of payment was regarded as vital, especially as the gold reserves tended to be concentrated in those countries with the greatest balance of payments difficulties. The problem was that the IMF rules prohibited the exchange of gold between central banks at rates above the official price of $ 42.44. Because the free market price was well in excess of $ 100, Gresham's Law had once again taken effect, and no significant settlements were made in gold after 1968.

In an attempt to make it practical for central banks to use gold in settling payments imbalances the Finance Ministers of the Community, meeting at Zeist in the Netherlands on 22 and 23 April 1974, called for central banks to be able to buy and sell gold at market related prices. Although there was little objection to sales of official gold at market prices, at least in principle, there were considerable differences of opinion within the Community, as well as outside, over official purchases of gold, for this raised the issue of the future role of gold in the international monetary system. Clearly the potential sellers of gold had a practical interest in foreign authorities buying gold so as to maintain a floor price. Moreover, this was consistent with their view of gold's role in the international monetary system. France, for example, had long asserted that gold should be the principal international reserve asset into which all other currencies were convertible, a system that would reduce the dollar's importance and impose 'discipline' on American economic policy. On the other hand, several member states not only objected to an obligation to buy gold in order to guarantee a minimum price but also opposed any net purchase of gold by monetary authorities because they felt gold no longer had a role to play in the international monetary system. To further complicate the situation, any mechanism for mobilizing gold reserves would have to be sanctioned by the IMF, especially since the bulk of gold sales would have to be to purchasers located outside the Community if this were to help finance the Nine's balance of payments deficits. Approval by the IMF, however, presupposed approval by the American authorities because an 80% majority would be required. The Zeist declaration got around the divisions among the Community countries and the problematic global environment by specifying that there should be no net increase in official gold holdings and by positioning the member states to move forward on two paths. The Nine would make a united demarche vis-à-vis the IMF while they would be prepared to move towards a 'European' solution should a global resolution prove impossible or unduly time-consuming.

The European proposal for allowing gold transactions at market-related prices was considered by the Committee of Twenty in June 1974. In its final report published in July, the committee recommended a reduction in the role of gold in the international monetary system. Although there was a consensus in favour of permitting official gold sales, the issues involved in the reform of the international monetary system were far too complex to allow a rapid decision to be made on amending the rules governing sales of gold. It was only in December at Fort-de-France, that the United States accepted in principle that central banks should be free to buy and sell gold at market prices, so long as there was no net increase in monetary holdings and it took the Interim Committee, which replaced the Committee of Twenty, until 31 August 1975 to recommend that the official gold price be abolished, that ⅙ of the IMF's gold holdings be returned to its members, that a further ⅙ be auctioned publicly with the proceeds going into a trust fund to benefit the less developed countries, and that there should be no increase in official gold stocks for at least two years. This set of proposals was formally approved by the IMF Governors in Kingston, Jamaica on 7–8 January 1976 and marked a major step in the demonetizing and, incidentally, mobilizing gold reserves[20].

While this slow progress was occurring at the international level, the Community countries had elaborated an interim solution based on the fact that although gold could not be exchanged at market rates, IMF regulations did not prohibit its being used at market rates as collateral for credits extended from one official institution to another. This idea was considered by the Group of Ten in June 1974 and was first put into practice on 5 September 1974, when the Bundesbank lent the Banca d'Italia $ 2000 million, secured by a deposit of 16 778 523.49 ounces of gold valued at just under $ 120/ounce[21]. Although the amount involved represented only a portion of Italy's financing requirements and although it was not followed by any similar transactions, it nevertheless set an important precedent and, by making it clear that gold reserves could in fact be mobilized at market rates, had the effect of psychologically bolstering the Italian reserve position.

Mutual financial assistance

The generally small size of national reserves even with the mobilization of gold holdings together with the need and desire to maintain a certain minimum level of international assets implied for most Community countries that the massive increases in the cost of imported oil would have to be financed by loans and credits from public and private sources until their economies adjusted to the changed economic situation. Although the balance of payments position of individual member states in the aftermath of the oil crisis differed considerably, there was general agreement that funds had to be made available to countries in balance of payments difficulties so that they could undertake the necessary adjustments in a gradual and controlled manner; after all, it was clearly in the interests of the surplus countries as well to avoid the breakdown in economic relations that sudden and drastic actions by countries in desperate situations would inevitably have entailed. The first step in providing international assistance came on 13 July when the IMF approved the first 'oil facility', designed to provide funds for up to seven years to help the less developed countries, which were hardest hit by the rise in oil prices. Intended to 'recycle' funds, the facility raised much of its money amongst the oil exporting countries; by the end of 1974, over $ 3000 million had flowed through this conduit. In mid September the IMF expanded its activities by making assistance available for up to eight years for countries with fundamental structural problems as well as oil-induced payments problems. Although Community countries did in fact receive substantial assistance from these facilities, there were strong political considerations militating in favour of mutual assistance at the Community level. Besides the obvious benefits in terms of strengthening the Community's identity, a new mutual assistance mechanism would help relieve the otherwise extensive demands of the member states on the IMF facilities upon which the less developed countries were dependent.

The need for a Community facility had already emerged from the Italian Government's request in early 1974 to draw upon the 1562.5 million unit of account credit line it had been granted in autumn 1973. Although there was some dispute whether the commitment had already expired, it was unthinkable on political grounds that the aid not be forthcoming, and on 18 March 1974 the full amount was made available for three months under the short-term financial support system[22]. Neither this nor the medium-term system was, however, really suited to the needs of the deficit countries, because they both were for limited periods of time and drew their resources from amongst the member states. The Community consequently moved to establish a new mechanism more appropriate to the situation.

Since it was expected that the Community as a whole would be in a balance of payments deficit, the Commission proposed on 16 September 1974 that the Community use its borrowing ability to raise funds externally which could then be on-lent to member states experiencing balance of payments difficulties as a result of the oil crisis, conditional on the borrowing country adopting a stabilization programme approved by the Council. Moving with surprising speed, the Council agreed in principle to this 'Community loan' on 18 November 1974. After resolving questions about the amount, duration and guarantee structure of the loan, the Council formally authorized on 17 February 1975, the raising of not more than $3000 million for not less than five years, with the member states provided guarantees for the same per cent as their quotas in the short-term financial assistance mechanism[23]. The Community loan was to be denominated in terms of the unit of account, which was itself in the process of being redefined because the move towards abolishing the official gold price made the existing definition rather anachronistic. That the Council approved on 18 March 1975 the Commission's proposal that the value of the unit of account used by the European Development Fund and the European Investment Bank be fixed in terms of a basket of currencies, such as the SDR, had therefore an important effect on the Community loan[24]. Because the loan was to be managed by the EIB, the Council's decision meant that the debt of borrowing countries would fluctuate in response to daily movements in intra-Community exchange rates, not just official revaluations and devaluations. This was a major departure in Community financial affairs, and as a result the 'Community loan' would operate more like a foreign currency borrowing with an exchange risk than the insulated type of financial transfers which occurred in the Community budget.

It was almost a year before the 'Community loan' system was actually put into operation. On 16 February 1976 the Council approved the Irish Government's request for $ 300 million and agreed to open negotiations on raising $ 1000 million for the Italian authorities. The terms of the $ 1300 million loan were formally approved on 15 March 1976, and the first funds raised under this mechanism were disbursed to these two countries the following month[25]. While the Community was creating this new mechanism it had been providing assistance to Italy by other means. The short-term support, first extended on 18 March and renewed on 18 June and 18 September for two further periods of three months, was replaced on 18 December 1975 by a 1159.2 million units of account loan for three and one-half years under the medium-term assistance system. As the United Kingdom was experiencing balance-of-payments difficulties at the time, it declined to participate and the credit consequently fell short of the 1562.5 million units of account that had been extended under the short-term monetary support system.

Italy was once again the recipient of funds from a Community loan in 1977. On 18 April the Council authorized the Commission to open negotiations on floating a $ 500 million loan, and on 17 May agreement was reached on borrowing two tranches of $ 200 million and $300 million for five years at 7½% and seven years at 7¾% respectively[26]. On 29 June, the member states agreed to test the capital markets with an issue of $ 100 million to re-finance the portion of the March 1976 loan coming due. Following the successful placement of this offering, the Council decided in January 1978 to authorize an additional $ 1000 million in borrowings to finance Community assistance to the member states.

While funds provided from the mutual assistance systems were an important symbol of Community solidarity and constituted a key element in the financial programmes of the deficit countries, the bulk of the credits received by the member states nevertheless came from other organizations. Besides the oil facility of the IMF, which furnished some $ 8000 million, the OECD countries created a $ 25 000 million support fund (Kissinger fund) to aid members in balance-of-payment difficulties, the Bank for International Settlements as on previous occasions made facilities available to the British authorities to cover any withdrawal in official sterling balances, and of course national governments made funds available on a bilateral basis. In addition to the $ 2000 million the Bundesbank lent to the Italian authorities, it provided $ 250 million to Portugal, which also received a further $ 250 million from the BIS. In June 1976 the BIS, the Group of Ten and Switzerland jointly extended a $ 5300 million line of credit to the British authorities. In December the German and American central banks made available an additional $ 350 million and $ 500 million respectively. This support was expanded the following month with the extension of a $ 3000 million line of credit from the Group of Ten central banks on top of almost $ 4000 million from the IMF[27]. Two conclusions clearly emerge from this pattern of assistance: first, the major economic powers were committed to providing the financial resources to permit deficit countries to adjust gradually to the changed environment and avoid sudden and disruptive effects on international trade, and second the Community played a significant role in this mutual support operation, but only as one of several conduits for assistance. Once again, member states made use of the Community system to carry out their national policies.

Initiatives to strengthen the international monetary system

With the example of the self-defeating competitive devaluations and trade restrictions of the interwar period in mind, the major western countries were determined to avoid a free-for-all in the aftermath of the oil crisis and instead foster an orderly adjustment process. The official statements of early 1974 promising to eschew beggar-my-neighbor policies were translated into deeds as well as words, for although there were significant exchange rate movements over the following two or three years, no country was accused of holding its currency down to unrealistic levels in order to boost sales abroad. Currency movements basically corresponded to balance-of-payments positions, and indeed the most marked depreciations, those of sterling and the lira, were resisted by the authorities. Undeniably, there were occasions when national reserves were allowed to grow more than was perhaps appropriate from an international point of view, but this reflected individual governments' concerns about maintaining sufficient reserves to ensure their ability to meet future import bills or official attachment to stable exchange rates rather than efforts to boost domestic employment. What is remarkable about the post-oil crisis international economy is not the intensified debate over policies pursued by other countries but the high degree of co-operation.

While the pragmatic approaches adopted worked well enough in practice, there was a desire on the part of many countries to come up with a set of formalized rules of conduct in international economic affairs. Ever since the gradual dissolution of the link between the dollar and gold in the 1960s, culminating in the official suspension of convertibility in 1971, international monetary relations had evolved away from the system envisioned at Bretton Woods. Conceived in the context of a system of fixed exchange rates, the IMF Articles of Agreement no longer provided a framework for national interaction in the world of floating exchange rates. The initiatives on the exchange rate front of the EMU Project were one attempt to come up with a new set of rules, but this was at best an incomplete solution. Efforts at the world level to reform the international monetary system had been underway for a number of years, but the knotty issues of reserve assets and adequacy, gold's future role, conversion of official dollar holdings, and appropriate exchange rate adjustment mechanisms evoked different responses from individual governments, giving rise to disagreements that impeded the formation of a concensus. Nevertheless, in a manifestation of the general disenchantment with freely floating exchange rates, especially in terms of the effects of sharp fluctuations on international trade, the heads of state of the major economic powers did agree at Rambouillet on 15–17 November 1975 to take concerted action to foster greater stability in exchange rates, particularly by conducting national economic policies so as to minimize strains at the international level[28].

As on previous occasions, it proved easier for the powers to agree on intervention policies than to co-ordinate their economic policies. At its meeting in Jamaica on 7–8 January 1976 the IMF took an important step forward in enunciating the principles to govern the international monetary system, approving an accord that enshrined fixed, but adjustable, exchange rates as the goal of the member countries. Recognizing that this would not be feasible for the present, the IMF formally endorsed the existing situation in which governments were free to maintain the fixed parity of their currencies or float them individually or jointly against other national monies. At some future date, however, the IMF would by an 85% majority decide to reinstitute the system of fixed but adjustable rates, and from that point on, individual currencies could float only if authorized by a similar majority[29].

At the regional level the European Community played an important role in combating the proliferation of trade barriers. When the Italian authorities introduced an import deposit scheme and other regulations designed to reduce imports in 1974 and again in 1976, these were attacked as contravening the provisions of the Treaty of Rome guaranteeing free trade among the member states. Although the Commission approved these actions retrospectively, it did so by classifying them as emergency measures taken by a country in a critical balance-of-payments situation, thus placing the burden on the Italian authorities to remove these barriers within six months[30]. Admittedly, there were complaints from certain member states, especially Germany whose beef exports were particularly severely affected, that the Commission had taken the expedient course of action and failed to confront the challenge to the principles of the Treaty of Rome. But realistically the Community could probably not have prevented the erection of trade barriers while it did help ensure their removal.

The Community played an even more important role in resisting the pressures for trade barriers in the steel industry. Because of over-investment in the late 1960s and early 1970s as well as the emergence of major new producers in the less developed world, the supply of steel far exceeded the demand in the years following the oil crisis. The natural consequences of this overcapacity were a series of price reductions that threatened to drive some major producers into bankruptcy. Because the steel sector was an important employer in certain regions of the Community – generally regions where unemployment was already high and alternate sources of work not available – and because it was also nationalized in certain countries, a scenario of rising national barriers to protect domestic producers was not difficult to envision. To prevent this, the Commission, using its extensive powers under the Treaty of Paris, acted to impose production quotas and rationalization programmes throughout the Community. Admittedly, the Community also had to limit steel imports from outside, especially from Japan, but once again the point is that the Community made a real contribution by creating an environment in which the necessary changes could be made in a logical and orderly manner, without the destructiveness of a proliferation of national trade barriers which might have set an unfortunate precedent for international trade.

The European monetary system

At the same time that the pragmatic co-ordination that had followed the departure of the franc from the snake in January 1974 was making a tangible contribution to exchange rate stability among its participants and the extension of the mutual aid system to include a 'Community loan' was providing member states with financing for their payments deficits, a series of reviews and reappraisals of the Community's strategy for European integration was beginning to bear fruit. Prompted by the failure of the EMU Project and the pervasive feeling of malaise and paralysis in the Community in 1974 this reassessment was resulting in proposals for the initiatives that the member states should take in the second half of the decade to re-vitalize the Community system. As in 1969, economic and monetary union was seen as a vital element in the efforts to construct a united Europe. The Tindemanns Report, commissioned at the Paris summit of December 1974 and completed about a year later, asserted that creating an economic and monetary union was an indispensable part of establishing a united Europe, although it recognized that for the time being differences among the member states ruled out common monetary or fiscal policies, 'doubtless because there is not sufficient mutual trust to permit the transfer to common controlling bodies of the powers which they would of necessity have to be given'[31]. Initiatives would therefore have to focus on making improvements to existing arrangements, such as the snake or the economic policy consultation procedures, rather than on introducing major innovations that would require the Community countries to make the 'qualitative leap' they were not yet prepared to take.

The first set of formal proposals for new steps in economic and monetary unification was submitted during the Dutch presidency of the Council in second half 1976. Known as the Duisenberg Plan after the Dutch finance minister, it called for the reintegration of countries not currently participating in the snake by establishing 'target zones' for their currencies in terms of the members of the joint float. National authorities would not be obligated to intervene on the exchange markets if their currency began to move away from the target zone, but they would be required to consult with the other Community countries and to forgo any policy measures that would lead to further divergence in intra-Community exchange rates. Resurrecting an idea first enunciated in the Barre Plan, the Duisenberg Plan also proposed that the mutual financial assistance systems be used to complement and reinforce the efforts on the exchange rate front. Funds would be available to help participants keep their currencies within the target zones, but this aid would be provided in tranches and be contingent on the country meeting certain conditions laid down by the Community authorities in advance, just as with the IMF[32].

Although reaction to the Duisenberg Plan was generally favourable, conditions were not yet propitious for a step in this direction. The departure of the franc from the snake for the second time was still a recent memory for the French authorities, and neither the British nor the Italian governments, both of which were trying to strengthen their balances of payments under the guidance of the IMF, were inclined to link their currencies, no matter how loosely, to the relatively 'strong' currencies of the snake. Moreover, exchange rates remained fairly stable for the first half of 1977; the decline of the dollar set in only in July. Consequently, the Council took no action on the Duisenberg Plan, merely referring it to the Monetary Committee and the Committee of Central Bank Governors for further study.

With the Community once again at a standstill in economic and monetary unification, at least in terms of formal initiatives, the Belgian Government tried to make use of its presidency of the Council in the second half of 1977 to infuse some new momentum. It proposed a doubling of the quotas and *rallonge* of the short-term financial support system as well as of the quotas of the medium-term monetary assistance system, as a first step towards providing the kind of support that would be required if the Duisenberg Plan, or something like it, were to be implemented. Because the principal aim of the Belgian proposals was to ensure that sufficient funds would be available to meet several simultaneous calls on the Community's resources, the maximum any individual country could borrow was increased by only 50% in the case of short-term support and limited to 50% of the total fund for medium-term assistance. Furthermore, as with the Duisenberg Plan, medium-term aid was to be granted on a conditional basis and in tranches so that the Community could ensure that the recipient was taking appropriate corrective action[33].

Because the proposals responded to an obvious need and were structured in a way that would not relax the discipline in the international monetary system, the only opposition arose because certain of the member states, such as the Netherlands, were against changing the quotas for the short-term financial support system before the five-year review scheduled for March 1979. In typical Community fashion, the Committee of Central Bank Governors, which was responsible for administering the short-term aid mechanism, approved the uncontroversial doubling of the *rallonge* from U.A. 1500 Million to U.A. 3000 million and on 13 December agreed to study further the issue of increasing the quotas. Six days later the Council, acting on the favourable opinion of the Monetary Committee, raised the quotas for the medium-term assistance system from U.A. 2725 million to U.A.5450 million[34].

At the same time that these practical steps were being taken, developments in several areas were moving the Community towards launching the first major initiative in economic and monetary unification since March 1973. Towards the end of 1977, Roy Jenkins, the President of the EEC Commission, delivered an important address in Florence, in which he called for a renewed commitment to EMU. Although the initial reaction was tepid and guarded, this bold and decisive step sowed an idea which fell on fertile ground, as the weakness of the dollar was once again disrupting monetary relationships among the member states. Between June and December 1977 the mark, which as usual was the currency most strongly affected, rose 11% against the dollar, placing a severe strain on exchange rates within the snake. Even with interest rate increases in Belgium and the Netherlands, sizeable interventions were required to keep the franc and the guilder inside their lower intervention limit vis-à-vis the mark. The Swedish kroner left the multilateral intervention system altogether on 28 August as Sweden was facing increasingly serious economic problems, and the Danish and Norwegian kroner, while continuing to participate, were both devalued by 5% on the same date[35, 36].

Perhaps even more important than the tensions inside the snake were the movements in intra-Community exchange rates involving countries floating their currencies independently. In the course of 1977, the French franc fell some 6% against the mark; the pound declined around 4%; and the Italian lira dropped by almost 15%. Even after allowing for the relatively higher rates of inflation prevailing in these three countries, this pattern of exchange rate movements clearly impaired the price competitiveness of the members of the joint float. Because exports were a key part of their economies, this was a cause of serious concern to their governments, especially as France, Italy and the United Kingdom were some of their principal foreign markets. It was this concern about the effects that exchange rate movements between currencies floating against each other could have on the economies of the snake participants, and particularly Germany, that was at the root of the proposals for a new initiative in monetary integration – the 'European Monetary System – advanced by Chancellor Schmidt at the Copenhagen Summit in April 1978.

Chancellor Schmidt's proposals were aimed at reintegrating the pound, Italian lira and French franc into the exchange rate concertation system by increasing the amount of mutual financial assistance available to participants. The German initiative called for the member states to pool 20% of their gold and dollar holdings in a reinvigorated European Monetary Co-operation Fund. As under the existing arrangements, the fund would credit the contributor's account in European units of account, but the individual countries would continue to bear the exchange risks on the assets they furnished. The fund's resources, projected to increase to roughly U.A. 50 000 million, would finance the short-term monetary support and the medium-term financial assistance systems, which would now finally be large enough to provide the aid that could be required by a country in balance-of-payments difficulty[37]. Interestingly, these proposals resembled very closely the ideas advanced several years earlier by the Commission and the French Government and rejected at that time by, among others, the

German authorities. Indeed, the same arguments were made as had been used previously by the 'monetarists' that usage of a European currency unit for settlements and lending in the context of the snake system as well as possibly for intervening on the exchange markets and holding reserves in the future would strengthen the Community's identity and provide a real alternative to the dollar in international finance.

Although Schmidt's proposals marked a significant departure from the German Government's position during the first stage, this was not the first time the Federal Republic had held out the prospect of very substantial financial assistance in exchange for a commitment to maintain fixed exchange rates vis-à-vis the mark. A similar proposal had been made in 1971 but had been rejected by the other member states. These incidents suggest that the provision of mutual assistance was the one area in which the German authorities were prepared to make concessions in order to attain their objectives in the exchange rate field. Significantly the proposals advanced at the Copenhagen Summit did not envisage any reduction in the discipline in the snake system: interventions were to be made in the currencies of the participants, with even stricter limitations on the use of dollars than in the existing system; settlements were to be made in the month following the interventions, with the debtor bearing the exchange risk; the very short-term credit facility could be extended by three months but it was then limited to the size of the debtor country's quota in the short-term monetary support fund; and settlements were to be made in a European currency unit (écu) that comprised gold as well as dollars. That the new exchange rate concertation system be as rigorous as its predecessor was essential to the German authorities because it was intended to be an instrument for reducing the divergence in price stability, seen as one of the fundamental causes of exchange rate fluctuations. In addition to the creation of a zone of stable exchange rates, the German initiative had, therefore, as an avowed objective promoting the adoption of less inflationary policies in the states not currently participating in the snake.

Predictably, the British, French, Irish and Italian Governments focused immediately on the relationship between their currencies and the mark in responding to the German proposals. None of them were prepared to enter into arrangements that would effectively tie their currencies to the mark, even with unlimited financial assistance. On the other hand, however, they recognized that the unstable exchange rate situation in Europe not only impaired international trade but also because of the ratchet effect exerted inflationary pressures on each individual economy. As a result, exchange rate movements were seen as less effective in correcting balance-of-payments imbalances than had initially been thought and as a contributing factor to the problem of stagflation afflicting many of the economies. The response of the countries outside the snake was, therefore, not to reject the German initiative but to suggest two modifications. First, target exchange rates should be set not only amongst the Community currencies but also with respect to third currencies, such as the dollar. This would place a limit on the upward pressure to which the new system would be subjected by an appreciation of the mark, and it would in addition help guard against the exports of its members becoming uncompetitive in terms of price on international markets. Second, the regional aid provided by the Community should be greatly increased so that the more backward and inflation-prone areas would receive the new investment and infrastructure necessary for them to survive economically. Since Ireland and Italy at least expected to be major recipients from such a fund, this flow of resources would help counterbalance the deflationary fiscal and monetary policies participation in the new initiative would probably entail.

As on many previous occasions, the heads of state clearly had to overcome major differences before they could achieve agreement on the way in which the new initiative in exchange rate concertation was to function. Nevertheless, at the Bremen Summit in July, they affirmed their commitment to resuming progress in economic and monetary unification and reintegrating all the member states into this endeavour. The Brussels Summit, scheduled for 4–5 December 1978 was set as the deadline for launching the new intitiative. For most of the autumn, however, the Community remained divided over the two issues raised by the non-participants in the snake. The latter had come to advocate a system in which intra-Community exchange rates were fixed in terms of the unit of account, itself defined as a basket of the currencies of the member states; this would insulate the snake from the gyrations of the dollar and prevent the movements of any one currency, i.e. the mark, from setting the course for the Community as a whole. The snake participants, especially Germany, naturally opted instead for the existing system of bilateral limits. As to the size of the regional fund, Ireland, which was particularly concerned about the effects on its economy of participation in the new arrangements if Britain stayed out, and Italy asserted that more than U.A. 500 million annually would be required to meet the needs of the less developed regions.

An intensive round of meetings between the leaders of different countries in November had, it was thought, eliminated the major differences on these two issues in time to reach agreement at the Brussels Summit. A meeting between the French President and the German Chancellor at Aachen had resulted in a compromise on the way in which the limits on currency movements would be defined. Following the familiar Community strategy of incorporating elements from both positions when agreement on one proved unattainable, the two leaders had reached accord that in the new system intra-Community exchange rates would be fixed in terms of both national currencies and a basket of currencies. Even though the basic differences between those inside of the snake and those outside remained, the Brussels Summit approved this formula and specified that the existing system of limits on the value of one currency in terms of another should be retained as the basis for the new system, the only change being that for currencies rejoining the snake the bands could be expanded from the 2¼ to 6% if requested. In addition, an upper and lower 'threshold of divergence' was set for each currency, which represented 75% of its maximum permissible movement (2¼ or 6%) against the écu, adjusted for the effect of the currency's own fluctuation on the value of the écu. Unlike the bilateral limits, there was no obligation to intervene when the 'threshold of divergence' was approached, but as the idea was to provide an early warning system it was implicit that the country involved should consider changing its economic policies or, in consultation with the other participants, entering the exchange markets. In practical terms, this meant that the German authorities would not be required to relax monetary discipline when the mark started to drag the other currencies upwards, but it would clearly focus attention on the mark as the currency introducing strains into the exchange rate concertation system.

Agreement on the size of the regional fund, could not, however, be achieved through such a nice compromise. Although Germany and the other major contributors – a grouping incidentally very similar to the snake participants – were prepared to accept sizeable increases, France balked at adding more than U.A. 200 million annually, for political as much as for economic reasons. Ireland and Italy thereupon refused to take part in the new exchange rate arrangement. That the Brussels Summit approved the new initiative, named the European Monetary System, was consequently a hollow achievement. Unless the Italian and Irish Governments could be persuaded to change their decisions, this successor to the EMU Project of which so much had been made in previous months would be nothing more than a continuation of the snake, with the French franc once more taking part.

In part because the European Monetary System initiative would have been stillborn without their participation, the Italian and Irish Governments reversed their decisions. Both countries had a considerable stake in the Community, in terms of their commitment to a united Europe as well as the benefits they received from the Common Agricultural Policy, social policy and regional policy. After reconsidering its fundamental goals and the role of European integration, the Italian Government announced that it would join the EMS despite the objections of the Communist Party. Ireland followed suit three days later, taking the momentous step of breaking the pund's 150-year link with the pound sterling and joining the Irish currency instead to the continental currencies. It was a significant political statement, not so much in terms of the relationship with the United Kingdom as an indication of the authorities' view of where the country's destiny lay, a perception that mention of increased Community aid in the future helped to strengthen. As to Great Britain, the Government remained firm in its resolve not to join the EMS. In spite of the potential problems arising from the participation of the pund, the authorities were not prepared to commit themselves to maintaining fixed rates: the behaviour of sterling on the exchange markets and the effect of North Sea oil on the economy were seen as making it important to retain a high degree of flexibility. The British did, however, undertake to try to keep sterling's movements in line with the EMS. That they lobbied successfully to have the pound included in the European Currency Unit, an arrangement which would create major problems for EMS if sterling and the other currencies evolved in different directions, suggested that they saw all the currencies moving basically together and furthermore that they wanted to have the preparations made so that Britain could easily join EMS at a later date. For the time being, though, they opted for a strictly informal relationship.

As the target date of 1 January 1979 for putting the new European Monetary System into operation approached, it appeared that this new initiative would get off to a smooth start. At the last moment, however, the French government tabled a proposal that monetary compensation amounts (MCAs), the border levies and rebates used to insulate farmers from the effects of exchange rate movements on the intervention prices set by the Common Agricultural Policy, be gradually phased out. Although the elimination of MCAs would have been of considerable economic benefit to France as a major agricultural producer, it was largely political considerations that motivated the government's action. And it was the electoral consequences of exposing farmers' incomes to the full force of currency variations that led certain countries, notably Germany, to reject totally the French idea. After appropriate posturing by both sides, a compromise was reached according to which MCAs would not be increased if exchange rate movements were less than 1% and that efforts would be made to reduce existing MCAs in strong currencies, which kept food prices artificially high, whenever intervention levels were raised. With this, the European Monetary System was able to enter into operation on 14 March 1979.

Like the launching of the exchange rate concertation system (better known as 'the snake in the tunnel') in April 1972, the inauguration of the European Monetary System was almost an anti-climax. The exchange rates among the currencies of the member states at the close of business on 13 March were used to establish the central rates of the new system, and applying the formula for the European unit of account (EUA), which had been employed by the Community for statistical purposes since 1974, the value of the new European Currency Unit was defined in terms of the participating currencies. The introduction of limits on the movement of the Irish pound against the Community currencies and their re-establishment of such for the French franc and the lira after roughly three and eight years of floating respectively passed without noticeable effect on the foreign exchange markets. Only minor intervention was required during the remainder of March and April to keep the seven currencies within their new bounds. Commenting on the ease with which the new arrangements had been implemented, however, the president of the Bundesbank pointed out that this had taken place under a propitious set of circumstances. The foreign exchange markets had in general been relatively stable, with the dollar reacting favourably to de-control of oil prices in the United States and the prospect of a downturn in the American economy, while within the Community discount rates in excess of 10% in Ireland and Italy and 8% in Denmark, reflecting the stringent monetary policies being pursued, strengthened their currencies against the mark, which indeed was one of the weaker currencies in the EMS[38]. That these conditions might not persist indefinitely and that the new initiative might come under the same pressures that had dismembered earlier efforts in exchange rate concertation were observations which could conveniently be brushed aside in the atmosphere of success created by the introduction of the European Monetary System.

As in the exchange rate field, the new arrangements in terms of credit facilities, settlement procedures and the introduction of the European Currency Unit were effected smoothly and almost imperceptibly. The very short-term credit facility, which finances automatically and without limit the claims and liabilities resulting from the multilateral intervention system until the settlement date 45 days after the end of the month in which the balances have arisen, was modified to allow for one automatic extension of three months. This was limited however to the country's quota under the short-term monetary support system. This debtor quota as well as the creditor quota and the *rallonge* were increased about two and one-half times to ECU 7900 million, 15 800 million and 8 800 million respectively, implying a maximum total short-term credit availability of approximately ECU 14 000 million, and the term of this assistance was extended by permitting renewal for a third three-month period. A corresponding increase in the funds available under the medium-term financial assistance system raised the maximum there to about ECU 11 000 million, resulting in a Community mutual assistance system totalling ECU 25 000 million[39]. Even taking into account the fact that no one country could draw more than a fraction of this total, at most some ECU 10 000 million, these changes meant that for the first time the Community would be able to provide assistance on the scale needed by member states in balance of payments difficulties. This was a very significant development. It signalled not only a determination that the EMS not fail for want of practical co-operation and support but also a perception that while external organizations such as the IMF would continue to have a large role to play in helping countries with payments problems, the primary responsibility rested with the Community as the body most directly involved and concerned with the exchange rate and payments policies of the member states.

The unresolved issues concerning the valuation of gold that had prevented progress in reserve pooling during the EMU Project once again necessitated a tedious arrangement whereby central banks effectively lent the required 20% of their gold reserves to the European Monetary Co-operation Fund through a series of revolving three-month swaps. But at the expense of this extra book-keeping, the member states were able to take a first step in the direction of combining their external reserve assets in a central fund in exchange for ECUs to be used in intra-Community settlements. As with the increase in the size of credit facilities, the implications of these new arrangements were at least as important as their practical consequences. By endowing the EMCF with its own financial resources as opposed to keeping it dependent on the central banks, the member states had begun to resolve some of the institutional issues concerning the role of a central Community monetary authority. Although disputes over the powers and responsibilities of such a body precluded agreement on establishing a European Monetary Fund as part of launching EMS, the member states demonstrated their confidence in being able to achieve a consensus by committing themselves to setting up the EMF within the next two years.

Under the circumstances, it was perhaps inevitable that the launching of the European Monetary System should give rise to unrealistic expectations. It was all too easy for the ringing declarations to be taken as commitments to monetary integration and for statements citing EMS as a means of working towards the ultimate goal of economic and monetary union to be misconstrued as meaning that EMS would result in monetary union, or at least a common currency. After all, though the resolution of the heads of state on establishing a European Monetary System, just like its predecessors in the field of exchange rate concertation, expressly provided for the modification of existing parities, it was clear that the intent of all these efforts was to reduce if not completely eliminate parity changes as well as limiting the amount of day-to-day fluctuations. On the one hand the experience of the eight years since the Community embarked on the EMU Project should have indicated how tenuous a foundation on which to build the commitment of national governments to maintaining specific exchange rates really was. On the other hand, the aspirations that were associated with the EMS were perhaps not as unfounded as might first be thought, because the snake had shown that under certain conditions and to a limited extent the existence of a formal exchange rate concertation system could contribute to the authorities' resolve to defend a given exchange rate.

This optimism in the results that were expected from the EMS was bolstered by the fact that at least two major drawbacks that had hampered earlier attempts to foster greater exchange rate stability appeared to have been corrected. First, the amount of financial assistance available through the Community mutual aid system had, as already discussed, been substantially increased so that a country would not feel forced to alter its parity because of a lack of reserves. In this context it is worth emphasizing that fully 40% of the assistance available was provided through the Medium-Term Financial Assistance System for periods of up to five years. As a result governments were able to obtain financing not just for immediate payments requirements but also for their needs during the adjustment period while corrective actions were taking effect.

Second, by defining the ECU in terms of a basket of currencies and by introducing the 'threshold of divergence indicator' attention was focused on the movements of individual currencies with respect to the group, not just on the strongest and weakest. This was of particular value in (i) identifying situations in which one or two currencies were moving opposite to the others because of external pressures, such as speculation involving a third currency; (ii) promoting timely responses before the bilateral exchange rate limits were reached; (iii) diffusing the intervention burden across all the currencies affected rather than just the one or two that happened to be most affected; and (iv) directing corrective action towards the specific problem rather than its exchange rate manifestations. True, countries exceeding their 'threshold of divergence' were expected, but not actually required, to take corrective measures: the only binding constraints were the bilateral exchange rates. There is, however, a clear presumption that the authorities concerned will strive to reduce the 'divergence' by adopting adequate measures, namely

(a) diversified intervention;
(b) measures of domestic monetary policy;
(c) changes in central rates; and
(d) other measures of economic policy[40].

Moreover, should appropriate action not be taken, the resolution laid down that the reasons were to be explained to the other participants and consultations held. Furthermore, while changes of parity remained an option, the operation of the basket of currencies meant that a modification in the value of one currency affected all the others, so that a government deciding to respond in this way rather than through domestic economic or monetary actions was faced with a much more complicated procedure than had heretofore been the case. Admittedly the 'threshold of divergence indicator' did not necessarily reduce the likelihood of a parity change, but by gently pressuring currencies that diverged from the others, this threshold encouraged national governments whose policies were causing the strains to reconsider their courses of action rather than placing the burden effectively on the government having the weakest currency, which was frequently in a situation where it had no alternative but to modify its exchange rate.

The guarded optimism that the new system might more effectively foster exchange rate stability than its predecessors was confirmed and strengthened as the EMS entered the third quarter with the original set of parities still intact. In both the 'snake in the tunnel' initiative in 1972 and the snake in

1973, the central rates had to be modified in June because of the weakness of the pound and the Danish kroner in the first instance and the strength of the German mark in the second. But in 1979 the mark, as well as the historically strong Dutch guilder and Belgian franc, remained below its official ECU parity, while the endemically weak lira was significantly above its central rate. As for the British pound, it had risen approximately 5% against the ECU since March, a development which demonstrated the beneficent effect of the North Sea oil production on the United Kingdom's balance of payments. Indeed, the only similarity with the earlier patterns was the decline in the value of the Danish kroner in response to a deterioration in that country's payments position.

As the summer wore on, however, a familiar pattern began to take shape: the dollar, which had been gaining against most of the Community currencies since the beginning of the year, began to lose ground towards the end of June as American inflation remained at historically high rates, prospects of a firm energy policy receded, and the money supply continued to grow faster than the economy. The combination of price increases that kept the consumer price index rising at an annual rate in excess of 13% and an easing of interest rates created a situation in which real yields were less than elsewhere and at times even negative. The resulting deterioration in the capital account was accompanied by a worsening of the current account, as rising oil prices and only slightly diminished energy consumption conspired with a relatively robust demand for goods and services to result in record trade deficits. Although a considerable improvement in the flow of services during the course of the year somewhat offset the weakness of the trade account, the exchange markets reacted to the discouraging trends in the American balance of payments in predictable fashion, and the dollar's decline steadily gathered momentum in July.

As on previous occasions, the flow of funds away from the United States put pressure on exchange rates not only between the dollar and the Community currencies as a bloc but also within the European Monetary System, because the dollar's weakness had different effects on individual countries. Following the familiar pattern, Germany was the principal target for funds leaving the United States. The increasingly tight monetary policies pursued by the Bundesbank in its efforts to combat the inflationary pressures revealed by the annual rate of increase in producer prices of industrial goods escalating from less than 3% in first quarter 1979 to over 4% in second quarter had resulted in attractive yields on DM placements. Whereas three-month money had cost 3.6% in January, it had climbed to 6.2% in May. Consequently, some DM 13 000 million flowed into the Federal Republic during June and July, almost entirely offsetting the DM 14 000 million outflow in the first five months of the year which had accompanied the strengthening of the dollar[41]. Although the pace of the capital inflow moderated appreciably in August as the exchange markets stabilized, it began to gather momentum in September as mistrust of the dollar intensified and the underlying strength of the mark became recognized. That the German current account deficit widened to DM 2900 million in August was regarded more as indicating the high level of domestic demand than any deterioration in the country's international competitive position, an assessment substantiated by the fact that the appreciation of the mark had not kept up with its relative advantage in price stability[42]. This combination of demand outstripping supply, inflationary pressures, a restrictive monetary policy and a currency undervalued in terms of purchasing power created a situation reminiscent of several previous occasions when the authorities had had to choose between stability in exchange rates or domestic prices. As the prospect of a revaluation began to appear on the horizon in late summer 1979, the pressure on the mark started to come from within the Community as well as the United States.

By September the mark was straining against its upper limit with respect to the Danish kroner, the weakest currency in the EMS, and the flow of funds into the Federal Republic was assuming an increasingly speculative character. Rumours of an impending revaluation sparked a major attack on 13 September, necessitating intervention on a large scale both in dollars and in Community currencies. Although the anticipated parity change did not materialize, the determination shown by the German authorities that weekend during a meeting of the major western finance ministers when they declined to relax their efforts to combat inflation in spite of the strains these actions were placing on interest rates in other countries strengthened the view that a revaluation was inevitable. A new wave of speculation set in on 21 September, prompted by concern that the Federal Reserve was not sufficiently committed to fighting inflation and might move to lower interest rates in the event the American economy showed signs of entering a recession. By the end of the week the Bundesbank's reserves had increased DM 9500 million over their level at the start of the month, half of which reflected intervention to support other EMS currencies and the rest purchases of dollars[43]. Faced with the alternatives of watching their reserves and the money supply continuing to swell in response to inflows from abroad or easing domestic financial conditions, the German authorities chose to relax the external constraint and announced a 2% revaluation of the mark on 24 September. At the same time the Danish kroner was devalued by 3% in recognition of the deterioration in the Danish payments position that had occurred over the previous six months.

Although the finance ministers of the Community cited 'tensions on the foreign exchange markets caused by the movements of currencies outside the EMS'[44] as responsible for the parity adjustments, the fundamental factors causing the tensions within the European Monetary System were internal to the Community. The continued decline of the dollar against European currencies for the rest of the month, just like its recovery after the tightening of monetary conditions in the United States on 6 October, may have reflected forces emanating primarily from the other side of the Atlantic. That France, for example, experienced a net inflow of only FFr 662 million in the third quarter in contrast to the deluge of funds on the Federal Republic was, however, a manifestation of the differences among the Community countries in terms of economic conditions, objectives and strategies[45]. In other words, the revaluation of the German mark, while undoubtedly precipitated by the decline of the American dollar, was in the last analysis the product of the policies of the German authorities. It was the German commitment to price stability, revealed yet again by the Bundesbank's raising of the re-discount and Lombard rates by 1% on 1 November, not the weakness of the American currency, that caused funds to flow towards the Federal Republic rather than into Denmark or some other country.

Seen from this perspective, it is clear that the 24 September parity changes have a far greater significance in terms of exchange rate stability than merely indicating that the countries participating in the European Monetary System had not renounced parity changes. What the events of September demonstrated was that the member states continued to formulate their economic policies, including their exchange rate strategies, on the basis of the same national interests on which they had acted heretofore. The new European Monetary System, in short, did not represent a major advance over the snake. All the grand pronouncements notwithstanding, these new arrangements differed from their predecessors in very little that was essential. Financial assistance had always been available in one form or another; EMS did not change the fact that credits had to be repaid and, beyond limited amounts, were conditional on the recipient adopting certain economic policies. The 'pooling' of gold and dollar reserves in the European Monetary Co-operation Fund altered the bookkeeping for certain transactions, but it did not alter the reality that the reserves belonged to individual central banks and that imbalances among the member states had to be settled by transferring ownership of these assets. Moreover, the failure to agree in 1979 on the next set of steps for setting up the European Monetary Fund effectively not only precluded meeting the March 1981 deadline but also demonstrated that beneath the veneer of consensus on the European Monetary Co-operation Fund the conflict over the institutional aspects of monetary integration which had prevented agreement in the Werner Committee still persisted. Defining the unit of account in terms of a basket of currencies and introducing an 'indicator of divergence' helped differentiate movements between participating currencies from movements against external standards, but all the same exchange policies were still formulated by national governments on the basis of their individual interests. Indeed, the only respect in which EMS represented an advance over the snake system was that it included more of the member states, an important consideration, but one whose real significance depended on the degree to which EMS represented progress towards economic and monetary union. Ironically, the new elements in EMS adumbrated here reflected preconditions set by countries for rejoining the exchange rate concertation system rather than efforts to make real strides in economic and monetary integration.

That the pursuit of divergent economic policies by the Community countries precluded the maintenance of stable exchange rates was demonstrated again on 30 November, when the Danish government announced a second devaluation of the kroner in terms of the other EMS currencies, this time by 5%. Although the timing of this action, coming so shortly after the adjustments of 24 September, was largely attributable to political developments in Denmark, the need for a further modification of the kroner's parity reflected the country's relatively poor economic performance, especially in terms of inflation and the balance of payments. The current account had deteriorated steadily since the beginning of the year, with the seasonally adjusted deficit growing from DKr 1400 million in the first quarter and DKr 2900 million in the second to DKr 4600 million in the third. The rising cost of imported oil was the major factor, accounting by itself for almost the entire deficit, but as the authorities pointed out, this merely emphasized the importance of adopting an effective policy that would reduce dependence on imported supplies. The big increase in excise taxes on energy enacted during the summer represented a first step in this direction, but clearly a basic transformation of the Danish economy, changing the flow of goods and services as well as redistributing income, would be required to restore balance on the current account. That the value of exports in the third quarter of 1979 was approximately 20% above the amount in third quarter 1978 seemed at first glance to indicate that the necessary adjustments were beginning to be made. On closer examination, however, it was evident that higher prices rather than a significantly larger volume of exports were behind this growth[46]. A further cause for concern about the balance of payments was introduced by the increasing burden of debt service. Payments of interest to overseas creditors accounted for almost ⅓ of the current account deficit in the third quarter of 1979, and this was projected to rise to ⅔ in 1980. The bleak outlook was summed up in a finance ministry report submitted on 21 September, which concluded that the balance of payments as well as inflation and unemployment would continue to worsen unless there were a major shift in economic policy[47].

As the grim realities of the Danish balance of payments situation became more widely recognized, the flow of funds towards Denmark that had followed the September devaluation and had pushed the kroner towards the top of the EMS reversed direction. The terms of payment shifted back against Denmark, and the first flurries of speculation set in towards the end of October, prompting the new government to issue a formal denial on 26

October that a devaluation was being planned. But it had few alternatives. Monetary policy had gradually become more restrictive during the course of the year, partly in response to the rise in international interest rates and partly in recognition of the need to limit the growth in the money supply. Already money market rates were around 20%, and despite income rising at a rate of about 10% the authorities were reluctant to tighten monetary conditions any more, given the economic encironment. Household consumption had turned downward in real terms, registering a 2.5% decline for 1979; investment was weakening, and with economic activity slowing down abroad, a fall in exports was projected for 1980. Moreover, even had the authorities wanted to adopt a more restrictive course, the need to finance government spending would have frustrated any such attempt. In the first ten months of the year, the government had borrowed DKr 9900 million in the form of direct credits from the central bank; this represented almost 30% of its gross borrowing requirement and virtually half of its net requirement. As the central bank noted,

> 'This injection of liquid funds by way of government operations made possible a corresponding outflow of foreign exchange to be financed without detracting from the banking system's liquidity. It is undesirable and at variance with the practice adopted in other countries to accommodate such a large proportion of governmental financing requirements by means of drawings on the central bank.[48]

Restrictive measures in the area of fiscal policy were also not a realistic alternative. The government had fallen on 24 September because the Liberal Party had not been able to accept the governing Social Democrats' budget proposals, which had called for restraining the growth in incomes while introducing limited price controls and a modest form of industrial democracy which would give workers a greater voice in the management of their companies. A compromise with the right had also proven unattainable because the more conservative parties rejected measures to increase worker participation. Since the 23 October elections had not produced any significant change in this constellation of forces, the Social Democratic minority government was denied for all practical purposes the use of fiscal policy in its efforts to remedy the country's economic ills, all too clearly revealed by the current account deficit of approximately DKr 15 000 million in 1979 and prospects for 185 000 unemployed in 1980. Consequently, a devaluation of the kroner formed a crucial part of its economic strategy. With the budget proposals being presented to the Folketing during the first week in December, the devaluaion of the kroner by 5% was announced on 30 November.

The difficulty in securing legislative approval for restrictive fiscal measures was illustrated by the fate of the new government's budget proposals, which were intended to be the other half of the assault on the country's economic problems. Of the measures proposed on 4 December, the 14-month price and wage freeze was rejected in favour of stricter controls on prices, profits, dividends and rents through 1 March 1981, an increase in the minimum wage, and a six-month wage freeze after which increases would once again be linked to the consumer price index except that energy costs would henceforth be excluded from the calculation; the higher wealth and personal and corporate incomes taxes were replaced by an increase in wealth tax rates together with an exemption for holdings of less than DKr 1 million, a modest increase, from 37 to 40%, in corporate income tax rates, and abolition of the tax allowance granted for investment in machinery and other capital goods; and the reduction in government spending was not mentioned at all. In short, fiscal policy was not to become significantly more restrictive. Given that the finance minister himself had admitted on 5 December that the original measures would at best hold the 1980 balance-of-payments deficit to 1979 levels, one has to agree with the president of the central bank, who commented on 10 January 1980 that the policies being pursued were inadequate and that unless decisive fiscal and monetary action were taken Denmark could find itself in a severe balance-of-payments crisis[49].

While Denmark did encounter balance-of-payments problems in 1980, the combination of having devalued the kroner by some 8% in the second half of 1979 and substantial borrowing abroad enabled the Danish currency to maintain its place in the European Monetary System. To a considerable extent, however, this reflected the exchange rate policies the other participants happened to be following, which permitted a divergent set of economic policies to coexist in an admittedly unstable equilibrium with the fixed exchange rate relationships. The fortuitous preference for maintaining the status quo in exchange rates was, of course, the result of independent calculations of interest by individual member states and reflected primarily the uncertainties introduced by the rise in oil prices in 1979, the largest since 1973. All the EMS countries had experienced a marked deterioration of their current accounts. Germany, for example, had recorded its first deficit in two years in May and had by the end of August amassed a cumulative eight-month deficit of DM 4400 million[50]. France's current account had turned negative in the third quarter despite a significant improvement in earnings from work abroad, largely a reflection of the growth in joint projects with the oil exporting countries[51]. Denmark's current account deficit had worsened sharply, and generally similar patterns had applied to Belgium, Italy, and the Netherlands. Given the experience of the worldwide recession unleashed by the 1973–74 rise in oil prices and the long anticipated decline in economic activity in the United States, as well as the delicate situation they faced domestically where their economies were poised above a downturn, national authorities were understandably cautious, wishing to guard against the risks of excessive payments deficits and price increases on the one hand and recession and unemployment on the other. Inclined to avoid both an appreciation of their currencies, which might impair the competitiveness of their products, and a depreciation, which might exacerbate inflation, they consequently followed along with the rise in world interest rates, as much for external reasons, but otherwise refrained from tightening or relaxing monetary policy.

The Bundesbank steered a course between restraining monetary growth and restricting the availability of credit. It raised the discount and Lombard rates by 1% each on 1 November, but at the same time increased rediscount quotas by DM 4000 million. The intent of these seemingly inconsistent actions was to eliminate tensions in the financial systems that had emerged as a result of the central bank allowing the capital outflows in the aftermath of the September revaluation to push day-to-day rates as much as 3% above the discount rate: the interest rate increases would signal the authorities' determination to maintain tight monetary conditions, while the quota increase would replace some, but not all, of the outflow that the banks had experienced with a more stable source of funds than the Lombard credits, which were really reserved for temporary liquidity problems. The Bundesbank defended its actions by pointing out that bank credits had increased by 12½% in the six months ending September 1979 and that the growth in 'central bank money', composed of notes, coins and deposits with the Bundesbank, was likely to exceed the 6–9% target set for the year. Moreover, the higher interest rates would keep Germany in line with the upward movement in international rates and help attract the capital inflows needed to finance the deficit on the current account[52]. In reality, though, the November measures represented not a significant tightening of credit but merely an adjustment, necessitated by the stronger than expected level of economic activity and hence monetary growth, to bring monetary conditions closer to the Bundesbank's original target for 1979. That unemployment rates were starting to rise and economic growth was slowing, admittedly normal occurrences in this phase of the economic cycle, constituted potent arguments against a more restrictive monetary policy at this time.

As in Germany, economic activity in France was more robust in the autumn than had been expected in view of the oil price increases. Along with the positive effects on employment and growth, this brought about a deterioration in the balance of payments, despite a particularly strong upsurge in exports, and gave a further boost to inflation. After an increase of 2.9% in the second quarter, the consumer price index rose by 3.2% in the third, more than twice as fast as in Germany and almost as rapidly as in Denmark. Even though the rate of domestic credit expansion slowed from 4.0% in the second quarter to 2.6% in the third, the Banque de France, like its counterpart across the Rhine, moved to bring the economy back onto the course it had originally charted, increasing from 20 to 30% the fraction of credits exempt from ordinary reserve requirements, such as export financings, that had to be included in calculating overall credit limits. At the same time, it allowed overnight rates on the money market to rise from 9¼% in mid July to 12¼% by mid November, roughly in line with the movement in world levels[53].

By early 1980 monetary policy was beginning to assume a more restrictive orientation as financing the rising cost of oil imports had become a major consideration in the formulation of national economic policies. Even though exports were rising rapidly, with Germany for example exporting 21% more in January 1980 than the year before, the even faster increase in imports occasioned by the climb in oil prices resulted in growing payments deficits. Consequently, interest rates in the Community countries closely followed the upward movement on international markets. The German discount and Lombard rates were raised 1% and 1½% respectively on 29 February 1980, and overnight money rose to almost 10%[54]. In France the day-to-day rate climbed past 12%, while the Lombard rate in Belgium rose above 12%[55]. That interest rates throughout the Community were raised to these levels, the highest in five years, was not just because of a desire to attract and hold foreign funds. True, the German authorities were keen to reverse the DM 5200 million decline in reserves that had occurred in January and February and to begin generating the private capital inflows they were expecting to finance half of the projected DM 20 000–25 000 million current account deficit; such considerations lay behind the reduction from four to two years of the minimum maturity of debt securities that could be sold to foreigners.

Demand levels and inflation rates, however, also gave monetary authorities in the Community countries good reason for tightening credit conditions. Retail prices continued to rise at almost 12% in Denmark and France and even in Germany came up to about 6%. Furthermore, monetary growth was substantially exceeding official targets, M_2 rising over 14% between the end of 1978 and the end of 1979 in France and M_3 increasing at an annual rate of 8½% in Germany in the first quarter of 1980. Finally, economic activity was more resilient than anticipated, as industrial production continued to rise in France and remained at high levels in Germany. A more restrictive orientation in monetary policy, consequently, became appropriate to internal conditions in the EMS countries. The Banque de France charted a course for 1980 that was in its words 'légèrement plus contraignant' than for 1979, increasing from 30 to 40% the fraction of credits exempt from ordinary reserves that were to be included in calculating overall credit limits and allowing virtually no increase in the ceiling for major banks in the first half of 1980[56]. For its part, the Bundesbank lowered its target for the growth in central bank money in 1980, selecting a range of 5–8%, and stressed that it intended to expand discount quotas only to the extent required to prevent capital outflows from having a deleterious effect on the banking system's financial structure[57].

During the late spring, a subtle change in national policies occurred as the persistently high rate of inflation made price stability more and more important in calculations of national interest. The effect on policy-making was most noticeable in Germany, where the traditional priority accorded to price stability was combined with a fundamentally sound reserves and balance-of-payments position, but it was discernible to a lesser extent in other countries as well. So long as countries were preoccupied with the balance-of-payments implications of the oil price increases, they were prepared, indeed predisposed, to accumulate reserves and to maintain a lower rather than higher rate of exchange, for this would not only confer some advantages for their exports in terms of price competitiveness, but would also strengthen their balance-of-payments position and hence encourage capital inflows. Once priority was accorded to inflation, however, the presumption shifted in favour of higher exchange rates. Although official strategies were never as simple as this, appreciation did become more attractive to Germany and other EMS countries as a means of reducing the cost of imports and indirectly reducing inflationary pressures domestically by introducing a better balance between supply and demand.

The situation in which the mark declined relative to the dollar and held stable only against the more inflation-prone currencies did not, therefore, last long into 1980. When American interest rates began to decline towards the beginning of the second quarter, the Bundesbank kept monetary conditions tight, and the value of the mark gradually rose inside the EMS as well as outside. The discount and Lombard rates were raised to 7½ and 9½% respectively on 2 May to bring them up to the levels prevailing on the money market and to signal once again the authorities' commitment to monetary restraint. That reserve requirements were reduced by 8% on 1 May for both domestic and non-resident deposits, which had the effect of releasing DM 5000 million in reserves to the banking system, and that the rediscount quota was increased by DM 3000 million on 5 May did not indicate any relaxation of the Bundesbank's policies. On the contrary, the DM 8000 million in new liquidity was intended to compensate for the outflow of almost DM 18 000 million on the capital account in the first four months of the year, which had sharply boosted rates on the money market and compelled the banks to borrow DM 6000 million from the Bundesbank in the form of Lombard credits in March and DM 10 000 million in April. As the Bundesbank once again made it clear that the Lombard facility was to be used only for temporary financing requirements, emphasizing this by raising to 2% the differential between the Lombard and discount rates, the end result was a significant reduction in bank liquidity[58].

The Bundesbank reinforced the message of monetary stringency by announcing its intention to hold the growth in central bank money to the lower part of the range set for 1980. Monetary growth had been high in the first quarter, with M_3 rising at an annual rate of 8½% and central bank money not far behind. Moreover, developments on the price and demand fronts suggested a more restrictive stance in monetary policy was consonant with the needs of the economy. Even though the cost-of-living index, which at the end of April was 5.8% higher than a year before, might not by itself give rise to concern about inflation, industrial producer prices were rising at almost 8%, construction at 12½% and imports, strongly influenced by the higher oil costs, at 24%. At the same time, the level of economic activity was firm and if anything increasing. Capacity utilization rose in the first quarter, led by strong orders in the capital goods sector. Overall, industrial orders were 13½% higher than the previous year, and consumer spending was not far behind, stimulated in part by speculation that goods and services would be more expensive in the future. Finally, unemployment was running at approximately 830 000 or barely 3% of the labour force. In short, economic conditions militated strongly for monetary policies designed to achieve a greater degree of price stability.

On previous occasions, this kind of policy orientation in the Federal Republic had invariably led to upward pressure on the mark, ultimately culminating in a modification of parities within the exchange rate concertation system. That this pattern was not repeated in the first half of 1980 reflects the specific circumstances of this period, such as the marked deterioration in the German balance of payments and the legacy of the exchange rate adjustments in the second half of 1979, and possibly also the timing of events, which because of the lag before changes in policy produced their effects, deferred the build-up of pressures in the EMS until the exchange markets had entered the summer doldrums. That the very different policies pursued by the Danish and German authorities, to cite only the most obvious example, could coexist within the framework of the European Monetary System raises interesting questions about the forces that impel exchange rate alterations. In the last analysis, however, what matters in terms of economic and monetary integration is that the economic policies of the member states had once again diverged. As long as economic policies set independently by the individual Community countries on the basis of their own national interests can, and in fact do, diverge because of different objectives, conditions and policies, stable exchange rates will prove an elusive objective.

This must be recognized in assessing the significance of the European Monetary System. That it should represent such a modest advance on the snake arrangements was inevitable. As was discussed in Chapter 9, exchange rate stability, like the other elements of economic and monetary union, can only be achieved by a once-for-all decision, namely abjuring parity modifications as a tool of economic policy. Short of taking this step, there is very little in the way of specific actions that can directly contribute to this objective, and the same applies to reserve pooling as well as interregional transfers or policy co-ordination. The member states were not prepared to cede their authority in 1971 or 1973, and they are certainly not prepared to do so in 1980. Under these circumstances, the only feasible and productive course is, as suggested earlier, to concentrate on making those small and frequently dull advances that foster an environment in which the member states perceive economic and monetary unification to be in their own national interests.

This, in terms of economic and monetary integration, is the function of the European Monetary System. It maintains the arrangements developed in the snake for the member states to work together in the exchange rate field. It promotes the interchange of information, the interaction of national officials, and the formation of common Community positions on issues affecting the Nine as a group. And it contributes in a modest way to exchange rate stability in the Community by reducing the day-to-day fluctuations between participating currencies and perhaps even by marginally increasing governmental determination and ability to maintain established central rates. Paradoxically, while EMS cannot realistically be expected to achieve the ambitious results initially anticipated from it, it has an important role in signifying and symbolizing the Community's commitment to economic and monetary unification. This is particularly important because it provides a sense of direction for the small steps being taken in often very disparate areas and helps to gradually establish economic and monetary union as a vital and attainable objective for the member states.

In practical terms, the significance of the European Monetary System, like that of the snake, is that it provides a vehicle in which those member states willing and able to maintain a specific set of exchange rates can work together towards this end. That it is an instrument for the execution of national economic policies determined on the basis of considerations among which economic and monetary unification has little weight implies that governments will defend these specific parities and accept the constraints of the EMS, loose as they are, only so long as this course is perceived to be in the national interest. Parity changes within EMS and even, *in extremis*, withdrawal from the system are, therefore, inevitable as long as the economic conditions, objectives and strategies of the Community countries continue to diverge. While it is beyond the scope of this book to attempt to estimate whether and how rapidly these differences could be reduced, the material presented in preceding chapters indicates that these dissimilarities have not markedly diminished in the course of the past decade and suggests that they are unlikely to do so in the near future.

What, then, has the Community accomplished since economic and monetary union was first made a formal goal at the Hague Summit ten years ago? Unquestionably, it has achieved a much better understanding of what EMU means and what its practical implications for the member states are. It has also certainly acquired a much greater appreciation of the magnitude of the task it has set itself, and with this has come the recognition that fixed and immutable exchange rates, a common market in goods and services, a system of interregional transfers and co-ordination of economic policies cannot be introduced in the space of a few years. It has learned, moreover, that in this, as in many other of the endeavours in which it is currently engaged, it can only proceed, no matter how sincere or binding the commitment to the final goal, if each specific step conforms with the individual interests of the member states and it has had to recognize that at least in the calculus of national governments progress in economic and monetary unification frequently does not lead to welfare gains. It has realized that progress comes through adopting a pragmatic strategy taking advantage of the opportunities inherent in each set of circumstances, rather than legislating a formal plan that fixes in advance the steps to be taken. It has attained a deeper understanding of the differences between the economies of the member states, in terms of philosophies and objectives as well as policies and conditions, and it has realized that the elimination of these differences is a precondition for real progress in this endeavour. It has introduced a system of exchange rate concertation allowing the participants to maintain the values of their currencies within bands considerably wider and at parities changing much more frequently than those of ten years earlier. It has established systems of mutual financial assistance now becoming large enough to meet the needs of the smaller countries. It has adopted a formal system of interregional transfers on a scale more modest than within individual countries and an informal one in the form of the Community budget which redistributes wealth on a basis defying rational explanation. And it has instituted a set of procedures for co-ordinating economic policies that have yet to have a discernible impact on decision-making in the Community. But perhaps most important, against all these disappointments and shortcomings in what has been achieved, the Community can set an accomplishment of capital significance. Over the course of the past decade the member states have come to accept the value of economic integration and have repeatedly reaffirmed their commitment and determination to achieving their ultimate goal of establishing an economic and monetary union among the countries of the European Community.

1 *Geschäftsbericht der Deutschen Bundesbank fur das Jahr 1975*, p.50
2 *Bulletin* (of the European Communities), September 1974, pp.5–22
3 *Geschäftsbericht der Deutschen Bundesbank für das Jahr 1974*, pp.30–39
4 *Geschäftsbericht der Deutschen Bundesbank für das Jahr 1974*, pp.6–9, 21
5 *Geschäftsbericht der Deutschen Bundesbank für das Jahr 1975*, pp.35–45
6 *Geschäftsbericht der Deutschen Bundesbank für das Jahr 1975*, pp.1–13
7 Banque de France, *Compte rendu* (Exercice 1975, pp.25–39
8 Banque de France, *Compte rendu* (Exercice 1974), pp.25–39
9 Banque de France, *Compte rendu* (Exercice 1975), pp.9–23
10 Banque de France, *Compte rendu* (Exercice 1975), pp.43–63

11 Banque de France, *Compte rendu* (Exercice 1975), pp.29–35
12 Banque de France, *Compte rendu* (Exercice 1974), pp.11–14
13 Banque de France, *Compte rendu* (Exercice 1975), pp.9–17
14 *Geschäftsbericht der Deutschen Bundesbank für das Jahr 1975*, pp.41–45
15 Banque de France, *Compte rendu* (Exercice 1976), p.17
16 Banque de France, *Compte rendu* (Exercice 1976), p.14
17 Banque de France, *Compte rendu* (Exercice 1977), pp.1–6
18 De Nederlandsche Bank, *Report for the Year 1975*, p.112
19 *Geschäftsbericht der Deutschen Bundesbank für das Jahr 1976*, pp.49–56
20 Banque de France, *Compte rendu* (Exercice 1975), pp.35–39
21 *Geschäftsbericht der Deutschen Bundesbank für das Jahr 1974*, pp.36–39
22 *Journal officiel des Communautés européenes*, XVIII(C174), 31 July 1975, p.3
23 *Bulletin* (of the European Communities) February 1975, pp.15–18
24 *Bulletin* (of the European Communities) March 1975, pp.17–19
25 *Bulletin* (of the European Communities) March 1976, pp.30–34
26 *Bulletin* (of the European Communities) May 1977, p.38
27 *Geschäftsbericht der Deutschen Bundesbank für das Jahr 1976*, pp.61–65
28 *Geschäftsbericht der Deutschen Bundesbank für das Jahr 1975*, pp.47–52
29 Banque de France, *Compte rendu* (Exercice 1977), pp.36–39
30 Banca d'Italia, *Abridged Version of the Report for the Year 1976*, p.22
31 De Nederlandsche Bank, *Report for the Year 1975*, p.113
32 De Nederlandsche Bank, *Report for the Year 1976*, p.114
33 Banque de France, *Compte rendu* (Exercice 1977), pp.33–34
34 De Nederlandsche Bank, *Report for the Year 1977*, pp.108–109
35 Banque de France, *Compte rendu* (Exercice 1977), pp.27–28
36 *Geschäftsbericht der Deutschen Bundesbank für das Jahr 1977*, pp.43–45
37 *Europe* (Magazine of the European Communities), No. 211, pp.6–9
38 'Europe's Money Pact: Calm Start, *New York Times*, 9 April 1974
39 *Resolution of the European Council of 5 December 1978 on the establishment of the European Monetary System (EMS) and related matters* (Document of the Council of the European Communities), p.6
40 *Resolution of the European Council of 5 December 1978 on the establishment of the European Monetary System (EMS) and related matters* (Document of the Council of the European Communities), p.4
41 *Monatsberichte der Deutschen Bundesbank*, September 1979, pp.29–35
42 *Monatsberichte der Deutschen Bundesbank*, October 1979, pp.9–10
43 *Monatsberichte der Deutschen Bundesbank*, October 1979, p.10
44 'West Germany Revalues the Mark', *New York Times*, 24 September 1979
45 Banque de France, *Bulletin trimestriel*, No. 33, December 1979, Table 39
46 Danmarks Nationalbank, *Monetary Review*, XVIII (3), November 1979, p.5
47 Kjobenhavns Handelsbank; *Denmark Quarterly Review*, No. 4, 1979, p.11
48 Danmarks Nationalbank, *Monetary Review*, XVIII (3), November 1979, p.6
49 Kjobenhavns Handelsbank, *Denmark Quarterly Review*, No. 1, 1980, p.8
50 *Monatsberichte der Deutschen Bundesbank*, October 1979, p.4
51 Banque de France, *Bulletin trimestriel*, No. 33, December 1979, p.9
52 *Monatsberichte der Deutschen Bundesbank*, November 1979, pp.5–8
53 Banque de France, *Bulletin trimestriel*, No. 33, December 1979, pp.3–7
54 *Monatsberichte der Deutschen Bundesbank*, March 1980, pp.5–7
55 Bank of England, *Quarterly Bulletin*, March 1980, pp.12–15
56 Banque de France, *Bulletin trimestriel*, No. 34, March 1980, p.13
57 *Monatsberichte der Deutschen Bundesbank*, March 1980, pp.6–8
58 *Monatsberichte der Deutschen Bundesbank*, May 1980, pp.5–7

Appendix

Exchange rates between Community currencies, the dollar, and the European unit of account, 1968–79

Period	DM	Currency HFl	BFr
21 Nov 1967 – 10 Aug 1969[c]	4.00	3.62	50.0
11 Aug – 29 Sept 1969[c]	4.00	3.62	50.0
30 Sept – 26 Oct 1969	3.73[d]	3.62[c]	50.0[c]
27 Oct 1969 – 9 May 1971[c]	3.66	3.62	50.0
10 May – 15 Aug 1971	3.47[d]	3.55[d]	50.0[c]
23 Aug – 20 Dec 1971	3.33[d]	3.32[d]	46.5[d]
21 Dec 1971 – 22 June 1972[e]	3.22	3.24	44.8
26 June 1972 – 11 Feb 1973	3.22[e]	3.24[e]	44.8[e]
12 Feb – 1 March 1973	2.90[e]	2.92[e]	40.3[e]
19 March – 28 June 1973	2.70[f]	2.82[f]	38.4[f]
29 June – 31 July 1973	2.33[f]	2.59[f]	35.6[f]
1 Aug – 16 Sept 1973	2.46[f]	2.68[f]	37.6[f]
17 Sept – 31 Oct 1973	2.43[f]	2.53[f]	36.8[f]
1 Nov 1973 – 20 Jan 1974	2.70[f]	2.82[f]	41.3[f]
21 Jan – 31 March 1974	2.72[f]	2.85[f]	41.4[f]
1 April – 30 June 1974	2.50[f]	2.64[f]	37.8[f]
1 July – 30 Sept 1974	2.61[f]	2.67[f]	38.9[f]
1 Oct – 31 Dec 1974	2.53[f]	2.60[f]	37.5[f]
1 Jan – 31 March 1975	2.34[f]	2.41[f]	34.9[f]
1 April – 30 June 1975	2.36[f]	2.41[f]	34.9[f]
1 July – 30 Sept 1975	2.55[f]	2.62[f]	38.4[f]
1 Oct – 31 Dec 1975	2.60[f]	2.67[f]	39.2[f]
1 Jan – 31 March 1976	2.57[f]	2.68[f]	39.2[f]
1 April – 30 June 1976	2.56[f]	2.71[f]	39.3[f]
1 July – 30 Sept 1976	2.53[f]	2.67[f]	39.0[f]
1 Oct – 31 Dec 1976	2.41[f]	2.52[f]	36.9[f]
1 Jan – 31 March 1977	2.39[f]	2.50[f]	36.8[f]
1 April – 30 June 1977	2.36[f]	2.47[f]	36.2[f]
1 July – 30 Sept 1977	2.31[f]	2.45[f]	35.6[f]
1 Oct – 31 Dec 1977	2.22[f]	2.39[f]	34.8[f]
1 Jan – 31 March 1978	2.08[f]	2.22[f]	32.3[f]
1 April – 30 June 1978	2.08[f]	2.22[f]	32.4[f]
1 July – 30 Sept 1978	2.01[f]	2.17[f]	31.6[f]
1 Oct – 31 Dec 1978	1.87[f]	2.03[f]	29.6[f]
1 Jan – 13 March 1979	1.88[f]	2.00[f]	29.3[f]
14 March – 30 June 1979[g]	1.89	2.06	30.3
1 July – 23 Sept 1979[g]	1.82	2.00	29.1
24 Sept – 30 Nov 1979[g]	1.76	1.96	28.7
3 Dec – 31 Dec 1979[g]	1.73	1.92	28.2
1 Jan – 31 March 1980[g]	1.78	1.95	28.7
1 April – 30 June 1980[g]	1.81	1.99	29.1

		Currency			
DKr	FFr[a]	Lira[a]	£	$	U.A.[b]
7.50	4.94	625	0.42	1.00	1.00
7.50	5.55	625	0.42	1.00	1.00
7.50[c]	5.55[c]	625[c]	0.42[c]	1.00[c]	1.00[c]
7.50	5.55	625	0.42	1.00	1.00
7.50[c]	5.55[c]	625[c]	0.42[c]	1.00[c]	1.00[c]
7.29[d]	5.55[c]	612[d]	0.40[d]	1.00	1.00
6.98	5.12	582	0.38	1.00	0.93
6.98[e]	5.12[e]	582[e]	0.42[d]	1.00[c]	0.93[e]
6.28[e]	4.60[e]	565[d]	0.40[d]	1.00[e]	0.83[e]
5.97[f]	4.34[f]	582[d]	0.39[d]	1.00[d]	0.80[f]
5.55[f]	4.09[f]	585[d]	0.39[d]	1.00[d]	0.73[f]
5.85[f]	4.30[f]	565[d]	0.41[d]	1.00[d]	0.78[f]
5.75[f]	4.23[f]	570[d]	0.41[d]	1.00[d]	0.76[f]
6.45[f]	4.70[f]	610[d]	0.43[d]	1.00[d]	0.85[f]
6.45[f]	4.95[d]	647[d]	0.44[d]	1.00[d]	0.84[f]
5.96[f]	4.87[d]	638[d]	0.42[d]	1.00[d]	0.78[f]
6.06[f]	4.79[d]	653[d]	0.43[d]	1.00[d]	0.81[f]
5.90[f]	4.65[d]	664[d]	0.43[d]	1.00[d]	0.79[f]
5.53[f]	4.29[d]	638[d]	0.42[d]	1.00[d]	0.73[f]
5.47[f]	4.09[d]	629[d]	0.43[d]	1.00[d]	0.73[f]
5.91[f]	4.35[g]	664[d]	0.47[d]	1.00[d]	0.79[f]
6.07[f]	4.42[f]	680[d]	0.49[d]	1.00[d]	0.81[f]
6.15[f]	4.53[g]	766[d]	0.50[d]	1.00[d]	0.80[f]
6.08[f]	4.71[d]	863[d]	0.55[d]	1.00[d]	0.79[f]
6.08[f]	4.91[d]	840[d]	0.57[d]	1.00[d]	0.79[f]
5.88[f]	4.99[d]	863[d]	0.61[d]	1.00[d]	0.76[f]
5.89[f]	4.98[d]	891[d]	0.58[d]	1.00[d]	0.76[f]
6.01[f]	4.95[d]	886[d]	0.58[d]	1.00[d]	0.75[f]
6.06[f]	4.89[d]	883[d]	0.58[d]	1.00[d]	0.73[f]
6.06[f]	4.83[d]	878[d]	0.55[d]	1.00[d]	0.70[f]
5.68[f]	4.76[d]	862[d]	0.52[d]	1.00[d]	0.66[f]
5.65[f]	4.61[d]	863[d]	0.55[d]	1.00[d]	0.66[f]
5.51[f]	4.39[d]	838[d]	0.52[d]	1.00[d]	0.64[f]
5.21[f]	4.30[d]	832[d]	0.50[d]	1.00[d]	0.62[f]
5.16[f]	4.27[d]	839[d]	0.50[d]	1.00[d]	0.75[f]
5.37	4.38	847	0.48	1.00	0.75
5.24	4.23	816	0.45	1.00	0.72
5.26	4.16	814	0.45	1.00	0.71
5.37	4.07	811	0.45	1.00	0.70
5.53	4.15	825	0.44	1.00	0.71
5.65	4.17	853	0.44	1.00	0.72

Notes

(a) Rates for the French franc and the lira are those for the commercial franc and the commercial lira during the periods when a two-tiered exchange rate system was in effect, namely from August 1971 to February 1974 and from January 1973 to February 1974 respectively.

(b) The unit of account used in economic and monetary affairs by such Community institutions as the European Monetary Cooperation Fund was originally defined as 0.88867088 grams of fine gold, the equivalent of one dollar at the then prevailing official price of $ 35 per ounce. In January 1979 with the advent of the European Monetary System, it was redefined to be a 'basket of currencies', composed of the following amounts of the currencies of the member states:

Currency	Amount	Weight as of 13 March 1979
Deutsche Mark	0.828	33.0
French Franc	1.15	19.8
Italian Lira	109.0	9.5
Dutch Guilder	0.286	10.5
Belgian Franc	3.66	9.3
Luxembourg Franc	0.14	0.3
British Pound	0.0885	13.3
Irish Pound	0.00759	1.1
Danish Kroner	0.217	3.1

The value of the new unit of account, called the European Currency Unit (ECU) was initially set equal to that of the European Unit of Account, used by the Community for statistical and other purposes. Rates of conversion between Community currencies and the unit of account are based on the existing parities if they were being defended or on cross-rates through currencies that were defending their value in terms of the unit of account. Rates of conversion between the unit of account and the dollar are based on cross-rates through Community currencies.

(c) Rate listed is the official parity with respect to the dollar, which was being defended by the authorities over this period. Under the European Monetary Agreement, actual exchange rates were allowed to fluctuate within 0.75% of this parity; European currencies consequently could fluctuate against each other within 1.50% of their par value.

(d) Rate listed is a representative exchange rate for this period as an official parity either did not exist or was not being defended. Except for the case of the Belgian franc/Dutch guilder in 1971, this sign indicates that the currency was floating against all other currencies.

(e) Rate listed is the official parity with respect to the dollar, which was being defended by the authorities over this period. Under the Smithsonian Accords of December 1971, actual exchange rates were allowed to fluctuate within 2.25% of this parity; however, exchange rate concertation arrangements within the European Community limited the size of fluctuations to 2.25% (instead of the 4.50% that would otherwise have been possible) among the currencies of the member states from 24 April 1972 to 1 March 1973, except for the pound sterling and the Danish kroner, which participated in this system only between 1 May and 26 June 1972. Within this system, the Belgian and Dutch authorities maintained the stricter 0.75% limit on fluctuations between their currencies.

(f) Rate listed is a representative exchange rate with respect to the dollar for this period as the currency was participating in the common European float against the dollar. Within the joint float, exchange rates were maintained within 2.25% of their official values (0.75% between the Belgian franc and the Dutch guilder until March 1976) defined in terms of the unit of account as follows:

	DM	HFl	BFr	DKr	FFr
19 March – 28 June 1973	3.39687	3.52282	48.6572	7.57831	5.55419
29 June – 16 Sept 1973	3.21978	↓			↓
17 Sept 1973 – 20 Jan 1974		3.35507			
20 Jan 1974 – 10 July 1975					n.a.
10 July 1975 – 14 March 1976					5.55419
15 March – 16 October 1976					n.a.
17 October 1976 – 3 April 1977	3.15665			7.89407	
4 April – 27 Aug 1977				8.13822	
28 Aug 1977 – 14 Oct 1978				8.56655	
15 Oct 1978 – 13 March 1979	3.03524	3.28928	47.7031	↓	↓

(g) Rate listed is a representative exchange rate with respect to the dollar for this period as all the European currencies except the British pound were participating in the European Monetary System, which floated as a group against the dollar. Within the EMS, exchange rates were maintained within 2.25% of the central rates (6% between the Italian lira and other currencies) defined in terms of the European Currency Unit as follows. Additionally, participating countries were expected to keep the value of their currencies in terms of the ECU within the 'threshold of divergence' indicator, defined as 75% of the maximum possible divergence (2.25% or 6% for the lira), adjusted for the weight of each currency in the composition of the ECU. Because exchange rate movements among the currencies taking part in the EMS affect their weights in the ECU, the 'threshold of divergence' changes each time the central rates are modified.

	DM	HFl	BFr	DKr	FFr	Lira	£Ire
14 March – 23 Sept 1979	2.51064	2.72077	39.4582	7.0376	5.79831	1148.15	0.664705
Threshold of divergence (%)	1.13096	1.51014	1.524993	1.6362	1.352868	4.07295	1.668262
24 Sept 1979 – 30 Nov 1979	2.48557	2.74748	39.8456	7.36594	5.85522	1159.42	0.669141
Threshold of divergence (%)	1.12536	1.51184	1.52657	1.63779	1.35606	4.07694	1.66836
3 Dec 1979 –	2.48208	2.74362	39.7897	7.72336	5.8470	1157.79	0.668201
Threshold of divergence (%)	1.12456	1.51159	1.52634	1.64009	1.35560	4.07635	1.66833

Sources: Bank of England, *Statistical Abstract Number 2 1975*, pp. 162–163.
Deutsche Bundesbank, *Monatsberichte*, Statistische Beiheft, Zahlungsbilanz, Table 19.
European Communities, Statistical Office, *Eurostat: Monthly Bulletin of General Statistics*
International Monetary Fund, *International Financial Statistics*

Index

Accords of Grenelle, 33
Arab–Israeli War, exchange markets and, 152
Authority, transfer of, 219
Azores meeting, 100, 104

Balance of payments, 32, 197, 213, 234, 242
  deterioration of, 43
  equilibrium of, 13
  France, 33, 36, 37, 87, 155, 156, 227, 229
  Germany, 33, 36, 47
  oil crisis and, 150, 151, 154
  U.K., 114
Bank for International Settlements, 236
Banks,
  central, 75, 138
  co-operation among, 144
  regulations for, 74
Bardepot, 117, 119
  introduction of, 113
Barre Report, 22–25, 56, 64, 65, 68, 69, 71, 72, 94, 239
  EMU and, 57, 63
  monetary integration before, 16
  proposals, 23
    mutual assistance, 24
  second, 63
Belgian franc, flotation, 100
Belgium, 44, 230
  attitude to EMU, 45, 70
  decline in reserves, 49
  discount rate reduction, 113
  effect of oil crisis, 155
  in August 1971 crisis, 91
  in dollar crisis of 1972, 118, 119
  inflation, 137
  in May 1971 crisis, 88, 89
  monetary policy, 48
  reserves, 136
Benelux countries, oil crisis and, 157
Border taxes, 102, 176, 200
Bremen Summit, 243
Bretton Woods agreement, 3, 20, 42, 83, 92, 131, 237
Brussels Summit, 243

Budgetary Committee, 23
Budgets, 7
  co-ordination of policy, 139
  national proposals, 181, 182
  policy, 71
  policy committee, 18
  Werner Committee on, 74

Capital,
  inflows of, 89
    August 1971, 93
    national interests and, 93
  market regulations, 175
  movement of, 41, 46, 136
    across Atlantic, 112
    constraints from, 47
    control of, 88, 97, 107, 175
    effects of, 48
    effect of Smithsonian Accord, 102
    forcing exchange rates up, 97
    in dollar crisis of 1972, 117
    in dollar crisis of February 1973, 126, 127
    into Germany, 32, 34, 49, 84, 127, 145, 146, 249
    into Netherlands, 148
    restrictions on, 14
    short-term, 90
Central Bank, 75, 138
Committee of Central Bank Governors, 23, 74, 78, 123, 138, 144, 162, 170, 179, 240
  co-operation fund and, 122
  exchange rates and, 111
Common Agricultural Policy, 4, 16, 17, 20, 23, 35, 54, 84, 200, 217
  and the dollar, 104
  difficulties of, 21
  effect of exchange rates on, 102
  EMU and, 142
  exchange rates and, 94, 99, 205, 245
  floating and, 85, 89
  potential dangers to, 21
  price fixing, 19
  safeguarding, 57

267

Common currency, 27, 60, 65, 66, 72, 132, 178
  arguments for, 5
Common Market, completion of, 174–176
Communications, 200
  improvement in, 196
Community, enlargement of, 54
Community loans, 235
Company law, 176
Convertibility,
  national interest and, 59
  Treaty of Rome and, 14
  unrestricted, 5, 19
  U.S.A. and, 44
Copenhagen Summit, 242
Council of Europe, 15
Council of Ministers, 180
  co-operation fund and, 122
Council resolution March 1971, 75–79
Credit conditions, Barre report on, 23
Credit facilities, 246, 247
Crisis,
  August 1971, 90
  dollar, of 1972, 117–121
  exchange 1968–69, 41
  June 1965, 20
  June 1973, 146
  May 1971, 88
  May 1973, 145
  sterling, 121
  sterling, of 1971, 115
Currency, common, 27, 60, 65, 66, 72, 132, 178
Customs, 200
Customs union, 15, 16, 17, 20, 23, 54, 217
  establishment of, 19
  safeguarding, 57

Decision-making,
  by Community, 28
  EMU and, 9
Deflation, 153
Denmark,
  and the snake, 224
  inflation and, 157
  leaving snake, 116, 121
  relations with France, 230
  union and, 124
Devaluation, 39
Dollar,
  as key currency, 83
  as reserve asset, 95
  CAP and, 104
  convertibility, 99
    restoration of, 95
    suspension of, 91, 92

Dollar, (cont.)
  crisis February 1973, 125–133
  crisis summer 1972, 117–121
  decline of, 101, 146, 249, 250
  devaluation of, 128, 129, 130
    effect on Germany, 95
  exchange rates and, 100, 143, 256
  fixed exchange rate against, 147
  flight from, August 1971, 90
  mistrust in, 113
  oil crisis and, 152
  overvalue, 20
  problem of, 112
Duisenberg Plan, 239

Economic and Monetary Union (EMU) 1, 11
  abandonment of, 135
  accomplishments, 253
  after oil crisis, 221–254
  as challenge to America, 42
  as instrument of further integration, 25
  Barre Report and, 56, 57, 63
  basic principles, 61
  Belgian attitude, 45, 70
  benefits of, 10, 27, 55, 216
  birth of, 54–80
  CAP and, 142
  causes of failure, 202–206
  commitment to, 203, 206, 241
  Council resolultion March 1971, 75–79
  crisis of June 1965, 20
  crucial flaw in, 217
  deadlock in, 141
  decision-making, 9
  definition of, 2, 4, 7, 9, 77
  dollar crisis of 1972 and, 118
  Dutch attitude, 69
  economist strategy see Economist strategy
  elements of, 7
  end of, 158
  European Monetary Co-operation Fund, 137
  failure of, 10, 171
  first stage, 205
    accomplishments of, 201
    end of, 198
    ruination of, 90
  fixed exchange rates and, 103
  French attitude towards, 57, 61
  German attitude towards, 57, 60
  goal of, 2, 3, 55, 71, 215, 216
  Hague summit, 2, 8, 54–58
  Italian attitude, 70
  loss of snake, 171
  monetarist strategy see Monetarist strategy

Index

Economic and Monetary Union (EMU), *(cont.)*
  motivation for, 13–30
    as instrument of further integration, 25
    national interest, 13–30, 31–53
    political, 27, 28
  national interests and, 51, 55, 58, 68, 116, 133, 163, 202, 204, 206, 214, 228
  need for, 104
  Paris summit, 121
  perspective, 9
  political implications of, 26, 27
  political will and, 133, 164, 202, 214
  pragmatism and, 218
  pre-Hague attempts, 56
  process of, 213
  results of project, 200–202
  second stage, 158
    draft decisions, 158
    end of, 133
    formal proposals, 161
    proposals for, 135
  snake in the tunnel and, 132
  stages of implementation, 63, 67
  time factors, 215
Economic goals,
  harmonization of, 185
  national interests and, 209
Economic interdependence, 46
Economic policy,
  authority for, 140
  common, 65
  concerting, 140
  conduct of, 10
  co-ordination of, 6, 23, 24, 25, 60, 67, 71, 77, 78, 81, 107, 123, 159, 165, 177–185, 216
    advantages of, 44–51, 183, 195
    communication, 196
    consultative procedures, 179
    limits of, 193
    national interest and, 184, 193
    political will for, 184, 185, 194, 197
    Treaty of Rome on, 14
  harmonization of instruments, 165
  national interests, 65
  regional, 60, 76, 78
  supranational decisions, 61
Economic policy committee, 159, 165
Economic policy-making, 28
  common, 7, 60, 72
Economic targets, 186, 208
Economic union, 55
  definition, 58, 60
  meaning of, 4
  motivation, 29
  relation to monetary union, 3
Economies, interaction of, 9

Economist strategy, 66–70, 71, 72, 73, 75, 76, 78, 79, 81, 125, 135, 138, 141, 160, 163
Employment and unemployment, 140, 186, 189, 223
  directive on, 160, 162
Energy, common policy, 16
European Atomic Energy Community, 16
European Currency Unit, 245, 246
  definition, 248
  value of, 245
European Defence Community, 15
European Development Fund, 235
European integration, process of, 217–219
European Investment Bank, 6, 235
European monetary agreement, 64
European monetary co-operation fund, 64, 251
  establishment of, 129, 137
European Monetary System (EMS), 8, 239–253
  concepts of, 8
  environment of, 8
  expectations of, 247
  inauguration of, 10
  national attitudes to, 244
  proposals for, 241
  significance of, 252
European Union, creation of, 141
European Unit of Account, 8, 245
  conversion of gold into, 161
  definition of, 21
  revaluation of mark against, 230
Exchange controls, 5, 86, 88, 112
  Belgian preference for, 88
  France, 34
  national attitudes towards, 105
  relaxation of, 19
  Treaty of Rome on, 14
Exchange crises 1968–69, 41
Exchange rates *see also* Parity, etc., 157, 256–259
  and the dollar, 100
  Barre report on, 23
  changes in, 26
  concertation *see also* Snake, 10, 71, 81–110, 178, 216, 242, 245
    after franc's withdrawal from snake, 221
    August 1971 crisis, 90
    common position, 95
    developments in, 82
    dollar crisis of February 1973, 125–133
    limits of parellelism, 158
    March 1972 resolution, 103–108
    May 1971 crisis, 83
    national interest and, 116
    relaunching of, 103
    second stage, 158

Exchange rates,
  concertation, *(cont.)*
    snake, 135–173
    snake in the tunnel, 111–134
  constraints on policy, 13
  co-ordination of, 18
  dollar crisis of 1972 and, 119
  dollar crisis of February 1973 and, 127
  effect of August 1971 crisis, 94
  effect on CAP, 94, 99, 102, 205, 245
  effect of capital movements on, 97
  fixed, 5, 14, 19, 99, 103, 145, 243
    against dollar, 147
    attractions of, 31
    freeing of, 20
  fixing as political decision, 100
  fluctuations, 63, 64, 82, 200, 201
    effect of Smithsonian Accords, 101
    reduction of, 106
  free, 237
  importance of fixing, 89
  investments and, 205
  irrevocable fixing of, 27
  loss of national control of, 6
  movements of, 31, 241, 242
    effects of, 21
    national interest and, 15, 39
  national interests and, 15, 39, 59, 106
  national policies, 143
  policies, 184
    political will for, 184
  relationships, dollar crisis of 1972 and, 120
  stability, 81, 194, 202, 248, 251, 252
    in 1971, 105
    maintenance of, 82
  two-tiered, 97
  Werner Report, 78
Exchange reserves, German, 69
Exports, 241

Factors of production, 206, 215
  EMU and, 4
  free movement of, 15, 26
  movements, 5, 78, 81, 175, 176
Fécom, 159, 170, 177
  Council of Administration, 142
  creation of, 138
  development of, 142
  finances of, 142
  significance of, 138
  strengthening, 161, 162
Floating, 82
  CAP and, 85, 89
  disenchantment with, 97
  in August 1971 crisis, 93
  in dollar crisis of February 1973, 128, 130, 131

Floating, *(cont.)*
  joint, 142
  rejection of, 32
Foreign aid, effect of suspension of dollar convertibility, 92
Franc,
  appreciation of, 96
  devaluation of, 36, 40, 168
  effect of oil crisis on, 167
  flotation of, 168, 169
  gold parity, 113
  overvalued, 36, 38
France,
  attitude to EMU, 57, 61
  attitude to interregional transfers, 50
  balance of payments, 33, 36, 37, 87, 155, 156, 227, 229
  economic policies, 183
  economic targets, 186, 187, 208
  economy, 225, 226
  effect of oil crisis on, 167
  employment in, 186
  exchange controls, 34, 98, 112
  exports, 45
  GDP deflator averages, 33
  GNP, 211
  gold reserves, 231
  in August 1971 crisis, 91, 93, 96
  in dollar crisis of 1972, 118, 119
  inflation in, 157, 209, 227, 229
  inflow of capital, 118
  in May 1971 crisis, 87, 89
  interest in EMU, 45
  interest rates, 47, 148, 156
  labour supply and productivity, 210, 211
  monetarist strategy, 62
  parity changes, 39, 40
  policies, 207
  price rises, 33, 50, 97, 154, 188, 229
  production in, 98
  reserves, 136
  return to snake, 227
  snake and, 224
  two-tier exchange rate and, 97
  views of parity changes, 33, 35
  withdrawal from snake, 150, 165, 221, 228, 239
Free trade, 4
  removal of barriers to, 26

Germany,
  as speculative target, 117
  attitude to EMU, 57, 60
  attitude to exchange controls, 105
  attitude to mutual assistance, 69

Germany, (cont.)
  aversion to interfering with free market forces, 105
  balance of payments, 33, 36, 47
  Bardepot, 117, 119
    introduction of, 113
  economic targets, 186, 187, 208
  economist strategy, 66–70, 71, 72, 73, 75, 76, 78, 79
  effect of dollar devaluation on, 95
  effect of oil crisis on, 155
  employment in, 186
  exchange reserves, 69
  flow of capital from, 112
  flow of funds into, 32, 34, 49, 84, 127, 145, 249
  GNP, 211
  in August 1971 crisis, 93
  in dollar crisis of 1972, 117, 119
  in dollar crisis of February 1973, 127
  in May 1971 crisis, 84, 85, 89
  interest rates, 47, 86, 136, 146
  interests, 207
  labour supply and productivity, 210, 211
  leadership in snake, 222
  parity changes, 37, 39, 40
  pooling of reserves and, 143
  price rises in, 33, 50, 154
  response to American challenge, 94
  taxation, 137
  views of parity changes, 33, 35
Gold,
  conversion into units of account, 161
  initiation to mobilize reserves, 231
  price of, 143, 144
  role of, 43, 232, 233
  selling of, 233
  two-tier market, 22
  valuation of, 246
Gold Pool, 20
Gold reserves in U.S.A., decline of, 92
Goods, movement of, 26, 81, 175, 176, 215
Government spending, 190, 191
Gross national product, 190, 191, 223
  comparative figures, 212
  in France and Germany, 211
Group of Ten, 95
Growth, directive on, 160, 162
Guilder,
  decline of, 152
  flotation of, 89, 100
  revaluation, 145

Hague Summit, 2, 8, 29, 43, 54–58, 70, 106, 164, 203, 214, 253
Health and safety standards, 4

Ideas, interchange of, 196
IMF, 24, 41, 95, 108, 196, 239, 240
  Articles, 237, 238
  gold and 231, 232, 233
  loans from, 236
  oil facility, 234, 236
  on parity, 32
Import deposits, loss of national control of, 6
Industrial policy, 176
Industry, 153
Inflation, 120, 137, 160, 188, 209, 211, 233, 241
  checking spread of, 46
  fight against, 191
  in France, 157, 227, 229
  in U.K., 114
  oil crisis and, 155, 157
  parity changes and, 46
  target rate of, 189
Information,
  flow of, 196, 197
  interchange of, 252
Insurance, regulations for, 74
Interest rates, 136, 148, 156
  French, 47
  German, 47, 86, 136, 146
  rises in, 112
International monetary system strengthening, 236
Interregional transfers, 6, 8, 10, 201, 205, 253
  institution of, 177
  reaction of member states to, 50
Investment, 160, 206, 215
  exchange rates and, 205
Ireland,
  attitude to EMS, 244
  union and, 124
Italy, 165
  attitude to EMS, 244
  attitude to EMU, 70
  gold reserves, 231
  in dollar crisis of 1972, 118
  in May 1971 crisis, 89
  leaving snake, 116
  loan of funds to, 236
  policies, 207
  request for funds, 144
  support of floating, 88
  withdrawal from snake, 128

Kroner, 250
  decline in, 249
  devaluation of, 241, 250

Labour, 206
  in France, 210, 211
  in Germany, 210, 211
  mobility of, 176

272 Index

Lira, flotation of, 125, 130
Luxembourg, 44

Mark,
 appreciation of, 96
 decline of, 152
 flotation of, 85, 89, 96
 fluctuation of, 32
 influence in snake, 222
 overvalue, 38
 parity of, 37
 revaluation of, 230, 250, 251
 revalue of, 145
 undervaluation, 84, 86
Medium-Term Economic Policy Committee, 23
 creation of, 18
Medium-term financial support, 23, 58, 71, 72, 78, 234, 240, 241, 248
Medium-term policies, 56
 co-ordination of, 24, 25
Minisnake, 169
Monetarist strategy, 62–66, 69, 70, 71, 72, 73, 75, 78, 81, 116, 122, 123, 135, 138, 139, 141, 143, 163, 195
Monetary Committee, 14, 23, 57, 78, 85, 144, 159, 162, 179, 196, 240
 and co-operation fund, 122
 establishment of, 17
 formation of, 18
 mandates, 18
Monetary co-operation fund, 106
 creation of, 122
 national interest and, 122
Monetary integration before Barre Report, 16
Monetary policy, common, 5
Monetary union, 55
 conditions for, 2
 definition of, 4, 58, 60
 relation to economic unions, 3
Money supply, growth in, 190, 191
Monopolies, 4, 216
Multinational companies, 26
Mutual financial assistance systems, 14, 56, 104, 116, 144, 200, 234–236, 239
 advantages of system, 41–42
 Barre Report on, 24
 establishment of system of, 21
 German attitude, 69
 medium-term, 23, 58, 71, 72, 78, 234, 240, 241, 248
 shortcomings of system, 41
 short-term, 23, 57, 124, 158, 234, 240, 241

National authorities controlling monetary conditions, 49

National interests,
 and response to American challenge, 94, 99
 capital inflows and, 93
 conflict of, 58–62
 convertibility and, 59
 co-operation fund and, 122
 divergence of, 206–213
 dollar crisis of 1972 and, 118
 EMU and, 31–35, 55, 58, 68, 116, 133, 163, 202, 204, 206, 214, 216, 228
 exchange controls and, 105
 exchange rate concertation and, 116
 exchange rates and, 59, 106
 Fécom and, 143, 144
 in August 1971 crisis, 96
 in dollar crisis of February 1973, 130
 in May 1971 crisis, 89
 in policy-making, 65
 interregional transfers and, 50
 parity and, 59, 62
 policy co-ordination and, 184, 193
 snake and, 146, 149, 222
National sovereignty, 204
 loss of, 49
 retention of, 7
Netherlands,
 attitude to EMU, 69
 attitude to exchange controls, 105
 balance of payments, 213
 capital movement into, 148
 discount rates, 113
 economist strategy, 60–70, 71, 72, 73, 75, 76, 78, 79
 effect of oil crisis, 155
 exchange controls, 118
 in August 1971 crisis, 93
 in dollar crisis of 1972, 118
 in dollar crisis of February 1973, 130
 in May 1971 crisis, 87
 pooling of reserves and, 143
Norway, 170
 leaving snake, 129
 mutual assistance and, 132

Oil,
 cost of, 152, 154, 155
 dependence on, 151
 sharing of, 153
Oil crisis, 149–158, 218
 balance of payment and, 150, 151, 154
 causing strains on snake, 154
 effect on France, 167
 effects of, 150, 151, 153
 EMU after, 221, 254
 inflation and, 155, 157
Oil facility, 234, 236

Parallelism, 70–75, 81, 123, 144
  in second stage of EMU, 139
  limits of, 141, 158
Paris summit, 121–125, 137, 141, 177, 198
  significance of, 124
Parity see also Exchange rates, etc.,
  adjustments, 34
  aversion to changes, 32
  changes in, 17, 20
    factors responsible for, 32
    French and German views, 33, 35
    political and economic costs of, 39, 40
    political considerations, 35
  France and Germany, 36, 37, 38
  inflation and, 46
  irrevocable fixation, 62
  national interests and, 59, 62
  permanent fixation of, 68
  reducing fluctuations, 64
  reduction in, 73, 74
Parity bands,
  enlargement of, 101, 103
  reduction in, 84
Political factors,
  in economic integration, 16
  in EMU, 26, 27, 133
  of parity changes, 35
Political union, 28, 29
Political will,
  EMU and, 133, 164, 202, 214
  policy co-ordination and, 184, 185, 194, 197
Pound,
  crisis of 1971, 115, 121
  devaluation of, 20, 21
  ECU and, 249
  flotation of, 115, 125
  gold parity, 113
Power in Community, national concentration of, 11
Prices,
  desire for stability, 45
  increases, 154 188
    France and Germany, 50, 229
  stability of, 46, 188, 211, 223
Production,
  factors of see Factors of production
  oil crisis and, 153

Regional balance, 16
Regional Fund, 70, 165
  creation of, 107, 177
  size of, 244
Regional policy, 60, 76, 78
Reserve currency,
  Bretton Woods system, 20
  dollar crisis of 1972 and, 120

Reserve currency, (cont.)
  pooling of, 8, 63, 68, 124, 143, 158, 161, 247, 251–252
  recycling of, 42
  size of, 234
  special requirements, 107
Reserves, 136, 237
Resources, utilization of, 26
Revaluation, 39

Schiller Plan, 67, 222
Short-term credit facility, 246
Short-term financial support, 57, 124, 158, 234, 240, 241
Short-term policies, 56
  co-operation, 23, 25
Short-term policy committee, 23
Smithsonian Accords, 82, 101–103, 111, 113, 126
  consequences of, 101
  failure of, 117
Snake see also Exchange rate concertation, 8, 135–173, 200, 218, 243
  deflationary courses and, 153
  economic policies and, 157
  exchange rates with dollar, 143
  France and, 224
  freeing of, 136
  French return to, 227
  French withdrawal, 150, 165, 221, 228, 239
  influence of mark in, 222
  mini-, 169
  national interests and, 146, 149, 222
  new character of, 169, 170
  Norway and Sweden entry into, 132
  oil crisis of 1973, 149–158
  reasons for failure, 166
  strains within, 145, 148
  U.K. withdrawal from, 115
  vulnerability of, 128, 148, 149
Snake in the tunnel see also Exchange rate concertation, 82, 111–154
  countries leaving, 115, 116
  dollar crisis of 1972, 117
  EMU and, 132
  Paris summit, 121–125
  withdrawal from, 129
Social policy, 176
Statistics, 196
Steel industry, trade barriers in, 238
Sterling see Pound
Structural differences, 209, 215
Structural policies, 140
Sweden, 170
  mutual assistance and, 132
Switzerland,
  in dollar crisis of 1972, 117
  in dollar crisis of February 1973, 126

Target zones, 239
Tariffs, 4, 176, 219
  loss of national control of, 6
Taxation, 160, 176
  direct, 5
  harmonization of, 60, 78, 159
  indirect, 4
  in Germany, 137
  national systems, 175
Third Medium-Term Plan, 185
Threshold of divergence, 244, 248
Tindemanns Report, 239
Trade barriers, 238
Trade movements, 78
Transport policy, 15
Treaty of Paris, 238
Treaty of Rome, 5, 13–16, 23, 26, 29, 174, 178, 201, 215, 219, 238
  on exchange rates, 18
  provisions for monetary union, 3
  ultimate object of, 15

United Europe, 55
United Kingdom, 165
  attitude to EMS, 244
  Azortes talks and, 104
  balance of payments, 114
  economy 1971, 114

United Kingdom, *(cont.)*
  flow of capital from, 114
  inflation in, 114, 211
  leaving snake, 121
  union and, 124
United States *see also* Dollar, etc.,
  appetite for imports, 43
  balance of payments, 83, 112, 126, 249
  common response to challenge, 93, 99
  decline of gold reserves, 92
  dominance, challenge to, 42–44
  gold reserves, 20, 233
  import surtax, 102
  inflation in, 249
  national interest in response to, 94
  pre-eminence in monetary affairs, 42
  relation of economy to Europe, 104
  reserves, 126

Value added tax, 60, 74, 175, 200

Werner Committee report, 58–62 70–75, 76, 77, 78, 79, 83, 85, 88, 106, 141, 159, 164 168, 175, 178, 180, 181, 203, 219
  endorsement of, 75,
  formation, 59
  on budgetary policy, 74